Stephen Dudeney was brought up in London's East end, and for as long as he can remember wanted to be a Fireman. In 1987, he joined the London Fire Brigade and began his career at Bethnal Green Fire Station. He was promoted through the ranks always remaining within East London. Finishing his career as Borough Commander, covering the area of the East end where he grew up and plied his trade, over the course of his career he attended some of the most significant incidents to befall London in recent decades, this is his story.

For all of those I served with, for the friendship, camaraderie, and support through laughter, tears and tragedy. For everyone who has or will in the future answer the call and become a firefighter, this is your story.

For my wife, Joanne, and my three daughters, Charlotte, Abigail and Imogen. Thank you for being the better part of me. Special thanks to Charlotte for her assistance in editing and correcting as this book took shape.

Stephen Dudeney

LONDON FIREFIGHTER

AUSTIN MACAULEY PUBLISHERS™

LONDON • CAMBRIDGE • NEW YORK • SHARJAH

A CIP catalogue record for this title is available from the British Library.

ISBN 9781398463240 (Paperback)
ISBN 9781398463257 (ePub e-book)
www.austinmacauley.com

First Published 2022
Austin Macauley Publishers Ltd®
1 Canada Square
Canary Wharf
London
E14 5AA

20221102

A special thanks to my eldest daughter, Charlotte, for editing this book whilst recovering from breast cancer.

Table of Contents

Introduction

As I jumped down off the fire engine, I was stalled by the sight in front of me. The whole building seemed to be alive with fire. A large wall of flame came from the double-fronted shop window that made me squint from the radiated heat and brightness. The wet roadway in front of the building had been dried by the heat of the fire and it steamed further out where it was still damp. I looked up, inside every window it was brighter than day itself, large transparent flames rolled around inside with tiny brighter yellow flames clinging to the underside of the wooden floors, the ceilings long having surrendered to the flames eating them.

Even the tiny holes in the air bricks in the building pushed out white smoke, which was then sucked into the skyward plume of fire, heat and smoke. On the top floor the flame was less clean, here it mixed with dark smoke that was illuminated by the fire underneath.

Along the street people stood. Alone, in pairs or bigger groups, they looked from behind curtains and out of doors at the drama unfolding in the street, the light of the flames more powerful than the orange of the sodium street lamps, casting bright light and dancing shadows onto everything I could see.

The old Leading Fireman grabbed hold of me and broke me from my trance.

"Come on boy, come with me and let me show you the fire."

Dutifully, I followed him towards the building. The heat on my face was as intense as the fear in my gut. The old fellow crouched low, I held my hand up to my face to shield the heat, and we ducked into an open doorway.

This brought some respite from the severe radiated heat but in here the air was hot and acrid. I felt as though I was breathing the flame and the first couple of breaths were short, as if I had just jumped into a freezing pool of water. There was very little smoke although I could taste the unmistakable tang of burning wood already so familiar to me in my short career.

Inside, the hallway was bright from flame coming from a panel above the door, this flame was drawn along the hall away from us and up the stairs out of sight. I hesitated to go back, the 'leading hand' beckoned me on. Looking on along the hallway a mass of flame was headed up the stairs from the rear of the building. Embers fell to the floor and sparks were drawn up into the plume. We started to move up the stairs, I felt compelled to say something, I screamed to be heard above the noise.

"I-is this… I mean will, will we be OK?"

"Don't be stupid, of course we will. Follow me."

He stamped hard on the stairs and nodded as if the response of his feet against the timber satisfied him that the staircase was still strong enough and up we went. I crouched low with my face close to the stairs and began to creep up behind my grizzled companion.

"Get up…what's wrong with ya, young boy like you crawling around like an old man."

I looked up and saw him standing on the half landing eerily illuminated by the light of the flames. I took a breath and ran up behind him. It was hot; my eyes were streaming a little and it was hard to breathe. But I was not burning, as anyone would expect to be deep inside a building that was alight from top to bottom, without any breathing apparatus or water. Up another flight and we were on the first floor. He elbowed a partially burned door out of the way and we went up again, half a turn, then up to the second floor.

It seemed like a long time since we had been in the street and although still relatively comfortable, I would have been a happy lad to be standing back down there right now. After a look into the burning second floor, we went halfway up the next flight where he stopped and crouched.

"This is as far we go, above us is the top floor… that's where all of the heat will be, we are OK up to here but all of that coming up the stairs is bottled up above us. Always remember in these jobs. If the fire is well ventilated you will be OK to move about inside just watch out for the heat, it's always at the highest point…and the structure, stay near the walls, the floor is strongest there, wooden staircases can burn though, stone staircases will go on forever but as soon as you hit them with water they will contract and shatter in an instant."

As we headed back down the hoses began to come to life, water hit the blazing ground floor and we were enveloped in a sudden cloud of scalding steam and smoke. I held my breath and ran for the front door. Once back in the street I saw the front of the building beginning to darken down and watched clouds of expanding white smoke roll out from the ground floor and obscure the building. I savoured the cool damp air and went to work.

The Boy

My grandparents lived on the 11th floor of a tower block in Limehouse in East London. As a child I used to look from their windows at the fire engines screaming past on their way to another emergency. More often than not, if I followed the direction of the fire engine, I would see a pall of black smoke in the East London sky. I don't know why, but for as long as I remember, I was fascinated with the big red engines with the wheeled ladder on the back, the blue flashing lights on the roof, the noisy air horns, clanging bell and the men who came to the fire in them.

The East End of London had been more or less razed to the ground by the Luftwaffe in the Blitz of World War II. Night after night from September 1940 until May 1941 tons and tons of bombs were dropped on this district. The East End was home to a multitude of docks covering a twelve mile stretch of the River Thames from The Royal Docks at North Woolwich, through the East and West India Docks in Poplar, across the river to the Surrey Docks right down to the London Docks at the Tower of London.

Inevitably stray bombs missed their targets and many of the tightly packed streets of terraced houses were flattened during this period. Casualties were high but still the spirit of the East Enders shone through. 'The Blitz Spirit' is a phrase that was coined to reflect the resilience of the East Enders during that time. It is a phrase that has since been used to describe everything from embattled communities from flood ravaged third world disaster areas, to the City of New York in the aftermath of the 9/11 attacks, to those trying to live as normal a life as possible in the war-torn streets of Syria.

After the war, many of the bombed streets were flattened to make way for faceless post war council housing estates; people who were once talking over garden fences were now bearing witness to the re-birth of an area and a whole new way of life from their windows on the 20th floor. The docks were re-built with large warehouses of lightweight construction, replacing the large Victorian warehouses that had fallen victim to bombs. The period just after the War saw more ships coming into the Port of London than at any time in history. However, the rise of the motor vehicle, road and rail freight in the 60s and 70s, as well as constant trouble in industrial relations saw the gradual demise of the docks and shipping in London. The docks were all but derelict by the late 70s and many other bombed properties remained derelict until the early 1980s when the area saw another massive metamorphosis.

This ensured the firemen of London's East End were among the busiest in the world during the post-war years. Massive warehouse fires raged along the river, ship fires took firefighting crews into what seemed like hell itself, and entire families succumbed to tragic fires in run down housing, caused by an overturned paraffin heater in a crowded two up two down. The aftermath of terrorism was also brought on to the menu of a fireman's duties when the Northern Ireland troubles spread to the mainland in the 70s. If it was happening to firemen anywhere in the world it was happening to the London firemen. Even during my tender years, I saw fire engines go past the top of my street almost as often as London's famous red double decker buses. The sound of two-tone fire engine horns was a familiar lullaby to the slumbers of many children in our area.

One summer, Saturday afternoon, I was sitting on the sofa at my grandparents' while my mother, father and both my grandparents were watching a Saturday matinee film. Bored, I got up and went to go into another room when something caught my eye. From beyond the net curtain, I could see a cloud of black smoke obscuring the River Thames, a mile or so from the block. At the source of this smoke was a riverside warehouse with flames belching from its upper windows and a mass of fire from the roof.

I called to my dad; his generation were witness to the nightly ravages of the Luftwaffe during the Blitz. They had seen flames beyond the imagination of even the most seasoned firefighting veterans of today. He raised an eyebrow at the fire and led me to the balcony for a clearer view. As I stood upon a plant pot to see over the wall, the first ladder pushed up from the ground to add even more silky threads of water to the inferno consuming the building.

After much persuasion, my dad eventually agreed to drive me over to the fire to get a better look. We got out of the car and walked as far as we could get. Standing among a crowd of onlookers and displaced local residents I was perched on a wall watching black clad firemen rolling out hose, pitching ladders and shuffling fire engines to allow aerial ladders and hose laying lorries better access to the building. I was awestruck, I knew what firemen did, and I had seen and smelt fire. But never before had I tasted the soot, felt the heat from a hundred yards or heard the deep malevolent bonfire like sounds of a hundred-year-old building being eaten inside out by fire, a fire that had in all probability started as a flame no bigger than my finger but had consumed this Victorian giant in less than a couple of hours. The fireman in me was born on that day.

Steve with the Red Watch at Poplar Fire Station on his first visit on Bonfire Night, Nov 5th 1982

As I got older, I became more fascinated and ventured further in pursuit of the big red engines. I'd hear the two-tone horns turning out of Poplar fire station, just a few streets up from where I lived, and race up to the main road to see if they were headed my way. I'd get a head-start on them and follow the sound into the distance, around the streets of Poplar until I saw the tell-tale pall of smoke. A derelict building, a burning car, a pile of rubbish burning on wasteland, I got to know a few faces and always got a humorous welcome, usually along the lines of, "He's here again, I swear we'd be nowhere near as busy if it weren't for that kid."

It was two nights before Bonfire Night in 1982, I was 14 and already knew the shifts that the firemen worked; two days followed by two nights. I decided I wanted to help the firemen out on what was and still is the busiest night of the year for the country's firefighters, November 5th. I talked my friend Billy into coming with me.

"'Scuse me, can we come to the station and help you out on Bonfire Night?" we asked.

"Wait there kid, I'll get the Guvnor."

Shortly after, a man in a white shirt with black epaulettes, each with two white 'pips', on both his shoulders came to the door.

"Can I help you boys?"

"Er…yes…we want to help you out on Bonfire Night, do some cooking or the washing up or something."

"It's for our scouts firefighting badge," lied Billy enthusiastically.

The Guvnor looked us up and down. "Well…thanks for the offer lads…"

But, I thought.

"We'd be delighted," said the Guvnor. "Get here at 6:15 on the night and we'll get you sorted."

"Cor…thanks, that's great, we'll see you then."

On the night we turned up dead on time, I think they were as surprised we came back as we were that they still let us in. We were taken up to the mess room at Poplar and introduced to the Mess Manager: 'Judgy'. He poured us each a cup of tea and soon we were joined by the rest of the Watch noisily arriving in the mess.

I looked down at the neon lit appliance room below, the first two bays were empty, in the third bay was an old Merryweather turntable ladder and beyond that a Ford Transit Divisional Control Unit. The pump ladder and pump were out on calls, I had heard them darting along the road since I had got in from school. The Red Watch had come on duty at 6 pm, but the Blue Watch had been responding from one call to another since just after school turned out, not surprisingly.

As if on cue, one fire engine returned, a few younger guys necked their cups of tea and got up. Some more looked up from their conversations and someone farted loudly, Billy and I giggled to each other. The pump ladder had returned from a bonfire call somewhere, this was followed some minutes later by the pump.

We were hustled into the kitchen where Judgy chucked us a bag of potatoes and a couple of peelers.

"We're having stew tonight, lads, get peeling… everything in the bag," he said in his broad Yorkshire accent.

We set to work as Judgy returned to a massive pot on the stove. Another fireman wearing a blue shirt with a loosely fitted black tie walked in. He had a mop of black hair that went below the collar on his shirt.

"Alright boys…what the? Oi Judgy you 'orrible git, why you making them peel the spuds when there's a machine over there?"

"Eff off, Codsy, they need to learn the hard way," replied Judgy.

"Come on, give us 'em 'ere, we'll put 'em in the machine." Codsy picked up the bowl.

A small bell began to ring in the mess followed by loud bells, all of the lights that were not on burst into life. Billy and I looked up, Codsy ran from the kitchen and Judgy carried on at the stove. We looked at him.

"I thought you were here to help? Go on then, go and have a look, we're over tonight so I am off the run to do the cooking."

Billy and I ran across the mess and down the stairs, a group of firemen including the Guvnor were gathered around a massive antiquated printer that chattered out in the room.

"All the lot" was cried out and someone reached over to drop three coloured switches on an equally antiquated looking box of lights and switches.

All of the men hustled out of the room, one by one the engines on the pump ladder, pump and turntable ladder burst noisily into life and they pulled into East India Dock road with a twofold mêlée of noise and light. We looked down at the old printer and looked at a message full of codes but managed to make out they were going to a fire in a scrap yard, in Ditchburn Street, Poplar.

"I know that," I said to Billy. "It's behind Blackwall Tunnel, shall we go, it'd only take us a few minutes to run there."

"Nah," he said, "we're meant to be helping here, not running after them."

A young fireman came out of the office. "Alright boys, where have they gone?"

We both stepped back, and he looked at the printer.

"Do you understand all of this?" he enquired, we both shook our heads.

18

He explained the cryptic message that had been hammered out on the old Home Office teleprinter, we could see that they had been called to a fire in a scrapyard in Ditchburn Street in Poplar but that was about it. He then carefully explained the meaning of the various letters and numbers which were short-hand code from the fire control room at Stratford for what fire engines were attending from what station, the risk code, map reference and so on.

He reached over flicked up the three coloured switches and pressed down another, some of the lights went off, he then explained how "this box of tricks" controls the lights in the station that come on when a call is received and the coloured buttons matched the coloured lights in the bay where the fire engines sat to show which fire engines were called to the incident.

"There you go, as clear as mud."

"Oh right, thanks," we said.

"Come on then, let's get you back upstairs to get our dinner on."

We walked out of the Watchroom and towards the stairs.

"Why didn't you go?" asked Billy.

"Oh, I'm on outduty. I'm being sent to another station tonight…Millwall, the one at the bottom of the Island, d'ya know it?"

"I know it," I said, "the old one on the corner."

"That's it, F23 Millwall, should be a bit quieter than this place tonight."

The turntable ladder came back within about ten minutes, followed by the pump ladder and eventually the pump. As Bonfire Nights go, it wasn't too bad, about 18 calls in all plus to the 10 or so that Blue Watch had attended before 6pm. We all managed to eat together, although the TL got a call towards the end of the meal. In between calls, Billy and I got a tour of the station and fire engines or 'machines' as they were colloquially called. We looked at the equipment, went into F Division Staff and got shown over the Divisional Control Unit by a friendly old Sub Officer called Ron. Ultimately, we were shown to the dormitory where we were given a small tie on sheet, a pillow and a blanket. I didn't sleep much between the calls and we were told in no uncertain terms to shut up…or words to that effect every time we whispered a little too loudly.

So, I'd had my first stay at a fire station, Poplar fire station. An experience I was to repeat on hundreds of occasions over the coming twenty odd years in a place I came to regard as a second home.

The following years Billy came back to the station once or twice more but didn't share my enthusiasm for the Fire Brigade. He ended up as a Policeman funnily enough, although we still laugh about that night on the station all those years ago.

I regularly used to turn up at the station, always greeted warmly by most as 'The Boy'. I got to know everything about firefighting, Poplar fire station and its proud, busy and sometimes tragic history. I eventually got to go out on the fire engines and as it happens; saw some pretty good fires, most of them as an observer. There were a few occasions though where I got to do a little more.

I went to Stepney Green Boys School, a modern office block style Comprehensive that was about 8 floors high. One afternoon I was in one of the higher floors on the east side of the building facing Poplar, just as the lessons were winding up for the day, I noticed a large pall of smoke rising from in front of the old power station near East India Dock. Soon after this the 'bell' went and I was off. I ran down and got my push bike from the compound and cycled off towards home. I rode along Ben Johnson Road, over the hill by the stadium and on towards Burdett Road, still seeing the pall of smoke from time to time between the buildings. In no time I was into East India Dock Road, indoors, quickly changed and out again heading for the smoke. It had died down somewhat but smoke was still coming up from behind the containers, I hadn't heard anymore sirens and as I flew past the fire station, I noticed through the open doors that the TL and Divisional Control Unit were in the station…whatever the fire was it was not serious.

I got to the gate of East India Docks at the junction of East India Dock Road and Leamouth Road, this dock had been empty for years and apart from a big shipping container yard the dock was populated with scrapyards and derelict buildings so there was no security. I rode in and through the now cooling smoke that was banking down across the cobbled roads. Soon I got sight of a dripping fire hydrant with two lengths of hose attached. I followed them as they snaked through the dock until they came to Poplars pump ladder and parked a little further up was the pump.

I saw a couple of jets run out from the PL over to a great big pile of burnt tyres. There were still several fires burning underneath the deeper parts of the pile. I saw a few of the White Watch firemen and as the smoke parted I saw atop a smouldering pile the charismatic White Watch Station Officer 'Twizzle'. He was an outspoken character known throughout the Division for his no nonsense approach and obsessive love of fishing…in actual fact after his retirement he went on to become a writer for a number of fishing journals and spent a lot of his time fishing all over the world before his untimely death in 2003. He had also been awarded the British Empire Medal for his part in the 1975 Moorgate Underground Disaster, where he was one of the first firemen on the scene.

After the usual round of insults about where I had been since I had 'lit this one' and one or two other remarks in dispute of my parentage, I found myself on a jet with Matt and Dean, both were young firemen on the White Watch although as was typical of Poplar and the standards of the officers they were already vastly experienced hands.

I was passed a small one and three quarter inch (45mm) jet that had been divided from a large 2 and a half inch (70mm) hose line into two to assist in the damping down. I perched myself on some old car body parts while the guys saw I was settled with the weight of the hose, after a few moments of encouragement and direction for the hose, Matt and Dean crawled over the pile and began to expose more of the burning tyres below for me to extinguish. After a while everything was cool, I helped make up a few of the lengths of hose from the hydrant while others, filthy and black from the fire, were bundled onto the back of the fire engine. Me, an equally filthy teenager happy as Larry with my firefighting, got back on my bike and pedalled off home down East India Dock Road. I came home filthy so many times I can't remember my Mum's reaction to this particular event, but I suppose it was the same as always: "Good money on clothes…dress you in rags in future… bloody fires…."

Sometimes I think back to some of the things I did and shudder, but I think of them in the context of today's culture, where probably the Fire Brigade and my parents would have been taken to task for letting me go to fire stations and fires. But to be honest I was a sensible kid, or at least I thought I was, and this kept me out of trouble that others of my age were quickly discovering.

Eventually, as the years moved on, I got a little less interested in chasing around on my bike and started to get attracted to the other side of fire station life. I regularly started to socialise with the men I came to know as a second family. There were football tournaments, charity bath races, barbeques, all of which cemented the family bond that is almost unique to the Fire Brigade. Finally in 1986 as my eighteenth birthday approached, I saw an advert in the Daily Mirror asking for applicants for the position of Firefighter in the London Fire Brigade. The rest of my life was about to begin.

Training

Steve as a Probationary Firefighter at Bethnal Green Fire Station in 1988.

I sent off the application and was eventually invited up to Fire Brigade HQ at Lambeth to sit the educational tests. A maths test, followed by a written comprehension test and finally a dictation test, a bit of a breeze for a kid only a couple of years out of school.

This was followed in a couple of months by an interview. At the time, interviews were being conducted at local Area Headquarters. The 11 Divisions had gone, and the Fire Brigade had just changed over to five Areas. The area I lived in was now part of North East Area. Poplar was at that time the area HQ having previously been the Divisional HQ for the F Division. Not surprisingly as I lived locally, my interview was at Poplar. I arrived at the station and entered a familiar place, but for the first time I was on official business. The Green Watch were on duty that day they all came by the reception to give me their own piquant wishes of good luck. The Green Watch Guvnor Olly led me up to the offices where I was welcomed by a uniformed Officer who greeted me with a knowing smile. Nevertheless, I was shown no favours and had quite a difficult interview.

The fact I had hung around the fire station for the past four years or so meant nothing. The interview was properly structured around what experience I'd had of teamwork, trust, manual dexterity, working under pressure, dealing with equalities issues among other things. For an eighteen-year-old who had left school just about two years earlier and then gone and worked in a bank in the City, this is where it all started to go wrong.

I hadn't heard anything for weeks, the first few telephone calls I made told me that there was a high number of applicants and it may take a while, after this I got the impression that if I hadn't heard I hadn't been successful. As a last chance I decided to have a drive up to LFB headquarters to see the recruitment people face to face. Luckily for me, I got there during lunch, there was only one guy in the office in Queensborough House, one of the old HQ Buildings. I gave him my name and he looked through a pile of buff coloured cardboard folders all of which had a big 'A' marked on them. My folder was not there, I must have failed the interview, as if to confirm this; he started looking through a pile marked with a 'B' he got about half a dozen down and withdrew a folder, it had my name on it, my stomach sank.

I looked at the folder, at the same time the recruitment guy and I were drawn to a big character marked on the folder…it was an 'A'. I had passed, but for some reason my folder had been put in the wrong pile. He smiled and told me I would be hearing from them soon. Delighted, I bounded out of the room glancing over my shoulder to see the guy urgently looking through the rest of the folders for anymore 'passes' in the reject pile.

I got another letter soon after; I was to report to the Greater London Council's County Hall on the South Bank to get through the last hurdle of the recruitment process; the medical. This is where I had the advantage; I was young, very fit and a picture of health. It was only a formality, or so I thought.

I felt a little ill on the day before the medical, it was the early part of 1987, cold and miserable. I guessed I was just a little bit under the weather with all the worrying about getting through. I didn't sleep well the night before the medical, tossing and turning, hot and cold, drifting into restless dreams of the medical I was due to have. Eventually I woke up at about seven in the morning, and I felt terrible. I had come down with a heavy cold.

Undeterred I got up, got showered and changed and made my way over to County Hall. I was shown into the medical suite and asked to wait. Eventually a doctor came out and led me into a room where he made a thorough examination of me, despite the fact I was obviously ill I seemed to get through everything. I was then taken to a booth, sat down and given a set of headphones. The hearing test was explained to me; whenever I heard a sound, I was to push the little button in my hand. All ready, I waited for the tests to begin and I waited and waited.

Eventually, the doctor came into the booth and led me out. I enquired what was wrong why we hadn't done the test and he explained that I had done the test and scored zero. Then it came to me, I was so blocked up I was as deaf as a post. The hearing test is a series of very quiet high- and low-pitched bleeps, although I could hear things reasonably well in the world outside; I was so blocked up, I did not hear a thing during the test.

The doctor explained that he could not pass me, but noted I did appear to be suffering from a heavy cold, which was to be my salvation. I took myself straight off to my GP; he had been my doctor for my whole life and knew me very well. I begged him to write a letter to the Fire Brigade, although he couldn't do this, he told me that if I got some sort of appeal, he would inform them I was suffering from flu on the day.

I went home and got busy putting pen to paper; I followed this up with the usual telephone calls but felt like my chance had passed me by. Miserable I went to the fire station where the Green Watch were again on duty. I told them the story and they sympathised, some being positive others saying it didn't look good for another run at the medical. Would I have to wait another year?

What I didn't know as I left that day was that Olly had been down to see the Area Commander, Joe Kennedy. Joe was a firefighting legend who had cut his teeth in the East End of London during the early sixties and had been promoted up through the ranks to Assistant Chief Officer now in charge of the entire North East Area of London. Joe, who I didn't know at the time, but had always asked after me, was horrified. I was later informed that a few telephone calls were made that afternoon, the result was, thankfully I got called back up to County Hall in early spring.

This time round I had the hearing test again and cringed when I heard the array of pitches going through my now clear head, what must they have thought on the last medical seeing me sitting there like a lemon with a silly grin on my face doing nothing. This was followed by an allergy test; I had hay fever so they had to check I was not allergic to everyday items that the firefighter may come into contact with, such as dust and water. I left on top of the world and walked along the South Bank on a lovely spring morning confident I was through.

Early in May 1987 I had a bad car accident, bad for the car fortunately and not for me. I was pulling out of a side turning just off Ben Johnson Road in Stepney when some idiot came hurtling over the canal bridge at about 50mph and straight into the side of me. I had just pulled away when this happened and for some unknown reason did not have my seat belt on. Seeing this Ford Fiesta XR2 looming up on me I dived across the passenger side of the car and bounced off just about every surface of the car when the other one hit. Apart from feeling a little bruised and having a few cuts in my mouth I was OK. But I was really not happy. I had seen my pride and joy written off and despite the fact I was hit by a car doing almost twice the speed limit, I was deemed to be in the wrong because I was emerging from a side road and to top the lot, like most youngsters I could only afford third party insurance and so found myself the proud owner of a pile of scrap metal. My treasured Mk5 Cortina was gone, and I was left rattling about in a 1970 Mini Clubman with holes in the floor that I'd bought for a few hundred quid.

One fine morning around this time, I wandered downstairs with my own personal black cloud over my head and picked up a pile of mail from the passage. I scanned through the envelopes bringing more bad news about my accident when I came across a thick A5 Envelope. It had a London SE1 postmark; it could only be one thing. I frantically tore through the envelope and started to read the London Fire Brigade headed letter.

'Dear Mr Dudeney

You are invited to take up appointment as a Fireman with the London Fire Brigade. You should report to the London Fire Brigade Training Centre at 94 Southwark Bridge Road, London SE1 on 13 July 1987.'

Was I happy? I ran into the kitchen laughing so much I was somewhere between laughing and crying, my mum cried and my dad shook my hand and congratulated me. I got on the telephone and called my girlfriend, giving her the good news. I had done it, all my life for as long as I remember I had wanted to be a fireman and now I had been given the chance.

13 July 1987 was a warm day with white fluffy clouds occasionally blocking the sun across London. Surprisingly I slept really well and got up at about six, ready for the tube ride to Borough Station, from which there was just a short walk to the Training Centre.

When I got to reception of the Training Centre there were already a couple of other lads there. We sat there in silence occasionally giving each other nervous glances or looking up at each new arrival. Sometime after 9 o'clock a man dressed in a Station Officers uniform came and called a register. All present, we were taken up some stairs and given a brief introduction to the London Fire Brigade and the Training Centre. About half of the group were then led away by the Officer. The rest of us were to wait and we would be dealt with shortly. Eventually another two Officers came up to see us, one was a Station Officer, the other a Sub Officer. We were to be taken to the GLC supply warehouse over at Tottenham Hale to be kitted out in our uniform.

We loaded into a personnel carrier, which still to this day I swear were the most uncomfortable vehicles I ever travelled in, and made our way to Tottenham. We arrived and disembarked, and were lined up in alphabetical order, being a 'D', I was third in the queue after two 'C's.

Up in the warehouse we were called up to a large wooden counter a few at a time, we were roughly measured up and issued with four blue shirts, four pairs of socks, four blue T-Shirts, two pairs of blue 'workwear' trousers and an off the peg undress uniform consisting of black trousers and a black double-breasted jacket with silver buttons with the GLC crest on them. This was followed by a sleeping bag, tie on sheet, pillow and pillowcase, two caps, two ties and two pairs of leather shoes. Then we got the good stuff. I was given two Melton wool double breasted fire tunics with the same silver buttons as the jacket, two pairs of yellow rubber waterproof over trousers, two pairs of rubber debris gloves, a pair of rubber steel toe cap fire boots, two large canvas belts, a pouch with a short personal line and finally a yellow cork fire helmet.

I had all the kit, this was it, now I was a proper fireman – or so I thought. We were crestfallen when we got back to Southwark to find out we were to be put into a 'holding squad' and start training the following week. This shouldn't be a problem, after all we were here. But we soon found out that the holding squad were the 'lowest of the low' in Training Centre terms. As the hundreds of others lined up at each parade in smart uniforms with highly polished shoes, spotless trousers and tunics, we were over in the last line with blue trousers and shirts.

We spent our days cleaning equipment, stuffing circulars into envelopes at HQ, picking weeds from the front of the building and generally being abused by everyone from the Commandant down to the other half of the entrants on that day that had been taken straight into a training squad.

After a week in the holding squad, we returned the following Monday to be met in the locker room by our instructor Trevor, who had returned from leave. Trevor was a young officer who was already quite experienced due to his time served at busy South London stations including Brixton. His Dad had also been a fireman and had retired a few years earlier so firefighting was the family business. Most of those early days were spent with Trevor shouting at us like a Sargent Major, his face getting increasingly red to match his red tinged moustache.

All of a sudden, we were proper recruits and as if to prove this we were taken over to the 'grotto', a little playground behind the Training Centre where we spent a couple of hours doing squad drill; standing to attention, marching, left wheels, rights wheel, about turns, the lot. By the end of our training, we would have given a troop of Guardsmen a run for their money on the drill square.

Over the coming days we were gradually introduced to the equipment, from running around the drill yard with heavy lengths of hose until we nearly fell over exhausted, only to be ordered to keep going at a run and not to "dare walk on my drill ground, Dudeney."

We were introduced to ladders and pumps and gradually bit by bit, with the assistance of detailed classroom sessions that explained the workings and science behind the equipment, and a couple of hours of self-study every evening, the mystery of the equipment began to unravel. From single ladder drills that took four of us ages to complete, we practiced and practiced, barking our shins and knuckles and pushing ourselves to levels of endurance that seemed impossible in the weeks before this training began.

Once we had the basics and the drills became a little more sophisticated, the classroom seemed to beckon a little more often. Now we were looking at building construction, fire prevention legislation, chemistry and hydraulics. All of the time I had spent around the fire station in the years before never prepared me for this. It wasn't such a big deal for me being young and relatively fresh out of school. I'd trade with the older guys; they would assist me with some of the tricky practical elements or push me that little bit further when I was close to collapse, because although arguably fitter than some of my squad mates, I was immature in terms of stamina and the ability to mentally push myself to and beyond the limits. Meanwhile I'd sit there and explain a hydraulics formula to them, or go through various chemistry problems like how many hydrogen and carbon atoms and structural isomers were needed to bond, to make methane or propane or even octane for that matter.

Once we got to about week eight of our training, we were due to move onto the hardest part of the course; breathing apparatus, and for these two weeks, we had another specialist breathing apparatus instructor.

"This laddie is a Siebe Gorman firefighter breathing apparatus set. You will get to know this over the coming week better than you know your wife, girlfriend or mother, because none of them will save your life while your arse is on fire in a burning sub-basement."

He was not wrong. We learnt that BA set in and out from every single part of the demand valve system, to the design and construction of the air cylinder. Along with this were all of the very strict breathing apparatus procedures used in the UK fire service.

After we got through the BA course, definitely the hardest part of training, it was all downhill, apart from the final examinations and practical tests at the end of the twenty weeks. Sadly, I contracted food poisoning at the Training Centre and missed a few days. I was 'back-squadded' for a week and had to get to know a whole new group of recruits and a new instructor. Of the twelve of us in this new squad only a handful of us had not been in the military; most had seen service in the Falklands or Northern Ireland and had come into the fire service after their military discharge. I was the youngest and felt very intimidated by some of the guys who were more than 10 years older than me and who had "fought a war while you were still at school, kid." Nevertheless, as time went on, I began to fit in with the squad, and although I never quite got along as well as I did with the original squad, we eventually headed towards the final weeks.

One night during October 1987, I was woken by a strange howling noise. My bedroom backed onto Poplar High Street and as I had no heavy curtains or blinds, there was normally quite a bit of light in the room from the orange street lamps. I laid there taking in the noise and felt a little unnerved in my semi-conscious state by the lack of light in the room. After a few seconds there was a flash followed a roll of thunder. I jumped out of bed and looked across the playground of the school at the back of the house. The trees were almost bent sideways and the air was filled with debris like something off The Wizard of Oz. I went across the house and into my parent's room. They were awake.

"What's happening?" I asked.

"Dunno, some sort of storm, the wind is terrible."

I looked out of their window at the front, we lived in a small square formed of 25 small red brick council houses on three sides of the square, the fourth side was a small row of garages and the entrance road which went around the square and back onto itself. In the middle was an area of around 12 parking bays with trees in the middle. Two of the trees were blown down, one on top of cars, the other into the road, this was some storm. I went back into my room and looked at the clock; it was around four in the morning. Unable to sleep or do anything because of the power cut, I decided to get dressed and like a crazy man have a drive around the area.

I managed to get my car out of the parking bay and around the tree; I drove up to East India Dock Road and unbelievably the car seemed to be lifting off the road in the wind. I turned right and the road looked like a rubbish tip, leaves, twigs branches, rubbish bins and a whole host of litter was being blown down the road at unnaturally fast speeds. Further ahead I could see a large shadow looming in the road with flashing blue lights bouncing off it. A large old sycamore tree had fallen into the road and crushed a van. The White Watch were on duty on this night and the pump ladder and pump crews from Poplar were trying to cut through the trees and into the van. Luckily, the driver was not injured but was trapped by the tree crushing the van.

Unable to help, I looked across Poplar Park to Woodstock terrace. Two friends of mine; Joanne, who was later to become my wife and Sarah, her older sister, lived there. Things looked OK and as if to testify I saw Joanne's car being driven down the road. Why would a seventeen-year-old girl be out at this time I thought? Then I remembered Joanne was in Arizona with friends and her dad Joe was using her car. He was leaving to start his shift at the Post Office.

After driving around a while longer it began to dawn on me that I had so far been lucky not to have met up with a lump of debris being blown past at 90mph. I decided to quit while I was still in one piece and drove back home.

I got a little more sleep and later, on my dad's battery radio we discovered that the whole of the South East of England had been battered by a hurricane that had taken over 20 lives, including two firemen in Dorset, who were killed when a tree fell on their fire engine. The storm had caused millions and millions of pounds worth of damage. I left for Southwark Training Centre with a fellow recruit Andy at about 7am. We managed to make our way across East London and the deserted City of London, taking shortcuts and diversions around roads that were blocked from fallen trees, cranes and scaffolding. We eventually managed to cross the River at Southwark Bridge, and what should have been a 20-minute four-mile journey took over an hour and covered twice the distance with diversions. Expecting the whole of training school to be up and running as usual we walked under the arch to find the place almost deserted.

We found a few people sipping tea by candlelight in the canteen. Hardly anyone had got there; it was only those of us who lived nearer the centre of London who managed to get in. Only a handful of the Training Staff managed to get through, so it was decided, with permission from HQ on this exceptional morning that the instructors and recruits would drive around the local area helping out as best we could.

While others got a host of equipment ready; saws, axes, brooms, salvage sheets and so on, my instructor Dave and I took a fire engine to a DIY hire shop to 'borrow' a few tree saws for the day. Back at Southwark we loaded up a crew and started on our way. Firstly, we stopped just around the corner on Borough Road where a tree had fallen across the pavement. We managed to cut away the branches and clear a path through the tree to allow pedestrians to walk through. Part of the tree had crashed into an old lady's roof. We managed to secure a salvage sheet to the roof to keep out the worst of the remainder of the storm.

After a few hours of trawling around Southwark we eventually ended up driving north over Tower Bridge. I think London Bridge was closed, but as we turned into Tower Hill we were met by a tree that was taking out all but one of the three lanes on our side of the road. Dave decided this was to be our next stop and we set to work clearing this ancient tree that had fallen from the grounds of the Tower of London. As we beavered away it soon dawned on us that there were hundreds of tourists in London, who due to the power cuts were stranded with very little to do. We got quite a crowd and all of us at some point had to stop to have our picture taken by a smiling Japanese tourist or to line up next to a heavily tanned Texan who wanted to get a picture of the damage caused by the storm. It was even better that we got filmed by ITN and appeared on an extended TV news bulletin that night.

A year before I joined, the film 'London's Burning' hit our TV screens. It was so successful that they commissioned a series to follow which went on for over 14 more years to become staple viewing for tens of millions on a Sunday night. The cast for the new series was largely unchanged, but three new actors were joining the cast. Glen Murphy, Ross Boatman and Treva Etienne. Originally, our instructor Dave had trained the cast for the film, so he disappeared in the early part of one week to give the new actors the basics. After a couple of days, they joined our training squad when we were on the drill ground to put what they had leaned into practice, he'd done a pretty good job with them in a couple of days as they did OK alongside us. On the final day of that week, the rest of the cast from the film came and had a refresher day at the Training Centre. Our deputy instructor took care of us that day as Dave put them through their paces before filming started again.

I have to admit I absolutely loved *London's Burning* back in the day, especially when it was on before I went on duty, it made me look forward to going on duty the next day. Sadly, towards the end, most of the cast had changed and the production was much less gritty than in the early days. I never watched the last couple of series.

All of a sudden, late autumn was upon us and that day in July when I first walked under the arch at Southwark seemed like a lifetime ago. Training was all but finished and everything was heading towards the final tests. Kit was prepared and polished; drills were practiced over and over until they were accurate, with every wasted second shaved off the time we took to complete them. Books were read at home at night or on the train, even in the pub after work. I bothered everyone I could to ask me questions about the weight of a ladder, the formula to get 500 gallons of water per minute up a 300-foot building, the chemical formula and UN number for a whole host of hazardous materials. I swear any one of my friends or family could have sat the written exams for me and passed.

Week 19 of training arrived, the week when we could have failed as an individual in the written or oral interviews, or failed as a whole squad on the drill ground. Over the course of the week all of the skills honed in the previous months were now tested in a variety of ways before we were let loose on the public of London. We were tested as a group on pumps and pumping, carried out BA drills and placed ladders up to the most inaccessible places. We sat in classrooms and had exams covering all of the topics that we digested over the course of training. Then it was the dreaded face to face examination with the Senior Instructor where he could ask five questions on anything, written or practical from what we had learned.

Finally, on the last day of the week we had our final practical examination. The Divisional Officer stood glowering at us with his peaked cap and double-breasted overcoat as Station Officer Dave detailed the drill we would be performing. It was raining heavily and the two fire engines we had scrubbed and polished in readiness for the final looked grim under the dark London sky. We were lucky enough to have a 1981 Dodge that had just been moved from the operational fleet into training, as well as the trusty 1975 Dennis F109 that had served us so well throughout the course. We mounted up; I was in the middle on the back of the Dennis. I fiddled nervously with the harness of my breathing apparatus set hanging in front of me in the cab.

Soon, the order "Squad 13/87, as far as detailed, get to work" boomed around the drill yard and we were off. I was part of the crew that was to put the 35ft wooden Dewhurst ladder up to the second floor next to and in time with the other crew who were placing the 45ft '135' ladder up to the third floor.

"Underun…Well! Extend…Well! Head in! Get to work," orders were barked as the drill unfolded.

"Water on, number one delivery, branch working on ground floor, four bars pressure."

Water coursed through the first of the hoses run out to 'protect' the crews from the imaginary fire devouring the drill tower. I jumped on the back of the Dennis and pulled my BA set off the bracket. I laid it on my lap, passed my hands through the harness and hoisted the set over my head and onto my back. I jumped down from the Dennis and as I jumped, I cursed. We had been taught to dismount the fire trucks properly and not to launch ourselves out like we were "on a fucking Hollywood movie set."

Before I hit the floor, I heard the instructor shout at me, "Dismount that machine properly, Dudeney."

I looked over to the DO, still glowering and even more miserable and damp than when I last dared glance his way. He looked at me and made a note on his clipboard. If I thought for a minute this had gone unnoticed by everyone in the confusion I was soon left in no doubt as a fellow squad member deliberately bumped into me as we rounded the corner and called me a prick!

I started my BA set, reported to Entry Control with my partner and made my way up the ladder to the second floor to fight the 'fire'. As we were pushing up the stairs with a high-pressure hose reel some others on the third floor were lowering a drill dummy over the edge of the parapet on a lowering line. I missed this, but as the dummy got to the ground another recruit tripped and fell flat as he moved the dummy to the casualty clearing area. This was one of the ex-military guys so I stopped feeling so bad about my mistake.

We soon made our way back down and all of the equipment was made up with the same theatrical timing and skill as it had been deployed. We fell back into our line at the end and I gasped for breath whilst standing to attention with water falling from the brim of my helmet onto my face. The Divisional Officer marched out in front of us and we were stood at ease while he de-briefed us. I swear he'd seen a different drill to us by the way he tore us to pieces. The only way I knew he'd been watching us was his reference to my jumping from the machine and his comment on how much use did I think I'd be to his Fire Brigade and the public of London if I had a broken ankle. By the end of it, we were all crestfallen, my exhaustion had given way to nausea and I was convinced that if we had maybe have scraped through, my acrobatics had seen our chances of passing fly straight out of the window. I was going to be so dead it was unreal.

I looked at the DO, his glower lightened and his face turned into a smile.

"Well, apart from that it was a good display, your casualties were out of the building in less than five minutes, the ladders went up a treat and the pumping was well done, especially as I know you haven't had that much time on the Dodge. Well done 13/87, I think you are ready to be unleashed onto the public of London…fall them out, Station Officer."

That was it, we were through! We had made it past the final hurdle. We fell out of line and heartily congratulated each other. After 19 weeks of blood, sweat and tears, literally. Whatever we had been previously; soldier, sailor, builder, banker, had been broken down and remoulded into a London firefighter.

Later in the day we were handed our London Fire Brigade helmet transfers, all through training we wore our helmets with just our names on the side. The LFB badge was only given to those who had passed the training. We thought we were the business that Friday afternoon. All of the appliances were cleaned by the recruit's last thing on a Friday. We were strutting around with our helmets on with badges like we were seasoned veterans. As senior squad we were dispensing our wealth of knowledge to all the other recruits about the best away to do this and that. Jack the lads every one of us.

That night we went out on the town, as we normally did. But instead of a few pints after work we hit the West End for a major celebration. I remember trawling through Covent Garden and Soho eventually ending up in a club called

Samantha's in Old Burlington Street just off Regent Street. One of the lads in the squad met a girl that night that he ended up marrying. The last time I saw him on a big job a few years back he was still happily married to her with a couple of grown up kids.

The following week was a bit of an anti-climax. We spent four days doing our First Aid certificate and getting all of our kit together. Midweek we got our postings. One of my squad Ian, a 25 year old ex-Marine and I got posted to F26 Bethnal Green. I got the Blue Watch and he got the Green Watch. As I remember everybody did fairly well. Soho, Plaistow, East Ham, Croydon. A couple got sent to Wembley another to Peckham, all fairly busy stations in those days. Ian and I were well made up. The East End was a lively area in those days before the developers came to town. I grew up there and hung out at the fire station so I knew this, but the entire east was very busy back then. Bethnal Green, Whitechapel, Poplar, Homerton, Stoke Newington, right out to Stratford, Ilford and Dagenham. There weren't many places a fireman could get posted to in East London that wasn't getting a lot of work.

So last thing on Friday 13 November 1987, we jumped into one of those uncomfortable personnel carriers. One for each Area that we were posted to, four of us jumped onto the North East Area one. Paul who was off to Plaistow Red Watch, Pav to East Ham Red Watch and Ian and I to Bethnal Green. When we arrived, The Green Watch were on duty and we were wheeled in to see the Green Watch Station Officer who read us the riot act just for the hell of it and then told us about the station. A little later, because the Blue Watch were on that night, I met my Station Officer, a very well-spoken calm cigar smoking gent called Keith. He told me a little more about life on the blue watch and then told me to go off and take it easy and to report back at 8 am for a 9 am start the following Wednesday, 18 November.

Inferno

Unlike my first morning at training centre, I did not sleep very well before my first day on full duty. I had a fitful sleep dreaming about missing work, being late, not getting on the Fire Engine, the whole shooting match. I eventually woke up at 6 am and sat downstairs checking my uniform over and over until my Mum and Dad got up at about 7 am.

I showered and changed, then went around to the shop to get my dad a newspaper. Wednesday 18th November was an overcast and mild day, nothing unusual about the day at all. I was the only one on my squad who had been posted on to the Blue Watch. Those posted to the Red and White Watch had already started their shifts on either Monday day for the Red Watch, or night for the White Watch. The Green Watch wasn't due to start until Friday so Ian, who was posted with me, and another couple still had a few days to go. So of all of the 7000 operational firefighters in London only one was due to start today...me.

I left at 7:30 and got to Bethnal Green in about 15 minutes. I parked my car and walked into the station. I met up with the White Watch Station Officer. A lean grey-haired man with a small pointed chin beard.

"Good morning Sir, I'm starting here on the Blue Watch today."

"Oh hello, yes I knew you were coming, you are a little early, but make yourself at home and your Watch will be in shortly."

I wandered out into the appliance bay and looked over the fire engines. The pump ladder was a 1982 Dodge, not unlike those at Poplar and the pump was a 1977 ERF, again with a similar set up to the old Dennis, so I was quite confident I knew were everything was. I wandered back into the office where the White Watch had now come down from their breakfast. The Leading Fireman on the White Watch, Terry, had a chat with me and showed me up to my locker.

I was already changed, but my fire kit was still inside where I'd placed it the previous Friday. I took this downstairs and started to nod nervously to the firemen who were coming through the station and giving me the eye on the way up to the locker room. I got into my fire kit at about 10 minutes to nine and went and hid myself away by the pump, too nervous to open the lockers but trying my hardest to remember what was where, in the space of half an hour I'd forgotten everything.

Just before 9 am I wandered back in near the muster area, there were quite a few there getting into their fire kit, some friendly, some looking at me like I was something on their shoes, still here I was. The Station Officer came from his office and we had roll call. I was detailed to ride the pump with a fireman called Dave on the back, the Station Officer sat up front in charge and another fireman called Pete was driving, as well as being nominated to look after me. The Watch were quite short so we were only riding 4 on the pump, it would normally be customary to ride with 5 on a recruit's first day.

Most of the Watch had joined in the 1970s and were all in their 30s or older. There were a couple of younger firemen but again they'd all been around for between three and five years which at the time seemed like forever to me.

We got our gear on, checked our BA and then went upstairs for tea. The Station Officer took out a Villager Cigar and lit it. Almost everyone else pulled out a packet of cigarettes and started smoking. It is bizarre but all of the time I worked at Bethnal Green where the majority of the Watch smoked, I was never interested. When I later transferred to Poplar, where only a couple smoked, I started smoking for the first time in my life.

Once we'd finished with our tea, we went downstairs and carried out more checks on the equipment. I was taken into see the Guvnor and after another brief look through my report from TC I was given an in depth look around the station; from the top floor to the basement; every room, store, cupboard and so on. I was told I'd have to know them all because it would be me who was sent to fetch things from them or clean them more often than not.

After this I was asked a few questions by more friendly members of the Watch while the not so friendly members asked more testing questions as if to try to trip me up. Soon enough it was 10:30, a couple of times the teleprinter warning bell went, leaving my heart in my mouth but still no call had come. I was expecting my first call at any second – what would it be, how would I cope? I hope I don't mess up was all I could think. We headed upstairs for 'stand easy', which according to Fire Brigade tradition at the time, consisted of a round of thick cheese and onion sandwiches and big mugs of strong tea. I ate nervously and the questions directed towards me were more about my time at Poplar.

Bethnal Green bordered Poplar to the south east, so they knew of my time there as a kid. I began to think it wasn't such a good thing, both Poplar and Bethnal Green are busy stations; there was obviously some rivalry between them and I was the butt of a number of ribald jokes. After 'stand easy' they all went off to smoke in the quiet room. One of the fireman there, a dark-skinned muscular guy called Mark had been talking to me while we were eating and having a go at some of those who had been giving me a hard time, I followed him into the TV room as he also didn't smoke. I sat quietly behind Mark watching some daytime TV show, the teleprinter warning bell rang. I tensed, then calmed down as it rang on. All of a sudden, the fire bells clanged into life and the lights came on. I had heard this sound a hundred times before, but it made me jump. This was it; this was for real, this was my first 'shout' as a London fireman. I felt my heart beating hard in my chest and an instant brow of sweat formed on my forehead.

I ran out of the TV room towards the pole house behind Mark and slid down to the ground floor. I ran to the pump, kicked off my shoes and stepped into my boots with the yellow plastic waterproof legging folded down over them. I looked up to see a green light showing in the ceiling. Pump only, I thought, can't be anything that serious; then again there were less people for me to hide behind.

I felt sick as I climbed up into the rear cab. The others climbed on, the Guvnor shouted something to Dave in the back with me, I didn't hear it, I didn't want to know and was not going to ask him to repeat it. I pulled my arms through my fire tunic and began to fasten the buttons, I looked across at Dave, and although he had got on the back after me, he was already rigged and looking out of the opposite window, helmet hanging in front of him off the BA set bracket. I pulled on my belt to secure it around me and instantly the heavy yellow hand lamp fell off. I re-threaded it and again attempted to get the belt on. We had belts at training centre but they didn't have the torch or axe on them to slide off the minute you lifted it up. I eventually got the whole ensemble on and popped my hat on my head. I looked out of the window and noticed we were coming to the end of Roman Road and appeared to be heading right.

As if to confirm this I was thrown hard against the side of the machine as we made the right. I guessed this was Bow's ground so decided that obviously weren't going to a small call on our ground, but on something more serious elsewhere. I decided to ask Dave.

"What have we got, Dave?"

"Fire…on Poplars ground, dunno where."

"Oh, thanks."

"Don't play football at all, do ya?" enquired Dave.

"Nah, not really…not since school," I replied.

And with that Dave turned back and looked out of the window. We then went left onto Mile End Road and on into Bow Road. I couldn't work out where in Poplar we were going, I lived there, it was straight across into Burdett Road in my book. Soon we made a right into Campbell Road, now I knew it must be the top of Poplar's ground. But surely Bow would have gone onto this with Poplar and not us? I began to worry, what if it was a big job and Poplar and Bow were already there. What if they were elsewhere and we were going to be first, it may be a raging inferno by the time we get there. This part of Poplar is as far from Bethnal Green as I could imagine.

As we swung into Devon's Road, I started scanning the sky, I couldn't see much and knew that we must soon be there or we would be leaving Poplar's ground. We turned right into Empson Street and drove onto the industrial estate. Soon I saw a couple of fire engines and a small cloud of white smoke. As we arrived, I followed Dave off the machine. The Guvnor was on the radio and a crowd of firemen looked at me. I recognised some from Poplar, and I nodded sheepishly. Others from Bow just looked at me and a happy looking Fireman with grey hair made a wisecrack and winked at me.

There was some rubbish burning over a wall on the side of the canal. Poplar Blue Watch had got a recruit a few weeks ago and he was busy seeing to the fire like an old hand already. My Guvnor had a chat with Bow's Guvnor and soon we were climbing back on the machine. Ironically my first shout had been on Poplar's ground and a bit of an anti-climax. I'd soon get to know that for every decent job there would be ten or more of these 'nothing shouts', but you never know when the next decent job is coming.

Later that day, I slammed my locker shut and bolted out of the dormitory and down the pole. I ran past the Watchroom where Paul the Sub Officer was looking at the teleprinter. The Guvnor, tie loosened off and cigar in mouth, joined him. I jumped into my boots and pulled on my tunic, Pete came running to the front driver's door so I decided to jump on in case I got left behind. I noticed both the green and red lights were on, Pump Ladder and Pump—this was obviously a more serious incident. I did a little better with the belt this time and left my helmet off in imitation of Dave over on the left of me. I thought I'd look like a cool fireman instead of the raw recruit I really was.

I heard something about Poplar again and we seemed to be heading off along Roman Road towards Bow but made a sharp right into Globe Road. I managed to catch something about "St Paul's Way", and "Poplar are not on it." I knew St Paul's Way, this was more near Bethnal Green's border with Poplar. We turned left onto Mile End Road and made our way up towards Burdett Road. As we cleared the Canal Bridge, Mile End Park opened up on the right. In the sky about a half a mile away I saw black smoke blowing across the sky. I came alive with adrenalin and was willing the machine nearer its destination with a mix of fear and excitement.

"What is it, Dave?"

"Dunno, we ain't there yet," came the reply, "but I guess it's something, so you'd better get the hydrant set in."

"OK I will."

As if in confirmation, the Guvnor called over, "When we get there grab the hydrant gear and go find a hydrant, Mr Dudeney."

"Yes Guv, OK."

I struggled to see ahead of me for some more signs but didn't pick much out between the BA sets hanging in front of me. I went to look out of the window but struck my helmet on the top of the door frame. Ducking, I saw we were approaching the railway bridge in Burdett Road, St Paul's Way was just a hundred yards beyond it. The smoke was visible to the right, I knew there were a lot of derelict houses on this side of St Paul's Way. I'd actually seen a good fire there a few years before while chasing the fire engines on my push bike. As we cleared the railway arch, I looked at the houses and the smoke was across from them. I was momentarily confused until we began to make the turn; ahead at the next junction was a small second-hand car dealers. Black smoke was coming through the large open doors and roof, tongues of flame came from the end window of a single storey white painted workshop.

The Pump Ladder had pulled up just past the workshop, Poplar's TL had arrived just before us and seeing as the ladders were unlikely to be used, they had pulled into Turners Road to the side. We stopped just beyond the workshop where I got off and ran around to the other side of the machine. The owner of the garage was an enormous man who seemed as round as he was tall. He was frantically trying to throw buckets of water on a caravan parked right next to the workshop; I guessed the caravan was his office. The workshop itself was well alight; I guess he wanted to save the rest. He was shouting at anyone who would listen about "getting some water on the fuckin' fire."

I realised I had come to a halt—the hydrant! I spun around and went to the locker of the Pump and lifted the middle locker door. I looked to my right and saw that Pete had already got the hydrant gear and was running towards a hydrant on the opposite kerb. I saw that a high-pressure hose reel had been pulled from the Pump Ladder and was already being got to work by Stuart who was on the Pump Ladder. Mark and Archie were securing their BA sets as Dave was running out a larger diameter inch and three-quarter jet that the guys would take into the fire.

Steve driving the Pump Ladder, Poplar Fire Station 1991.

I opened the next locker and pulled out a length of two and a half inch hose. I threw this out towards the hydrant and ran towards the hydrant with one end; I took the other end towards the PL and obediently offered it to Steve who was driving the PL.

"What the fuck is that?" he spat.

I looked down and realised I had run with the wrong end of the hose. I had left the female end at the hydrant and taken the male end to the pump. The simple rule is 'female towards the fire'. No matter what, the male end of the hose is always to the supply the female end to the fire.

"Ohh…I…"

"Sort it," was his reply as he turned his back on me. I ran off and swapped ends I don't know how in the confusion, but everyone including the owner of the site, seemed to have spotted me and were looking at me with varying levels of disgust. Once this was done, I was told by Paul the Sub Officer to help Dave out with the hose reel. The BA crew were inside, and the flames had given way to thick columns of white and grey smoke that pulsed out of the shattered windows. Dave was cooling the caravan and squirting the burning façade above the windows, he handed me the reel with a smile and pointed me towards the remainder of the façade.

"Up there, that's it…bit down the side of the caravan… over there just above the window." He spoke encouragingly to me. Soon the fire began to subside, Mark and Archie came out of the fire and pulled off their facemasks, this was the cue for Dave and me along with Stuart to go inside and finish the job off. The air inside was smoky and hot, at once my eyes began to water and I stifled a cough. I remembered to try to breathe through my nose but with the adrenalin still pumping I needed more air than my nose would allow in, so I returned to a pattern of breathe, cough, breathe, cough, trying for the life of me to slow my breathing, stop coughing and breathe through my nose. I felt even worse as Archie came back in after dumping his BA set, sucking on a cigarette.

We were there until just after three o'clock when a Pump turned up from Plaistow as a relief. We packed the remaining kit back on the old ERF Pump and headed back to Bethnal Green. So, three quarters of the way through my first day and I'd had two shouts and my first job, both on Poplar's ground. I bet myself Vince, the recruit at Poplar was well pissed off he had missed this one. It turned out however that Poplar was attending a flat fire not far from where I lived so I guess it didn't matter anyway.

The remainder of my first day was much less eventful. I managed to get through my first ever Automatic Fire Alarm call. This was at the Royal London Hospital on Whitechapel Road. We were on it with Whitechapel and Shadwell. Apart from standing around outside, nothing else happened. I'd go on to attend thousands of AFA's during my career along with rubbish fires, persons shut in lifts and false alarms. These made for the soup of 'nothing shouts' that kept us busy between real jobs.

At six o 'clock, in common with the other 113 fire stations across London, Blue Watch handed over to the Red Watch. More than one hundred and fifty of these Red Watch firefighters would come together that night for an event that would change the course of firefighting and go down in the history books of London.

I got home, got changed and decided to go to the pub with my friend Brian. We used to frequent the Phoenix at the end of my road at the junction with East India Dock Road. For some reason we decided to go up to the Resolute in Poplar High Street that night, I don't know why, this was my dad's local not mine. From the Phoenix we may have seen the fire engines from across London headed west along East India Dock Road into the centre of London, as it was I was blissfully unaware at the Resolute and at 11'O clock went home and jumped into bed in preparation for my second day on duty.

I got up a little later on the second day. I had a shower and came downstairs; my dad had just walked in from getting his newspaper.

"See, a couple of firemen got killed last night," he said throwing the paper across the table towards me. I went cold and looked at the newspaper 'Thirty two dead in Underground inferno' screamed the headline. There was a picture of a paramedic lifting a blackened casualty into an ambulance, the casualty had tubes down his throat and wore a London Fire Brigade fire tunic.

After I had got home and gone down to the pub a fire had started below the escalator at King's Cross Underground Station. The fire developed and exploded into the ticket hall, killing thirty-one people in the end, including the Station Officer from A24 Soho Red Watch; Colin Townsley.

King's Cross Station is one of London's major transport interchanges. As well as the Main Line King's Cross Station serving the North of England, four separate underground lines interchange at this station, which handles up to one hundred thousand people per hour. King's Cross is in the north eastern section of Central London on the Euston Road. It is on A23 Euston fire station's ground.

At approximately 7:32pm on Wednesday 18th November 1987, passengers coming up the Piccadilly Line escalator noticed a small fire showing through the wooden steps of the escalator about 20 ft or so from the top. After being alerted to the fire by passengers, the first call to the London Fire Brigade was received at 7:36pm from station staff. As if by a wicked turn of fate the local station A23 Euston, that was just half a mile along the same road, were out on a fire call elsewhere. Consequently, appliances from C27 Clerkenwell, A24 Soho and A22 Manchester Square were ordered onto this incident.

The crews from Clerkenwell and Soho fought their way through the dense London traffic arriving at 7:42pm. The most senior officer at the scene was

Station Officer Colin Townsley from Soho. Station Officer Townsley and a crew went to the concourse of the station, where they were directed to the Piccadilly Line escalator. By this time, the flames had reached about 4 foot in height. Townsley ordered his crew back to the surface to fetch a hose line and get more crews into BA. The Leading Fireman from Clerkenwell was detailed to send a 'make pumps four' Assistance Message to Control.

The officer in charge of Clerkenwell's Pump had descended one of the adjacent escalators to stop members of the public; who were still at this point going about their business as if nothing was happening. The remainder of the Clerkenwell crew, rigged in BA passed, the Soho crew who were going to fetch the hose line.

The time was now 7:45pm; Station Officer Townsley had now been joined by Station Officer Osborne from Manchester Square. Hearing a commotion at the top of the escalator, Station Officer Osborne moved that way, noticing dense smoke and flame at ceiling level. He descended the Victoria Line escalator to prevent more people from coming up to the concourse. Almost instantaneously there was a very rapid build-up in heat and smoke, the area was plunged into darkness and temperatures became unbearable. The remaining firefighters who had returned to the street to help collect hose were met with thick black smoke suddenly exploding from all of the entrances to the station and a large number of screaming burned passengers exited to the street. Station Officer Townsley was guiding passengers from the station and was last seen helping a woman to the exit when the fireball erupted.

The BA crews, armed with a powerful 2 and1/2-inch jet tried to enter the station, they compared the experience to 'entering a volcano'. Progress was slow and torturous with crews fighting the fire being cooled by other firefighters. Assistant Divisional Officer (ADO) Shore arrived amid chaos at 7:49pm; finding no Incident Commander he sent a further assistance message requesting more resources. The crews from Soho had managed to make a little progress with the protection of another hose line; they came across Station Officer Townsley and removed him to street level. Sadly, efforts to resuscitate him were in vain.

By 8:15pm Deputy Assistant Chief Officer (DACO) Wilson was in attendance and in charge of the incident. He had been informed that several firefighters were missing and a roll call was being carried out. Faced with what was fast becoming a disastrous incident with bodies being discovered by the minute by crews still battling the inferno, Wilson sent a 'make pumps twenty' message. He was further informed that 3 firefighters (including Station Officer Townsley) had been removed to University College Hospital. Unknown to him, Station Officer Osborne from Manchester Square and Sub Officer Bell from Clerkenwell were still below the fire, all trains were ordered to bypass the station once the remaining passengers were evacuated from the platforms.

The incident was ultimately commanded by Assistant Chief Officer 'Joe' Kennedy, Commander for the North East Area of London, and the Brigades Third Officer. The incident reached 30 pumps before being brought under control late in the night.

The 'Stop' (under control) message read:

From ACO Kennedy

Stop for King's Cross Underground Station

The whole of a circular main concourse, 50 Metres in diameter serving 4 Underground lines and 1 British Rail line, 2 pedestrian tunnels from street to concourse to platform level 100% damaged by fire.

3 jets, breathing apparatus

Unknown number of persons rescued by Brigade from concourse and platforms

23 persons injured

34 persons apparently dead

All persons not yet accounted for

Same as all calls

The Brigade remained on the scene until the following evening.

A week and a half later, thousands of British firefighters took to the streets of Central London to line the route (that passed King's Cross Station) for the funeral of Station Officer Townsley. Six firefighters were awarded the Chief Officers Commendation, including Station Officer Townsley, who received the award posthumously. Fourteen further firefighters received letters of congratulation for their bravery.

Following the fire, one of the biggest enquiries ever seen in the UK was undertaken. Lasting 91 Days, the enquiry heavily criticised London Underground for the lack of maintenance and cleaning on its escalators. Ignoring advice following an earlier fire at Oxford Circus in 1984, they did not fit sprinklers. The fire was believed to have been started by smoking material dropped onto the escalator that then rolled into the edge. The enquiry also uncovered a previously unknown type of fire growth; the trench effect. The following passage is taken from part of the official LFB investigation team report:

This trench effect was seen to cause hot gases in the buoyant plume to lie along the escalator surface and create a rapid airflow which caused these gases to curl over and over towards the next steps above. The airflow in the trench increased in proportion to the size of the fire, eventually creating a flamethrower type effect up and into the ticketing hall.

Beyond doubt, at the enquiry was the bravery and commitment of the London fire crews who attended the incident that night. LFB brought forward its new fire kit project that was being trialled in 1987. At the time of the fire, London's firefighters were still issued with heavy double-breasted woollen fire tunics, yellow waterproof leggings and rubber gloves. In many cases the rubber gloves melted onto the facemasks of the BA sets as firefighters attempted to clear their facemasks of debris.

I got to work on my second day and found the Red Watch in a subdued mood, the Pump from Bethnal Green had been called on to the job when it got made up to a twenty pump fire, they had pretty much been there through the thick of it. That day most of the talk was about the fire, the loss of a firefighter and a load of other 'grown up' stuff that went above the head of me, a mere recruit.

I watched the news at lunchtime and saw a friend of mine at the fire. Barry was in my original squad at training. He had been posted to A21 Paddington Red Watch the week before me. He had already done a week at Paddington and this was his first call on the first night duty of his second week. Barry was about 6'5" and twenty-one years of age. Being fresh from training there was no way they were going to send him into the inferno below ground. In a lot of the press photographs from the fire you will see an extremely tall young bewildered looking fireman standing at the entrance to the station holding a Field Telephone Unit while hell is unfolding around him. That is Barry. I spoke to him many years after the fire about that night; he said it was absolutely unbelievable. Most of us who joined in those days soon had our 'baptism of fire', but Barry's was like no other. Whilst on the subject, another training school mate of mine was posted to Soho. He's first day was Friday, two days after the King's Cross fire and he had to report for his first day to a station that had just lost one of its Officers… again I'm glad I wasn't in his shoes.

First Fires

The Red Watch at F22 Poplar Fire Station 1992, Steve back row holding name plate.

On Friday, I met my Girlfriend for lunch and got into Bethnal Green for my first night duty early. My mate Ian had had his first day, not as exciting as mine had been but he'd had a few bits. At about 5pm a few of my Watch started to drift in. Archie asked me if I fancied a pint, being my first night I declined and he ribbed me a little bit about being soft and "shit scared of the Guvnor", he wasn't wrong.

Soon enough 6pm was upon us and I was about to find out what it was like to be a fireman in the East End of London in the 1980s. As I placed my gear in the middle of the Pump, I was riding with Dave again and another bloke, Pete who was one of the nicest men I ever met, too nice to be a fireman, but who also had a bizarre sick sense of humour and was probably one of the unluckiest people ever.

"Friday night is 'make up' night young Stephen," he said.

"Uhh?" I replied with a smile.

"Fridays…we always get a job on a Friday, normally a four pumper either on our ground or someone else's, that's why they call Friday night 'make up' night, normally some punter comes in from the pub half cut and ends up torching his place," Pete offered me by way of an explanation.

I didn't get upstairs before the bells went down, I was rigged and on the Pump in seconds. I was looking over a brand new Dodge Pump that had been delivered to the station as a replacement for the 1977 ERF that we had on the run as a spare. It was going to be placed on the run as the Pump Ladder during the next few days, so it'd be a few weeks before I got to go on it. These were the first batch of London fire engines to be fitted with sirens instead of the older two-tone horns.

I climbed on the Pump and sat in the middle. We were going to a person shut in a lift somewhere behind the station. When we got there Pete took me up to the lift motor room to wind the lift car down while Dave and the Guvnor stayed down to release the trapped passengers once the lift had been brought level with the floor. Pete explained the workings of the lift room to me, and how the brake release and winding wheel worked. He also told me to be aware of needles as 'druggies' often used these motor rooms. This was before Aids had really become an issue, so it was all about avoiding unnecessary injuries.

From there we got back to the station and I was in the Watchroom when the bells went again. Once more we were off down Roman Road, this time to Bow for a fire in a flat in Tredegar Road. The job was just around the corner from Bow fire station, so things were well under way when we arrived. A line of hose reel was hanging from the fourth-floor balcony and some light smoke came from a nearby window. On the instruction of Pete, I'd grabbed a 9-litre water extinguisher. It was a cardinal firefighting rule that a firefighter should always have something with them on job, a line (rope) an axe, an extinguisher, but never be without anything.

We were soon on our way back and already the two quick calls in succession had begun to get me a little hyped – what else? I hadn't even been upstairs yet. Back at the station we went up to the kitchen where I was told to help with the washing up and the meal. I heard loud shouting and swearing coming from the kitchen and felt a little embarrassed to find Mark in a heated debate with the other Pete, the guy who had been driving me on the first day. Mark was challenging some of the more established views on the Watch. He was about 28 at the time and like me had joined young and came from the local area. He had a good part time job and drove around in really nice cars, but did not like the views of some of the older blokes on the Watch.

Mark stormed out and left Pete and me in the kitchen.

"What you looking at?" he said, then smiled.

"Peel about half of those spuds then wash up the cups, Stuart is the mess slut tonight, but you can help out, do another pot of tea as well while you are at it."

I obliged and got on with the spuds, looking at myself in the reflection of the kitchen window with the night sky behind. The teleprinter bell rang out, but it was a copy of the stop message from the job at Bow.

The curry had been cooking since the afternoon, Pete had left a note for the cook to hand over to the Green Watch to get it going before we came on. All we had to do was cook the curried potato and boil the rice. I guess it was about 8pm when we settled down. I was gulping a glass of water to wash my curry down when the bells went down again. I slid down the pole and got on the machine, the others got on and the Guvnor shouted, "Car alight…Malcolm Place" as we pulled out. Pete told me to look out of the left window as Malcolm Place was in a road adjacent to the Roman Road where the fire station was. Sure enough through the trees in the park I saw a plume of smoke with bright flames dancing towards the night sky. We soon pulled up and Pete told me to grab a hose reel. We may have used two high pressure hose reels on a car but this was only a small car so it would not be a problem for the high-pressure reel to overcome.

I opened the nozzle and turned it to a slight spray, I directed it into the burning passenger compartment and it darkened down and engulfed me in a cloud of hot steam. Pete directed me around the car, again the adrenalin was pumping and straight after my dinner I felt slightly nauseous as well as anxious. After the fire was out Dave and Pete went around banging the doors, roof and so on. I didn't understand why until I saw a few embers drop down. I turned the nozzle back on and gave the car another good wash down. The Police turned up and the Guvnor exchanged details and reference numbers for the fire report. Pete explained that as it was only railway arches around this street it was a regular place for us to get torched cars. People would drive them here and torch them to get the insurance money. "We get a load of car fires round here, wherever the railway arches are and away from houses. Fucking pain in the arse, but a good bit of flame for you I suppose."

Back at the station we all washed up after the dinner. Everyone helped to clear the bulk, then Stuart and I finished up. He told me to get my bedding down, because "If we are busy tonight, you'll get hung trying to get your bedding out in the middle of the night." I went to the dorm and unpacked my sleeping bag, pillow and sheets. I made up a bed near my locker, it was right opposite the double doors, I wasn't allowed a bed tucked away around the corner in case I missed a shout and anyway the doors to the dorm were glass so light got through them. I went down to see the Guvnor. He was in his office in a white T-shirt, smoking a cigar and writing in some sort of log book.

"Hello Steve, settling in OK?" he asked.

"Yes Guv, I'm OK…er is there anything else you need from me?"

"No, you take it easy and get a feel for the place this week, we'll get you started properly next week… lose the shirt Steve, t-shirts are fine after supper."

"Oh right, thanks Guv, thanks, see ya."

I ran back upstairs and changed into a t-shirt. Most of the others had changed into t-shirts and the older ones into old overall type trousers that I guessed were a throwback to the 60s and 70s. Waiting for the next call I crept into the TV room behind the Guvnor who had come up from downstairs, someone had put a video on, the room was heavy with cigarette smoke. I sat down at the back of the room, the smell of the Guvnor's cigar and the warm atmosphere reminded me of being at home when I was younger when my dad would smoke a cigar whilst watching TV on a Saturday afternoon with a glass of Barley Wine and a Scotch as a chaser. I was feeling on top of the world. Here I was doing the job I loved, the job I had always wanted to do. All the years of wanting to belong but never quite being there, for as welcome as Poplar made me, I was only ever a visitor, now I was a fireman in my own right. Not at Poplar but at a station that was equally as busy and in the same area.

Before long we were on our way again. This time we were called additionally on multiple calls to a fire in a house north of Victoria Park on Homerton's ground. Just off our ground, they had a minute or two on us from the original call. We pulled into a side turning and stopped behind Homerton's machines. Smoke was blowing across the headlights and the blue lights on the machines were cutting through the smoke like a lighthouse through fog. A few of Homerton's guys were pulling more hose reel off and their Sub Officer was standing on the street encouraging the crews.

I followed Pete as the Guvnor went to have a word with Homerton's Sub Officer. The house was three floors with a basement. As with many of these properties the basement had been converted into a self-contained flat. I stood at

49

the edge of the front garden as Homerton's crews piled in. The window was black, and brownish dark grey smoke pushed out of the door from about shoulder height. Pete acknowledged someone behind me.

"Come on Dud," he said. "We need to check the property above," and I duly followed.

There was a light haze of smoke in the house above, Pete told me to open the back door. I did this, but the garden was heavy with smoke from a basement window that had been vented by the crews fighting the fire, so I took the initiative to shut it and tell Pete. I wandered into the front room and Pete was feeling around the edge of the floor. I started doing the same guessing I was feeling for heat but not really knowing. As if guessing my thoughts Pete explained that I should feel around the floorboards for any heat. It was unlikely that the ceiling below had been breached as the fire seemed more smoke than anything else, but we were always to check. We went back outside and I was venturing towards the basement flat. Most of the smoke had cleared and the BA crew were out taking their sets off. I felt a tug.

"Come on, we're all done here. Homerton will finish off, this is their job." We got back on the Pump, the Pump ladder had already gone and I heard the Guvnor book available on the radio.

As we turned back towards the fire station, I heard the radio call the Pump Ladder up: "Foxtrot two six one, Foxtrot two six one from 'F.E priority over.'"

I heard Paul the Sub Officer on the Pump Ladder reply, and then it was us.

"Foxtrot two six two, Foxtrot two six two from F.E priority over," The Guvnor acknowledged.

"Foxtrot two six one and foxtrot two six two... you are ordered to smoke issuing from a shop, Bethnal Green Road near Valance Road, taken as Bethnal Green, east two..."

Both appliances acknowledged and I detected urgency in the engine note as Steve, the driver tonight, changed the pace from sedate to urgent.

"Sets please gents," the Guvnor called into the back. My stomach dropped, the Guvnor wanted us in BA...was I going to go in? "Grab the BA board if we have anything Steve," came the reply that had let me off the hook. In any case it was customary for probationers not to go into fires in BA in their first 6 Months, there would be plenty of time for that later. You only got to wear BA after the fire was under control and there was ventilation and cutting away to do. Pete and Dave grabbed their sets from the bracket in front of them. They placed the sets in their laps put their arms through the straps and pulled them over their heads, securing all of the straps. I pulled the BA board from in front of me and checked the clock against my watch, it was 10:30pm.

We slowed down but with Pete and Dave hanging out of each window I didn't see much, I guessed that there was obviously not that much of a fire in Bethnal Green Road or we would see it. We pulled up just short of the lights near Valance Road and got off. Nothing showing at all, the Pump Ladder's crew disappeared around the corner into Valance Road. I looked up and down and stepped off the kerb to check the opposite side. I heard a shout and got back on the kerb. Stuart was waving us from around the corner. We went that way while the Guvnor stayed at the front with the drivers.

I rounded the corner and no one was there. I then noticed a small alleyway behind the shops. Dave and Pete passed by me, and as I turned into the alleyway, I saw some flames at the back of a shop. I still had the BA board as we approached, I guessed I'd be dumping this to get the hose reel so I could put the rubbish out. Paul the Sub Officer was talking to the Guvnor on the radio and told Pete and Dave to get back to the front. They parted and I could better see what was burning. There was a metal roller shutter in a wooden frame at the back of the shop covering what seemed to be a loading hatch to the basement. The wooden frame was burning and part of the metal roller shutter was glowing red. There was clearly quite a fire going on in the basement of the shop. Shoreditch's Pump Ladder had turned up, we had all three machines due on the initial attendance here now.

I was ordered back to the front where I was told to put on an armband from the back of the Breathing Apparatus Entry Control Board that identified me as the 'Entry Control Officer', an illustrious sounding title normally reserved for the junior member of a crew or the driver, unless the job was really sticky. As two firemen were going into this job in BA it was my job to take the tallies from their BA sets and place them in a board where I would record where they were working, how much air they had and calculate the time of their low-pressure whistle. The UK had very strict procedures for firefighters wearing BA after a couple of jobs in London in the late 1940s and 1950s where firemen had got lost in smoke or simply run out of air and died. As Dave and Pete started their BA sets, I took their tallies and checked the content written on the tally with that on the pressure gauge. I panicked a little trying to work out their time of whistle on the clock in front of me. A simple exercise I had done time and time again in training, but this was real, a real fire in the middle of the East End on a Friday night.

I looked up as they disappeared inside, a light smoke was evident inside the shop, a drab place that sold fireplace surrounds, the smoke soon thickened, indicating Pete and Dave had found the door to the basement and had entered it. More sirens came along the road. The Pump Ladder from Whitechapel pulled up, the crew got off wearing their BA as their Sub Officer went over to our Guvnor. Obviously the attendance of both the Pump Ladders from Shoreditch and Whitechapel meant to me that their Pumps; usually the first mobilised, were already on other calls. The Guvnor had obviously requested extra resources and had 'made pumps four' bringing Whitechapel to join us and Shoreditch. Friday night clearly was 'make up' night.

Another crew fed a larger jet into the shop to back up the high pressure hose reel that Dave and Pete had took in as an initial attack line. Soon enough the smoke began to lighten and the boys appeared to have the job. Dave and Pete came out; their tunics were steaming in the cool air. They took their facemasks off and I gave them back their tallies. The Guvnor spoke with them to ascertain that the job was best part over. Pete opened a delivery on the Pump and filled his fire hat with water that he then dumped over his head. Dave dumped his set on the floor, loosened his tunic and lit up a cigarette. It had clearly been a very hot job.

Soon the other crew withdrew and I shut down BA control. I then joined some others in turning over the basement to extinguish the last of the fire. The basement had been used as a recording studio. This explained the dozens of empty egg boxes that had burned; they were used as sound insulation in the studio. It appeared from what was being discussed that an electrical fault in one of the amplifiers was responsible for the blaze. Also, in amongst the wreckage was the body of a big old Alsatian dog, kept there overnight to protect the studio from intruders, it had slowly choked to death in the smoke from the growing fire. I looked down at it and felt a little sad at the limp beast that a couple of hours ago would have loyally faced anyone who dared to try to get onto his master's property.

It was past 1am as we got back to the station. Bow's Pump was parked in one of the bays, they had been sent to cover Bethnal Green while we were out on the job, they had been out a few times on stuff in our absence. Their crew appeared in the bay and began helping to get our machines ready to go again while a couple of the guys cleaned up. I was unceremoniously handed a BA set. "Clean that up and get it ready to go again," was the order barked at me.

I was joined in the BA room by the friendly looking grey-haired fireman from Bow who had briefly spoken to me at my first shout on Wednesday. "Hello young'un how are you?"

"Oh, I'm OK thanks."

"I'm Tom, from Bow."

"I'm Steve, Steve Dudeney."

"Nice to meet you, Steve."

I came to know and respect Tom because we met up with Bow almost every day back in those days. Later in my career when I served at Bow, a chat with Tom one afternoon when I was feeling miserable about the job saved my career. I was a junior officer and came close to throwing it all in and going back to being a firefighter, but Tom talked me round.

The radio was on in the machine as I climbed up to replace the BA set. It had been chattering away all the time with the bleep, bleep, bleep of the busy signal interspersing each message to and from Eastern Control at Stratford. I listened harder. It seemed every station in the North and East of London was out; from Holloway and Tottenham, down into Stoke Newington and Homerton across where we were, to Poplar, Plaistow and Stratford, and right out onto Barking and Dagenham. The crews were out and about; flat fires, derelict buildings, rubbish and car fires, drunks fallen asleep halfway through cooking a midnight feast. I jumped into the front of the machine and turned the channel switch on the radio. The South and West were busy too; Brixton, Peckham, Old Kent Road in the South and Paddington, North Kensington and Hammersmith in the West; it seemed the inner-city districts of London were keeping their firefighters busy on this Friday night as I would learn they did on most nights.

I lay on my bed sometime after 2am. I was shattered but knew I could not let myself go to sleep. Most of the guys were still upstairs chatting and smoking in the quiet room. Soon we were on our way again, an automatic fire alarm at the London Hospital in Whitechapel, where a candle had tipped over in one of the nurses' homes and set the alarm off. A call to smoke in a hallway of a block on Shadwell's' ground, that was actually a rubbish bin burning followed soon after.

Back into bed again and this time I drifted off. The bells woke me with a start and set me on my way with a nauseous adrenalin that would shake me back into consciousness thousands more times in my career. Having fallen asleep, I felt terrible. I was glad of the fresh air that came in through Pete's window as we cut through the dark streets. We were called to a house fire in Cranston Cottages off Maroon Street in Limehouse. Right on the borders of our ground and Poplar's. We pulled in at the opposite end of the terrace of cottages from Poplar's crews. The courtyard was shared with a rough looking block of flats. I knew this estate well, like a lot of the East End the tiny cottages and low-rise blocks of flats were built before the Second World War as the Victorian slums were cleared. It had now fallen into disrepair with many of the flats boarded up or burnt out. I remember seeing a fire in one of these blocks as I made my way home from school a few years earlier.

Poplar were running so we started running, all of a sudden, I stared to feel a little breathless. I began to heave, I was convinced I was going to throw up, I guess I was on adrenalin overload. Not wishing to embarrass myself, I ducked into the lobby of the block of flats. I retched a couple of times but thankfully nothing came up, I heaved again taking sips of air between each heave trying to calm myself. Eventually I composed myself and slipped back into the forecourt. I joined the rest of my crew, Poplar's guys brought out a smouldering pot…another drunk I guessed. For Christ sake it was gone 5am by now, surely the world should be sobering up? I nodded at Vince the new guy at Poplar and he nodded back at me. I hoped I would look as calm as that in a month instead of the wreck I seemed to be right now.

Back on the machine we headed back to Bethnal Green, and for the first time I began to doubt myself. I had been on a load of calls and a couple of good jobs and just about survived, what if I had to face a King's Cross like the Red Watch had faced just over 48 hours earlier? I crept back to the dorm my head full of nightmares.

The last call came in just before 7am. It was to a car on its side in King Edward's Road in Hackney. We pulled up and the police were already there. I felt a little better but sank again when I saw a pretty police woman who looked not much older than me giggling and flirting with the others. She had probably faced a night of fights, domestics, and drunks but still looked fresh and confident. The car was a Mini, it had been turned on its side, quite easily I imagined, by a few lads with a load of beer inside them. We righted it and I spread some sand on the petrol that had leaked. Safe, we left it with the police who were waiting to find the owner.

I got back to the station, had a wash and went downstairs to wash the machines. We had breakfast and slowly the Green Watch began to appear for their second day duty. I got off at 9am, having attended about 10 of the 18 calls that had come into the station during the shift, including two decent fires. The others were attended by crews covering our ground while we were attending our fires.

I got home, spoke to my Girlfriend on the phone and slept like a baby until about 3pm. I got up and showered for my second night duty. The sleep had made me feel better, and with renewed energy I set off to face my second night duty. We were off soon after 6pm to a litter bin that someone had set light to along the road from the station. Soon after that we got call to Mile End Underground Station; the fire at King's Cross had unleashed a paranoia across London that every hint of smoke or smell of burning was going to end up in another inferno. This went on well into 1988, when as with most things, people's memories begin to fade.

We were in and out for the rest of the night; a few flames, a couple of false alarms, a near promise. We got ordered to standby at C22 Kingsland Road who were attending a fire in a clothing factory. I was on the back with Stuart, who expected that the job would increase from the four Pumps that were already attending it. In the end they held it at the four and we sat and watched Saturday night TV for a couple of hours at Kingsland.

Eventually I began to settle into a routine. The calls kept coming in as we headed towards Christmas; false alarms, rubbish fires, people stuck in lifts, car fires. Around about once a week we would pick up a good job somewhere in the area or be called onto someone else's ground as assistance to a job they had.

It was around this time I had my first fatality. Poplar Red Watch had attended a fire on a houseboat in the early hours, the guy inside was unable to get out. They went off duty at 9 in the morning, so we were ordered on as a relief crew from Bethnal Green assisting the fire investigators. I edged slowly into the cabin where the body was. I didn't know what to expect but in the end, it was not at all bad. The poor guy was badly burnt but did not look human anymore. Everyone has different things they find repulsive. I have always tried to look beyond what I am seeing and think about the human life that once existed in the body and treat them with the respect they deserve. The one thing that always put me on edge though was when someone's eyes were still open. Even if the body was not burnt or mutilated, I would get a little spooked if the eyes were looking at me.

Christmas came and went, and I had my first Christmas period on duty, my shifts fell lucky, working either side of the main days, but thankfully we were pretty quiet over that period. However, Christmas 1987 had been tragic in other parts of the UK. Several fires had occurred in homes, each one killing a number of children. This caused outrage and saw changes in the laws governing the construction of furniture. All new furniture had to have flame resistant foam and coverings. Also, as a result of this, smoke detectors were pushed for the first time. The uptake was slow but now, years later the majority of homes in the UK are fitted with a working smoke detector. This has seen fire deaths across the UK drop massively over the years.

New Year's Eve night I was on duty. I missed a couple of parties, but I could live with that. Back then Bethnal Green was a big weekend nightlife area. Most of the pubs in Bethnal Green Road and Hackney Road attracted revellers from all over the East End and beyond. We hung around outside the station chatting to people passing by, earning ourselves a few kisses and cheeky comments for our trouble.

Not long before midnight we were called to a person shut in a lift at a factory nearby, this had to be a 'Mickey' (fire brigade slang for a false alarm) – who would be working this late? We soon found out. There were some Pakistani men working in a factory just off Bethnal Green Road, they were the ones working late, a little too late. The power in the building was timed to shut down after 11pm. They had pushed it right to the last minute and got into the lift, unfortunately the power cut halfway down. It took about half an hour or so before someone realised they were in there and then we got called to release them. We got the power back on to the building pretty quickly, but the lift motor had tripped out. We had to go up to the motor room to wind them down to where the Guvnor had opened the door. Running down the stairs the shouts and fireworks from outside indicated I had seen in my first New Year as a fireman in some stinking factory in Bethnal Green. I was not happy with our friends who were nodding and smiling gratefully at us as we left.

We got into Bethnal Green Road and blasted the two-tone horns on our machine, much to the delight of the revellers outside the pubs. One young girl was exceptionally grateful and thanked us by lifting her top and flashing us. Things always have a habit of turning in your favour when all seems lost.

After Christmas the quiet spell continued, I was on duty one Saturday and we didn't move for the whole day. A far cry from the usual duty we had been picking up in my first couple of months. One of the older blokes explained how modern central heating had 'killed the job'. Back in the 60s and 70s no one had gas fired central heating, they all had open fires or even worse, paraffin heaters and electric blankets; a double whammy of potential accidental ignition.

"Now," he told me, "now, we have to wait for them to get pissed and burn 'emselves out or have a ruck and go and torch each other's places before we get a look in."

One afternoon around this time I had my first proper 'wear' in BA at a fire on Homerton's Ground. We were called to a fire in a derelict nursing home somewhere off Mare Street. I was on the back of the Pump with Steve, one of the more experienced guys who was also a driver. We pulled up at the same time as Homerton and saw black smoke coming from a doorway. Our Guvnor was in conference with Homerton's Guvnor as the crews laid out hose. The Guvnor beckoned us over.

"Steve," he said to the other Steve, "there's a big pile of rubbish burning in that storeroom, it has no windows and only one door, so it's pretty bottled up in there. Take Young Steve here and get your sets on, I think it's time he had a wear."

I was right up for it, getting rigged in my BA set ready for my first 'hot' wear. Back in those days we never did hot fire training like the new recruits do now. They told us about all the fires we would go in and how they had all had their ears burnt but we never experienced it. I was fully conscious of the heat of a fire but didn't think of it all the same.

I got started up and still didn't take the hint as Steve dropped to the floor below the smoke. I was immediately enveloped by total blackness and felt my way in through the door. It was hot and my ears began to sting straight away. I don't know what part of my common sense gene was missing at that time in my life but instead of getting down below the heat I stumbled on in getting hotter. Somehow, I ended up in front of Steve and decided that this fire lark was not for me. I blundered out, treading right on Steve who was on the floor as I went. I had effectively committed another cardinal sin, leaving a fellow firefighter in a job. I got outside to be met by several surprised faces. Their surprised turned to anger when they heard me whining that it was "too hot." Without any further ado I was 'kicked' back into the job and told to "buck my fucking ideas up, I was a fucking disgrace to Bethnal Green leaving a man in a fire like that." I went back in, keeping low this time, and saw the fire was already put out. After I got back to the station, I was torn up by the Watch to ensure never again would I bottle out, or moreover act before thinking.

That was a turning point for me. I realised that I was in a serious job where people expected me to be there for them, not just my colleagues but the public. What good would I be to a person trapped in a fire if I lost my bottle? Over the years I have cringed when I think about this, but now I put it down to inexperience, immaturity and lack of training. As for Steve, he is long retired now. He was a decent bloke who forgave me my stupidity. Although I saw him on a big high-rise fire in an office block in 2003, a year or so before he retired, and as I made my way up the stairs towards the burning upper floors with another officer, we greeted each other and he offered to "lay down on the stairs for me" should I feel the need to come running back down in the next few minutes.

I soon picked up another job and with some quiet words from my Sub Officer Paul, I was sent into a fire in a maisonette in Stepney. The top floor was going fairly well and as I started to make my way up the stairs, I lost all of my vision and began to feel the heat. I felt my way to the top of the stairs and became aware of heat on my right side. I was against the left wall and realised I had reached the top of the staircase. The other Steve, there were three of us on the Watch, was behind me and feeding the hose up. Laying my head on the floor I tried to peer through the smoke, but the best I got was the feel of heat through my mask. I gave the fire a toot of water from the hose reel and listened. It got a little hotter, I had hit something.

I crawled onto the landing and felt the heat right in front of me. I detected a slight glow through the smoke, this fire was well bottled up as I could not see a hand in front of my face, literally. I struggled to read my BA air gauge. Steve encouraged me to hit the fire, I did so by aiming up at the ceiling and down around the floor. I edged forward some more and became aware I was in the room. I opened the nozzle again and gave the room a good drink. In the noise I heard the sound of glass, the water hitting the hot window had cooled and shattered it. The conditions in the room soon lightened up and I began to pick out a few shapes. Soon we were able to stand and we felt our way around the rooms to ventilate the rest of the floor.

I had done it. No big deal, just a regular domestic fire but with the farce from the week or so before hanging over me I felt a lot better. I headed back outside to the Pump to drop my BA set off and get some gear to carry out salvage work. Pete rubbed my head and told me I had now been broken in.

We got busier again as the year pressed on; big fires that I soon discovered involved little more than standing outside pouring water on the building. Regular fires with just the local stations were the best. I began to feel more comfortable in my role. I kept the butterflies, but the original horror of what I had let myself in for passed. I was still only nineteen. On reflection I guess I was a little too young and unprepared, despite my time spent hanging around Poplar.

One night I was in the Watchroom as the 'Dutyman' and riding the Pump Ladder. The Pump had been fairly busy running around to the usual collection of rubbish fires, calls on other grounds and so on, but we had only been out a few times. The teleprinter warning bell went off above my head in the little partitioned area of the Watchroom where I was laying down trying to rest. I swung my feet to the floor and by the time I stood up the lights came on and the main bells crashed into life. Squinting in the bright fluorescent light I looked over the old teleprinter as it slowly chattered out its message. The Pump was ordered to standby at C24 Whitechapel for fire cover, obviously they had something on their ground. We were the take station (next out) for the eastern part of their area so the job had to be on the other side of their ground with Shoreditch or Dowgate with them. I turned the radio listening post on and ripped off the sheet of paper passing it to the Guvnor as he came into the room.

"Standby at 'Chapel'," I announced loudly to no one in particular but let everyone know what it was, as was customary.

The Pump pulled out and headed off down the road, no lights and sirens as they were simply relocating to cover the empty fire station. I wandered back to my bed. I laid on it as the radio chattered in the background. All of a sudden Whitechapel's call sign caught my ear.

"M2FE from Charlie two four one priority over."

"Charlie two four one from 'FE go ahead over."

"Charlie two four one, make pumps 6, Turntable Ladder required over."

I was up and out of the bed, certain that the Pump was going to be ordered on to this job and that maybe we would too. I was annoyed that the guy on the radio hadn't repeated the address, but I guessed they were a little busy right now. I got fully dressed and hovered near my boots and leggings. I thought better of getting rigged as I would probably curse our chances. I stared at the map looking for a clue to the whereabouts of the job, it could have been anywhere. I waited for the teleprinter and bells summoning us to the incident.

The radio came to life, Control called up our Pump and Kingsland's Pump who were obviously going in to cover Shoreditch. Then I found out where the job was. They were ordered to a six Pump fire, Turntable Ladder required at Woodseer Street, Whitechapel E.1. I scanned the map tracing the roads with my fingers. I knew the area but not every road over in Whitechapel. Then they gave the route card detail to the machines, I looked up the grids and found the address. It was just off Brick Lane.

Brick Lane back then, as now, was the main thoroughfare in the middle of the Bangladeshi area of Whitechapel. That community has spread all across the borough now, but then before Brick Lane became famous for its curry houses, it was a real ghetto full of run-down housing and clothing sweatshops. Fire and death were synonymous with the area. From fatal blazes in sweatshops to fire bomb attacks in overcrowded Bangladeshi households by racist gangs, that area had seen it all.

I ran off to the toilet in case we were going to get called and as I came back, I heard the back end of an informative message being read back from control. I did manage to hear 100% of something alight but didn't hear what. I was buzzing with anticipation for the next message, hopefully asking for more help. I was not to be disappointed. Soon enough Whitechapel came over the air with another priority, this time making pumps eight. We were sure to go on it now. Less than a minute later I was already fully rigged, the bells went off and we were on our way. Paul the Sub Officer was in charge, Pete was driving and Dave and Stuart were on the back with me.

"Do you want sets Paul?" I asked across the front.

The others looked at me and tutted, I felt embarrassed.

Paul, as decent as ever, replied, "No don't worry Dud, we don't know what we'll be doing when we get there…we may be right up the road pumping water or something."

I hoped not, I wanted a piece of the action. We drove down Bethnal Green Road and then left into Valance Road, then we started making our way through the back streets towards the job. I got a glimpse of some orange tainted smoke but had to wait until we arrived.

Paul told us to wait by the machine until he booked in at the Control Unit. I stared at the fire. It was like a few I had seen before, but the building was much bigger. It was an old Victorian warehouse, only 4 floors but 4 tall floors making it about 60ft in height, it was also very deep. Flames came from most of the windows at the front and from the roof. I hoped we got to go in and do some work here. I scanned around for hydrants, hose was snaked all over the road and water pressure appeared to be good from the jets that were already in place. I felt sure we were not going to be tied up getting water from a larger main several streets away as I had done at a couple of other big jobs that I had been to. They had been in big lightweight construction buildings such as storage warehouses, those jobs had been all about surround and drown, nothing but a big bonfire with four walls. This building was different; it was a proper building, so I hoped it needed proper firefighting.

Steve who was driving the Pump came over to us. The Pump had arrived a while earlier on the six pump make up. The others were off on a roof somewhere pumping water into the fire, Steve had stayed with the Pump, pumping water to Dowgate's Ladders. Steve was talking about getting me a turn at the head of the Turntable Ladder when Paul the Sub Officer returned. "Right, get your sets on, they need a crew to take a jet into the building." I was ecstatic. I was off, back to the PL to get the set on like a light, while the others ambled back. Unlike a fire in a house or flat where someone may be involved, there was no rush for this, apart from the rush of boyish enthusiasm from me.

Soon we were standing outside the building rigged in our BA, Pete, Dave, Stuart and I made up a crew of four. A jet was being laid by Shoreditch, and I nodded at a girl I had trained with who was posted to Shoreditch a few weeks after me; she looked well pissed off at me getting to go in and gave me a sarcastic grin in return.

We were approached by an Assistant Divisional Officer; he briefed us that we were to take a two and a half inch jet into the building for firefighting on the ground floor. Most of the floors had given way so we were to stay close to the walls. After the briefing we started our sets and reported to BA Control where we handed our tallies in.

Pete led the way followed by Stuart, me and Dave at the rear. As we approached the door, I could feel a strong breeze behind me. As we got closer and began to enter it got stronger; the fire was so big it was sucking air in from the street like a howling tornado. We got into a passageway and saw a door off to our left. The glow from within the building was fantastic, like a furnace. Pete and Stuart looked through the door as Dave and I looked up a staircase to the right.

Dave and I discussed maybe getting up the stairs but in the event, Pete called us to help with the hose. As we got into position, I managed a look into the ground floor; a mass of burning rubble from the floors above rose up in the middle of the floor, massive flames leapt up from everything and disappeared up through the broken floors towards the sky above us. We persevered with the jet for a while but facing such a mass of fire it was having little effect. Even though we were throwing near on a thousand litres per minute at the fire, it was probably turning to steam before it got to the heart of the blaze. Soon Pete decided, as team leader and senior hand, that we'd be better off fighting the fire from elsewhere, we knew that our Pumps crew and Whitechapel were operating jets from adjacent buildings, and we needed to find our own vantage point.

We dropped our BA sets and were re-united with Paul our Sub Officer. Paul had been asked to break into a building in the street behind to look for another way into the job. Apparently, the burning building linked with a large shop in a terrace behind. Even with my limited experience of the Brick Lane area, this came as no surprise, as every building seemed to have been altered or knocked through to make it so you could walk in a door in one street and come out in another street entirely.

Armed with breaking in gear, we trooped round the block and found the door. A few cracks with the 14lb sledge hammer; known as the 'key', made short work of the door. We crept up the stairs, in the darkness we could smell smoke but this was not unusual for firemen in inner city areas. The majority of the smell probably came from the smoke from previous fires clinging to our gear. At the top of the first flight of stairs we opened a door and came into another hallway that seemed to connect the shops. We turned right along this hallway, then left and up a few more steps where there was a steel door that was padlocked. The paint on the door was blistered and there was a slight mist of smoke in our torch light, as well as a smell of hot metal and burning paint. Bingo! We had hit gold. Paul studied the door and reasoned we were right up next to the fire.

We backed out and got a Pump pulled into the street, a hydrant was located and a jet laid out. The time taken to do this was agonising for me, but obviously we were working as part of a major operation. We couldn't just get a Pump, tap into a hydrant and go for it. Plans had to be consulted, were we depleting another sector? Would this new jet compromise the jet of a crew already inside? Did the Incident Commander want us working from the rear?

Eventually we were ready; using a crowbar and the 'key' we started working on the steel door. The noise in that enclosed corridor was deafening, all the more reason to get though quick. I took my turn swinging the hammer; I was soon exhausted but encouraged to carry on by a chorus of abuse from the crew. Once the lock gave out, I pulled back and allowed Paul to crack the door open, it had expanded due to the heat, but as the roof of the burning building had collapsed and the heat was escaping to the heavens, the door had cooled down a little.

We were all ready to pull out and let a BA crew take the jet but there was only a little smoke so we managed. As the door opened, we were looking right into the fire, the floor on the other side of the door had gone and it was thanks only to the steel door that these buildings in the next street were not on fire now too. I looked right across into the part of the building where we had just been. I could see jets coming in the windows from the flat roof to our right and high above I could see the head of Dowgate's TL between breaks in the smoke.

Every so often another bit of the building would give itself up to the fire; we would scuttle back down the stairs for a few seconds and then come back. This little game repeated itself over the next hour or so until the building, like many others when fire takes hold, ended up as a steaming foggy mess.

There is always this big thing among firefighters around the world about 'stopping a fire'. The trouble is though; Mother Nature in all of her forms is a very powerful force to contend with. Once a fire takes hold, there is only so much water from man-made hydrants, pumped through man made fire hoses, can do. The only way to get control of a fire once it has consumed a large building is to match it with something equally as powerful such as a waterfall, or a 'building sized' bucket of water, which is not going to happen. So, in reality, we surround it and play the game until most of the fuel is consumed and the fire dies down to within our comparatively 'tiny' ability to move water around and cool things down.

If I turn up on a fire that is small or even medium size when we arrive and it's easy to access, then I expect to put it out. If it is already through the roof of a several thousand square foot warehouse, I'm not to get upset about not putting it out quickly. I know what the odds against us are at big fires, so I'll get a good water supply, protect the surrounding risks and play the waiting game.

I had already been through my six-monthly interview at Area HQ and was drilled hard in preparation for my yearly exam which would decide whether I was to carry on in the fire brigade or get extended probation, which really, was not an option, I was informed on more than one occasion.

I was also spending a lot of time learning various operational procedures, all of the equipment that was at our disposal and the routes around the local area. I was OK with the southern part of the ground, but to the north towards Hackney I had to learn every little back street. I knew my way around the Pump Ladder and Pump like the back of my hand; every piece of equipment, its uses, its specifications, strengths and weaknesses.

November 1988 was soon upon us. It seemed hardly possible that I had been at the station for a year, it had gone so quick, but I had seen so much. I used to keep notes of all of my jobs – I had worn BA in fires well over a dozen times, not a bad feat seeing as I wasn't allowed to wear for the first few months. Some of the youngsters coming on the job now only get a couple of wears in their first year. In the East End back then, common with lots of inner cities across the UK, we had a hell of a lot of property fires; flats, houses, derelict buildings, factories, sweatshops, it seemed every week we had something decent. If we went a couple of tours without anything everyone would be edgy.

I had my yearly drills with the Station Commander, followed by a very in depth walk around the machines being asked questions about random pieces of equipment. A week or so later, we made our way to the new North East Area HQ at Stratford. I was wheeled in to speak to the Divisional Officer responsible for our group of stations. He asked me questions about the area, the brigade structure, and various operational procedures, all of which I answered confidently. The hard work had paid off. I was sent out of the room while the DO spoke with my Station Officer, and after 5 Minutes I was called back in. The DO congratulated me on completing my probation and shook my hand. Keeping hold of my hand he pulled me closer to him without breaking his gaze, the smile fell from his face.

"Know it all individuals like you Mr Dudeney do not always get on in this job. Just because you got through this doesn't mean you'll be sitting here in my chair one day lad. I'll be keeping a very close eye on you in the future so tread very carefully… good day."

I was crestfallen, I thought I had done really well. My Guvnor explained it was all 'part of the psychology' and not to take any notice. I had passed and that was that. Back at the station the lads all seemed genuinely pleased for me, my early unease and inappropriate foot in mouth comments had passed, and I was settling in well, but that was all about to change.

My Guvnor Keith was given a temporary promotion to ADO somewhere in the area. We had a couple of temporary Station Officers over the course of a few months, but then the Old Guvnor was promoted, and we were given a newly promoted Station Officer from a nearby station on another Watch.

I didn't really click with the new Guvnor, he didn't seem too keen on me and seemed to find a reason to have a go at me quite often. One night, I was trying to tell him something quite important while we were out on a job and he turned around and shouted at me not to interrupt him, which made my neck prickle with anger. Back at the Station we had words in his office. This cleared the air somewhat, but I decided that enough was enough. I had still kept in touch with the gang at Poplar and a position was coming up on the Red Watch later in the summer. I put in a transfer request and waited my turn.

Meanwhile, during the summer of 1989 things remained busy, it was a lot warmer than 1988 so we were out and about a lot more. One night when I was on leave, the Watch had picked up three good fires in one night. A six-pump fire that had burnt out a sweatshop in the early evening, a flat fire with a rescue, and after midnight a fire in a derelict pub off Hackney Road that was burning in every room on all floors.

When I returned to work, I was disappointed, although I didn't have to wait long. Days were pretty active with one thing or another, and straight after roll call on nights we went out to play volleyball in the warm evening air. We had been playing for about half an hour when Mark pointed across to the north east.

"Look at that, I think we're on our way out."

I turned around with everyone else, a thick black pall of smoke was rising in the sky about half a mile away. With that the bells went down and we were on our way.

"Fire in house, Old Ford Road," the Guvnor shouted across to us. We were only a few streets away and as we turned into Old Ford Road, we could see the big old detached house going like a train.

I was on the back with Lee, a fireman who had done about three years and had just transferred over from another station.

"When we get there, we'll grab the hydrant Dud," he said. I had other ideas; he was right of course, but someone needed to get water on this. I hit the ground running and pulled a length of two-and-a-half-inch hose from the rear locker. I grabbed a nozzle and the driver threw out another length. I saw Lee run off down the road with the hydrant gear looking at me disapprovingly.

The force of a 'two and a half' was tough to handle alone. So as I called for water on, I knelt on the cobblestones of the tiny dead end road that the house was on the corner of. Because this old road had been cut off by a post war housing estate no one bothered to tarmac the road, I was therefore perched on shiny slippery cobbles.

The water coursed through the hose and soon I was hitting the flames from every window; into the door, right window, up across the top windows and down to the left window. The power of the jet was pushing me back on the cobbles. I braced against the kerbstones and the fire darkened down. I have put out thousands of fires in my career, everything from extinguishing a small fire to being one of a dozen jets at a massive blaze, but nothing comes close to standing outside a burning property that is well alight, but not so big that you can't make a difference; and being the first to get water onto the fire, straight through the doors and windows. Of all the fires I have attended I can remember each occasion where I got to do this and the feeling never goes away.

Lee soon joined me from the hydrant, backing me up on the jet, and we pushed in towards the front door and along into the hallway. The hose was cumbersome and we struggled to bend it into the first room. Enveloped in swirling steam, smoke and debris we gave the room a drink and backed out into the hallway again. With our eyes streaming and mucus running from our noses, we coughed and spluttered as we went around a corner and pushed the fire further back down the passage, before going into another room to extinguish that. We had given the ground floor a decent soaking, and keen to keep going, headed towards the stairs to make our way up, knowing we were now being backed up by the others. But before we could reach the upper floor, and having been given a good bash at it, we were pulled out, as Stuart and Mark who were assigned to wear BA on the PL took over, with a slightly more manageable inch and three-quarter jet.

Within an hour the fire was out. We turned over and cut away with crews from Bow, who had made up the four Pumps. We made up all of our equipment and headed back on this sultry evening to a hearty dinner that had been prepared by Archie, who was off the run to do the cooking.

We were in and out a few times, but it went quiet after 1am. At 5am as daylight had broken, we were back out of the doors to Old Ford Road. As we approached, white smoke was rolling out of the upper windows and roof of the house we'd been to earlier. The Guvnor was furious, even more pissed off than he usually was. There is a great shame attached to a re-ignition, and I can now say I never had one as an Incident Commander in all of my years in the job. So as not to attract the inevitable senior officer cavalry that would attend this re-ignition, the Guvnor had to send a false alarm message, book us available and then immediately put in a call to another nearby 'fire'. We allegedly found several tons of rubbish burning on a nearby site that would tie both the PL and Pump up for the next hour. We worked like demons to get control of the job. The whole of the underside of the roof was alight, and every man on the job gave 110% to knock this fire out in double quick time. God knows what would have happened if one of us had gotten hurt, but there you go.

On a Sunday night just after this I was driving around bored. My Girlfriend was out with her mates and I didn't fancy the pub where my mates were. Listening to the radio it came on the news that there was a massive fire in a cold store at Smithfield meat market. I went home and grabbed my camera and headed across the City to Smithfield. I ducked and dived a little bit around the City, avoiding a couple of the more obvious road blocks, and eventually parked up around the back of Farringdon Station. I walked through a couple of streets with my camera over my shoulder, found a friendly looking policeman and with a flash of my ID I was through the cordon.

As I walked around the corner onto Charterhouse Street, smoke was banking low across the street causing an eerie mist in the orange street lights, which was made even more surreal by the pulses of blue lights coming from the top of the fire engines.

Looking up at the building, it was about 6 floors high, but with nothing but cream bricks right up to roof level. A cold store had no need for light and ventilation so windows were not a feature when the architect put this one down on paper. Smoke was rolling over the building from the roof and also from the row of large loading doors along the base of the building, the crews must have been taking a real beating in there with no windows in the place. I took a roll of film, but to be honest there wasn't a great deal to see. I spent a little while longer trying to get to see the back of the building then called it a night.

The following morning, I arrived at Bethnal Green for my first day duty. I looked at the teleprinter and read the daily news bulletin. Among other incidents I saw that the fire at Smithfield had been a 15 Pump fire involving most levels of the building. One of the White Watch guys who had been on the job, explained further that most of the cork insulation was alight in the building. It had gone right up inside and out through the roof, but even with the roof gone conditions were pretty brutal inside. At one point everyone had been withdrawn and the adjacent railway line closed as a massive crack appeared across several floors of the building at the rear. I half guessed we'd be there at some point during the day on a relief. I just hoped there was some good stuff to do.

We got on with our usual daily business, and the day progressed in time as well as temperature. Just after lunch, full up and sweltering, we had a couple of nothing calls just to keep the sweat pouring. Just as we got back from one call we were ordered, as I had predicted, onto the cold store relief along with another fourteen Pumps. We drove through the East End and into the City at normal road speed, no lights and horns for a relief. After parking up and shunting around a few of the machines that would soon be leaving, Dave, who was acting up as Leading Fireman for the day and in charge of the machine, came back with a job for us.

Steve was to stay with the machine and use it for pumping, the rest of us, the two Dave's and I, had a job to do. I was disappointed when LFM Dave explained we had to find our way into the basement and see how deep the water was. Apparently, the building had three basement levels and there was some concern as to where the firefighting water was going to.

We went in through one of the loading bay doors, inside was full of white smoke that was blindingly bright from the reflected afternoon sun outside. Beyond the platform where the lorries unloaded was another set of large doors, we headed that way and as we walked out of the light we were amazed at the sight in front of us. We were in another large room, it was like walking towards a large darkened auditorium. The entire floor was a sea of glowing embers, it must have been like watching the World War II Blitz on London from an aircraft thousands of feet above. Silently, more embers fell from above like an illuminated snowfall.

We turned right into a doorway and onto a staircase. It was pitch black, lit only by our torches, and warm water fell on us from the floors above like a tropical rainstorm. We headed down the stairs and the water falling from above, added to what was falling from the ground floor became a torrent, and we were instantly soaked through. Down another level and unable to hear anything above the noise of the falling water, I began to sense that I was wading in water.

Another step and the water went over the top of my boot. We peered into the darkness and the bottom basement level had been completely submerged in water from the hoses of the past eighteen or so hours of firefighting.

LFM Dave decided we had seen enough and we withdrew up the stairs. We came onto the street squelching across the road, and although the day was warm I let off an involuntary shudder. I unzipped my tunic and tried to ring out some of the water; I also sat down and tipped my legs up to allow the water to run from my boots.

LFM Dave was soon back with us, followed by an ADO I had seen before in the area.

"Right lads, time for some good old-fashioned firefighting. This job was a bit of a cock-up last night. They are stuck at 15 Pump reliefs, but there are too few crews to use breathing apparatus. We'd have to make it up to 20 Pumps and that just ain't gonna happen. The roof is off, so the smoke isn't too bad, but it's very hot in there. No one has been beyond the second floor yet. There is a jet laid out to the second that I want you to extend. Go and have a look on the third and see if you can do a bit of firefighting. I've picked you Bethnal Green lads' cos I know you won't let me down."

We were soon off again into the building. We crept up the same staircase in darkness until the first floor, at the second it got a little lighter, although it was still very eerie and dull. LFM Dave told us to sort the jet out by adding another length of hose while he went off upstairs. Dave and I coughed as we exerted in the smoke, it wasn't too bad but anything more than softly drawing breath through the nose caused a coughing fit. My eyes and nose were also weeping tears and snot like a two-year-old having a tantrum.

LFM Dave came back down the stairs, his face streaked black then clean again by tears. "Right," he coughed, "We should be OK up there, it's shitty but not too severe, but its fucking red hot up there. Run the jet up the stairs and I'll radio down to get it charged."

Dave and I crept up the stairs, this floor had burned through in places as had the floor above, but the roof above was gone so there was quite a bit of light up there. The floor was covered in rubble; concrete from the roof, burnt timber, cork and all sorts. Dave took the nozzle and we pushed forward on the floor. LFM Dave wasn't wrong – the smoke was annoying but as it was only wood and cork burning and as it was escaping above us it was tolerable. The heat was a different matter. As I breathed in it was searing my lungs, a bit like trying to breathe in over a boiling kettle, I was laying on the floor in a puddle of steaming water trying to find some cooler air.

LFM Dave soon re-joined us and the jet snaked its way to life as water coursed through it. So there we were; Dave, then me, then LFM Dave following up the rear. As Dave opened the nozzle we were engulfed in steam as the water cooled the superheated atmosphere above us. I buried my head a little lower and held on for dear life as Dave worked the jet around the large landing, extinguishing the burning contents.

We pushed a little further and tried making our way into a room on the right. I was suffering a bit now, and as if reading my mind, Dave pulled back and I pushed up to the nozzle. I opened it and aimed in the direction of the fire. I got some relief by breathing in the cool clean air that was being forced out of the nozzle with the water. Soon we had pushed a good way forward but we were taking a real beating. I could feel my skin scalding as the wet fire tunic steamed in the heat. The others did not have the comfort of the air from the nozzle so LFM Dave soon decided that we needed to get out.

He told me to back out after them; I clung to my nozzle as long as I could, then seeing them on the stairs took a gulp of clean air, got to my feet and ran. As I stood up the heat was really searing my ears and exposed skin, and when I turned for the stairs, one of my feet became caught in some conduit that had fallen from the wall. I tried dragging it out but it was pulling my foot from the boot and going barefoot wasn't an option just yet. I looked around and the conduit was connected right along the floor behind me and moved in a twisted mass as I struggled. I was getting short of breath and panicking a little. "Stay clam…stay calm," I was thinking, but not doing so well. As my lungs began to burst, I made a final thrust forward, this did the trick releasing my boot, but now with all that forward energy I was flying through the air down the stairs. I braced for a painful impact and as I hit, I rolled over again, landing at the feet of the two Dave's who were by this time on their way back for me.

I guess the adrenalin was running because I didn't feel a thing, I was up on my feet in a shot excusing my idiotic behaviour to the Dave's. We made our way out and over to the Salvation Army canteen van for some repulsive so-called 'lemon flavour' drink that was designed to replace the salt that we had sweated out. After his de-brief, LFM Dave came back and we cleared away some equipment and then 'made ourselves busy' around the back of the Pump to kill the rest of the afternoon. It was so hot outside that our dripping gear was almost dry by the time we were headed back to Bethnal Green.

Later in July of 1989 I tuned 21, my Mum and Dad gave me the choice of a personalised number plate for my car or a 21st birthday party. I opted for the party although seeing the value of the £400 number plate now I often wonder if I made the right choice.

The party was booked for mid-August about three weeks after my birthday. This was also to be my 'leaving party' as the transfer to F22 Poplar had come around. I finished at Bethnal Green on the day of the party. My new Watch were on duty that night, so they didn't come. I was a little in two minds by now. I had grown up over the past twenty months and even the new Guvnor and I had 'an understanding'. But, the dye was cast, I was due to start at F22 Poplar on the Red Watch the following week.

Back to Poplar

'Pushing in' Firefighters from F28 Homerton White Watch making an attack on a house fire in Hackney in 2005.

I still lived just around the corner from Poplar Fire Station in Saltwell Street. Having already moved all of my gear over to Poplar, I contemplated walking the few hundred yards to the station on this warm late summer morning.

In the event, I decided to drive in case I got an out duty to another station, so I was in the car for all of a couple of minutes. I parked up got out of the car and headed pensively towards the station. On the stairs I came across a member of the Green Watch, I had still been in to visit the watches at Poplar ever since I had joined so my face was still known.

"Hello boy, welcome home, looking forward to being here…back on the Red Watch where it all started eh?"

Keith was the Leading Fireman on the Green Watch. He was one of the longest serving members at Poplar, and at well over six foot he was a larger-than-life character in many ways. A first-class fireman who had served on the Red and Green Watch at Poplar and a veteran of thousands of incidents.

I got changed and went down to the office where I took a few minutes abuse from the Green Watch before checking my riding position for the day. The board had me riding the Pump Ladder and in the Watchroom as Dutyman. I cursed thinking I'd be given a day to settle in, just ride the Pump and get used to being at Poplar.

My New Sub Officer came into the room. "Alright, how's it going?"

"Not bad Paul, you? Ere, why am I in the 'box' I thought I'd get at least a couple of days to settle in."

"Settle in? You know this place better than most of us here! Get lost, you're in the box and that's it."

I grudgingly accepted my fate and got on with the day. The day passed without much fuss and second time around was a bit easier. Compared to Bethnal Green, Poplar Red Watch was a young Watch, a lot of those who I'd known in the earlier years had moved on and had been replaced by newer younger men, there was now about seven of us who were in our early twenties so the social life was a lot more active than at Bethnal Green.

The work rate was slightly different at Poplar although the two areas were adjacent to each other. Poplar seemed to go out more, but the fires were different. Part of Poplar was the old Docklands area that had already been mostly burned to the ground and was now being redeveloped. Bethnal Green still had a lot of old derelict properties especially in the north of the ground around Hackney Road. Fires at Poplar seemed concentrated to the housing estates to the north of the station, and more than any man's share of rubbish and car fires. The big difference was the risks; we had the River Thames, a few miles of urban motorway, road tunnels, industrial areas and the beginnings of the biggest building site in Europe at the time with the fledgling Canary Wharf beginning to dominate the Docklands skyline.

It wasn't long before I got into the diet of life at Poplar, I was a lot happier here and the confidence that came with knowing every inch of the stations ground and all of the nuances of the area gave me some extra credit, sometimes to the annoyance of the other younger members of the Watch.

The summer of 1989 was drawing to a close and apart from a few flat fires here and there and some interesting incidents over at Canary Wharf, including workmen uncovering unexploded World War II bombs at an alarming rate, things had been a bit slow. I was beginning to think that I'd been sold a pup, and life at Poplar wasn't all that I'd imagined, but I needn't have worried.

Just before the end of shift one day in October the Pump Ladder, Pump and TL were called, along with Bow's Pump, to a fire in a derelict pub in St Leonard's Road near the Teviot Street estate. As we pulled up, I was on the back with John and Gary, we were all rigged in BA, as was the norm for the PL's crew on receipt of a call to fire in a building.

It was clear that a fire was burning somewhere within the building as smoke was rising into the darkening autumn sky. It was also evident that the pub had been burnt before; all the windows were boarded up with corrugated iron sheets and there was black smoke staining and scalded brickwork from the upper windows. This was confirmed by Ken, the White Watch Sub Officer who had come in early to let one of our Officers go home – he said that the White Watch had attended a fire here about a year ago.

The Pumps crew laid out a hose reel as Paul the Sub Officer gave Gary, John and me a briefing. Part of the corrugated sheeting was removed, and armed with our hose reel we made our way through the small gap. The bar area was pitch black, but my torch cut through a mist of smoke that was bottled up in the ground floor. Loud banging from behind me told me that the crews outside were removing more of the sheeting to ventilate the place.

I was behind Gary and John as we searched for the fire; Gary seemed to think the fire was upstairs and made for a ladder that had been placed up to the first floor in lieu of the staircase, that had been removed following the previous fire. I backed up a bit to allow them some room on the ladder and as I did, I felt a waft of hot air come over me. I looked behind me and could see nothing; all of a sudden, I saw a lick of flame in the darkness near the floor. I called Gary and John back and knelt down towards the flame. I then felt more heat; it was now obvious that the fire was in the basement.

I let the others know, then all of a sudden Gary pushed past me with the hose reel and was on the stairs, John also pushed past me and I felt a little peeved at this. Gary found the staircase and we all bunched up behind him, he tried to get into the basement but took a beating as he attempted to descend through the heat barrier. He hit the heat with a blast from the hose reel but this just enveloped us in a cloud of scalding steam. Gary cursed through his BA mask as his neck blistered, and backed up. I saw this as an opportunity and grabbed the hose reel from him, still pissed off from being pushed past; I promised myself that whatever happened I was going to get into the basement.

Finding the stairs with my feet I started guiding myself down the stairs and then got it big time from the heat barrier. I wasn't going to give this up, so I positioned myself so that I could slide down the stairs on my BA cylinder. Stupid really, as I could have gotten a few steps down then fallen through a weakened or burnt staircase right into the fire, but I guess that's another one chalked up to youthful enthusiasm.

I was soon at the bottom and the ceiling above me danced with dark crimson flame. I looked to the source of the flame and saw a doorway illuminated through the smoke, beyond it was a bright orange glow from another room that was obviously well ablaze. I hit the flames with the hose reel and after sending another ball of steam rolling up the stairs, it became obvious that the hose reel wasn't man enough for the job. I called to the others who had now come down behind me that we needed a larger inch and three-quarter jet, I heard Gary send the message over his comm's set.

Eventually the jet came and with it another crew, I began giving John, who at that time was the Junior Buck the benefit of my whole two years' experience. I was rattling on about this and that, how you should stay low, what we should do next, when a deep voice rudely told me to "shut the fuck up and get on with it." When the jet had come in, the crew from Bow had come down the stairs, I now had Steve from Bow behind me. Steve had done plenty of time at Poplar and at Bow and had been badly burnt on the M.V. Rudi M ship fire on Poplar's ground in 1980, where his partner Steve Maynard had died. This was a no deal job for him and he unceremoniously shoved past me with his BA partner to make a search of the remainder of the basement.

Eventually we knocked the fire down and withdrew from the job. The TL was up checking for extension upstairs and the street was a hive of fire brigade activity. The cool air was as refreshing as a mountain stream when I stripped my BA set and tunic off. I lit up a cigarette and drew heavily on it as Neil, one of the Leading Firemen was inspecting Gary's burnt neck.

As we were riding the Pump Ladder, we loaded up the BA sets and made our way back to the station. The good thing about an end of shift job is that the oncoming Watch have to clean and service all of the gear while we just get showered, book our overtime and get on our way. I stood under the shower letting the water relax me, pleased with my performance at my first challenging fire at Poplar.

I had decided before I joined the fire brigade that promotion was on the cards for me. I didn't know how far I wanted to go or why, but I fancied it nonetheless. At this point I had been operational for about two years and was eligible to act up to Leading Fireman. I had already taken and passed the written exam for promotion in 1988, so felt that I was ready to start learning a little more.

Back in those days, promotion wasn't the free for all that it seems to have become these days. If an individual wanted to do it, he or she showed an interest to their own officers, took the exams and also started helping out in and around the office of the station, learning all of the systems and paperwork. What form to fill out for what task, always typed in triplicate on the old-fashioned ribbon typewriter. After this, when an opportunity presented itself, you would be able to act up for a day or two here and there, maybe even a couple of weeks at your own place to cover leave. Once this had happened a few times, your 'reputation' began to build, and you might get offered some other temporary promotion at another station or on another Watch.

Back then, I was considered too young and green for long spells of temporary promotion, despite the fact we were all fast building on our experience in those days. When temporary promotion did come up, I ended up in charge of the turntable ladder. I use 'in charge' very tentatively as the operator of the ladders was always an experienced firefighter with great expertise, who could manoeuvre the ladder delicately into a host of tight spots. Even senior officers at large fires would always ask the ladder operator for their opinion on a particular pitch to a building.

As if to underline this, one old operator who came to us on a standby for the shift once called me 'Brick'. Puzzled I enquired further. "Well, the only thing you are useful for is working the siren on this machine. I drive it, I operate it…anyone can go to the top of the ladder at a fire. The only thing that you can do is operate the siren from that foot pedal on the floor. If I had a brick with string tied to it, I could throw it at the button when I wanted the siren and pull it off when I'd finished. Thus, you my son are as useful as a brick on this machine."

Nevertheless, I started acting up and spending time on the TL. At the time Poplar's TL was as busy as any across the brigade. There were plenty of TL's in Central London, but apart from one further east at Dagenham and another south at Greenwich, we had a good slice of North East and South East London to take care of, especially as the aerial ladder at Greenwich seemed to spend a lot of its time in workshops. We would spend many days chasing around the area on a whole host of calls, mostly nothing, but I got to see some great views from the head of my ladder at fires, and when we didn't get to work, got to see a wide variety of incidents, before the driver got bored and 'got us away'.

The 23rd December 1989 was a bitterly cold morning. London's three mobilising controls were in the process of being changed to a central control at Lambeth HQ, so we were on paper mobilising. The old Home Office Teleprinter was now eternally quiet, waiting to be replaced, and all calls came in via a red phone in the Watchroom. The bells in the station were temporarily wired into the telephone so shouts were announced by a brrringgg…brrringgg of bells instead of the traditional long ringing. The bells went down and we all piled out into the Watchroom. The Dutyman was busy writing the message but mouthed up to me "Ladders only" indicating it was the TL only to go.

As he put the phone down, he handed me the sheet and I read it.

'Man in precarious position on pylon

Elmcroft Avenue

Wanstead E.11

F30 Ground

F30 PL and P, L21 ET, F22 TL'

Had been hastily scribbled down on the form 9 used to take calls when the printer was out of service. I checked the map reference and walked out across the cold bright bay where Keith, the driver, already had the engine running.

"Leytonstone's ground, man up a pylon," I shouted as I pulled myself up into the cab.

"Do you know it?" replied Keith.

"Nah, it says Wanstead so head up towards the Green Man and I'll look it up." I pulled the A-Z atlas from the dash in front of me and stabbed at the siren button with my right foot as Keith eased the TL out onto East India Dock Road.

It was one of those days when squally sleet showers would give way to a blinding winter sun. Keith struggled to keep the windscreen clean from all the muck and spray as we weaved our way through Bow, Stratford and Leytonstone, northward towards Wanstead. Eventually tracing the route on the A-Z with my finger we worked our way into Elmcroft Avenue. At the dead end of the road, a policeman waved us into a large school field with a 200ft electricity pylon perched over in the far corner. As we slowly crossed the field towards where Leytonstone were parked, I saw a figure sitting upright on one of the cables just off the pylon, silhouetted against the bright sky.

"He's dead," said Keith.

"No, he's sitting upright," I argued.

"Nah, that's the current doing that to him," replied Keith… "You'll have to go up and get him down," he added for good measure. I gulped and sighed at the prospect.

As we pulled up, I looked up and saw, to my relief now we were closer, he was still alive, God knows how because there were thousands of volts of electricity running through the pylon. I jumped down off the machine and pulled my helmet onto my head as Leytonstone's Station Officer approached. 'Jock' was a tough Glaswegian Station Officer, who, legend had it was a cop in Glasgow but was thrown out for being too tough. He was well known for not suffering fools gladly and was not shy of grabbing a luckless individual in a head lock between his massive arms and squeezing until the poor soul almost passed out.

The rescue of the man from the pylon in Leytonstone, Steve on ladder facing camera.

With that fact burned into my mind, I smiled my most defensive smile as he approached and waited for him to speak.

"Alright son? There's a wee laddie perched up there upon the insulators, I'm all in favour of leaving the headcase up there 'til he fries himself and falls to the ground. But ah s'pose we'd better look willing and do something about it. Can ye get yer ladder pitched beneath him and try making contact wi' the mad bustud?"

Roughly translating Jocks request, I went back to Keith and told him the plan. The ladder was soon pitched underneath the pylon, and armed with a loud hailer, I was on my way up to make contact with the man who was believed to be a local man called Michael, who had gone missing the night before. I climbed to the top of the ladder, clipped on, and gave an arm signal letting Keith know I was ready to be shot up to the full one hundred feet of extension.

Once up there, I was still about thirty feet short of 'Michael' and I noted somewhat surprisingly that he appeared to have his trousers round his ankles which added to the bizarre scene 130ft above North East London. I wondered with a smile what Jock would make of it when I went back down to tell him. I raised the megaphone to my mouth and began calling out to 'Michael', all the usual incongruous stuff that flows from the mouth of would be rescuers or negotiators at times like this.

"Michael, are you alright."

"Can you hear me Michael?"

"Are you cold or hungry Michael?"

He looked down at me once and then looked above and all around him. Discouraged at my attempts to be a negotiator I signalled to be brought back to ground level. I stepped off the TL and was met by the gaggle of fire and police officers that had now assembled at the scene.

"It was no good Guvnor, I tried but he ignored me…just kept looking all around him when I was calling Michael."

The Police Superintendent smiled and explained to me, "We've just had some more information lad…your man isn't who we thought. He's an Irish lad called Patrick who escaped from the mental wing at UCH last night. He's probably been up there most of the night. Christ knows how he ended up here, but here he is, and we need to get him down."

Patrick! No wonder he was looking all around him. I can see it now, him thinking, "They think I'm mad, but there's a lad with a yellow hat on at the top of a ladder looking for someone called Michael, up the pylon…my pylon! They're all crazy!"

I went on to paint a full picture of what was actually going on up the pylon and the group of senior officers walked away from me deep in thought, thinking it was time for another plan to be hatched, as negotiation in light of the new information clearly wasn't going to work.

An engineer from the Central Electricity Generating Board had been requested to attend the scene to earth the residual current and give us any advice they could, after all these were their pylons, so supposedly, they climb up and down them all day. A Royal Air Force rescue helicopter had also been called for by the Guvnor's, they seemed to think he could be 'plucked' from his perch by the chopper like they do with people stuck on cliffs or mountains.

The next half hour was filled with more chin rubbing and head scratching and debating by those in charge. The CEGB guy also arrived and after confirming that the power was off and the residual drained, he joined the chin rubbing and head scratching group. I had been Plan A, you know, go up make contact and then he would wave back, realise he was stuck on a pylon and wander down as happy as you like. Plan B appeared to be the helicopter and as if on cue, the sound and sight of a Sea-King helicopter appeared from the south east.

The chopper closed in on us, descending and slowing as it got nearer. The pilot circled the pylon a couple of times and the winch man hung from his door like one of those cool Vietnam gunners. After a couple of loops, they set down in the school field about 200 yards from us. A couple of khaki fly-suited chaps jumped out and made their way over. The chin rubbing and head scratching crowd greeted them enthusiastically, the chin rubbing had now been replaced by excited pointing and gesticulating between the pylon and the RAF crew. Their response was to start chin rubbing and shaking their heads again, Plan B did not look good.

Soon, the RAF crew walked back to their aircraft, the DO came across to us and explained that the gusty winds meant that the rescue was too risky for the helicopter crew. Had he have been on top of the pylon, they could have chanced it, but the prospect of the winch becoming entangled in the power lines was not one the crew of the chopper welcomed. I looked up at the helicopter as it lifted off and ascended over to the pylon, I made them right.

As the helicopter disappeared into the distance, I envied the fact that they would be back at base within half an hour warm and cosy, although I couldn't get the image of the chopper parked in a field, with the crew sitting on old

Leather armchairs, pipes in hand and a Labrador lying next to them like an old war film, out of my head.

Plan C was soon hatched; it looked like it was going to work because as usual it was the hardest and least desirable. As the DO let us know the plan, the sky once again darkened and opened up in sympathy with my miserable snotty nosed plight. This plan became all the more urgent, as bored by our inaction, Patrick had gotten up, half pulled his trousers up and somehow shuffled off his perch. There were a few sharp intakes of breath as he moved from the insulator to the stanchion, followed by more gasps every few seconds as he shuffled, half-dressed, along a slippery piece of steel 130ft above the ground. Against all odds he made it to the main part of the pylon and paused briefly to get his breath back. Then we all "ooh'd and aah'd" again as he slid down an angled cross member, completely ignoring the vertical one that would have been a more natural 'fireman's pole' type descent. For the time being he seemed happy where he was so it was time to act.

The GECB guy and the ADO were going to go up to get Patrick down; a couple of us would go up after them and assist him down the rest of the way. I had previously volunteered to go along with one of the lads from Leytonstone; Jeff. Our TL had broken down and had been replaced by another TL from Lambeth. By rights we should have gone back to Poplar to wait for a mechanic to turn up to fix the problem, but I was involved now, much to the annoyance of Keith, the driver, who was sucking on a soggy roll up giving me daggers, thinking of the warm lunch, cup of tea and game of snooker that were not going to happen for him this lunch time.

Soon we had taken our leggings and helmets off, put our boots back on and tucked the trousers in. The logic being that the yellow rubber leggings may catch on the pylon, and as for the helmets – well, if we fell, they weren't going to save much so we got rid of them too. The GEGB guy went up, followed by Alf the ADO. They climbed the TL part of the way, then transferred to the pylon. Jeff and I waited on the base of the TL for the order to go up.

If any of you have ever had the good fortune of climbing an electricity pylon, you will be aware that the only way up is by standing on three-inch bolts spaced about a foot apart, on the outside edge of the pylon. Not such a problem for the first fifty foot or so, but between fifty and a hundred foot, one rapidly begins to lose confidence in these tiny bolts, which is all that is keeping you between where you are and an untimely meeting with your maker. Added to this is the fact that between you and the pylon will be a person who up until a few moments ago, thought that sightseeing on a 400,000 volt pylon was a good way to spend a Saturday morning just before Christmas, you may understand why I felt that twenty one was not a good age to die.

Jeff and I made our way up the pylon. Looking above me, I saw Alf was making slow progress with Patrick; it appeared as though he was trying to adjust his trousers that had obviously not been secured, and gravity was having its natural effect on them. Jeff went up and took over from Alf, and then after what seemed like ages, Patrick's feet were near my head. Somehow on these three-inch bolts, Jeff managed to manoeuvre Patrick from in front of him, down and now in front of me. I felt as if my feet were going to slip off and throw me into a rapid and ugly descent at any moment.

Painfully, one foot at a time I managed to get him nearer the TL. Offering words of encouragement. All fear had now been replaced with an adrenalin fuelled determination to get us both onto the relative safety of the ladder. More than once, I had to let go with one hand to pull up Patrick's trousers. I could have done with two hands to secure the button, but that would have been the last thing I did, so we pushed on.

Eventually my foot reached the head of the ladder; I pressed Patrick against the pylon as I mounted the ladder. The officer on Lambeth's TL came up behind me to support me and between us we managed to get Patrick between us and walked him down to the base of the ladder.

I had never been so pleased to be on a soaking wet playground in all my life. The Police Chief was ecstatic; he was promising medals all round which prompted the DO to say he would pass our actions up to the Honours and Awards Committee. As a postscript to the story, on a cold February day in 1991, similar in many ways to that December day, the London Fire Brigade held its first Honours and Awards Day for a couple of years. As can be expected with a big busy city fire brigade there were many meritorious and brave stories told that day, from fires and rescues over the past few years. In among them was a story of a rescue of a young man from a pylon just before Christmas 1989. ADO Alf and The GEGB engineer were awarded Commendations from the Chief Officer. Jeff and I received Chief Officer's Letters of Congratulations. It transpired that Patrick had returned to Ireland and was living with his family.

January saw the arrival of a new year and a new decade. It also heralded the arrival of the tenth anniversary of the death of Leading Fireman Steve Maynard in a fire on board a boat in Regent's Canal dock. The night of the 25th January 1980 had been busy for the London Fire Brigade. There had been a number of major fires across the city; one of them was at the disused flour mill in Lots Road, Chelsea. The Pump from Poplar had been sent right over to Chelsea on a relief late in the night, so stretched were the resources available. It was a tired Red Watch who were passing the last minutes of their shift before Green Watch took over on the morning of the 25th. A number of Green Watch riders were already with the Red Watch, replacing those who had opted to leave early, as the bells went down for a fire on board the MV Rudi M in Limehouse, just before change of shift that morning.

The station had already attended a fire on the boat a few days before. The boat, a former Panamanian Gas Tanker, was being converted in the dock for a new role. It was while the contractors had been using hot cutting equipment that they had started a small fire in the hold of the ship. The fire was quickly dealt with and a Fire Prevention Officer was called to advise them on a safer system of work and warn them of the consequences of not following the advice.

Sadly and fatally, they did not heed the advice, as a few days later the Pump Escape and Pump from Poplar, along with the Pump from Shadwell were again on their way to Limehouse Basin for a fire on the vessel. Upon their arrival, it was evident to the Station Officer that a significant fire was developing in the hold of the ship. Further pumps were ordered on and a BA crew armed with a jet were ordered into the hold to begin firefighting.

After a short time, it was apparent that the firefighting attempts were not as successful as hoped. The smoke issuing from the hold was growing thicker and angrier by the minute. It was decided to withdraw the crew and fill the hold full of high expansion foam. As the crew didn't have radio communications, a crew of two firemen were despatched into the hold to tell the others to withdraw.

Steve, was the first into the hold and immediately met up with the original crew who had also decided that things were not going so well. Steve passed the message and they began to withdraw. Within a few seconds Steve was alone in the hold with the last of the crew Steve Maynard. For some reason, maybe as Steve Maynard was the Officer, he edged Steve towards the ladder.

Steve was almost at the top and Steve Maynard was making his ascent when the whole hold was enveloped in an explosion of bright red-hot flame. Burning, Steve managed to find the strength within to keep hold of the ladder and climb out of the hold. Steve Maynard, completely engulfed could not hang on and fell back into the hold. As he landed, the joint on the BA cylinder broke off adding litres of compressed air to the inferno.

Friends, colleagues and 'brothers' fought to get back into the hold in vain. Jets were played onto the flames, but sadly it was too late. Steve Maynard was 26 years old and recently married. Once again Poplar Fire Station was witness to the death of one of their own in their struggle to protect the people of the East End.

It hardly seemed possible that ten years had passed since that cold January day. I remember my Nan, her flat overlooking the dock, telling me later that the firemen had been there all morning and the fire was bad. Little did she know until she saw the Lunchtime News on TV that one had given up his life and others had been severely injured.

Steve spent many weeks in hospital with severe burns to his legs and arms. His bravery and determination met every new challenge and he was back to work at Poplar a year later. In 1985 he transferred to Bow, but on the tenth anniversary, he was detached back to Poplar for the day as we were going to the cemetery on Poplar's Pump to lay a wreath for Steve Maynard.

The day was cold, wet and windy. No one took much notice of the severe wind that had blown up by mid-morning. The background hum of the radio got steadily busier as London's firefighters began to respond to more and more calls. It wasn't until we started seeing things blowing down East India Dock Road that we began to realise there was a problem.

A message was passed to all stations that 'all outside duties were cancelled due to severe storms across Southern England and high call volume'. As if on cue the bells went down and the Pump was called out, with me in charge, Steve, and a few of the other veterans of the old Red Watch, who attended the Rudi M fire, riding on it.

We had been ordered to glass in a precarious position in a tower block right over on Homerton's ground. We were the next nearest available Pump. En route, the radio was going mad; people were fighting to get messages sent, it was as if every appliance in London was out, all three radio channels were the same. I remember the young girl on the radio was getting very flustered. In the end a senior and very experienced Control Officer came on the radio and with his calming tone took over the channel and miraculously seemed to get some semblance of order back.

The block we had been called to was one of a pair of twenty storey blocks on the Kingshold Estate in Homerton. They were largely empty because the estate was a haven of crime and drug dealing. Most of the flats in both blocks had been burnt out giving the blocks the name 'Beirut Towers' due to their similarity to the burnt-out bombed buildings in war torn Beirut.

Upon our arrival we were met by a solitary local who colourfully explained how he had nearly been guillotined by a shard of glass from one of the flats. Now if we had been dealing with one empty flat, we could have dealt with it. Send a couple up to secure the windows while the others kept the public back. But we had two blocks of sixty odd flats each, with certainly two thirds of them abandoned or burnt out. A quick calculation led me to surmise that we had well over 50 windows on the side of the blocks I could see that weren't secured. I would need dozens of firefighters all armed with lengths of cord or rope to tie these windows down…that wasn't going to be a call that I, a young Temporary Leading Fireman was going to make on the busiest day since the 1987 Hurricane. I turned to the others for ideas, it was decided that we would inform the police and council, but apart from taping off the base of both buildings there wasn't a great deal we could do. No doubt the police and council were as busy as us. There wasn't a great deal of people about in any case on this estate, so I crossed everything I could and we left.

I tried getting in on the radio but to no avail. Then I heard something I had never heard and have never heard since. Control, historically the most efficient and skilled of all the emergency service controls had, because of the imminent change of mobilising systems mentioned earlier, completely lost track of appliance availability across London. They were asking for appliances free to take more calls. I managed to get in and we were soon on our way across to Stratford where a roof had blown off a row of garages and onto a house. We weren't alone, we were to be joined by the Emergency Tender from Norbury, a suburb in the depths of South London near Croydon, a run of well over 40 minutes in the best of conditions. Although I guess probably 70 of London's 115 fire stations were nearer to us, this was the next nearest free appliance.

As we turned into the road, it was obvious where we had been called. There was a terrace of 1960's council houses with a 50 ft mess of timber and corrugated roofing material draped across it, flapping wildly in the wind. Next to the row of houses was a row of garages with bare brick work open to the elements, where the wind had torn the roof from its fixings.

As we jumped down from the machine, again I looked in astonishment at the power of nature and wondered how we were going to resolve this one. Looking at the row of garages, I did not have enough salvage sheets to cover the expanse of roof, nor would we have been able to secure them in this wind if the roof itself had been ripped off. I turned my attention to the houses – how on earth were we going to get this mess cleared?

Luckily, the practical experience of the crew with me that day soon solved the quandary. First of all, it was decided that we should use some of our lines to secure the roof from doing any more damage, particularly to ourselves standing right beneath it. This done, we then decided that we would dismantle it bit by bit, lowering it as we went.

The next hour was spent getting cold and wet, gradually breaking it down and piling it up. Pull off a few sheets of roofing, pile them up, then cut away the timbers, pull it down a bit further, re-secure and then start again. A few times we were forced to throw ourselves across it to hold it down, but bit by bit, we gradually reduced it to its component parts and relative safety.

Once this was done, we then had to decide what to do with the pile of materials, each of which, especially the sheets, a potentially lethal weapon if the wind caught them again. Fortunately, one of the garages was abandoned, so we stacked the materials in this garage and secured them. Having long given up trying to get through on the radio, I advised the occupier of the end house, who also had one of the garages, to let the local council know when things had settled down somewhat, as the chances of getting repairs done at the moment were almost zero.

I took a few details for the inevitable report and then we were on our way. We never got through on the radio so arrived back at the empty station after negotiating the debris strewn, traffic chocked rush hour roads. The guys made an 'executive decision' as they usually did with younger inexperienced officers, to use this time to get a brew and have a peaceful smoke break. After a while, I got through to Control where we were immediately despatched to someone shut in the lift of a tower block that had suffered a power cut due to the storm. That pretty much wrapped business up for the day so after another painful crawl back through the traffic we got back and were relieved by the oncoming White Watch, who had faced the previous Hurricane on one of their night duties a few years earlier.

It was a warm afternoon for April, 1989 had been a good summer and it seemed that 1990 was going to follow. All of the windows were open in the mess room and a few of us were still sitting around the table following lunch. A few others had moved off for a game of snooker or to watch the news on TV. The bells went down, chairs were scraped back, tea spilled as cups were placed roughly back on the table. We snaked out of the room and down the stairs as the cry of "All the lot" called out from the Watchroom.

"Fire…with a number," was the familiar cry for a report of a fire with a door number of the property, more specific and therefore more likely to be the real thing. My period of temporary promotion ended, I was now back as a fireman and riding the Pump.

"Where we going?" I called into the front to the Guvnor.

"Knapp Road, off Campbell," came the reply.

"Look up the hydrant," added Dave who was driving.

I reached for the book on the shelf between the front and back of the cab, but John, sitting next to me, was already there. I held on as we made a hard left into Chrisp Street, off East India Dock Road, peering up in front for the tell-tale smoke plume. Nothing was showing but I couldn't get the best view. John braced himself as he struggled to read the list of hydrants for Knapp Road; the swaying and bumping of the machine, always more pronounced with Dave driving, meant he had to hold his finger on the list, like a child reading a book, to keep his place.

We were thrown hard again as the Pump doglegged from Violet Road across Devon's Road and into Campbell. I pulled up my collar and put on my gloves. We swung into Knapp Road and pulled up by the first block. I jumped off the Pump as the Pump Ladder drew up behind us, I heard the two tones of the TL still a block or so behind us, and further away still, in the other direction, the horns on Bow's Pump making up the attendance. I pulled up the locker door nearest to me and hauled out a long line, running around the front to catch up with the Guvnor who was entering the block, I noticed John had got a water extinguisher and a large axe.

Upstairs the adrenalin drained as we reached the door. It was obvious from the adjacent open window that if anything was going on inside the flat it wasn't going to be anything exciting. A scruffy gaunt young man opened the door. His eyes were big with fear but turned to casual arrogance as he spotted us. He knew nothing about a fire and after a few darting glimpses over our shoulders to the street below, slammed the door shut.

"Wanker," muttered the Guvnor, who looked over the balcony and called "code six please Codsy" down to Dave.

I walked back down behind the BA crew who had come up behind us, and after putting the line back, jumped up on the Pump. I played around with the straps of my BA set in the bracket behind me and slunk back into the gap I had created, getting comfortable for the ride back.

"We've got a visit this afternoon lads, A CRR over by Canning Town, caps and ties please," said the Guvnor as we pulled back into the station. Afternoons were the preferred times for fire safety visits, with cleaning, maintenance, drills and office work being the usual morning pastimes. I went upstairs, stopping off to empty my bladder on the way, then went to my locker to get my cap and tie. I slid down the pole to the ground floor with my cap perched at an angle on my head.

We were soon pulling into the car park of a small industrial unit just off Stephenson Street in Canning Town; this end of the ground was more industrial, so we were here fairly regularly for inspections. I looked up at the warm sun as we approached the building not really that enthused by what we were going to be doing for the next half hour or so.

I was standing in the reception looking with disinterest at the pile of printing trade magazines spread out on the table where we stood. I looked up at the receptionist, a bitter looking skinny woman in her late thirties, with short hair and massive framed glasses, she didn't make me feel any better either. A blast of the two-tone horns in my right ear from outside, with a tinny "Shout" called over the hand held radio by Dave got me interested in life again. I was away through the doors as the Guvnor made his excuses behind me. I saw Dave with the radio handset wedged between his ear and shoulder as he took down the details. He had already gunned the Dennis Pump into life.

As we climbed on I heard him say something about a fire in a house in a road that I did not recognise, I then heard Star Lane, this I knew to be on Plaistow's ground, the next station east of us and not a great distance from where we were now. As we pulled out of the industrial estate, I struggled to get rigged, I loosened my tie angrily but didn't have the time to pull it right off. I heard rapid conversation from the front and the radio was calling up Plaistow.

"It's going," called the Guvnor, "look."

As we headed back up Stephenson Street, I looked across the railway, the end of our stations ground, and saw the feathered edges of the top of a plume of dark grey smoke, in contrast with the blue sky rising above the buildings, no more than half a mile away.

"Plaistow got this by radio too, we may be first in, get ya sets on," shouted the Guvnor into the back cab over the noise of the engine and two-tone horns. I struggled with my leggings as we turned out of Stephenson Street and rolled again as we screeched round Canning Town roundabout as I was fighting with my tunic. I was breathing hard as I did it up and slid my arms through the straps of my BA set. We pulled into Barking Road, looking ahead I couldn't see smoke, Barking Road was long and straight, Plaistow were nowhere to be seen. The adrenalin was really pumping now; my heart was racing and I had that slight nauseous feeling that is all part of the 'fight or flight' built into us. This was certainly going to be fight. We turned into Hermit Road and I could see nothing between the tall flats, we then made a hard right into Star Lane and across the green I could see a dark boiling pall of smoke from the row of houses off to the left of us. Dave made a hard left and then a hard right. The burning house was on my side as we pulled past it, and I got a brief blast of radiated heat through the window.

"We'll have a jet on this one," I heard the Guvnor say as I jumped down.

I looked at the house as I ran to the back of the Pump. The door was already open and dark orange flame rolled from the downstairs window of the terraced house, reaching the guttering and completely masking the windows above. I was aware of people running around and shouting and I now really felt the heat on my face from the flames, no more than twenty feet away.

At the back of the Pump, I made a grab for the flaked length of inch and three-quarter hose. Dave barged me out of the way.

"Don't fucking worry about that, get yourself started up," he said.

I threw my hat on the floor and the joined John already pulling his mask over his head.

"There's someone in there," the Guvnor said as he stood in front of us, "an old fella, probably on the ground floor. Watch how you go, knock that fire down a bit first."

My lunch felt heavy in my stomach, I looked at the flames rolling out of the window as I pulled my mask tight, this didn't look good for him.

Dave had plugged the jet into the delivery, cranked up the revs and opened the valve. He stood in the road in his shirt and trousers holding the hose, braced against the water snaking through it. The first spits of water evaporated into steam, then as the water flowed the flames darkened and were engulfed by a wave of billowing steam. John took the jet from Dave and hit the ground, pushing the jet through the window high into the ceiling of the room. Engulfed In scalding steam I crouched low and pushed open the door. I immediately hit the deck and crawled into the passageway. Bright flame was being pushed out of the door to my right and was causing an eerie light to fall around the blackened hell inside.

I felt John pushing in behind me, way back, seemingly miles away but in reality, only a few feet. I heard the Guvnor calling encouragement from the cool bright heaven that was the world outside of this place. I pushed past the door, looking briefly into the swirling maelstrom of steam, flame and smoke. The heat was stinging my ears and I winced as the hot metal rings on my mask came into contact with the side of my face. I could just see the carpet rise in front of me as I reached the stairs, and as I swept my arm out to the right, I hit something heavy but soft. I swept back and with my arm felt a foot and an ankle. I knelt up and heard a voice screaming.

"I got him; I've got him here… here John, I've got him," I realised the voice was my own as I got two hands on his leg. I pulled hard and in doing so pulled myself upright, the heat was really bad now and all of my face was stinging where it was exposed. The mask juddered on my face as I was pulling in such deep breaths, I was almost overcoming the continuous flow of air being delivered to me through my BA. I got the body moving and started to drag him. I dropped back down and pulled harder, John was behind me and I was kicking backward with my boot to try to get him to back out. He was soon beside me and found the other leg, we dragged the body to the door, then picked him up face down and turned him round.

We laid him in the kerb and I fell over. I looked up at a sea of horrified faces and down at the body. He was slightly burned but not so burned that he was beyond hope. I crawled towards the door again as Plaistow's machines pulled around the corner and went back into the house. I picked up the jet and opened it, aiming it high at the flames rolling from the door and up the stairs. Once again, we were enveloped in steam and we pushed towards the door on the right. I laid down and rolled onto my left side, the momentum of which pulled the jet up and to the right. I forced it forward and down swirling it all around the room. The heat began to lose its sting now, I knew we had it.

Within a few seconds noise behind us shook me out of the trance of swirling steam. A couple of blokes from Plaistow were in and they wanted to take the jet.

It was fair enough; we had made a grab on their ground and hit the fire, they needed to do something. I crawled out of the house on John's heels. Dave and a few others were working on the old fella with a resuscitator. The Guvnor was in the road talking to Plaistow's Sub Officer.

"Well done boys, lose your sets and get a breather," he smiled as we walked past. Drained, I pulled off my helmet and sat on the opposite kerb. I pulled at my mask and ripped it off. The cool, tasteless, odourless, clinical air gave way to the smell of the smoke and fire. This always seems really strong after taking off breathing apparatus, I guess because of the rapid change. I laid back on my elbows and let out a loud sigh. I was young, fit and had only done a few minutes of work, but it was extreme adrenalin filled work. As the adrenalin drained away so did my energy. The sharp drop in temperature was a welcome relief but also a shock.

***

Things in the job, my career and my personal life moved on at a steady pace. My Girlfriend Joanne and I had bought a small terraced house in Dagenham in the eastern suburbs of London. I was doing a little more in the office, helping out, learning the admin side, even when I wasn't acting up. From time to time, one of the officers would go off on a course or get acting up to a higher level, then I would get another spell for a few days or weeks.

I was having another of my temporary promotion spells, Dave was driving the Pump and once again I was on the back, but this time as temporary Leading Fireman. Del was on the back with me, and with the Guvnor away at the Fire Service College, the Sub Officer Paul was acting Station Officer. We made our way onto the Isle of Dogs for an Automatic Fire Alarm in a big supermarket and were waved away by Millwall as soon as we arrived as the incident was a false alarm.

As we came back over the Blue Bridge, I heard the radio call us up for another call. We were ordered to a fire in a block of flats in Rainhill Way in Bow. There was nothing unusual about this as the place was always having fires; rubbish chutes, the underground garages, flats, even a barbeque on a balcony that caused dozens of calls as it was on the 22nd floor and most of East London saw it. We were ordered on as the third Pump with Bows pair, and our TL also being ordered.

By the time we got to the bottom of Cotton Street, screeching left onto East India Dock Road, they were calling Bow up for multiple calls; again, not that unusual, it meant something was obviously happening, but lots of people had phones. The difference was, they were saying over the radio that there were people calling in who were trapped on the 6th floor, the 20th floor and the 15th floor. What on earth was going on?

We quickly made the right onto Chrisp Street and the PL was turning out of the station on the left in response to the multiple calls. They were soon up behind us as we made our way towards Bow. From the three tower blocks in Rainhill Way up ahead of us there were no flames spewing from floor upon floor, so that was at least one good thing. However, there were massive bright flood lights fitted to the tops of the blocks and even from a half a mile away we could see these were shrouded in smoke.

The access road into Rainhill Way had the most severe speed humps I have ever known. They are not so much speed humps as kerb stones laid across the road. You have to come to a halt to negotiate them and with all this going on, the radio still pouring out messages of doom for the inhabitants of the block involved, it made progress frustratingly slow. As we rounded the bend the TL and Bows machines were up in front of us. Thick black smoke was pouring from a number of windows up above. The radio burst back into life and as we jumped off the machine, and I heard Bow's Guvnor frantically "make Pumps six, persons reported."

We followed Paul, our Temporary Guvnor up to the block, he met up with Bow's Guvnor who quickly explained, "Someone has set light to the cable TV feed that runs right up the middle of the block in an open shaft, with ventilation grilles on every floor. It's run a few floors on us but the whole block is smoke logged. I've got people pouring down the stairs and others claiming to be trapped on every floor...do what you can Paul."

"OK mate, we're on it," came the reply and the three of us were off into the block. The stairs were choked with people, most of them pleading excitedly to us in a foreign language.

We gave up the stairs as a bad job and run for the lift. One of Bow's blokes was loading up with equipment, so we hitched a lift.

"Where you going?" asked Paul.

"Up to the 12th to get above the fire," came the reply.

"That'll do us," said Paul, then keyed his radio, "foxtrot two two Station Officer to foxtrot two seven Station Officer over."

"Go ahead."

"We are going to the 12th, I'll work down and send my blokes up to see how things are and we'll try to get people to stay inside."

"Received Paul, thank you, over."

Once on the 12th floor, we knew our job; some other Bow guys were waiting in the smoke logged lobby for the equipment being brought up. Paul briefed us quickly and Del and I decided to take alternate floors. I went up to the 14th and immediately encountered moderately thick smoke, it was a little pungent but bearable. One of the doors was open with a young Asian girl standing in it, holding a baby.

"Get in…get back in," I shouted at her, "you'll be OK as long as you get in and shut the door."

She was having none of me, she disappeared back inside and came out with another child and a much older man, who was wearing a vest and some type of sarong.

"Get inside will'ya?" I shouted at them, "you'll be OK."

They ignored me, pulled the door shut and had it on their toes. Blocks of high-rise flats designed in the 1960s were built of concrete, with each flat being its own fire resisting compartment. So, a fire could start and should – and in my experience always did – stay within the flat of origin, apart from the odd occasion where it may break out of the window and cause a little damage to the flat above. The principal being that people could stay safely in their flats and have no reason to evacuate unless it was their flat on fire. Designed by architects as a 'stay put' strategy, which, unknown to me at the time would become a very contentious issue many years into the future. I had to leave them to it, the staircase was free of smoke, so they would come to no harm, but with so many people panicking I worried for a disaster if someone tripped on the stairs and more people fell behind them.

I banged on the other three doors and lifted the letterboxes shouting for people to stay where they were. I got no response from two of the doors…good. But the final door opened.

"Hello…ohh, what's…"

"Alright mate, it's the fire brigade, there is a fire in the shaft but we've got it…" I lied convincingly, "just a bit of smoke, go back in, open a few windows and you'll be OK."

"Yer…righto…you sure?"

"Yeah, I'm sure, you'll be better off in there."

The door slammed shut. One more quick look round and I went into the lobby, the self-closing door shut behind me as I considered the little permanently open vent windows on the landing and the stairs, designed to ensure the staircase stayed free of smoke for anyone evacuating from a fire. I went back through the door, took a mat from outside one of the flats and wedged the door open, the smoke crept out behind me, it wasn't ideal ventilation, but it would do. I heard Del shouting from below, so I went on up to the 15th. Same procedure, knocking on the doors and shouting. I heard the lobby door behind me scrape the floor and saw Del, he turned on his heels and went up to the 16th.

I eventually ended up on the 18th floor when another crew came in. We had an exchange, they said the landings on the top two floors were fairly thick with smoke, but they got no answers from any of the doors. The smoke was getting better on the lower floors. I didn't have a radio, so I went to meet up with Del, before we made our way back down. The stairs were clear of most people now and I met up with a few firemen going about their business as we went. On about the 4th floor we again met up with Paul, this floor was hot, it was obvious that the cables and shaft had burnt up to this level. Paul kept Del with him and sent me to the ground floor to help out if I needed to.

On the ground floor, I met up with the Sub Officer from the control unit, he sent me off to return to the CU with a couple of roll boards from the appliances that he had gathered. On the back of the unit, I waited patiently as a Divisional Officer was being briefed. Once this was over, he turned to me, I smiled and went to pass the boards forward, to go in the rack that keeps a tally of who is attending. The DO felt it right that he should bollock me for something or the other as was customary in those days.

"Leading Fireman," he said to me, his breath making me flinch, "where are you from?"

"Poplar Guvnor," I answered.

"Well then, do your collar up properly if you are on my fireground, right?"

"Yes Guvnor," I muttered and said a few other things under my breath.

I jumped down off the unit and looked at the grassed area at the side of the block, there must have been well over a hundred people stood there with the odd policeman trying to make sense of it all, darting in and out of the crowd. Checking that the DO had disappeared, I theatrically pulled off my helmet and wiped my sweating brow, letting my admiring public see what a hero I'd been. None of them even noticed me so I made my way back to the front of the block.

Soon it was all over. The police kept the people out of the block while we made our gear up. The machines ordered onto the six pump make up, and our PL and TL were away, leaving Bow's pair and us at the job. Shortly after, as I had a sneaky fag inside the pump with Dave, the residents went back into the block and we were on our way, leaving Bow to assist the Fire Investigation team.

No one could recall what the shaft was originally there for, but regardless – with a grilled outlet on each floor there was certainly not meant to be any combustibles in there. Over the years, various utilities were conveniently placed in here, including the main cable TV feed which was made of heavy plastic. The day someone decided to light a bit of rubbish that had gathered in the base of the shaft was the day it all nearly went wrong. Thankfully, apart from a bit of panic, no one was injured and the guys held the fire a few floors up. It was a bad night for all those with cable TV though.

Shortly after this, we picked up another serious high-rise job, this time in the middle of the night on Plaistow's ground. My head spun as I jumped out of bed and slid down the pole. We had been out a couple of times already and I had fallen into a deep sleep. As I emerged blinking into the brightly lit appliance bay, I looked up to see both the red and green lights for Pump Ladder and Pump were illuminated.

"Fire in flats on Plaistow's ground…we have been ordered on multiple calls," the Dutyman cried.

I pulled on my boots and leggings and jumped onto the back of the Pump. The back of the Pump was silent as we all rigged, trying to clear our heads for the urgent situation that was facing us. The Guvnor gave us the full story, we had been called to a fire in a flat that Plaistow were already en route to. With several calls being received at Control, it was obvious at this time of the morning that this was going to be no false alarm.

The first of the very early rush hour traffic was beginning to head into London; lorry's delivering to the fish market, early morning cleaners. The big rush was still a couple of hours away at 7am. We quickly made our way along East India Dock Road, over Canning Town Flyover and onto the A13 proper.

"We've got something here," called the Guvnor from the front. The pair of us in the back looked through to the front. Ahead of us to the right was a group of high-rise buildings, from the side of one of the smaller 11 storey blocks came a jet of bright flame and a column of black smoke visible against the first threads of light in the sky.

We passed the block on the A13 and I saw a few more flames from the side windows of the building a few floors from the top. The fire was in a flat on the opposite side to where we were, so a full appraisal was still unclear. We slowed violently as we reached a crossover in the dual carriageway, the tyres screeching as we turned hard on the heels of the Pump Ladder in front of us. A quick couple of lefts and rights and we had pulled up beyond Plaistow's machines.

"Help with the riser," called the Guvnor as we jumped off the machine. I ran around the Pump and looked up. Flames were rolling out of a side window and a wall of flame came from the balcony of the flat where I assumed the entire living room was alight. Small pieces of flaming debris were falling to the ground, and bizarrely a woman was kneeling on the floor with a coat covering a little black cat.

"I'll take that Mel," I said to one of Plaistow's drivers who was throwing out a length of hose, he gave the ends to me, I placed one in the outlet of their machine and ran with the other to the riser, handing it to one of the Plaistow firemen who was attaching the first. Looking back to see that both were connected I called to Mel "water on." I stood there momentarily as I saw the hose begin to snake into life, then ran across to straighten out the twin lines of hose that had been laid from the hydrant. This done there was soon a good supply of water going into the building to allow the firefighting to begin.

I had a look around, everything else seemed to be done down here. Our drivers were rigging and beginning to look after all of the command support stuff and Plaistow's Guvnor was formulating his first message. The rest of my crew had disappeared inside the building, so I made my way towards the entrance. There were again a number of people in various states of undress wandering out of the building, shocked by the events that had prematurely interrupted their night's sleep. One of Plaistow's guys came out of the lift with a young woman who was crying and snotty. An ashen young man was behind her, these I assumed were the occupants. They were shocked and confused but seemed OK, their relative calm in the situation seemed to confirm that no one else was trapped in the flat, otherwise they would have been hysterical. I jumped in the lift and went to press a button but I paused... was it the eighth or ninth floor? It is good practice to always go to a couple of floors below the fire in any situation so you don't have the lift doors open up onto an inferno. Doubting myself, I pressed number six to be sure.

The lift opened up on the sixth floor and I could hear a lot of noise and activity above me; deep, metallic and echoing sounds reverberated around the concrete core of the building. I opened the door to the staircase where a few people eyed me up and carried on with their escape from the building. I was soon on the seventh floor, where a group of my guys were stood along with a fireman and officer from Plaistow. The two from Poplar on the pump ladder were starting their BA sets to go on and assist the firefighting in the flat, while the rest of us would check above the fire.

A small amount of smoke was in the stairway from the eighth floor. As I passed the entrance to the floor the landing was dark with smoke but I could see that the overhead light fitting was shrouded in swirling smoke. I got onto the floor above where there was light smoke but nothing too severe. I banged hard on the door immediately above the flat where the fire was. There was no answer, I looked through the letterbox and the light was on and there was again a small amount of smoke evident in the flat. The light pointed to the fact that someone had been in and had gone downstairs, there was nothing blazing in here at the moment, so I reasoned I had a bit of time.

I went downstairs to the seventh floor to get hold of a radio to try to get the keys to the flat. Shortly, a breathless Plaistow fireman joined me back at the ninth floor. He turned the key in the lock and the door opened. I followed him into the flat and let out an involuntary cough as the smoke in here although not thick, was quite pungent. We checked that every room was clear, finally standing in the living room directly above the fire. The side window was blackened and cracked. The balcony door and window had been offered a fair bit of protection as they were set back. Grey smoke and steam still curled rapidly over the edge of the balcony occasionally obscuring it as the fire below was being fought. I heard muffled noises of the battle going on immediately beneath me and shuddered a little as I imagined waking up trapped in a high-rise fire.

There was no sense in opening this flat up to ventilate it just yet as we would have only let the smoke from below in. I had a close look at the window, we'd need to take the glass out once the fire was out otherwise it could fall to the ground and injure someone as soon as we left.

The flat was tidy, and despite the misty smoke in the room, it had an air of cleanliness about it. Looking around I saw the flat maybe belonged to an older person, the furniture was simple but very tidy, the room was full of photographs including children and grandchildren. The items left around told me that a woman lived here. Ladies reading glasses, woman's magazines and so on, I also got the feeling after taking the scene in that she was here on her own. Her husband maybe having died some time before, I thought back to how they were probably moved into this block in the 1960s as a middle-aged couple, possibly with one adult child left at home. How they had moved into a new flat with central heating, hot and cold running water, a bathroom, full of post war optimism. Now twenty odd years later, she was stood outside her building wrenched from her sleep by a fire below her, probably caused by some careless accident. How she had seen the changes. The people of her generation slowly dying off and increasingly younger and poorer people were taking their place. The once clean stairways now reeked of urine and vomit. How lonely she must have been as one by one all those who once shared her hopes and fears had slowly left her alone with only her memories of better days gone by.

I found myself then thinking of my Grandmother, asleep in her bed three miles to the west of here on the 11th floor of her building. I realised that I knew nothing of this woman but had actually been comparing her circumstances to those of my Nan. I was probably not far wrong. Plenty of old people in the inner cities were seeing out their time like this. My Parents also recently retired with just their state pension to live on and were in a similar situation, although I was comforted that they at least had a house to live in and not a flat. I was glad I was a firefighter, I may never be a millionaire but I should at least have a house that I owned and be paid a pension to allow me to live somewhere pleasant so I could pass my last years away in relative comfort.

Soon I was awakened from my daydream by one of the officers; he came to see how it was going. I looked over towards the balcony, the occasional wisp of steam came up from the flat below, but the battle was won. I opened the door and felt a damp warmth on the balcony carried up from the aftermath of the fire below. I peered over the balcony into the ugly blackened mess beneath me. The steam made my eyes water.

We cleared the glass from the window and informed the official from the Council that it needed replacing, someone brought the old lady up from below and thankfully she was absolutely fine. I should have known, this generation of East Enders were dragged from their bed's night after night during the War, she had witnessed disasters our generation could only imagine.

We soon had her settled and all she was worried about was the cat from the flat below. Apparently, the cat had been in the room on fire and as the fire developed had in her panic squeezed through the open window and launched herself 80 foot to the ground. Only a miracle would have saved a human attempting a jump from that height, but the agile cat had managed to land on her legs, breaking a couple of them, but all things considered had a lucky escape.

***

Plaistow was another busy station immediately to the east of Poplar, so we spent a fair amount of our time there. One afternoon, when I was again acting up to Leading Fireman and riding the TL, the bells went down for a call for the TL. Ronan Point was one of about half a dozen twenty story blocks built in the Custom House area of Plaistow's ground in the late 1960s. With the demand for more and more modern housing, most of it being built increasingly taller in that era, pressure was put on architects and engineers to come up with quicker ways to produce mass public housing. Blocks like Ronan Point were basically a central concrete frame and floors with the outside walls of prefabricated concrete blocks lifted into place by a crane, then bolted together like a life-sized Meccano set. This type of block was known as 'system built'.

Early on the 16th May 1968, not long after the block was opened, a gas leak had developed in one of the upper flats. The resident of the flat had woken up, gone into a room and struck a match to light the cooker causing the gas to ignite violently. This phenomenon was not uncommon, gas leaks and subsequent explosions have happened many times. What was unusual though was a gas explosion in such a high building with this particular type of construction. The explosion caused the windows and walls to be blown out, but then the 'puzzle' of fixings that held the building together had been compromised. The result was an entire corner of this high building had fallen down. The resident had a miraculous escape, but four others in the block didn't. It was also a miracle that the explosion happened early in the morning when most people were still in bed, later in the day, with more people in their kitchens the casualty list would have inevitably been much higher.

The explosion at Ronan Point heralded the end of the ideology of building mass housing higher and higher. Although Ronan Point was re-built, by the early 70s surveys had identified that many of the concrete panels were resting on bolts instead of the bed of mortar they were meant to be on. Many of the gaps had been stuffed with newspaper and serious fires that had occurred over the years in many of the blocks had spread into adjacent properties, despite having been so called 'fireproof' compartments.

I was therefore surprised to be heading east on the TL en route to a fire in Ronan Point, musing about its notorious past knowing the building was now in the course of being demolished. As we reached the crest of Canning Town Flyover, I saw the inevitable column of smoke coming from the upper floors of the block. As we passed by on the A13, headed again for the cross over point on the A13 dual carriageway, I could see flames blowing from a flat on the floor below the top. We turned into Butchers Road, drove down and pulled up just outside of the block.

I walked into the site where I met up with the officer in charge of Barking, who were standing by at Plaistow covering for them while they were attending a fire elsewhere. He informed me that the demolition men had accidentally set fire to a flat, as they were doing some cutting. To make things worse, a lot of the rubble and furniture abandoned as the residents left was still on the upper floors. Worst of all, in their wisdom, the first thing the demolition men removed were the lifts and the dry riser; the pipe used to pump water up inside the building with an outlet on each floor for firefighting. The final irony came when we were told that to stop vandals and curious children getting into the building, the staircase had been removed from the ground to the second floor.

So, just about everything engineered into a building to allow fire crews to access and extinguish a fire had been removed. With most of the windows also gone, the fire was being fed by air currents from all sides of the 200 ft block. The fire was spreading rapidly across the floor and to the floor above. So, with us stuck on the ground with no easy way in it was decided to make the job up to six pumps while the Incident Commander started to get his head around the problem.

He decided that we should pitch the TL as high as possible then allow crews to gain access from that level. It was pointed out to him that this particular TL had a three-man cage on, so it might be better to take people up two at a time, with me in the cage operating the ladder. We got this started and after a couple of trips, including one with me, not the lightest of people, and two other big lumps in BA sets that caused the cage of the TL to sway and groan when we got to full height, eventually enough people and equipment were up there to begin an attack on the fire.

All we needed now was water. If the fire had been confined to a single flat then water pumped up a hose from the outside may have done the trick, the hose replacing the riser. As it was the building was just on the limits of operability of a dry riser, another floor in height and it would have required a wet riser; a permanently charged water pipe with booster pumps to assist in getting the water to that height, not that any of that was anything other than academic now that the building was being demolished.

With the best part of the top two floors now burning merrily, albeit the top floor was partly demolished and open to fresh air, it was decided that a light portable pump would be required at roughly halfway up the building to provide the pressure and, more importantly, the flow of water necessary to overcome the rate of burning without putting the crews at undue risk. The thing with fire brigade lightweight portable pumps is, they are exactly the opposite. Sure, compared to a fire engine they are small, light and portable, but they are still basically a small car engine with a pump attached, built into a frame. So heavy that it takes four firefighters to lift and carry it. There was no way that the TL could get it up there, it would have collapsed under the weight even if the inbuilt safety systems on the ladder could be overridden.

In the end, the supervisor of the demolition crews offered his crane with a large skip attached. So, with the crews up there joined by some demolition men who 'knocked out' a wall on the twelfth floor, the LPP was loaded, along with more hose, onto the skip where it was skilfully delivered by the crane driver into the newly created hole in the building. More crews were taken up in the TL and soon water was pumped up to the LPP on the twelfth floor ready for its onward journey. Two lines of hose were then threaded up the gap between the stairs until they reached the floor below the lowest one that was alight. Although the windowless flats had created a lot of air movement that allowed the fire to spread unhindered, it also made life more bearable for firefighting crews who, once their hoses were charged, were soon able to knock out the fire on both floors.

One other incident happened on Plaistow's ground while I was at Poplar that had an effect on me. We had been on a Friday and Saturday night duty and things as usual had been fairly lively. The last call we had was about 3am on Sunday morning, so we had managed to grab a few hours' sleep. It was a fine spring morning when I got up and had a shower, just as I was walking downstairs to get breakfast the bells went down.

"Pump ladder and pump," came the cry from the Watchroom and I picked up speed jumping a few stairs at a time until I reached the ground floor. I ran into the bay and jumped onto the back of the machine.

We were on our way to Pacific Road in Custom House, again, just off Butchers Road, to a fire in a flat. We pulled out into the bright warm morning and headed east towards the fire. As we were turning through our now famous gap in the A13, Control were calling Plaistow up with a better address; Pacific Road, the correct address that we had been called to. The first call was seen by someone a few streets away, so Plaistow lost vital seconds as they were sent to where the fire had been seen from by the first caller, which was wrong. So, they were pulling up just seconds before us by the time they had turned around. As we pulled into the close where the fire was, I saw a red brick block of maisonettes with dark smoke coming from the top window of one of them. As I jumped down, I saw a well-built woman in her night clothes being restrained by neighbours, next to her on the balcony were a couple of police officers, one stood on a chair on the landing outside of the maisonette trying to smash the smoking window with a long broom.

It was evident from the panic that someone was trapped inside. A surreal and shocking scene for such a fine Sunday morning, belonging more to the middle of a dark and wet night. Paul, who was in charge of the pump barked at me to go around the back of the block to check on the situation and whether anyone was trapped there. I ran to the back of the block and leapt up onto the high wall. I looked up at the flat and saw smoke pushing from the windows at the back. A look into the gardens below confirmed that no one had jumped or fallen. Running back to the front I met up with Paul who was in conference with Plaistow's Guvnor. I looked up to see dark orange flames belching angrily from the window that had now been broken or had failed from the heat. The first of Plaistow's BA men were going into the maisonette with a hose reel.

"There's a kid trapped in there," Paul told me as the Plaistow man walked back towards the fire.

"The PL's crew have got sets on and are going up to search as well. Get up there and see what you can do," he added.

"Will do," I replied.

Upstairs, I heard the woman's anguished wails from inside another home, I looked in and saw two frightened little boys in the passage with the policemen. At the door of the burning maisonette one of the Plaistow firemen was busy filling in the BA entry control board while another fed hose reel in. There were six firemen up the stairs looking for the little kid. I crawled up the stairs and drew up next to Plaistow's Sub Officer whose eyes were running from the smoke.

"Anything Steve?" I enquired.

"Nah, nothing yet," he replied.

I went back down the stairs and looked elsewhere in the maisonette. The living room had a large double bed in it which looked like it had been evacuated in a hurry. I figured that the mother had been woken by the fire, but had no idea where the father was. Having fully searched the lower floor, I waited at the bottom of the stairs expecting the limp form of the child to be rushed down the stairs at any second. From above I heard the desperate blind search by the firefighters, the crashing and banging of furniture being tossed around in a desperate but methodical search. Coupled with this was the sound of the fire being extinguished and anxious high-pitched voices trying to communicate in BA.

After a short time, the fire was out and the upper floor although still heavy with steam and residue smoke was now breathable. The BA crews had withdrawn once we got up the stairs and were able to stay there. Checks were going on with the mother to confirm whether the child was actually in there, as casualties, even those long dead, are usually found very quickly in a domestic fire where there are only a few small rooms to search.

The back room was filled with boxes of merchandise of some sort and lots of furniture that had been stacked but no beds. The place, as a result of the search, looked like a bomb had hit it. I moved into the front room where the fire had been. In here was another mess of bed remains and a couple of spilled wardrobes and drawers. The wall from about waist height was clean brick where the plaster had spalled off in the heat, a single charred wire hung from the cracked concrete ceiling where a light had once been. The air in the room was hot and humid and I had an ominous feeling in the pit of my stomach.

Steve came back in the room and confirmed the mother had said the child was in the front room. I sighed deeply and carried on with my search. Everything was covered in the steaming damp plaster that had fallen from the walls and ceiling. I stepped across the bed pulling up what was left of the mattress, but found nothing. There were the remains of a chest of drawers under the window opening. At its base was a pile of rubble with what appeared to be a burnt quilt. I lifted the quilt and the rubble fell away, then I saw a brightly coloured sock, heel upward. I looked closer and the heel was attached to a small black leg. I lifted up a bit more rubble and then uncovered the poor little boy who was buried in the rubble. His lower half that I exposed first was unburnt, sadly and beyond all hope, his upper half was horrifically charred. There was no hope that this little fella was still alive.

I called Steve back into the room and showed him my miserable find. I stood there and offered a prayer for one so young that had seen his life snuffed out before it had begun, and as the other officers arrived, I left the room. I walked downstairs out of the maisonette and then down the communal staircase to the ground floor. I spoke to a couple of people then snuck off around the other side of the pump to have a quick smoke. I didn't have kids at that point in my life. Something I was grateful for on reflection.

Back at the station we sat quietly through a late breakfast, I chewed miserably on it before going for a long shower and then home to get a few hours' sleep. The following Thursday when I returned to duty, as the person who had found the body, I had a number of statements and forms to fill out in preparation for the coroner's hearing. Life carried on and I almost forgot about it until the morning of the inquest where I was to report to Walthamstow Coroners Court in full undress uniform for the inquest into how the little boy died.

The case was opened and the coroner asked the Fire Investigation Officer to go through details of the case. He outlined what happened and then the Station Officer from Plaistow was asked to read his statement as Incident Commander. I was then called to stand and read my statement. I found it difficult to make eye contact with the mother of the little boy who was sitting in front of me with tears rolling down her face as I described my actions at the incident in detail. I was relieved when the coroner thanked me and asked me to step down.

It transpired that the mother and father of the three boys who lived at the maisonette had split up. Her new partner had recently moved in with her which explained the back bedroom being filled up with boxes and furniture and why they had been sleeping down in the living room. On the morning of the fire, the new boyfriend had got up early to go shopping at Petticoat Lane Sunday market. While he was getting ready upstairs, he had woken the three boys from their slumbers. Once he left, unable to get back to sleep, the boys; the eldest of which was five, the three-year-old who had died and a younger one, began playing. Somehow, they had managed to get hold of a cigarette lighter and the oldest one had set light to the bedding.

Kid being kids, they decided that if they ran out of the room and forgot about it, nothing further would happen, out of sight is out of mind. They went downstairs and woke their mother, who realised all was not right. She went upstairs and found the top floor filling with smoke. All hell broke loose at this point and she opened the door allowing a wave of fire, heat and smoke to wash over her and the kids. She screamed and told the kids to get outside, in this melee the kids were running around her feet, blinded by smoke and panic she felt the three boys around her and turned her back on the fire. Picking up the littlest one she ran down and out onto the landing at the front of the maisonette. Where she realised to her horror that one of her boys was missing. She ran back up the stairs but was this time beaten back by heat and smoke. For some reason that will always remain a mystery the middle boy ran into the room where he was very quickly overcome and succumbed to the fire.

The police who were patrolling in the area saw the smoke and tried to make a rescue, but they were beaten back. Thinking by breaking the window they would be able to release some of the heat and smoke, they tried to get to it with a chair and a broom which is when we arrived.

As the Coroner was getting around to summing up, the solicitor of the boys estranged father, who was sat behind us, asked to see the file on the inquest. The coroner agreed and gave the file to the clerk who took it to him. Within a few minutes, having seen what he wanted, the file was being passed to the front again, we all saw it coming and as if in slow motion before anyone could get hold of it, the file, with photographs of the fire was handed forward to the mother. The scream she let out when she saw the photo of her baby, now uncovered with all surrounding debris removed by the Fire Investigators, his now grotesquely burnt body staring up at her from the photograph, was truly the most desperate and anguished animal scream I have ever heard in all my life and still haunts me to this day.

I was fine after the fire, but after the inquest I was a little affected. I had a few weeks of disturbed sleep where I kept hearing the mothers scream. The worst incident of all came one morning when I was off duty. My Girlfriend Joanne had got up to get ready to go to work, at that time with two out of the three bedrooms in our house empty she used to get ready in the front bedroom with a dressing table facing the window. I was in that half-conscious state between sleep and waking and saw her sitting there as I drifted back into a sleep. Suddenly, she was calling me, I got up out of the bed and walked into the front room. I looked at her long shiny dark brown hair and the dressing gown draped over her shoulders, and she slowly turned around. Facing me was a hideous old wrinkled face, that of a woman who was well over 150 years old if there was such a thing.

I turned and ran for the stairs but coming up the stairs towards me was the little boy from the fire. Burnt on top with two big eyes looking at me, little shorts on and those brightly coloured socks that I had seen when I found his body in the fire. I stood there and screamed. I felt a jolt and all of a sudden Joanne was standing over me looking horrified shaking me. I had drifted momentarily back to sleep to be instantly haunted by the fire, or moreover the inquest and the tragic screams of the mother.

Gillender Street

Early morning after the night before, a fire in a warehouse in Poplar in 2006.

Gillender Street is a name that many firefighters from across the UK of a certain age will instantly recall. They may not know where it is exactly, but everyone knows the story. Gillender Street is the renamed remains of a road that used to run down the eastern edge of Poplar from Bromley-by-Bow to the Blackwall Tunnel. The road was called Brunswick Road and along its length among other things was the old Brunswick Road fire station, replaced along with Burdett Road fire station in the early 70s by the new Poplar Fire Station. Brunswick Road also contained a couple of housing estates, a library, several pubs, rows of terraced houses and a large old mill on the banks of the River Lea.

The construction of the second Blackwall Tunnel in the late 1960s and the impending increase in traffic required a large dual carriageway to be built running from Hackney all the way into the tunnel. This took away most of the buildings and houses in Brunswick Road and effectively cut off a small slice of the eastern end of Poplar leaving it as a virtual no man's land between the new dual carriageway and the River Lea. This new road became known as the Blackwall Tunnel Northern Approach or East Cross Route depending on which part you were on. One small section of Brunswick Road remained, which included the now isolated fire station (as good a reason as any to build a new fire station and close a second into the bargain). For some reason unknown to me, the remaining 500 yards of Brunswick Road was renamed Gillender Street and as well as the now derelict fire station, the only thing left there was part of the Coventry Cross housing estate, a pub, a small industrial estate and a couple of very large warehouses.

10 July 1991 was a hot day in London, the hottest day of the year so far in fact. Shortly after 2:30pm a fire alarm actuated in one of the warehouses, a large irregular shaped concrete monolith of three and five double height floors that stretched from its frontage on Gillender Street to the River Lea at the rear, it dwarfed the old Brunswick Road fire station right next door. Green Watch were on duty that day and the pump ladder and TL from F22 Poplar were ordered to the incident, along with the pump ladder and Pump from Bow, because Poplar's pump was on a call elsewhere. Because of the dual carriageway Poplar had to go past the warehouse, turn around at Bromley-by-Bow and enter Gillender Street from there, arriving just ahead of Bow's crews.

The warehouse was being used as a large storage facility by a company called Hays. Due to the dense concrete structure of the building, the fire developed to a point where there was significant heat and smoke inside, but little outward sign of fire. Coupled with this was the confusing layout, with vast open floor areas divided into wired cage storage areas with narrow passageways in between. The fire was located in a large compartment at the rear of the building behind two pairs of double steel doors.

The crews were met on arrival by staff and informed that the alarm was going off on the second-floor mezzanine. A crew made their way up the stairs to the second-floor landing. A smell of smoke was detected, so they withdrew so that a BA team could enter and search for the fire. Entering the floor, the crew progressed towards the back of the building in search of the fire. Reaching the first set of double doors, light smoke was detected and the doors were warm to the touch. They were opened and the next set of doors were found to be very hot.

The crew withdrew to a safe area whilst a firefighting jet was made ready and supplied from the internal fire main within the building. They made an entrance into the fire compartment, but the heat was intense, and thick black smoke completely restricted their vision. The jet had no noticeable effect on the fire so the crew, two from Poplar and two from Bow withdrew again. The two from Poplar closed the doors and remained outside while the two from Bow went to fetch a larger diameter hose to give them a greater flow of water to tackle the fire.

The conditions now deteriorated even further, heat and smoke filled the entire floor and staircase forcing the remaining two from Poplar to withdraw to the main staircase. Another crew entered and used the hose line to guide themselves towards the fire. Pinned to the ground by the heat at this point, they also had limited success and were also forced to retreat as their water failed. As they left, the hose that was left in the fire compartment kept the door slightly ajar and allowed more heat and smoke to fill the warehouse.

Reinforcing appliances from other local stations as well as senior officers from North East Area HQ at Stratford had now arrived. Crews were searching the building in an attempt to find another way into the heart of the fire, which was spreading across the entire floor, making access and firefighting increasingly difficult.

At that point, it was decided that BA guidelines should be used. BA guidelines had been introduced across the UK decades earlier following the loss of two firefighters at the Smithfield Meat Market fire in London in 1958. They are 60m lengths of 8mm plaited rope with a pair of nylon cord tabs spaced at 2.5m distances, one of these cords is knotted. The way the tab is laid out from its bag, the knotted tab will always be in the direction of the exit and firefighters are taught "get knotted; get out" as a reminder.

The rules around the use of the guidelines are very strict; with only two being allowed to be used from any one entrance to a building, and up to four 'branch' guidelines able to run off the two main guidelines, all of which will have a plastic tally fixed to them denoting A and B and so on. Just from reading the above, it's obvious to see how their use can be very confusing. They are rarely used, the training burden is immense because of the strict protocols, and I am glad to say that modern firefighting techniques and equipment are making them less relevant and I think the time will come soon when they are withdrawn.

It was decided at Gillender Street that because of the use of guidelines, that BA crews would number four members and be led by an officer. A crew made up of the Station Officer from Stratford and one if his firefighters, along with Terry Hunt and Dave Stokoe, two firefighters from Silvertown, would be the ones to lay the first main guideline to the seat of the fire. This process involves one of the crew wearing the guideline bag on their waist and paying it out as they go, while another loops and ties the line off, at around elbow to shoulder height, where at all possible, to make following it easy and natural, as well as keeping it from getting tangled around feet or getting buried by debris.

The line was secured at the entry point outside and the tally fixed to it. The crew entered and paid the line out up the stairs to the second-floor mezzanine and inside the vast caged floorspace. They met another crew coming out who told them they were still unable to locate the seat of the fire and that conditions were punishing. The first guideline came to the end and was tied off and another added to extend it. At this point, the heat had forced all four of them to their hands and knees, and Terry Hunt, the most experienced of the pair from Silvertown, began to raise concerns about the conditions, especially as Dave Stokoe had lost radio communications on his built in BA communications set, requiring the Station officer from Stratford to use his hand held radio to send garbled messages through his BA mask.

They reached the end of a hose line that had previously been laid, this one, a larger diameter hose, had not been charged with water, but they found a smaller one that was charged and pushed forward. Once they reached the compartment, they found the doors open but conditions were now untenable. The Station Officer decided that they should all withdraw and radioed this to BA Control.

Meanwhile another BA team had followed the guideline and reached a point where they thought it had ended. It had, but it was where it had been extended by Terry and Dave's crew. They then added a branch guideline to the line, effectively meaning three lines were now at one junction. They continued on but in the thick smoke actually reached the end of a passageway and inadvertently turned back on themselves all the while laying the guideline now heading back out.

Terry and Dave's team came back out of the compartment and came to the confusion of lines. Beginning to get anxious, the Station Officer radioed that they were lost on a guideline and started to work blindly on the tangled lines to try to work out the knotted tab which would lead the way out. By now they were all short on air and their low air warning whistles were beginning to go off adding to the growing sense of desperation.

Terry found the branch guideline, found the next set of tabs and informed the Station Officer of the fact and that he was going to lead them out. The Station Officer had also sorted out his tangle and insisted he now had the way out. They argued briefly and with Terry and Dave now agitated they moved off with such force that it snapped the short length of personal line that all of them were attached to each other by.

Fatally, although the "get knotted: get out" principle remained, because they had got onto the branch guideline this actually led them further into the building before it tuned and came back out. The Station Officer and his firefighter were now on the way out and called back but to no avail. A rescue team that had been sent in from outside in response to the message that the crew were lost came across the Station Officer whose air had now completely run out as they reached him, he collapsed and was carried out along with his firefighter.

Terry and Dave had now gone further into the second-floor mezzanine all the while tracing the branch guideline back, were now critically low on air, they sounded their distress signal units during this time. Sometime after this another crew, attracted by the piercing high pitched bleeping of the distress signal units, came across Terry and Dave. They were both found side by side, unresponsive and without a pulse, one of them had removed his facemask as his air had ran out. This rescue crew, themselves now quite low on air desperately tried to get both of them out of the building but as their own air was close to exhaustion one of the pair was left behind to be carried out by another crew who were on their way in to assist.

Paramedics worked on both Terry and Dave as they were brought out from the building, moments apart, by the rescue teams. They were transferred into ambulances and removed to hospital where they were both sadly declared dead upon arrival.

I was in Majorca at the time with Joanne, her parents and her sister and brother. This was before mobile phones and in the times when you'd go to a 'phone shop', be allocated a booth with a phone in to ring home and then pay for the time on the 'meter' at the end of the call. Having had a pleasant evening meal in one of the bustling squares in Alcudia, I said to Joanne that I'd give my Mum a call just to see how things were at home, as I walked past one of these phone shops.

Getting through to home on a crackly line, I asked my Mum how things were and told her about my holiday so far. In passing, she mentioned to me that "two firemen had been killed yesterday near Blackwall Tunnel." I was gobsmacked and went cold. With the mention of Blackwall Tunnel, I thought for some reason that there had been a road accident. I questioned her urgently and then it became apparent that there had been a fire. I urged her to find out the names, I had no clue who was on duty having been on leave for over a week and losing track of my days. After a bit of muffled talking, no doubt asking my Dad, she came back on the phone and gave me the names. Terry Hunt and David Stokoe.

I was shocked, I'd actually misheard Dave's surname and was convinced it was another Dave, a Green Watch firefighter from Bow, who I had worked a part time van driving job with, that had a similar sounding surname. It wasn't until I got the paper the next day, which in those days were a day old when they arrived, that I read the story and got the names right. Although I never knew Terry and Dave, I had obviously met them on out duties and calls at the change of watch, as Silvertown was a regular place for us to be sent to standby from Poplar.

Back home in London and back on duty a week later, the sense of shock and grief was palpable. The Brigade felt like it had been hit by a train. King's Cross a few years earlier, where Colin Townsley was lost, happened because of a tragic coincidence of the crews arriving just as the ticket hall exploded into flames. But Gillender Street was a slow-motion disaster, with LFB in attendance for several hours before it went wrong. A failure of procedures, a failure of policy, a failure of how equipment was used and a failure of command.

We all felt like we had failed, and for me, the honeymoon, four years into my life in London Fire Brigade, was now over. Despite all of the gripes and complaints from older hands, I was so proud of the LFB and being part of it, it could do no wrong up until that point. It never really felt the same after that for me. I lost my youthful rose-tinted view of it all.

In the following weeks, along with firefighters and officers from across London and beyond, we lined up twice, in a long guard of honour. First of all, in the roads leading to the East London Cemetery in Canning Town for Terry's funeral, then in the road leading to Corbet's Tey Crematorium in Upminster for Dave's. Although I didn't know them personally, like all of us who served through that time, I'll always remember them and do every year on July 10th.

Growing Up

'On arrival' The scene at a derelict building fire just as crews arrive, Turners Road, Poplar.

A short time after this in the autumn of 1991, I decided that I wanted to be a Brigade driver. Having been in the job long enough and having held a full car licence for several years I was eligible to apply. I had a medical and got my provisional HGV licence and a while after, on a Monday morning, I reported to North East Area Driver Training Centre at Plaistow fire station.

After a morning's theoretical input about the expectations of the course, some admin and other bits and pieces we were ready to start. After lunch the instructor, a long serving fireman called Ken, took me and the other candidate out for our first drive. Jeff, the other candidate, drove first; he had driven a few small lorries before so this seven ton 'bread van' was no problem for him.

After about 40 minutes of driving, we pulled up along a road in Barking and it was my turn. I eased myself into the seat and went through a check of the seat position and mirrors and we were off. Ken gave me left and right directions through the area and I soon got the hang of driving the vehicle, just remembering this was three times as long as a car and the front wheels were underneath me instead of in front of me as in a car.

The HGV test at that time also still required the candidates to 'double de-clutch', as although this vehicle was fitted with a synchromesh gearbox, many other HGV's were still fitted with crash boxes. Double de-clutching requires the driver, once he wishes to change gear, to dip the clutch, move the gear leaver into neutral and then dip the clutch again to push the lever into the higher gear. Coming down was harder because once the lever was moved into neutral a quick rev was required to match the speed of the engine with the gears.

The next couple of weeks were spent with us driving around a variety of different areas; from the country lanes of South West Essex, to a busy lunchtime on Hyde Park corner. All designed to give us as much practice and expose us to all traffic types. Later in the course, we were also taken to Greenwich gas works where we practiced the manoeuvres required for the HGV test. Reversing between cones, stopping accurately on a line from a run up and so on.

In a blink of an eye, the two weeks had passed and the tests were upon us. One of the officers at the Driving School was also a DOT qualified examiner. So, on the final afternoon of the two weeks, we were out on our tests. The manoeuvres had been completed successfully first off. Then in turn we were taken out for our road tests. I sweated nervously as we left Plaistow and made our way along the A13 towards Barking. Straight away I was on a 50mph road and needed to demonstrate I had the confidence to drive up to that speed limit. I drove through Barking, in traffic around East Ham, round by the Royal Docks and finally back to Plaistow.

He then asked me a series of Highway Code questions similar to those on the car test, but involving some more detailed questions about larger vehicles and their handling. Finally, he closed his folder and looked at me.

"Steve, that completes the test for today and I am pleased to say that you have passed."

"Aw great, thanks very much Guv, thank you."

We both managed to get through, so it was a relaxing weekend, with the next week then being used to train us on driving a proper fire engine, with its automatic gearbox; common to buses and fire trucks, whereas most other HGV's have manual gearboxes.

The final week was much more relaxed, we toured similar areas and were taken onto an old airfield up in Essex where we were given some emergency driver training, accident avoidance and had to learn to control the vehicle if the gearbox or steering failed. On the Friday afternoon, we were told to go back to our station and spend the next few weeks driving back from calls, and driving the pump to and from standby's and visits, in order to log ten hours of practice before we were to take our EFAD, emergency fire appliance drivers test. I said my goodbyes to the instructor and my fellow candidate and looked forward to getting back to Poplar to get my hours under my belt. It didn't take that long to log the hours, by November I had applied for the EFAD, but then had to wait another few weeks for the test. The test was pretty much a rerun of the HGV, but in a proper fire engine. Once again I followed the now familiar route and once again I passed. I was ecstatic! This was my first day duty, the next day was a Saturday, the traffic would be light and we should be fairly busy, and as a newly qualified 'MD', I would be driving the pump. As I was driven back to the station on this bright, late autumn afternoon, I was on top of the world.

The alarm woke me at 7:30am. I quickly turned it off, not wanting to wake Joanne who had been working all week at her job for a bank in the City. She could lay in for a while today. I crept out of the bedroom and went downstairs. As I walked towards the kitchen window, I was surprised it was steamed up. I peered under the curtain, it wasn't steamed up – a thick blanket of fog had descended on this, of all mornings, the first day I was due to drive. I got showered and dressed then made my way into Poplar. Where we lived in Dagenham wasn't far from Rainham Marshes, and our house was surrounded by lots of open ground, so I hoped the fog would clear as I neared London, but it didn't. I crept all the way along the A13 on my motorcycle and I was within about 50 yards of the fire station before it loomed up before me, out of the murk.

As expected, at roll call I was detailed to ride the pump. I got a fair bit of the usual stick from everyone, the Guvnor included, voicing that they thought they'd be safer on the pump ladder or turntable ladder, along with some other comments about the fog and having to walk in front of me with a torch.

At the time we had a 1984 Dennis SS131 as the pump. Although the older of the pair of front-line pumps, it was a much better vehicle than the 1987 Renault/Dodge that we had, which seemed to spend most of its life in workshops, where it had gone again late the previous evening. So with the Dennis now running as the pump ladder, an old 1981 Dodge was what I had facing me in the pump's space in the appliance bay.

Nevertheless, I got up into it and went through the full routine. I started it up and tested all the lights, road horn and two-tone horns, wipers and other ancillaries. I dumped the air from the air brake tanks and built it up again by revving the engine. I then engaged the pump and tested both of the hose reels and the main fire pump. Finally, after checking everything was stowed correctly, I shut her down and jumped on the back to test my BA set.

I was just finishing off the test when my senses, tuned to pick out heightened voices on the radio, picked up on a higher pitched voice calling in a 'priority'. It was Whitechapel, making pumps four and persons reported somewhere off Brick Lane. I went back to what I was doing, they were a few stations away, but there were plenty of others who would attend a four on their ground before us.

I filled in my log book, then my heart leapt as the teleprinter burst into life and the bells went down. "Here we go," I thought, "this is it, I am off on my first shout driving."

I moved over to the teleprinter and stood beside Paul who was the Dutyman for the shift. He had only been driving for about a year and in sympathy with my plight said, "Well let's see where you are going then…DON'T PANIC…DON'T PANIC," he added in mimicry of Corporal Jones from the TV show 'Dad's Army'.

There was no panic, we had been ordered to standby at Whitechapel to cover the 'four pumper' that was going on. On the line below on the slip I saw that Bethnal Green's pump had been ordered into Shoreditch to cover them, so now we knew that the four pumps from both Whitechapel and Shoreditch had made up the attendance for the job in Brick Lane.

So, my first 'shout' as a driver was a slow foggy drive, obeying all the rules of the road, just like other vehicles. I was just debating to myself that in this fog, it wasn't such a bad thing not to be racing around, when fate decided for me.

"Foxtrot two two two, Foxtrot two two two from FE priority over," I gulped, the Guvnor reached over and picked up the handset.

"FE from Foxtrot two two two, go ahead over."

"Foxtrot two two two, you are ordered to an automatic fire alarm actuating, Plantation House, Mincing Lane, City EC3. Route card four hotel, page two zero one, Foxtrot thirty-three Whitechapel's ground, Foxtrot two two two acknowledge over?"

"Foxtrot two two two, received, now status two, over," replied the Guvnor. He put the handset back in the cradle and his pen back in his pocket.

"Go on then, whatya waiting for?" he said to me with a smile. "Do you know it, Steve?" he added.

"Y-Yep, I know it Guv."

I reached across to the switch panel in the middle of the dashboard and switched on the blue lights. I pushed my foot a little harder onto the floor and the Guvnor hit the two-tone switch under his foot. We were just passing by Limehouse Basin in Commercial Road, the lights at the junction with Rotherhithe Tunnel at Branch Road were approaching. I saw through the gloom that the lights were red and a line of brake and fog lights showed me that the traffic was at a standstill.

I eased the machine across the middle line and slowed as I approached the junction, the cars coming out of Branch Road halted as they saw me appear from the fog. I eased back round the traffic lights onto the correct side of the road. Almost immediately I had to do the same again at Butchers Row, this road was wider and faster and fed traffic up from another main road, I passed through this junction, so far so good.

As we continued west, I felt a little more confident, the fog eased up just a little as we neared the City and I began to enjoy myself. All too soon we had arrived at the incident and my first drive on the bell was over. Like a well-seasoned driver, I sat, leaning forward over the wheel enjoying the warmth of the cab as the Guvnor and crew joined Dowgate, searching the building where the alarm had gone off.

Over the coming years I got to drive roughly about half the time I was on duty. We had eight drivers on the Watch for the three appliances, with leave, out duties to other stations and the odd spot of acting up, I drove on average one day and one night of every four-day tour of duty. The good thing about driving was, no matter what the job, even a boring time-wasting false alarm, the driver gets to enjoy the thrill of guiding the fire engine through busy inner-city traffic.

Later on, I also became qualified as a hydraulic platform driver operator, which meant that when I was riding the HP, I got to travel further afield, because aerial appliances are only based at certain designated stations. Poplar's HP or TL, depending what we had on the run, was often called south of the Thames into Greenwich, Woolwich and beyond, up towards Leytonstone, Stratford and Wanstead, into the City or right out towards Dagenham and the eastern suburbs if their aerials were off the run or on another call.

As time went on, more new people came onto the Watch and although, because of the young age I had joined at, I was still the youngest, there were three below me in the pecking order of the 11 firefighters and three officers on the Red Watch. I was picked to act up more and more, helping out in the office and riding in charge of the appliances.

I was given a new recruit to mentor early on in 1992 and really enjoyed the challenges of advising him and passing on my own now quiet wealthy range of experience. I was now approaching five years in the job, regularly acting up, driving and outside of work was paying a mortgage on the home I shared with my Girlfriend. The ball breaking and practical jokes often found me at the centre of their planning or execution, instead of on the receiving end and I suppose I began to realise that I had now grown up.

It wasn't long after this that I was to be married to my Girlfriend Joanne. Although as I said, we had moved out to Dagenham, we decided to get married in a church in the East End. The Church most of us had used from school as kids and the church where Joanne's parents had been married; St Dustan's Church in Stepney.

The Sunday before the wedding I was on a day duty, I was due at the Church at 6.30pm for a rehearsal of the ceremony that was to be held the following Saturday. It was a fairly warm day in late September and around about 4.30pm, after a fairly routine day, we were ordered to a fire alarm going off in a factory in Violet Road, on the top part of Poplar's ground. I didn't expect anything much, but as we rounded the bend where Morris Road turns into Violet Road there was a haze of white smoke drifting across the road.

We pulled up outside the Coutts cardboard factory and strained to see over the high wall and gates. Someone jumped up on top of the pump and called down that the fire appeared to be over the back of the yard behind a small building. We gained access through the main gate and was met by a member of the security staff. He informed us that a fire had started in a covered storage area at the back of the factory and involved a large area of stored cardboard and packaging.

"Go and have a look Steve," the Guvnor bade me, "and let me know what's happening."

"Will do Guv, I'll take Rodney with me," I replied.

We went into the factory and noticed there was a light fog of white smoke permeating through the building. I headed in the direction that I had seen the smoke coming from while outside, and soon went through to another portion of the factory where the smoke was slightly heavier, but still light enough to see all around us. I noticed another set of doors and saw that a red fire hose was pulled off the wall. We headed towards the doors and I soon noticed it was very smoky, and flashes of orange flame filled the area beyond the door.

As we walked out, I was hit by a wall of heat. I looked around, the covered area was full of burning boxes on wooden pallets as the guard had explained and the lightweight clear plastic corrugated covering that acted as a roof, was beginning to burn through. At least the fire was now an outdoor fire, with the roof burning off rapidly as we stood there. The hose reel was on the floor a couple of foot inside the door with the water spraying uselessly along the ground. I figured that security guard had been trying to tackle the fire and left to come and meet us when he heard us arrive.

The smoke instantly stung our eyes and they started to water. I instinctively started breathing through my nose as the nasal hair filters out a lot of the junk. The job was going to be a bit hard on the eyes and nose, but with it venting well we weren't going to need BA.

"Grab that hose reel Rod and hit the fire. No, actually, go back and tell the Guvnor we'll need a hose reel in here and probably a jet from the front," I told him, thinking it may not be wise to leave him alone as the Junior Buck and selfishly wanting to get a piece of the action.

I picked up the hose and aimed it into the heart of the first pallet of burning material, I was instantly engulfed in steam and stinging smoke, and I coughed as my lungs adjusted to it. I laid on the floor and clenched my eyes tight shut in reaction to the smoke. Tears rolled down my face but I soon got used to the sting, and blinking heavily to clear the tears, I carried on.

The Guvnor was soon behind me asking what was happening.

"I think this covered area ends just to our left, at the rear along the factory back wall, but I think the room goes on and towards the front a way, most of it seems like its alight."

"OK Steve, the PL's crew are getting in through that other gate at the front, they will get a jet going from there. Keep at it, I've got Gary to pull the pump into the yard and Rodney is bringing you a hose reel. Bow are here now; I'll send someone else through with you," the Guvnor said as he turned and walked off.

I was joined by Rodney and another lad from Bow, holding the hose reel, I got Rodney into position, and backing up him and the other lad, we were soon in among the cardboard blinking, coughing and retching but having the time of our life anyway. I got bored as the third man on the hose reel so went back to fetch the factory fitted reel. As the boys pushed forward, I was using the other reel to dampen down the piles of smouldering cardboard behind us.

Before long we had met up with the PL's crew and now had good access all around the burning area. The flames died, to be replaced by the stinging choking smoke and as the adrenalin began to ebb away my mind wandered to other things.

"Shit." I looked at my watch. It was now well after 5pm and I had remembered I had a wedding rehearsal to go to. Seeking out the Guvnor I reminded him of the fact.

"Well you are on a fire call Steve, what do you expect, you can't just walk away from this," he said.

"Yeah, but?" was my reply.

The Guvnor smiled at me, "Go and see if you can borrow a phone to ring her, I am going to get the PL away at the top of the hour and the pump will stay along with Bow's pump. See if anyone will do a swap with you," came his reassuring answer to my predicament.

I asked to borrow a phone in the office and the security guard obliged. I left a message with my Father-in-Law to be, sufficiently spiced up to make it seem as if I was facing hells fire, instead of a pile of smouldering cardboard in Morris Road, and he promised to get my message relayed. I got Del to swap with me and at just after 6pm I was on the back of the PL heading back to the station.

With no time to shower, and stinking of smoke, I quickly jumped into the car and headed off to the church. I got there just a few minutes late and with a few sideways glances, and plenty of toothy smiled shoulder shrugs from me, the rehearsal went ahead without any further upset. The following night shifts were pretty average, with just a few little bits, so it was to be that the fire at the cardboard factory was the last fire I fought as a single man.

After a week of various stag nights, ranging from a drunken pub and club crawl with my friends and colleagues, to a sedate drink at my old local in Poplar with my Dad and Uncle, the morning of the wedding was upon us.

Joanne had stayed at her Parents' house in Poplar and I drove down to my Parents' house with my soon to be Brother-in-law Steve and my best man Brian. We dropped Steve off and went to get changed into our morning suits at my Mum and Dad's. We were soon ready and decided with half an hour to spare that we'd pop round the pub for a quick livener each. On our return, I was amazed to see a lot of the neighbours out on this dull drizzly October afternoon. Through the crowd I saw the object of their fascination. As well as the bridal cars going to the church, the best man and I were to be ferried to the church in a vintage open top Leyland turntable ladder. It was a real surprise and absolutely took my breath away.

At the church I breathed a sigh of relief, as Joanne was gracious enough to turn up and not leave me standing at the altar. After the ceremony my new wife and I were driven to the hall on the old TL, amid much bell clanging, tooting and waving from people on the route back to Poplar, where the reception was held.

Within a few days we had flown off on our honeymoon and were soon lying soaking up the sun on the Spanish island of Gran Canaria. I don't know what made me look up from my sun bed, but looking out across the pool I noticed a large cloud of smoke coming up from somewhere in the middle distance. I should have known better, but, I was soon up in the room peering off the balcony for the source of the smoke. It appeared to be coming from somewhere across the town of Maspalomas where we were staying. I fully intended to go back down to carry on enjoying my break, but before you could say "Massey Shaw", I was dressed in a pair of jeans and a t-shirt, and with camera in hand I was off to find my fire.

I briefly explained this to Joanne, but having known me for a good few years now, she just rolled her eyes in resignation and carried on sun bathing. Outside I got into a taxi, and pointing to the smoke, I told the driver the only words I could think of "fuego" and "bomberos." He soon had me on the way to the fire. I paid the driver off on arrival and made my way through the crowd. The object of the excitement was a large shopping complex called the 'Jumbo'. It was slightly raised from the road with two entrances where steps led up half a floor to the upper level shops, and down some stairs to the remaining shops in the basement. It was from these basement entrances that two ominous clouds of black smoke rose into the clear blue sky.

I looked at the local fire brigade presence. There were only three fire engines and about a dozen firefighters, some clad only in shirt sleeves at an incident that I estimated would have attracted 8 pumps back in London. The two newer fire engines were pumping water through hoses that were being fed into the basement. The third, an ancient thing with a large water tank on the back, appeared to be pumping water into the other two. All of a sudden, the water ran out. An older man who appeared to be helping, disconnected the hoses and stood back as the old machine pulled back out of the road, obviously to get more water.

I decided to try to help in any way I could and approached the old man.

"Er, excuse me," I said as I held up my LFB ID card.

"Me bombero…London, English bombero."

"Oh, I see, OK," came the English reply in a German accent.

Relieved, I went on. "Oh do you speak English?" I asked.

"Yes, a little," replied the older man.

"I am a fireman in London, can I help?"

"I am not sure, I live near here, I am a former German firefighter," came the reply.

Feeling confident, I decided to try a few very obvious strategies.

"Is there a hydrant for the water?"

The man looked at me strangely.

"A water hydrant to get water from the ground," I added.

"I understand what you mean," said the German, "but there are none, this is why they are bringing water for the pumpers."

I now realised why he gave me a strange look; I, a mere spring chicken to this German firefighting veteran, should have known better than to question or insult his, or the local firefighters intelligence.

We were soon approached by a fireman in shirt sleeves. He appeared to have some sort of shoulder marking so I took him for an officer. I went through the London bombero routine again, this time with some added translation from the German, probably along the lines of "This silly English kid is a fireman and wants to help, he thinks he is Red Adare. Just tell him to go and play with the traffic."

The Spanish officer looked me up and down and shrugged walking off towards the fire, he had better things to do than entertain me I guess. Feeling more confident, I now approached the fire and again held up my ID and said "bombero" to a group of police officers standing on the pavement. Walking up the stairs I could see over onto the basement. Something was going good down there, I reckoned a couple of shops at least, judging by the smoke and size of the shops at the top. Once up the stairs, I saw some firemen with a limp hose talking to some police, they were peering over a ledge that looked into the basement, and with that another thick plume of black smoke escaped, adding to those blocking out the sky. Once again, I did the bombero routine and also took a few photographs.

Back in the street all of the action seemed to have come to a halt and the fire and smoke conditions did not appear to be improving. Soon the older fire engine returned and I humped a bit of hose to help the guys get water back on. The crews soon disappeared back into the fire, my officer friend got a BA set on and went to the other entrance on his own, following a line of hose into the basement.

I followed him at a distance and looked on in horror as he, just in his shirtsleeves went into the fire alone. He was breaking every principal of firefighter safety I had ever been taught. Not only was he wearing no protection from the heat and flames, but was alone, who would know if he got into difficulty? With my heart racing and firefighting spirit aroused, I then decided it would be my job to see that he was at least accounted for if anything happened, as I at least knew his whereabouts. I looked up the street for any spare firefighters; there was one running between the two pumps ensuring they were both pumping an adequate supply of water, and the old German fireman helping where he could. To make matters worse, I saw that one of the policemen was now donning a BA set. This had a strange effect on me for some crazy reason, me, an English fireman who could speak no Spanish, with no understanding of the way the Spanish operated or the dangers inside the fire. I threw away all remaining common sense and decided that I too was going to get into a BA set and join in the firefighting. To this day, I look back on this and as each year passes, I shudder in embarrassment and shock at my stupidity.

Still, the dye was cast, and handing my camera to the German to hold, I grabbed a BA set. After a quick look to figure out how it worked, it wasn't too dissimilar to the type we used in London, I was soon under air, noting that there was about 150 bars of air in the set, giving me around 30 minutes of air if I took it easy. Stupefied even then by my actions, I ran along the pavement to the other entrance and followed the hose down. Entering the smoke, I saw a deep red glow in front of me. I was only just inside the wide mall area and by getting low on the floor I could see the legs of the Spanish officer in front of me. All of a sudden, we were firefighters in a fire, language meant nothing, you can't understand a lot in a BA set at the best of times, let alone with the noise of the fire and the sound of water from the hose. I tapped him on the back and indicated that I was going to hang just behind him near the entrance to keep an eye on him. He instantly understood and nodded as if it was the most natural thing in the world and I was part of his crew.

From what I could gather, from what was in front of me, he was holding the fire from spreading along the corridor while a couple of other crews, the ones in full fire kit it turns out, were right inside the job putting out the heart of the fire, which appeared to be in a shop on our left. By this time, looking at the debris at my feet, that I could see from what little light was coming down the stairwell, I guessed that the fire had started in a shop and had come out into the corridor, and fed on the cladding and fittings outside of the shop. The situation was not as bad as I had originally thought and as the minutes ticked by things began to improve dramatically.

The Spanish officer shut his jet down and started to back out. He gave me a thumbs up and I crawled back into fresh air. Coming up the stairs I noticed that the smoke was much lighter and greyer in colour. I don't know how they had done it, but these Spanish fireman had managed to contain the fire and it was now under control. I took off the BA set at the back of the pump and the Spanish officer gave me a hug around the shoulder and a hearty pat saying something to me in Spanish.

I helped unplug the hose as the old pump drove away again to refill. I decided that I had ultimately been foolish in my decision to enter the fire, but nevertheless, felt I had a job to do in covering the back of the man who had gone in alone. From the perspective of a fireman in a large city fire brigade this was unheard of, but I suppose on an island with only limited resources, it was a fairly common practice when the chips were down. As I went to leave, the Spanish officer called me over, and with some translation from the German, he indicated that I should visit them at the fire station the next day, and the German explained where in the town it was.

I found another taxi and was soon back at the hotel where I found Joanne fretting in the room. She saw me and went mad; I was soaking wet and black with soot. She was quite right, berating me that we had hardly been married a week and I was trying to make her a widow. The point was further underlined as somewhere else in the Mediterranean a young British policeman, also on honeymoon, had drowned whilst trying to rescue someone from the sea, leaving his new wife a widow when the ink was hardly dry on their marriage certificate!

We were soon back home and settling into married life. Like many young couples at the time, things were tight financially despite both of us working and me taking an extra job. The house was in negative equity thanks to 'Black Wednesday' just before we were married, and the subsequent recession. Work continued as usual, fires began to pick up a little due to the recession, along with the number of properties having 'accidental' fires. By early 1993 I had decided I was going to take promotion a little bit more seriously. I had qualified to hold the rank of Leading Firefighter, having passed the written and practical examination. It so happens that just after this, one of the LFM at Poplar on my Watch went off on promotion, so as I was qualified, I was given the acting up despite some local protests – rules were rules. I was now acting more like an officer instead of one of the lads acting up for a night or two and I began to take the job seriously in preparation for the next promotion round.

One night in June I was preparing the runners and riders board for the following shift. I noted we were short on drivers for the night, so I put myself driving the pump instead of sitting on the back behind the Guvnor as was customary. I checked this with John the Guvnor, and he was fine with it. I hadn't driven in quite a while, so I was quite looking forward to it when I reported for duty on the Friday night.

After roll call I jumped up into the driver's seat and did my checks, I tested the pump and ancillary equipment, then got on the back to do my BA set. From there I went into the office, did my drivers log bookings, BA book and then got on with the administrative task of the Leading Fireman. After half an hour or so I wandered upstairs enquiring after dinner, at which point the bells went down and we all piled down the stairs and pole. The TL from Poplar had been moved to Leyton late in 1992 as part of a review of aerials, so I knew I was going out. The call was for the pump and was to smoke issuing from opposite Silvertown fire station. Obviously, Silvertown's pump was off the run, as the PL from Silvertown was on the call alone, along with Plaistow's pump and us.

The pump at Poplar at that time was a Dennis SS131 with a V8 Perkins engine. Dennis' were proper fire engines, built from the ground up, as opposed to a fire engine body placed on a commercial chassis as others were and just about all are today. Although the PL was a newer Volvo, I loved driving the Dennis, so fire or false alarm, I was going to get to have a bit of fun at least in the Friday evening traffic.

We pulled out of Poplar and I eased the Dennis across the road into the centre line as the eastbound lanes were still heavy with traffic heading out of London. The loud two-tone horns echoing off the buildings soon had the oncoming traffic pulling to their left, enabling me to make my way along the outside of the stationary traffic. Just after Cotton Street near the Blackwall Tunnel entrance, the traffic thinned out a bit and I got back onto the correct side of the road, and pressed a little harder on the throttle.

Further along we went down the side of Canning Town Flyover which took the mass of evening traffic onto the A13 and out towards Essex. I braked hard on the approach to the roundabout under the flyover and stabbed the throttle hard, as I confirmed the roundabout was clear. The echo of the two-tone horns became momentarily louder and multi toned as we passed under the flyover. I noted with a satisfactory nod to myself, as I heard a deep squeal from the tyres on the rear axle, but felt the steering wheel firm in my hands, that I had hit a sweet spot where my acceleration into the turn was at its optimum, allowing me to leave the roundabout at speed without having to build up again as I might on a wet road.

I hit a good speed along the long, straight Silvertown Way, and checking well ahead anticipating upcoming hazards, I noted a bit of brown smoke in the sky and looked across to the Guvnor as he noticed it as well. As we approached Silvertown fire station, I cursed as I saw Plaistow's pump turn into the gates 100 yards ahead of me opposite the fire station, and lifted off the throttle as I slowed to take the turn. We bumped into the turn and through the gateway and kicked up a cloud of dust as we drove down the road between the warehouses towards the river. Turning a corner into a large open area, there was an old brick built three storey warehouse on our right with brown smoke coming from the top floor. My mind flashed briefly back to the month before when a fireman from West London, Mick Hill, had been killed in a similar old building that was being used as a laundry.

"Draw up short," the Guvnor asked me and I pulled up to the left, allowing room in case other appliances needed to go through. I jumped down, noting Silvertown's Sub Officer approaching my Guvnor and saw others from Silvertown and Plaistow laying hose out. Another couple of blokes from Silvertown were up the top of an external staircase. I went to the locker where my fire kit was, quickly got rigged and joined my Guvnor.

"Get up those stairs and see what we've got Steve, it doesn't look too bad."

"Righto Guvnor," I replied and made for the stairs.

As I got to the top the other two lads had the door in and were tentatively looking inside. I peered past them, the building was largely derelict and there was some rubbish burning inside, with some wooden partitioning and panels alight. It wasn't too bad and I figured we'd sort it in no time.

"Call down for a small jet will ya?" I said to the two Silvertown firemen, and walked further into the room.

It was quite warm and the smoke was stinging my eyes but it was bearable. I had a quick scoot around to check it was clear, then waited until the jet came up. As the jet arrived along with the Leading Fireman from Plaistow, I guessed I wasn't going to get much action with three on the jet, so I squeezed past and popped back down to update my Guvnor. That done, I called Dave who was riding on our pump and after telling the guvnor we'd have a look at the other floors, we made our way into a door and up a darkened internal staircase.

The rest of the building was clear and we were soon back up on the third-floor kicking in bits of panelling and generally taking out any frustrations we may have had, such was the beauty of firefighting in a derelict building. As predicted, the fire was out pretty quickly, and frustrated that the fire hadn't been unseen and unreported for another half hour to get going properly, Dave and I skulked back down the stairs for a breather. After making the hose up, I took off my fire kit and shoved it back in the locker and thought about having a quick cigarette but the Guvnor told me he "didn't have time to hang around here while I slowly killed myself." So I jumped up in the cab, turned the machine around in the big yard and headed back to Poplar.

I finally had my cigarette in peace and stood in the yard in the warm evening breeze, making the most of it before going back to the office to catch up on the admin for the night. Dinner was soon served and we all settled into the routine of the night. Not a great deal happened, a couple of minor calls and after watching TV, I wandered up to bed just after midnight.

I woke blinking as the lights came on and bells rung through the station. Quickly dressing, I shuffled over to the pole house, kicking against the floor to get my shoes on and slid to the ground floor. I walked into the Watchroom and Del, who was the dutyman, said, "Fire, Norbiton Road, off Salmon's Lane."

"Didn't we have a mickey there once before in the early hours?" someone said.

"Yeah, we've been there a few times," replied Del.

I walked out of the Watchroom and around the PL to the bay where the pump was parked, and as I climbed up into the cab I called behind me, "Fire, Norbiton Rd, but it's the usual mickey I think."

I pulled out onto the forecourt of the station and held back to allow the PL to pull out and go in front of me. It was a quick drive down East India Dock Road at that time of the morning, with the PL just blipping its siren across the junctions so as not to disturb too many people from their slumber. We soon made a sedate right turn into Salmon's Lane and right again into Copenhagen Place. As I followed the PL down it was a bit misty around the orange sodium lamps, but on a decent summer's night that didn't seem right.

"Is that smoke?" I asked the guvnor.

"I think we might have something," he said.

As we rounded a slight bend, the brake lights of the PL lit up, and off to the left smoke poured from the upper windows of a maisonette on the third floor, with heads hanging out of every window.

"Pull into the side street and send a persons reported," snapped the Guvnor.

A second later I was stopped, having swung the machine into Norbiton Road. The Guvnor was gone along with the two on the back. I picked up the radio handset.

"FE from Foxtrot two two two priority, over."

"Foxtrot two two two from M2FE go ahead with your priority."

"FE from Foxtrot two two two, at Norbiton Road, persons reported over."

Not waiting for the acknowledgement, although I should have, I jumped from the machine looking up at the front of the maisonettes and saw light smoke hovering at the front. I was briefly thankful that the fire didn't seem too severe, no flames or deep orange glow. As I approached the back, I saw the 135 ladder from our PL struggling over an 8 foot garden wall and just happened to find myself at the back of Shadwell's PL, who had also arrived behind us. Steve and Lloyd were pulling their 135 ladder from their motor and I just slipped into position at the head of the ladder as it dropped from the gantry. I looked up again and counted two adults at one window and three kids at another.

We walked up towards the wall and having seen what had just happened with the previous ladder, we pushed the head up to the fullest stretch of our arms and the two already on top of the wall took it off us. Six of us now manhandled the 45kg ladder over the wall and into the small back garden, where once over, the two on top of the wall jumped down to join the other two from their original crew, and their ladder was already going up to one of the windows. Back as a foursome, with Steve and Lloyd still in their BA sets, we somehow managed to get our ladder up to the left window of the maisonette in the tiny space, just as the parents were coming out of the windows to the right. I still hadn't had time to rig in my fire gear and along with the other firefighter from Shadwell, we footed the ladder as the other two rushed up it.

The kids from the left window, three of them between the ages of seven and fourteen, were yanked out of the window and were passed with one hand, down the ladder. I had climbed part way up the ladder and effortlessly took the weight of a young girl, a hand on her trunk to support the weight and another clenched around her arm. It is true what they say about adrenalin, looking back, although this teenage girl wasn't at all large, she was almost weightless at the time, and with both hands holding her I was also unthinkingly just balanced on my feet, fifteen foot up this ladder.

I can remember realising I was just stood on a narrow ladder with no hands, and somehow in one movement, passed her over my head and down using the hand that had supported her trunk, quickly grabbing the ladder with my other hand. Mum and Dad were now down and so a couple more joined us on our ladder and made a chain for the remaining kids. Once the windows were clear, I climbed back down the ladder and then managed to plunge my foot into a small ornamental pond that I had completely avoided minutes earlier whilst wrestling with a large ladder.

"Fucksakes," I spat as I squelched towards the wall. Back in the road, the Guvnor was looking for me.

"Get rigged and get upstairs please Steve and give them a hand at the front, I don't think much is alight." I quickly rigged in my gear, cursing again as I slipped my wet foot into the boot. Looking up, white smoke was now banking down from the front door, the boys were in and water was on the fire.

As I got to the upper landing and turned left towards the front door, the smoke had pretty much cleared and I was surprised to see the BA crew backing out with their hose reel. I peered round the Sub Officer's shoulder and could see a relatively small area of damage involving the street door and hallway to the maisonette. Unusual because there are not many ignition sources next to people front door. As if on demand, two scrawny looking Bengali teenagers stood on the landing began shouting to no one in particular.

"This is a racist attack man; some fucking racists started that fire!"

"Get rid of them will ya?" the Sub Officer asked me.

"Come on, we're trying to work, go downstairs or along the landing," I said as I shepherded them away.

"This is a racist attack man," I got told again in case I hadn't heard it the first time.

Soon enough we were all done, Shadwell and our PL had gone and it was just us on the pump along with the Fire Investigation team and the police. It was indeed suspicious, as petrol had been poured through the letter box and ignited. We tidied up as best we could and left it to the Fire Investigators and police, as I wearily guided the pump back through the empty streets as dawn broke over Poplar. Funny enough, it later transpired that the kids who were claiming it was a racist attack were found guilty of the fire. One of them, aged about 16, had been spurned by the 14 year old daughter. They had poured a small amount of petrol through the letterbox and then lit it to 'teach her a lesson'. Thankfully with very little to burn in the passage, the fire remained small but a shocking and distressing incident for this family nonetheless.

At the time racial tension wasn't too bad in this part of East London, as more and more people had moved into the area through the 70s and 80s, mostly from Bangladesh. As their numbers grew, the tide began to turn against the high number of attacks on members of that community, that had peaked in the 70s. Thankfully, the tragic fire bombings in this area where whole families had perished were a thing of the past. But I found it disgusting that these kids had burned out another Bengali family and sought to blame it on racism.

Promotion

Toward the end of 1993, the Leading Firefighters promotion round came out and I thought I may as well have a go at it. It was rumoured to be the last ever promotion round for Leading Firefighters before a new system of promotion for LFf, known as the Crew Commander programme, came in. Instead of a straightforward hour long interview followed, if successful, by a straight promotion, there was to be a series of assessments to access the development programme, six weeks of training, then an NVQ style development folder, where the candidate had to provide evidence for assessment over a number of months, before being confirmed in post.

A number of incidents in the early 1990s, where firefighters had been killed or suffered near misses, had left LFB with a couple of improvement notices that had been given following investigations into these tragic incidents. A common theme identified throughout had been a lack of effective command and control at various levels, which brought about the plans for a new way of promoting people, starting off with the first level and eventually working right up the rank structure as it was to become in the coming decade.

Nevertheless, having held the qualification and preferring an interview and immediate promotion to that which was proposed and yet untried, I was happy my Guvnor had recommended me and I put in my application form forthwith.

Christmas 1993 was one filled with good news. Not only had I got through the application stage for promotion, but Joanne and I were blessed with news that she was pregnant with our first child, due the following July. It was to be the first Grandchild for both sets of Grandparents, so the thrill of delivering that news was awesome. Plenty of tears, excitement and glasses raised that Christmas.

In the new year, whilst poor Joanne battled with morning sickness and a surprisingly unsympathetic female boss, I battled with numerous operational procedures, Brigade orders, personnel notes, memorandums and technical notes in preparation for my interview.

Steve giving a radio interview at a large fire in Central London.

I was invited to interview at the South East Area HQ in Lewisham. All candidates were being interviewed outside of their parent area, just to make sure of a level playing field. Sitting nervously in the waiting room, the door opened and I was surprised to see that my training school instructor, now a Divisional Officer in the SE area, had come to call me for the interview. I felt a little less anxious as I followed him down the hallway into a large wood panelled office, where he sat down behind a desk with another Divisional Officer and a civilian member of staff.

After a brief explanation of the format of the interview by the other DO, who was obviously the chair of the interview panel, my questions began. I was asked a number of scenario-based questions, around personnel and property problems, that I might face as a junior officer and then I was asked a number of technical questions and given other tricky 'what ifs' as supplementary questions.

After what seemed an age, I was given an operational scenario. I was in charge of an appliance and called to a road accident with a tanker overturned on a stretch of fast road, with persons trapped in a car, the tanker leaking an unknown product and typically, the cavalry of assistance that I'd get on a call like this, being 'held up' due to the traffic chaos. I tried to think of the answer logically, looking at limiting risk to my crews, then saving of life and then preservation of property and the environment.

The 'whys', 'what ifs' and 'wherefores' that challenged every part of the answers I gave seemed relentless. But eventually, with a sudden smile, the chair of the panel thanked me, asked if I had any questions and I was dismissed. My old training school instructor got up and I searched his poker face for any sign of hope. As he escorted me from the room, we formally parted, but I noted with some relief that he winked and flashed me a quick smile as we shook hands. I fretted and played the whole interview over for the next couple of weeks, analysing what I could remember and convincing myself I'd failed miserably and that his wink and smile were just because he knew me from being one of his recruits. I questioned other more senior officers about my answers and their assessments varied so much I was left even more confused. Nevertheless, after a painful wait of a few weeks, I received a telephone call stating that I had been successful and would be promoted to Leading Firefighter in the near future.

In late spring I was called up to NE Area HQ at Stratford for a formal interview with the Group DO. I was acting up into a vacancy at Poplar, and despite my Guvnor John stating the best thing for me was a clean break to start somewhere else as a Junior Officer, as opposed to staying on my own Watch, I really hoped that I could stay at Poplar. The DO welcomed me to HQ, congratulated me and told me that I'd be posted to the Red Watch at Plaistow. My stomach immediately dropped, I wasn't getting Poplar, and this was now real, I'd have to go and face a new Watch as a newly promoted officer.

However, over the course of the next few minutes, I calmed down, I was staying on the same watch, going to the next station east of Poplar where I knew a good few of the watch from bordering incidents and standby's, as well as being satisfied that Plaistow was also a busy station in those days. The DO presented me with my customary white box, which included two pairs of black shoulder epaulettes for my shirt, with a single white stripe denoting the rank of Leading Firefighter, as well as a pair of single chrome bars to be sewn onto each shoulder of my undress jacket. Although as a Temporary LFf I had been wearing the shirt rank marking and a single stripe of the collars of my fire coat, as a substantive LFf I got to put a single stripe around my yellow fire helmet, as well as the chrome bars mentioned above on my undress uniform.

The DO jumped smartly to his feet, held out a hand and congratulated me for what he hoped was "The first of many Mr Dudeney." Off I went back to Poplar, excited but sad to be leaving. The next couple of weeks went by, without a great deal happening and my last night, a Friday night duty, we had a massive water fight, which pretty much kicked off on roll call at 6pm. John the Guvnor had also decided to transfer elsewhere, so it was his last night as well. After the water fight and the hour or so to tidy up, interrupted by one minor call, we sat down to a large meal, followed by a night of high jinks with flour bombs, more water and smoke bombs in the toilets. Lastly was a game of chicken in the basement, which entailed filling the room with balloons that were full of propane gas, attached to a lighted taper. The aim of the game was to see who would stay in the old basement store room longest; as the number of balloons filled with gas gradually increased and burst, the harder and harder it was to breathe.

The following morning after a relatively uneventful night fire call wise, I cleared out the last of my things from my locker and sadly said farewell to Poplar fire station. It had been twelve years since that first night there as a kid with the Red Watch, and with a heavy heart, I drove out of the bay and headed home, in preparation for my first day at my new station as a proper officer.

Plaistow Fire Station was a large single storey fire station built for the West Ham County Fire Brigade in 1932. It had five bays with a pitched roof at the top and accommodation at each end of the building that went off into the yard at the rear, making the building look like three sides of a square from above. At the rear was the NE Area driving school and a BA training complex that had been added in the early 1970s. The right-hand side as you looked at it, contained the Watchroom and office, with the Sub Officers room behind, then a tiny TV/lecture room with 12 chairs crammed into it behind that and finally the mess room and kitchen. On the opposite side, the end bay had been given over to gear racks to store the fire kit of those who were off duty. The Station Officers room was at the front, and behind that was a long fireman's dormitory with ablutions right at the back. An extension had been added sometime after World War II which included a large snooker room, with a small room off that which was once a bar, and had been unceremoniously converted into the Leading Firemen's room, with the addition of 10 metal lockers and a couple of beds.

Plaistow was also one of the stations that in 1994, despite there having been operational firewomen in LFB for 12 years at that point, didn't have any women's facilities. An out duty from a woman firefighter would inevitably mean the Sub Officer begrudgingly giving up his accommodation, God forbid anyone dare ask the Guvnor.

I arrived for my first day on a Wednesday in May 1994. I got in quite early and as I ferried my uniform, bedding, books and other stuff back and forth to my locker, I was generally stared at by members of the Green Watch, none of whom I knew, with just the odd one raising a hand or calling "Alright mate" to me. Not long after that Larry and Mel, two of the older hands, arrived. I walked over to meet them having known them since I'd been 'next door' at Poplar. My smile was met with Mel simply stating, "Alright Steve, I hope you ain't gonna start with a load of old bollocks now you've been promoted."

I laughed it off, but felt instantly depressed as I was obviously now being seen as 'one of them'.

What I didn't know until a couple of weeks later was that their old acting Station Officer who had been there for a few years, had been moved and replaced by a new Station Officer, who was a 'hot and cold' man, so no one knew where they stood with him. Shortly after that, a new Sub Officer had been posted in, who didn't gel particularly well with the Watch. I guess I was seen as making up the trilogy. Especially as I'd displaced one of the firefighters on the watch who had been acting up long term and hadn't made it through the promotion round that I'd just had success with. Still, I was here now so I had to get on with it.

After roll call I had a chat with the Guvnor, who I'd seen about, but drew my own conclusions on, after getting my gear set up on the front of the PL. I went into the mess and asked Mel, who was Mess Manager, how much he wanted for food and whether we paid weekly or monthly. I sat with the Watch and the air soon began to thaw as I spoke in great detail about my last night at Poplar and all of the nonsense we'd got up to. I had a bit of 'first day' anticipation again awaiting my first call. The aerial ladder platform, a 32m articulated boom with ladders at the side and a large rescue cage, which I'd previously qualified to operate, went out on a call somewhere up towards Dagenham, and the pump also went out a couple of times.

After lunch, the phone rang and the pump was ordered to standby at Leyton. I was to take the pump to standby, leaving the Guvnor at Plaistow on the PL. Bizarrely we were told to drive to Leyton fire station but not approach the station, and instead wait in a street nearby. A few phone calls into NE Area staff got the "you didn't hear it from me but…" answer we were looking for. Nothing out of the ordinary, something had gone on, a hit squad of senior officers had arrived and took the station off the run. They didn't want us snooping around, so we were to provide fire cover via radio from a nearby street.

Leyton fire station sits on a 'T' junction where two main roads meet. As we approached up the leg of the 'T' we could see inside the large glass doors of the modern fire station. Both machines were out the back, but there were a couple of senior officer's cars parked on the forecourt.

"There you go," commented my driver, "someone *is* being done."

"I bet it's Les, been caught going to the pub at lunchtime," a voice called from the back.

"I reckon Martin has stabbed Jim for coming out with another stupid plan," said the driver.

"Maybe one of Jim's stupid plans has gone wrong in work time," I replied.

We backed into an estate road just next to the fire station and began to speculate on ever more elaborate reasons as to who might have got into trouble and why. After a short time, sitting there wondering how long we'd be parked here, I was drawn to the radio, whose background chatter from across NE Area I'd tuned out.

"Foxtrot four five two, Foxtrot four five two from FE priority, over," I reached for the handset.

"FE from Foxtrot four five two, go ahead, over…"

"Foxtrot four five two, you are ordered to a fire in an electrical substation, rear of four one seven Lea Bridge Road E10, near Avondale Road, route card thirty-one CC, page seventy-two, CRR code Sierra Alpha Charlie, Foxtrot four five two acknowledge, over."

"FE from Foxtrot four five two, received, now status two, over."

The driver was already thumbing through the A-Z map as I called into the back cab, "Fire in electrical substation, not far from here, get a couple of sets on lads."

"Right at the top of the road then third left," the driver said to me.

"Yeah, Lea Bridge Road is just up the top," I replied.

I tried to think back over my recent studying, *"electrical substations, lay out a covering jet… contact electricity company… substation ID number…restricted zone… oil cooled… explosion risk."* I braced against the cab as we swung right into Lea Bridge Road, *"nothing showing",* we pulled round a line of cars and as we approached the junction, a man in overalls waved us into the side street. We pulled up and a small crowd of people were mingling and one or two pointed down an alleyway that run at the back of the shops. I jumped down from the cab and walked around the front of the pump.

"He's in the back of the house," someone said to me, "they are looking after him," another man called over my shoulder. I could see a double storey windowless extension at the rear of the shops to my right and smoke was coming from an opening in the building. The side of the first house in the street was on my left as I walked up the alleyway.

As I walked towards the back of the house, I looked into a door in a wooden lean-to and two women were helping a man who was leaning over a sink, as they poured water over him. He appeared to be in his late 30s and was burned on his upper torso; there was a burnt t-shirt on the floor, his hair was singed and his skin pink from burns, but not too bad. I felt another of the crew behind me.

"Get the first aid kit and some oxygen. Then call an ambulance – one male, conscious and breathing, burns to upper body," I said. "You OK mate, what happened?"

"Er, yeah… I-I was working on the switchgear and it arced."

"Anyone else in there?"

"My mate… he was…"

"I'm with him mate," came another voice suddenly, "will he be OK?"

"Have you isolated the power?" I asked him.

"No, I've requested another team, they need to cut it off from the street."

I heard the sirens of Walthamstow's pump ladder in the street, I looked down and saw their crew getting off. I ducked into the opening and looked beyond a large metal door with vents in it; inside smoke filled the upper half of the darkened room and I could see something burning up on the wall to the right, dripping molten flames to the floor. A large buzz came from the room followed by a loud pop that made me instantly consider my position and duck back outside.

I walked up to Walthamstow's Sub Officer, I explained to him what was happening and that my crew were getting first aid underway. He told his crew to get a covering jet laid out and then took a tentative peek into the room containing the substation, himself.

Back in the street, my crew were dousing the man with water, he was shaking violently by now, with his friend hopping about next to him looking very concerned. The smoke was getting a lot thicker, so we cleared the crowd from

137

the alley and told the people in the house to get outside. This was greeted with a series of even louder pops and bangs.

In a short time, the ambulance had arrived and parked behind Walthamstow's pump ladder, I also saw an ADO's car arrive. Paul, my old Sub Officer from Poplar who was now acting ADO, got out of the car, it was good to see a familiar face. The Sub Officer from Walthamstow and I briefed him on what little we'd done so far and that the power still needed to be isolated. We walked back up the now deserted alley and turned in under the building extension to have another look into the substation. All of a sudden, a series of very loud quick pops, followed by an enormous bang went off, the shock wave hit me like a train and I was instantly deaf. Nonetheless, within no time at all I found myself with Paul and the Sub Officer sprinting back down the alley, deaf but for a giddy ringing in my ears.

"Jesus Christ, JESUS! What happened?" I cried. Paul looked as shocked as I felt and opened his mouth, but I could only hear ringing. We regrouped, and as my hearing gradually came back, I became aware of the familiar engine note and rotors of the Aerospatiale Dauphin helicopter, used by London's HEM's medical team, as the bright orange helicopter circled looking for a place to land.

As soon as the HEM's medics arrived, I noted that they had moved the victim to the back of the ambulance and had given him a general anaesthetic to spare him further pain. We kept a check on the fire but the worst was over. The explosion seemed to have involved everything else within the substation and with us unable to put water on the fire, it slowly burnt itself out after a couple of hours.

We'd been there well over three hours and the other team from the electricity board were still trying to dig the road up to isolate the supply. Paul told us a relief had been ordered, so within a short time both Walthamstow and us were away. As the investigation at Leyton fire station had concluded, we went straight back to Plaistow. I felt disappointed that my first job as a newly promoted officer had not resolved itself. That was made even worse when Paul rung me the next week to say that the poor fella who had been burnt had sadly passed away in hospital.

***

By early summer 1995, I'd settled at Plaistow and had spent a couple of short spells acting up again, this time to Temporary Sub Officer. No big deal, the only difference being the Sub Officer was in charge of the station when the Station Officer was off, so I'd now been in charge here at Plaistow, and for a few weeks, was even back at Poplar covering someone who was off.

Life outside of work had also changed dramatically for me as well. In July 1994 my first daughter Charlotte, had arrived. I remember the day after she was born; we got her home, plonked her on the floor in her baby seat and I looked at my wife Joanne and said "what do we do now." The most important thing that had ever happened to us and like every other parent ever, we didn't have a clue. We soon got used to it; we got into a routine of nappies, feeds, sleepless nights and within a few months we were experts.

Joanne went back to work pretty quickly as finances demanded it, so I became a house husband on my days off. When I was on duty, my Mum and Dad took care of Charlotte, as my in-laws were both still at work, seeing as they were still in their late forties at the time. With money being such an issue, I decided I would undertake the 'Knowledge of London' again. I'd started it previously in 1991 and gave up on it, but this time the responsibility of a child took the option of giving up away from me.

The Knowledge is pretty much unique across the world, it is the long process undertaken by people wishing to be licenced to drive one of London's famous Black Taxi's. It required the student to initially learn around 400 routes (known as 'runs') across Central and Inner London, (usually on a moped) and also all of the 'points on interest' (churches, hospitals, theatres, clubs, cinema's, significant buildings, police stations, large shops and so on) within a quarter of a mile of the start and end point of each 'run'. This is no mean feat and it usually takes at least a year and a half before the student is ready for 'appearances'. These are oral tests by a Knowledge of London examiner, who were at that time all retired police officers. These tests entailed them asking you to take them from one random point in London to another, detailing the route between. At the earlier appearances it might be a number of simpler questions like the route from a major station to a famous theatre, but as the appearances became more frequent (initially every 56 days, then 28 days and so on), the questions would get tougher and involved complicated turnarounds to another location somewhere else. These routes had to be spoken to the examiner road by road and take the most direct route. "Leave on the left of Cannon Street, left into Gracechurch Street, forward into Bishopsgate, left into Wormwood Street"…etc., all the way to wherever the examiner decided you were going. The Knowledge and my new-found parental responsibilities pretty much took up all of my spare time for the next few years.

A few moves had happened at Plaistow, so I found myself, at the start of summer, being given long term acting up to Sub Officer. The Station Officer had moved on, so we also had a Temporary Station Officer, a bloke I knew from Bethnal Green called Andy. At the start of the summer Andy had been put on a long course at the Fire Service college at Moreton in Marsh and booked his summer leave to start as that course ended in mid-August. With me having a child who wasn't at school yet, I along with others on the watch who didn't have kids or kids at school, booked our summer leave at other times. So, I was going to be in charge of the watch right the way through July and August, until I went on leave at the start of September.

Early summer was pretty regular for the South East of the UK. The beginning of June had been mild and occasionally damp but had followed a pretty dry May. By the end of June, it was warming up nicely and rain was a rare occurrence. First of all, we didn't really notice, I was beginning to pick up a few interesting jobs where I was in charge and began to cut my teeth as an 'Incident Commander'. A little house job, a relatively simple car accident, a fire in a derelict park building in Beckton where I got to practice my messages back to Control…

"Mel, can you send the following from me please; from Sub Officer Dudeney, at Canning Town recreation ground, a single storey derelict park building, five metres by eight metres, one hundred percent alight, one jet and one hose reel in use."

"Why the fuck don't you just send a code two?" came the tired reply.

"Nope, I want to do it properly, send the informative message please."

"Whatever," Mel said as he reached into the cab and picked up the radio mike.

Over the next few tours, the weather got hotter and hotter, the grass in all of the parks and common land out to the east of us began to catch light, maybe by accident or not, and on every day shift, as soon as the middle of the day arrived and lunch was due, the stations out to the east; Dagenham, Ilford, Barking and Hornchurch, among others, were going out of the doors from one fire to the next. The more these stations were empty, the more other grass fires or incidents would require stations from further in to cover them. So began a regular pattern for us. All the work around the station would be done early, a 10:30 stand-easy and a

1pm lunch gave way to a hearty brunch in readiness for early afternoon and the calls that would start coming in.

"Pump only," called the duty man as the bells stopped. I looked up at the ceiling as I walked across the bay to see that the green despatch light for the pump was illuminated.

"What we got?" called Delboy as he came out of the snooker room.

"Rubbish in a park, Barking Road, East Ham's end... they must be out already." I turned and walked back into the Station Officers' room, sat down and picked up my pen.

"Fuck sakes," I said to no one, but felt my heart skip a beat as the bells went down again almost immediately, as I walked out of the room I saw the red light lit up on the ceiling for the pump ladder, I sped up into a jog across the bay and stepped into my boots and leggings. There was a huddle around the printer and map on the wall, as I pulled by braces over my shoulders and walked into the Watchroom.

"What we got?" I demanded.

"Fire in a shop, Loxford Lane, Ilford," Owen the dutyman called out.

"Us and Hainault."

"Blimey," someone said, "Ilford, Barking and Dagenham must all be out as well for us to get that with Hainault."

"Come on then me son... let's go," said Andy excitedly as the melee around the printer now turned and headed towards me in the small doorway.

We jumped onto the machine and I stabbed at the siren button with my foot as we pulled out onto Prince Regent Lane.

"D'ya know it Lal," I said to Larry who was driving me.

"Yes mate, I'll go A13, A406 over the top of Barking and into Ilford Lane," came Larry's reply as if to confirm the route in his head. I turned the radio up and tried to pick up any messages for our shout as we made our way down to the A13. Further calls would be forwarded to either myself or Hainault's PL en route if it was a job. Any decent fire this time of day would be sure to attract several 999 calls.

"Stick a couple of sets on lads," I called into the back as we headed east along the A13.

"We'll easily beat Hainault there," I said with the excitement rising.

"FE from Foxtrot four one one priority, over," came over the radio.

"Foxtrot four one one, go ahead, over."

"Foxtrot four one one, from Station Officer Camp, at Parsloes Park Dagenham, make pumps four over."

"Foxtrot four four one from FE, your make pumps four, received at thirteen forty two, FE out."

"Who was that?" came a call from the back.

"Dagenham… Jim Camp just made a job up in Parsloes Park, must be grass," I called back.

As we turned onto the A406 from the A13 and the road rose, I scanned the sky to the north east, looking for the smoke from my shop fire, but there was nothing. I saw a cloud of white smoke in the distance to the east.

"That must be the Dagenham job," I said to Larry who grunted a reply. We came off the A406 at the first exit and round the roundabout towards Barking town centre, and then made another left at the next roundabout to go on the bypass that ran north.

We then turned into Ilford Lane, and continued north. Just as we approached the junction with Loxford Lane an elderly Indian man was waving to us from the corner.

"There Lal, on the right," I said to Larry as he veered the machine to the right.

"Over here on the right," I called into the back. Larry drew up to the kerb and I jumped down from the cab and walked around the front of the machine. Owen and Andy were off in their BA sets and moved to the lockers.

"What's up mate?" I said to the Indian man.

"Fire, in back, in ceiling," he replied to me in broken English as he turned towards the shop.

"Wait outside," I said to the others, "I'll have a look."

I followed the man into the shop and he led me behind the counter of what was a typical grocery shop. As I entered the storage area at the back, the heat of the day in the small store room hit me. He pointed to a far corner. There was the smell of burning wood and a discarded bucket on the floor in a puddle, with water down the wall and all over a pile of goods. The first trickle of sweat ran down my neck and made me shudder involuntarily as I stepped forward. It appeared the fire had been on the outside and had smouldered away setting light to the wooden beam that held a plastic corrugated roof in place.

"OK mate, not to worry, we'll sort it."

I ducked back outside and spoke to the others.

"Get a 'short ex' off and put it up to that roof, it looks like something is smouldering."

"Righto," said Andy.

I was interrupted by the noise of a siren gradually increasing in my ears as Hainault were working their way down Ilford Lane.

Hainault pulled up facing my machine as the short extension ladder was slid to the ground with a metallic crunch. I walked up to their Sub Officer.

"Hello mate, you OK," I said, "it isn't much, just something smouldering in the roof," his crews got off and assembled behind him.

"Alright," he replied, "do you need us?"

"No, you are OK, we'll manage, I'll send a stop in a mo."

"Good, enjoy the rest of your day," he said with a smile.

"Hmmm, I may see you again at this rate," I replied, hoping that would be the case… well a busy day with lots of jobs that is, not that I had any feelings either way about seeing Hainault again.

I returned to the side of the shop.

"How we doing?" I called up.

"Yeah, it's fuck all," said Andy, "looks like someone threw a fag out from upstairs and it's caught light to all of the dried-up shit in the gutter, which caught the roof timber."

"OK, do we need to cut it away?" I enquired.

"Nah, we are all sides of it, about 8 inches of the timber is charred, and a bit of the plastic burnt. We'll give it a soak and pull it back a bit further, then we will be done."

I went back inside the shop and spoke to the owner, I explained the problem and showed him from the inside. I told him he'd need to get the bit of roofing cover replaced and he nodded enthusiastically. I also asked if he needed any help tidying up to which he shook his head equally enthusiastically and I got the feeling he was trying to usher me from the shop. I took a few details for the fire report and climbed up the ladder to satisfy myself everything was in order. I asked Larry to send me a 'code one' stop and we started to tidy the equipment away, I then got back on the machine and we were ready to go.

"I haven't been able to get in on the radio to send your stop Steve," Larry said. The busy signal was bleeping away on the radio while the operator at the other end tried to cope with all of the radio traffic. We did a circle of side streets to get back on Ilford Lane, facing south, and headed back towards the station. The radio suddenly went silent…

"FE from Foxtrot four five one," I spat into the mike desperately, lest someone else with a message would beat me to it.

"Foxtrot four five one, go ahead, over," came the reply, I was relieved.

"FE, from Foxtrot four five one, stop code one, over."

"Foxtrot four five one received… all stations wait," and the busy signal came back on. I booked 'available' from the button box terminal in the front cab and wondered how long until the next one.

Messages, ordering for other machines and the odd priority came in as we headed back towards the A13. The grass fire in Dagenham was still going, along with another few jobs, but nothing else to immediately concern us. Just as we were heading back towards the Plaistow turn off on the A13, my ears pricked up…

"Priority, priority, Foxtrot four five one over."

"He we go," I shouted, "Foxtrot four five one, go ahead with your priority, over."

And so, we were off. Nothing exciting happened for us that afternoon, we got back to the station a couple of times, only to head out again, either on our ground or further afield. We never saw the pump again as they were still out until after change of shift. After their shout at East Ham, they ended up standing by at Dagenham, where they picked up a few shouts and saw the day out at a field fire right on the edge of LFB area in Upminster.

One of our watch was sent to Shadwell on a standby duty for that shift. Unbeknownst to us until the next morning, they and Bethnal Green picked up a serious house fire just off Ben Johnson Road in Stepney. Sadly, and unusually for a daytime job, a couple of kids got killed in the fire. Two firefighters were taken to hospital with burns, including our bloke Des. Although thankfully the injuries were just steam burns to the neck, as Des and his oppo from Shadwell desperately fought their way up the stairs to the bedrooms searching for the kids, while the Bethnal Green crews hit the raging fire downstairs with water.

And so, the weeks of that beautiful summer went on. I was having a great time at home watching little Charlotte play in her tiny paddling pool and toddle round the patio in a tiny swimsuit and sun hat. Other days were spent sweltering on my motorbike as I was tackling the 400 blue book runs on my Knowledge. I'd got into the habit of getting up really early, so I could get a few runs done before the heat started to build, the emptier roads also meant I could get a move on and get from one run to another without negotiating the heavier day time traffic. As I've said, most people do The Knowledge on a moped. I'd had motorbikes since I was 16 and having a full bike licence, I was used to zooming around on a 'proper' bike.

Nonetheless, when I started The Knowledge in the autumn of 1994, I went off with what little money I had, and got myself a second hand moped. I was about a week into doing blue book runs and was pulling from West Halkin Street in Belgravia into Belgrave Square. A City of Westminster dustcart was lumbering around the square and with my 'motorcyclist' head I thought, "I can make that gap." Committed, I pulled onto the square and didn't move as quick as a might have expected. Using my left foot, I jabbed the gear lever to drop and gear, and increase my acceleration. Of course, motorcycle gears are 'one down, four or five up' whereas moped gears on these semi-auto things are the opposite. All of a sudden, I had lost all acceleration… I heard a loud blast of a horn and my mirrors were full of several tons of dust cart. I veered over to the right as the dustcart brushed past me, the driver questioning my sanity and parentage as he went. I came to a stop against the cars parked in bays in the middle of the square, my heart in my mouth.

"Fuck it," I said to Joanne as I bound in through the front door that evening. "I'm getting rid of that fucking moped, it nearly killed me."

"What? What do you mean?" she said with a shocked look on her face. Baby Charlotte in her arms sucking on her dummy looking warily at her dad with her big eyes, as he ranted in the doorway.

I explained the situation and then got moaned at for the money I'd lose on the moped. But after a few days of searching, I managed to find myself a 'proper' bike that I got without too much of a loss. I'd had some decent bikes before that, a couple of Honda's, a Suzuki and my last bike had been a BMW 800RT. I wasn't in that league anymore, but found my budget stretched to a Honda CB450DX. A curious bike made under licence in Brazil. Based on the Honda 'Super dreams' of the late 70s, but distinctly less dreamy. Still at least it was a proper bike and I could get home from Central London along the A13 at a decent pace, as opposed to the flat out 40mph of the moped.

The advantage of the moped of course was the fact they could be fitted with a plastic clipboard above the handlebars to affix the list of runs, points and maps I used learning the streets of London. Because of the shape of the handlebars on a proper motorcycle that wasn't really an option and although it made no odds on a moped, it might make the aerodynamics interesting on a bike that goes along much faster. So, the curious Honda 450 had a top box added to the back for me to pack my stuff into. I got a magnetic tank bag for the petrol tank with a clear plastic window for my maps and runs and because I had started the Knowledge at the end of 1994, as winter was approaching, I bought a Perspex screen to keep the worst of the weather off me. I was set, so off I went as happy as a sand boy.

Obviously, I also used the bike to get to Plaistow and back when I was on duty, and it usually sat at the back of the bay, taking pride of place between the aerial ladder platform and the pump. A couple of others on the watch also had bikes, so quieter spells of an evening would be spent standing out near the bikes cleaning them or maintaining them.

So, back to summer 1995. I was growing in confidence as an officer and had already faced down a few challenges on the watch, with personnel issues, as well as out on the fireground. One night it had quietened down after a few early calls and after supper we were sat in the tiny television room at Plaistow watching some TV. We were watching 'Heartbeat' a drama series about a 1960's London policeman and his doctor wife who had quit the rat race for life in a small Yorkshire village. The main character had an old police motorcycle that he pootled around on. During the programme, I heard some whispering and giggles but took no notice. I briefly glanced up as Delboy and Andy crept out of the room.

Sometime after midnight, I got up and wandered out the back for a quick cigarette. As I stood in the yard during the sultry evening I looked round at my bike. Something was amiss. I looked closer and walked towards it. "What the fuck?" I said to myself.

Because Plaistow also housed the North East Area driving school, some pair of twits had got into one of the officer's cars, parked over outside the driving school building, taken the magnetic blue light from it and stuck it on my top box. They'd also carefully blue-tacked a radio aerial to the top box and had taken the time to cut out and colour in the words 'POLICE' and taped them to the screen. Just as I was stood there taking the sight in, I was treated to a chorus of the song 'Heartbeat' which was also the theme tune to the TV show we'd watched earlier, which soon broke into peals of wild laughter. I feigned great offence and used some interesting descriptive words to let them know what I thought about it all.

146

But smiled to myself at their ingenuity as I began to pick off the letters from the screen.

I went to bed in the early hours and lay there thinking how all was good in the world and how my initial worries about moving on, a year or so earlier, were unfounded, as the Red Watch at Plaistow were a friendly bunch. I must have drifted off to sleep as the next minute I was blinking in the harsh bright light in the Sub Officer's room as the bells clanged out above me. I got dressed and stepped out into the bay, the layout at Plaistow was such that as I walked out of the Sub Officers' room I was immediately next to the nearside of the pump ladder, so I stepped straight into my boots.

"All the lot went up the usual cry from the Watchroom and all three appliance despatch lights illuminated on the ceiling; red for pump ladder, green for the pump and yellow for the aerial ladder platform."

"What we got?" someone called.

"Fire," called the dutyman.

"All three," someone else shouted back towards the main dormitory.

"Fire, Balaam Street, fire in a shop," another call went up.

The dutyman came out of the Watchroom and handed me a call slip, "Fire in a shop, Balaam Street Steve."

"Cheers mate," I replied.

I jumped up into the cab as Paul gunned the machine into life.

"Balaam Street Paul, fire in a shop," I said to him.

"Yep," came the reply as he palmed his eyes to clear the sleep from them.

We turned right onto Prince Regent Lane and headed north. The radio remained quiet, but that didn't mean much either way at this hour. We crossed Barking Road and kept going. In my head I was thinking of the shops at the Barking Road end of Balaam Street and was about to question why we didn't go left, then remembered the road we were on also led to Balaam Street. We passed the bus garage and I glanced left across Plaistow Park, on the other side I got a quick glimpse of bright flames through the trees.

"It's going," I called out, "We've got a job, I saw it through the trees, it's about halfway down Paul."

Greengate Street bore to the left and then we made a left into Balaam Street and started heading back down. As we cleared a small turn, I could see a corner shop with flames coming from all of the upstairs windows and dark smoke coming through the roof.

"Pull past Paul, so we can get the ALP in front of the shop."

I jumped down from the machine and saw the pump swing into the side road, I called back to Paul who had jumped down from the cab.

"Make 'em four Paul."

I walked along the front of the shop, it was boarded up, but smoke was pushing through the wooden shutters, I also felt the heat from the fire against my face, a little like sitting next to an electric fire.

"The whole lot is alight," I said to Nick who was riding in charge of the ALP.

"Get the 'alp' set up and get ready to get to work... get Paul to feed you from the PL," I added as an afterthought.

I barked out a few more orders, "BA with a jet into the side door, get upstairs to do a search... lay out a covering jet and get some of that fire knocked down."

I walked into the side street and took a kick at the door that led to the upstairs of the property, it gave easily, and a mushroom of white smoke bellowed out. The hallway was well alight, ducking down I looked to my right and saw the staircase, the whole hallway was alight but the stairs seemed pretty intact. Looking ahead and slightly to my left, I saw another door, partially burned through with bright flames issuing from the top of the door, that was the way into the shop, I reasoned. Looking around I saw that everyone was busy. The engine note of the pump increased as the first water was pumped onto the fire, I also heard the clank of a hydrant cover from across the road... "they are getting water; set it," I noted. The deep note of the ALP engine also increased, as Mel engaged the power take off to set down the stabilising jacks.

My mind was racing. "What else?" I thought as I looked around at the others all busily engaged. A quick shrill blast of a whistle as a BA set started up, the rubbery 'slap' as hose was rolled out on the tarmac. I started to think about a message when to my right I saw the two machines from Stratford turn up in response to my 'make pumps four' message. The crews dismounted, and I walked over to their Station Officer. He was a very experienced Officer, I'd known him a long time, but he wasn't the friendliest of people. As I approached him, he started barking orders at his own crew, he looked at me as I confidently stated, "Alright Guvnor, I've just..." but he carried on walking past me towards the fire.

I followed him and started talking to him about what I had done. He was half listening to me like a parent does to a child whilst engaged in conversation with another adult, then he gave some more orders. He eventually sort of acknowledged what I had said and more or less walked off telling me to look after the firefighting inside. I was furious, but the moment had passed. In those days, old school Station Officers were a bit of a law unto themselves, so the underlying narrative was never to question or challenge them.

I walked back to the side door and just got on with it, hurt and crestfallen as well as doubting my own ability, doubting the confidence I'd grown in these past few weeks as an Incident Commander. The rest of the job pretty much carried on and passed me by. I was encouraging my crews inside, then once the main body of fire had been knocked down, I made my way inside and was helping feed hose and pull debris out of the door. Thankfully no one was inside, it transpired the shop was now empty and someone had torched it.

Before long, the Station Officer approached me as the bright rising sun was sending shafts of light through the trees in the park opposite. "We are done Steve," he said to me bluntly, "I've sent the stop, we'll leave it with you. Make sure you get everything turned over and pulled out. Order a one pump relief for 7am and don't leave until they are here and you hand it over properly." Even his parting words were quite condescending. I didn't say much and I got the feeling I think the rest of the watch felt for me. As I sat on a kerb a little while later, sucking miserably on a cigarette, I analysed what I had done wrong. I came to the conclusion that I'd pretty much done all that could have been expected and reflection after many years and much experience later confirms this, I just think that was the way some officers were back in those days. I vowed two things, firstly never to let anyone walk all over me on the fireground again and secondly, wherever I eventually rose up the ranks within the fire service, I would never do that to an officer unless they were blatantly incompetent, and even then I'd have the decency to explain they were an idiot before taking the job off them.

Toward the end of the hot spell, things were becoming so predictable that they were sending Central London stations out to standby in the afternoons at the outer stations to ensure adequate cover was provided. One day we'd have the pump from Whitechapel turn up, the next day the pump from Clerkenwell. It was a great time and I recall that throughout that six weeks, on every single shift, one or the other if not both machines picked up a decent job somewhere.

One thing that plagued us at Plaistow that year, seemingly isolated to just a few streets in Canning Town, was a problem with open fire hydrants. It was just like the scenes familiar from films of New York City during long hot summers, where kids would open the fire hydrants and play in the water. Unlike New York

149

and the rest of the USA, fire hydrants in the UK are under ground and need a standpipe shipped onto the underground outlet to connect the hoses.

The kids, who must have had a hydrant key stolen from somewhere, would open the hydrant pit and turn the water on. With a US style fire hydrant, you'd get a stream of water directed through the hydrant across the street. Unfortunately, with our hydrants, you'd get a spout of water gushing from the ground from 30-60ft depending on the water pressure. Some poor sod on the back of the pump would have to get off the truck and walk into the spout of water, somehow try to affix the hydrant key then slowly turn the supply off, getting drenched to the skin in the process.

Between the four watches at Plaistow and surrounding stations, who came onto the calls if Plaistow were out, a number of solutions were attempted to save the poor firefighter from getting a soaking. Some tried an oilskin overcoat found in a store at driving school, others tried quelling the flow by laying a large board over the open pit, but the pressure would then blow the board off launching it spinning in the air much to the delight of the assembled kids. The bravest of them would simply strip down to a pair of shorts and walk into the water and turn it off.

This 'fun' soon lost its edge with the crews, the wet fire kit had to be changed, because if they were then called to a fire, the firefighter entering a burning compartment would be scalded and burned by the wet kit in the heat. It also got quite violent, older kids would start to pelt crews with bricks and stones for coming to turn the hydrant off, which inevitably meant they'd be stuck there for a considerable period of time, waiting for the police, who were also busy, to come along before we could get in and turn the water off. That then caused complaints from neighbours who had water running near their property or covering their cars and gardens while we seemingly stood by and waited. The accusation being we were doing it on purpose. There was more than one stand-up row between pissed off firefighters and angry locals over this.

"If you control your bloody kids, we'd be able to switch it off. Why should I get a brick in my head because of your bloody kids… you should stop them from turning it on if you don't like it."

At its peak, we could be called to four or five of these hydrants in an afternoon, not that we weren't busy anyway with all of the other fires. We never did find a suitable cure for it or a way to deal with them, long after I left Plaistow, the crews were still getting called to open hydrants in the summer, well into the mid-2000s.

All of a sudden, the end of August was upon us – it had been a spectacular spell and I'd been to dozens of good jobs. A massive scrap yard fire in Wennington, a large factory fire in Barking. We even had a row of shops alight in Barking, where the roof collapsed while crews were inside, prompting a frantic scramble to get to the crews, who had just climbed a ladder and gone into a window just seconds earlier... everyone blowing short sharp blasts on their 'Acme Thunderer' whistles; the recognised evacuation signal in the UK fire service. We had a difficult high-rise fire on our own ground in Plaistow, house fires in East Ham, Ilford and Dagenham, a man collapsed on a roof in cardiac arrest, high speed car crashes along the busy A13 in the dead of night, and grass fires... so many grass fires. Wanstead Flats, the chase at Dagenham, Hornchurch Country Park, they all made the list.

Firefighters shrouded in smoke on a hot evening at the Wanstead Flats grass fire in 2018.

It was my last night duty before going on leave. I was working from 6pm until 9am the following morning and was flying out to Menorca the day after with my wife, daughter and in-laws. By now, we'd taken to eating 'Al Fresco' as soon as we came on duty; we'd move all of the table and chairs from the stifling mess room out into the open 'washdown' area at the back of the bay. We'd eat our evening meal and breakfast out there on nights, and brunch on days.

The lads had completed their checks, I had a quick hand over with the off going Blue Watch Station Officer and signed for the keys and petty cash. I had a quick look through the station diary in the unlikely event something had been booked for the evening and was soon over in the make shift outdoor mess having a cuppa and a fag and catching up on what everyone had done since going off duty at 9am that morning.

It wasn't long before the bells went down sending the ALP off to a fire alarm in a building somewhere, followed by the pump on a rubbish or grass fire somewhere local. So far so good for us, as it was a Friday night, we were having a Chinese takeaway that Mel, the mess manager, was busy making a list for, before he went off on the ALP for their shout. Eventually we got the list made up and the ALP went to collect it from a Chinese takeaway up on Barking Road that would provide us with a heavily discounted feast for a few pound per head.

After dinner a few of us sat around the table talking rubbish and generally taking the piss. One or two others wandered off to do their own thing or ring their other halves to chat about their day, as most of the watch had second jobs and had been working all day between nights. Despite the rules stating that you had to have a clear 8 hours rest between shifts, everybody knew people had mortgages to pay, kids to feed and clothe, as well as the little extras like my impending fortnight in Menorca. A firefighter's wage, although arguably reasonable, wasn't a fortune.

It wasn't long before we were on our way to something or the other which didn't turn out to be much to write home about. As we headed back to the station in convoy, the last shred of daylight fading in the clear sky, the pump was called up for a car fire near New City Road and came racing past us, siren wailing and blue lights bouncing off the walls either side of the road, lighting up the inside of our cab as it went. We pulled back into the station and I elected to lay my bedding out for the night, before it was too late, hoping to spend some time in it on my last night.

I walked from the Sub Officer's room into the office to type up the call log for the incident's attended so far, when the bells went down. I got to the printer first and read the message. We were called to smoke issuing from a warehouse, in Jedburgh Road, quite close to the station. We were ordered as well as the pump, which had been called up by radio returning from their car fire. Delboy came into the Watchroom first as he was the dutyman that night.

"Smoke issuing from warehouse, Jedburgh Road," I said to him.

In response, he called out into the bay, "Smoke issuing, Jedburgh Road, pump ladder only."

"The pump will beat us there, they are only round the corner from it, Jedburgh runs into New City Road," Del said to me.

We got there in little over a minute, I had a standby driver from Barking driving me, but he knew the area. As we turned into Jedburgh Road, I could see the pump ahead, its headlights and blue lights picking up smoke that was hanging lazily in the road. Well over half of the north side of Jedburgh Road was taken up by a large old three storey building, a hundred yards or more long, that once upon a time must have been a large factory of some kind. In recent years it had been divided up into multiple business units of all kinds; storage, small manufacturing, offices. The place was a rabbit warren, I'd been here previously on a couple of shouts, as well as a headache of an inspection of the premises earlier in the year, which had required me to call out a Fire Safety Officer as it was so complex.

As we pulled up and jumped down, I heard the distinctive sound of a sprinkler gong going off along the road, reminding me that parts of the building had a sprinkler system fitted. Some relief and an indication as to why the smoke coming from the large roller shutter was so slow and lazy, as whatever was burning had been cooled. I initially toyed with the idea of making the job up due to the complexity of the building, but dismissed it immediately until I could see what was alight.

I noted water running out from under the roller shutter, it wasn't hot to the touch and with my ear up to the gaps at the edge I could hear water running. I spoke to Bob, the leading hand on the pump, and asked what he'd done. He said he'd sent his lads along the road to try to find a way in to save us forcing the shutter and damaging it. In the end, we found no other way in and had to force the shutter up a little to squeeze one of the lads in, who then found the chain to roll the shutter up. As it came up, I sighed to myself as there was tons of smouldering rubbish alight inside. It was still burning quite well over the back, out of the reach of the sprinkler, so turning off the sprinklers wasn't an option until we had pulled out the rubbish at the front, in case the fire took hold and got further into the building.

Inevitably, it was all hands to the task and we slowly got very wet dragging out rubbish bags, soggy cardboard and other packing, most of which was falling apart as it had been burned and was now wet. I got my crew to put a ladder up to check no smoke or heat had penetrated above and we spent the remainder of the Friday night pulling the soggy mess out, extinguishing as we went. Once it was all extinguished, I called the police via radio as the nearby car fire and this unexplained rubbish fire looked a little suspicious. In all probability, this fire had been caused by a cigarette or something earlier when the place was still open, but I was damp and irritated and couldn't be bothered to wait for a keyholder to arrange to secure the premises, as well as the local council to come and clear the tons of rubbish we now had outside. We pushed it as far over as we could, the main sprinkler valve had been closed, so I also informed the forlorn looking PC that it was important he inform the responsible person that the sprinklers were out of action and they'd need to be reinstated as soon as possible. With that we were on our way back to the station and a freshen up, as most of the lads had to change their fire kit as it was stinking and soaking wet. I hadn't fared as bad, as I was walking in and out of the loading bay and in any case, I was about to go on leave so I'd suffer it. I hung my fire coat over a large old radiator next to the machine and skulked off to the mess for a bar of chocolate a nice cold drink from the 'Nutty' fridge, and a cigarette before turning in for the night.

I'd chomped down a Wispa bar, swigged a few mouthfuls of Coke and was on my second drag of the cigarette when the bells went down again. "Ahhh fa fuck sakes," I spat in disgust as I stubbed out my cigarette and headed to the machine, both the red and green lights for the PL and pump came on.

"AFA West Ham United," shouted the dutyman. I groaned again as I pulled on my damp fire coat, although it was gone midnight, it was still very warm out, but the dampness of the coat just felt clammy on me.

West Ham United's Boleyn Ground was in Green Street in Upton Park, just off the Barking Road about a mile east of the fire station. Everyone knew the ground well, we'd have occasional calls there and lot of the firefighters at Plaistow worked there as fire stewards, something that had been in place for around ten years, since the tragic fire at the Valley Parade stadium in Bradford in 1985. In this part of London pretty much everyone supported 'The Hammers' anyway.

As we pulled into Green Street from Barking Road, someone was directing us into Castle Street, the side street before the main gate, which took us towards the recently opened Bobby Moore stand at the south end of the stadium. As we pulled up, another security guard was waiting. I jumped down and met him.

"Alright mate, the alarms are going off up in the executive boxes... we've checked it, there is no fire but a weird smell along the corridor."

"OK, we'll have a look." I asked Bob to take his crew to go and see what was going on. East Ham's PL had pulled in behind us and their Guvnor came up to me.

"Hello Steve, what have you got?"

"Alright Steve," I replied. "I don't know yet, the AFA is going off but there is a funny smell in the corridor."

We stood and waited for a few moments until Bob came up on the radio.

"I think we've got a problem Steve, I can smell ammonia up here, it might be a leak." I groaned to myself again, not for the first time that evening, but felt relieved when Steve, East Ham's Guvnor interjected.

"Look Steve, we'd better make it a hazmat job, I'll have to take it, we'll get my ET here to set up decon. In the meantime get your first two blokes rigged in CPS." Chemical Protection Suits, are an airtight and liquid tight rubberised suit that completely encapsulate firefighters and their BA sets for use in hazardous atmospheres where toxic gases or liquids have been spilt.

Steve took over from me and sent the required messages. Before we had my blokes rigged and ready to go in, the Fire Rescue Unit had made the quick journey down the road from East Ham. These large vehicles designed and equipped with everything needed for major rescues from road or rail crashes, persons trapped in or under things, as well as all of the equipment required to make safe hazardous materials and decontaminate firefighters. Up until the early 90s they had been called Emergency Tenders, shortened to 'ET' (long before the film ET gave those words a whole new meaning) and in 1995 the FRU was still habitually referred to as the ET.

The first crew in reported back that the small fridge inside one of the executive boxes was tipped on its front and was leaking refrigerant. One of the stadium managers who had by now joined us went ashen.

"Oh, we've had some work done in the boxes out of season including new fridges. It says they should be defrosted when not in use, we've tipped all of them in every single box on their front to let any water drain out." Steve and I looked at each other and both began to work out in our head exactly how many crews we'd need to call in to deal with this. The crew in CPS called up again, "the one next door is the same…" It seemed our fears were confirmed, "but the one past that is tipped forward but not leaking."

"Are you sure?" I replied with the manager looking at me anxiously.

"Yes, it's definitely not leaking, bone dry."

In the end roughly six or seven of the fridge's were leaking, so we managed to do the whole job with just the crews from Plaistow's pair and East Ham's PL wearing CPS, plus the FRU crew decontaminating. The ADO who attended as 'hazmat officer' was also satisfied, keen as he was to get back to his slumbers. All of the fridges were put the right way up in all of the boxes, those that had leaked were dragged out onto the terrace in front of the affected executive boxes and those rooms were ventilated. All in all, we were there for a couple of hours and soon left the situation with the stadium's staff and went back to station.

After doing a bit of paperwork while the crews serviced their BA sets and washed the CPS suits, I rang control to tell them we were now back 'on the run', but riding with no CPS as the suits needed to be left out to dry. I eventually climbed into my bed sometime after 3am and went out like a light.

As I awoke to the bright lights and bells, I was confused and alarmed. I had obviously fallen into a deep sleep, which is quite unusual when on duty as you always seem to sleep lightly, waiting for the inevitable call. I felt a bit shaky and slightly nauseous with the shock of it all and walked into the bay to a hubbub of shouting that I wasn't really deciphering, in my still confused state. I got something about a fire and multiple calls and heard Mark, the standby driver, shouting, "That's where my Mum lives." I pulled my legging on and jumped up into the cab. I shut the door and immediately we had flown out the door, with Mark desperate to get to the fire. I reached for my fire coat, but it wasn't there. I suddenly remembered that the coat that was wet from the earlier fire and no better after sweating away at the next job, was still on the radiator back at the station, which was fast disappearing as Mark pushed the machine frantically along the road.

"My tunic! Hold on I've left my fucking tunic behind," I shouted at Mark.

"I ain't stopping, my Mum lives there…"

"What the fuck are you talking about?"

"Look at the call slip, fire in house, opposite the school, Corporation Street, my Mum lives opposite the school, Stratford are already on it, we are going on additional for multiple calls."

I was very much awake now as we blasted through the lights at Barking Road, with just a cursory glance as we sped through the junction.

I read the call slip and confirmed what Mark had told me.

"OK mate just take it easy, we want to get there in one piece," I said trying to do my best to remain calm at such a high speed and work out what I was going to do with no coat at the fire. The tyres let out a deep squeal of protest as we swerved round the left and right bend in Greengate Street past Balaam Street. It felt like we lifted off the ground as we sped over the bridge at Plaistow underground station.

"I'll have to use your tunic," I said to Mark who was by now leant forward over the steering wheel as if to will the machine to go faster in response to the 'make pumps four, persons reported' message Stratford had just sent. I can't remember actually turning into Corporation Street it was so fast, but I felt the g-force of the turn and heard the noisy complaint from the tyres. It was quite a way along Corporation Street, which was a street on a long gradual bend.

"Oh fucking hell," Mark shouted as the fire came into view, but he was immediately calmed, as the smoke filling the street and consuming the front of his Mum's house on the left, was seen to be coming from the house opposite. As we pulled up behind Stratford, I said to Mark.

"Right, I'll take your tunic, keep out of the way and don't let anyone see you without it."

I quickly jumped off the machine and ran around the back, opening the middle locker on the driver's side, where he kept his fire kit, and pulled his tunic out. The next problem was immediately evident. I am just about six foot and quite broad with long arms. Mark is about 5ft 8 inches, of a much slighter build and has fairly short arms. As soon as I pulled the fire coat on, I had a good three or four inches of my wrist and forearm exposed, I also struggled to fasten the zip, but with a deep breath in, managed it.

I reported with my crew to Stratford's Guvnor, the first time I'd seen him since the fire at Balaam Street a few weeks earlier. "Alright Guv, where do you want us?" I said to him with a smile.

"Get your pump's crew to help with the water, and I want you and your crew in BA to go into the job."

"Sorry, ME and my crew in BA?" I replied somewhat surprised.

"Yes, all of you," he said looking me up and down. "We think there are people in there and I want the whole place searched quickly."

Now anyone who knows anything about the fire service in the UK will testify, at a smallish fire like a four pump fire in a house, it is almost always the crews on the back who will rig in breathing apparatus and go in to fight the fire. Officers riding in charge of the appliance will usually get some command or support role. Whole crews, including their officers in BA, is usually reserved for much larger incidents in complex buildings such as a hospital or factory. On any other occasion, I'd have pulled his arm off for the opportunity to get in and do a bit, especially as this long-term spell as acting Sub Officer meant I was always on the front riding in charge and would never get to go into a fast moving house fire in BA.

"How's my fucking form," I mumbled to myself as I jogged back to the machine to get my crew in BA and rig in my own set. I looked down at my exposed arms and back at the house with hot boiling smoke and small tongues of flame still coming from every opening.

We reported to BA control, started our BA sets, handed in our tallies and made our way into the fire, me desperately tugging at each sleeve trying to make the gap disappear. As it happens it wasn't so bad, my arms got a little warm but didn't get burned or scalded. We made a rapid search of the upper floor of the house and soon confirmed no one was inside, so I was quite happy as I came out that I'd had a little play and I'd got away with leaving my tunic back at the station. I walked out and in the fifteen minutes or so I'd been inside daylight had got the better of the night and things had calmed down in the street. We went back to BA control and closed down our sets, and I made my way towards the machine. I looked to my right and saw Mark, his boots and leggings on, talking to a woman who I assumed was his Mum outside her house, keeping out of the way as I'd told him with a fresh white bandage on his arm... a bandage?

He came over to a bit sheepish and smiled at me.

"What have you done?" I demanded.

"Well I was helping pass the hose reel into the window and I caught it on the broken glass."

"Hold on," I said, "I distinctly remember telling you to keep your head down and you were feeding the fucking hose reel though a broken window?"

"Well, erm yeah... I erm, there wasn't anyone else about."

"Jesus fucking Christ Mark, what's wrong with you?" I said shaking my head as I dropped my BA set to the floor.

"It's OK, I explained it all to the ADO and he said I could drive back and walk round to Newham General to get it looked at."

"ADO? What ADO, you've now told the ADO that the reason you have a cut arm is because the Sub Officer is wearing your tunic because he left his behind...? I don't believe it, I just don't believe my luck tonight..." I muttered to myself as I headed back to face the music.

As I walked back to the scene, I saw the ADO talking to Stratford's Guvnor. Thankfully it was Terry, the Station Commander from Poplar who knew me from when I was based there. "Guv, look I'm really sorry I..." I said to him.

"What's happened to you Steve? You are meant to be a Sub Officer now, what example are you setting?" I looked down at the floor and again winced as I saw my long arms sticking out of a short coat. I looked up again and detected a smile of his face, I don't know whether it was a smile of sympathy, pity or exasperation, but I was taking it as a good sign.

I explained the whole situation to him but felt by his nods and smiles that I was digging myself a bigger hole with every word. As if sensing my pain, he told me to get my crew together get back to Plaistow, send Mark around to the A&E and "get the paperwork started for the injury." I gathered the crew together and we made our way back to Plaistow.

After drinking a strong cup of coffee, I started filling out all of the forms. I spoke to the Officer in charge at Barking, Mark's home station, to let him know and finally sat down for my last ever 'al fresco' breakfast at a fire station. I'd have plenty more 'al fresco' dining at fire stations on fine summer days, but never breakfast. The last hour or so passed by and I did a long hand over with the oncoming Green Watch Guvnor who called me a plonker for leaving my coat behind and for causing him to have to go back to Jedburgh Road to carry out an inspection later, to check the sprinklers had been turned on again.

And so, as I climbed wearily onto my motorbike to head home to bed before going off on a well-deserved holiday, I reflected on the long hot summer of 1995 in the London Fire Brigade. I knew it was over, by the time I got back to work we'd be heading into the third week of September and as the heat was forecast to break imminently, it would be much cooler by then. I'd come a long way in that time, I learned a lot and felt that I'd vastly improved in that time. I'd also learned what not to do at times, from my own mistakes or seeing how others did things. All in all, it was one of the best summers I had in my career and I'll always remember it.

Bow

Earlier in 1995 I'd applied (again) to take the Sub Officers written examination, which I'd failed a couple of times previously, having not studied enough due to life getting in the way; buying a house, getting married, having a young child and generally being more 'in the moment' than thinking about the future. As autumn took hold, I'd clearly been too busy over the summer anyway, as well as my studying of 'the Knowledge' taking up the lion's share of my capacity for study. As the examination day approached, it was too late to cancel, so I decided I'd simply not attend, the penalty for which meant I'd have to miss the 1996 exam and wouldn't be eligible again until 1997, I wasn't concerned as I has too much on my mind.

After a couple of years with no promotions, LFB established the new 'crew commander' and 'watch commander' promotion processes. Had I have passed the Sub Officers written and followed that up with a pass in the practical examination, I'd have been eligible for the watch commander process. I wasn't, so at the end of 1995, a new Sub Officer, conditionally promoted on the new scheme, was sent into Plaistow Red Watch which put me back at Leading Firefighter on the watch. That was fine, it was nice to spend some time 'on the back' again, but more often than not I was stuck in charge of the ALP. The mobilisation and attendance standards had been altered recently, so all of a sudden, the ALP wasn't going onto as many calls as it had been removed from a lot of the 'pre-determined' attendances across the area.

Initially I was quite happy to be going out less, but this soon wore off and after a few shifts where I didn't go out at all, I started to get an itch that I couldn't scratch. In 1994, I had undertaken the three-week training course to ride the Fire Rescue Unit, I'd qualified to become a 'Rescue Firefighter' or "One of the SAS of the London Fire Brigade" as one of the instructors had proudly boasted when we passed. The qualification had given me some great shifts at East Ham riding their FRU on out-duties, as well as a few riding the FRU's based further away.

However, there were no vacancies for Leading Firefighters at East Ham, so I wasn't able to transfer there.

I was in contact with lots of people in the area, and a friend at Bow who was already a taxi driver on his days off, informed me that they had a 'leading hand' vacancy and that a few of the guys on the watch were doing their 'Knowledge'. Bow was a two-pump station in Parnell Road, at the eastern end of the famous Roman Road street market. It was a small modern station built in the 1970s and covered the NE part of Tower Hamlets. Bow was arguably the nicest part of the borough, less affected by the Blitz of World War II, and many of the old streets of terraced houses remained. There were a few modern council estates, a large part of the top of the ground was taken up by Victoria Park and to the east was a semi-derelict industrial area, now home to London's Olympic Park where the 2012 Olympics were held.

Bow was a relatively quiet station compared to what I'd been used to over the previous eight and a half years of my time with LFB, but it was surrounded on four sides by busy stations. Bethnal Green to the west, Homerton to the north, Stratford to the east and Poplar to the south. I knew from having seen Bow on so many fires over the years, it may be quieter locally, but was always going to be involved in the action when jobs kicked off on neighbouring stations grounds. So without further ado, I submitted a transfer request to F27 Bow and at the end of the year said farewell to Plaistow.

My first day on the Red Watch at Bow was Boxing Day 1995, I'd clearly had quite a time of it on Christmas Day, as I arrived for work feeling the worse for wear and in no mood for anything much apart from taking it easy and watching TV, as the fog in my head and storm in my stomach slowly cleared. Soon after roll call, the Governor called me into his office and I still clearly recall most of what he said going in one ear and out the other, as I willed the banging in my head to stop and took deep breaths to control the accompanying nausea. I managed to get through without running away from my new Governor mid-sentence to visit the little boy's room and after a hearty breakfast felt a lot more in love with the world. The day passed without drama and I began to settle into life there.

With a few other 'Knowledge boys' on the watch, a lot of the down time was spent in a study room 'calling over' runs across London, testing each other on points and the quickest routes from A to B. During the summer, I'd let things slip a bit, and as I was now at the stage of having 'appearances' with the examiners at the carriage office every 56 days, I recognised I had begun to stand still as opposed to getting better at the last couple of appearances. This change was what I needed and early in 1996 my progress improved, I became more disciplined, getting back to going out on my bike very early every morning to look at the most recent 'points of interest' that were being asked of other students and then attend one of the Knowledge 'schools', where you could study with other Knowledge boys and girls.

One night in February 1996, I was sitting in my living room on the phone to my best mate Brian, a friend I'd grown up with and who was my best man at my wedding. Mid-sentence, he suddenly exclaimed, "Fucking Hell what was tha—" Before he could finish the sentence I physically 'felt' a loud explosion literally roll down our street. He was in Poplar, I was around eight miles east in Dagenham. The delay of a few seconds was the time it took for the explosion to move at the speed of sound to reach me.

"Fucking hell, I just heard that," I said.

"I think there has been a bomb, the windows nearly came in," Brian replied, "Over at the 'Wharf'," he added.

"OK, I'd better go, I need to ring my Mum and Dad, see ya later." I put the phone down as Joanne came into the room holding little Charlotte.

"Did you hear that? I think it was a bomb," she said.

"Yeah, Brian heard it first and a second later it reached here, did you hear how it rolled from one end of the road to the other?" the hairs on the back of my neck stood up as they often do at times like this.

I turned on the TV but didn't have Satellite or cable TV at the time, so was unable to watch Sky News. In any case, in those days before such prolific live reporting and immediate social media feeds, I doubt I'd have found out much. I rang my parents who had heard it and told me there were lots of sirens in the area, and eventually a new flash came up on terrestrial TV stating that a bomb had been reported somewhere in the Canary Wharf area.

In 1994, the Provisional IRA had declared a ceasefire to allow their political wing the Sinn Fein party to get involved in peace talks. However, as the British Government had insisted on full disarmament, the fragile peace fell apart. Seventeen months after the ceasefire began, the IRA detonated 3000lb of ammonium nitrate, fertiliser and sugar packed into a low loader truck. A warning was sent, but the area had not been fully evacuated, 2 people were killed in the explosion and 100 injured. Although known as the 'Canary Wharf' Bomb, the truck was actually abandoned just south of the Canary Wharf estate in South Quay, next to a small precinct of shops and the South Quay Dockland Light Railway Station.

At 6pm on Friday 9th February 1996, the Green Watch had reported for their last night duty at the 114 fire stations across London. At 7pm, the Green Watch at F22 Poplar were undertaking their nightly routines, the mess manager was preparing dinner, officers completing admin tasks and the firefighters testing and checking equipment. A minute later at 7:01pm, the station was rocked by the explosion. Crews in the bays ran out to the yard and were joined by the officers. A decision was quickly taken between veteran Green Watch Sub Officer Keith and his Station Officer to immediately respond.

The pump ladder and pump from Poplar quickly turned out and headed south towards Canary Wharf. The Station Officer made a 'running call' on the radio, to be informed multiple calls were being received to both the area of Canary Wharf and the district of Deptford just across the river.

Poplar's crews quickly found themselves in the midst of the devastation along Marsh Wall by South Quay, they assisted with first aid and protecting the surrounding buildings from fires and collapses for the next few hours. I watched the news until late that night as the story unfolded, knowing I'd most likely be there the next day as I was back on duty.

The talk of the bomb was all around the station the next morning. The Green Watch at Bow hadn't attended the incident, but had spoken to others who had. We did our role call and equipment checks and had a quick cup of tea in the mess. As expected, not long after change of shift, the relief orderings came out and Bow's pump, with me riding in charge, were one of four pumps sent to the site.

We were to report to the rendezvous point at Westferry Circus. After booking in at the Command Unit, we had quite a long wait and then I was crestfallen as I was given the job of 'inner cordon' controller, logging everyone in and out of the inner area. Although a police incident, the fire service have the responsibility for safety at major incident, and in line with the London 'multi-agency' major incident plan, we take responsibility for keeping a log of anyone who enters the inner area.

Thankfully, a Command Unit officer relieved me of this role after a short spell, due to the high numbers of people who needed to be logged in, so the CU set itself up as a proper focal point. I headed in towards the immediate scene to join my crew, along with the crews from other stations and Paul, my old colleague who was an Assistant Divisional Officer and in charge of the LFB response that morning.

As I walked along a very familiar Marsh Wall towards South Quay station and the epicentre of where the bomb had gone off, it was very eerie. There wasn't a window in any of the buildings and a lot of the lightweight cladding had also been blown off. Worse still was the sound of dozens of burglar and fire alarms going off inside the buildings. Whenever I see a news report of the bomb years later, the sound takes me right back there. It was relentless and although it became background white noise for the few hours we were there, every now and again when you were not involved in the task at hand it would leak back into your mind.

We were being held back while the forensic recovery teams were cataloguing parts of the truck that had been recovered from the significant crater the blast had left behind. The truck was parked right beneath the dockland light railway overhead track, which although terribly scarred was amazingly intact. This had the effect of forcing the explosion down, thus the crater was larger than what I'd seen before at other bomb incidents. That along with the small shopping precinct, a couple of meters east of where the lorry was parked, had the effect of 'pushing' the blast in a south westerly direction. Everywhere I looked to the west of the explosion was devastated, even lots of the windows in the four high rise blocks on the Barkentine Estate over a quarter of a mile away. Yet when I looked east along Marsh Wall, the damage was much less significant by comparison.

Within a short time, Paul explained to us that two men who worked in a newsagent's shop, at the very end of the precinct where the truck was parked, were missing and presumed buried in the rubble. This was 1996, still several years before the British Fire Service undertook all of the 'New Dimensions' work following the 9/11 tragedy in the USA. There was no Urban Search and Rescue capability like we have today, with teams of highly trained firefighters and bespoke equipment for digging, shoring, searching and so on. We did have some equipment on the FRU's for searching for live casualties trapped beneath rubble, but sadly 15 or more hours after the explosion and amidst the carnage, this was definitely a recovery operation and sadly not a rescue.

Paul took me and the other officers inside what had been the shop. One of the outside walls was still partially standing and holding the building up, but the internal walls had gone and what were two shops was now one. One of the initial things I noticed was a cold drinks refrigerator that had been by the door. It had been blown over but was largely intact. The drinks inside had all been grotesquely deformed by the pressure of the blast and the carbonated sugary contents had become crystallised. The nearest thing I can describe it to is a can of fizzy drink that had bulged until it had split with what looked like crystallised candle wax, set 'mid-fizz' as if time had stood still.

I remembered the narrow shop before the blast, I considered the direction of the blast as I looked around and then noted the pile of rubble from the partial outer and internal walls of the shop, up against another wall that had held, like a pile of leaves that had been swept against a wall before being scooped up. There were one or two other indicators that I won't go into, and as if reading my mind, Paul came back into my consciousness.

"It's most likely that the two persons missing are under that pile over there, get yourselves and your crews to start to gradually remove the debris, under the watchful eye of the forensic teams and place it in the area that they have cleared for you outside. If you come across anything, stop what you are doing and let us know."

Fully briefed and keen to make a start, we armed ourselves with buckets, shovels and other hand tools to begin the painstaking work of removing the pile by hand. We did this for a couple of hours. It was painfully slow and we all wanted to get to the two men as they deserved to be recovered and their families informed for certain. We revolved crews, as although there was no heavy lifting, it took a lot of discipline to gradually unpick the pile, as the desire was to ferret away to reach them. We all took turns at digging, carrying buckets and keeping an eye on the fragile structure we were inside, lest it should collapse and entomb us all.

We had reduced the pile from about 6ft down to roughly waist height. We felt we were getting near, but then Paul pulled us out and said our reliefs were here. I was gutted that we couldn't finish the job we had been given to recover these poor men, but also partly relieved not to have had to bear witness to how they may have succumbed. Stratford's pump crew were reliving us and I took their Sub Officer Mick inside and showed him the pile and the evidence that made us so sure they were right there. After a debrief and a request to go back to the station and write statements of our actions, we were away. I had a long hot shower and then sat down to a late lunch as we were all surprisingly very hungry.

Mick rang me just before the change of shift when he got back to Stratford. He told me they came across the first man, right where we thought, around 15 minutes after we had left. The second man was found a little later on and thankfully both were recovered with dignity and handed to the police.

***

I arrived for work on another Saturday first day shift several months later. The Sub Officer had transferred elsewhere so I found myself acting up again. We also had a new Station Officer, a gentle and friendly man called Glenn who the watch really liked. We only had a handful on duty due to leave and someone going sick, and no drivers at all. The station was empty as Green Watch were out at a fire that had broken out in the early hours. They returned just after the change of shift and we had enough to keep the pump ladder on the run, but a Green Watch driver had to hang on. No one particularly fancied it, as they'd had a rotten night, so I volunteered to drive. It was unusual for the Sub Officer to drive, but as long as the Station Officer, who was a rank above me, was on duty, he would ride in charge, so we'd get away with it.

I always loved the chance to drive the machine and hoped we'd get a shout or two before the standby drivers arrived to drive the PL and put the pump back on the run, where I'd then take charge of that machine. Just as I came back into the Watchroom after doing my drivers checks, I saw Phil who was the dutyman, talking out of the window to a man who was very animated. At that moment the bells went down, as others were peering out of the window. The call was to a flat alight just off Old Ford Road, a few hundred yards from the station. It quickly became apparent the call and the man at the window were reporting the same thing.

"Fire in flat, Clare House," someone called.

"I know it," said Pasty, "left into Old Ford, first on the right."

"You can't miss it, it's going like a bastard," someone else added. I gunned the engine of the Volvo PL into life and pulled out of the bay. As I turned right, I could immediately see the top of the pale pink Clare House enveloped in thick black smoke. Flame was blowing hard out of a window on the top floor on the face of the building half hidden from our position. I looked back down as a few people crossing the street into the Roman Road market scattered out of my way. I lost sight of the block for a second and then it came back into view as I reached

166

the junction with Old Ford Road. I made a hard left and edged forward impatiently as the traffic at the lights in the narrow road shunted to let me through, I noticed a couple of 'pointers' stood in the road waving us in. A quick right and I floored the throttle and headed the hundred yards or so to the base of the building, looking again at the burning flat.

"Make pumps six, persons reported Steve," the Guvnor called as he jumped down. I engaged the pump and jumped down myself, after sending a quick priority message making the job up, calling out to Ross, who had been the third firefighter on the back, to help me with the hydrant and the dry riser.

"No I want Ross upstairs with us," the Guvnor called back, as Phil and Pasty threw the lockers up to gather equipment and hose. I went to argue, as the Guvnor could do BA control upstairs briefly while we waited for the rest of the attendance, but I had to get their water. I thought better of it as we had too much to do. As the crew ran around to the front of the building, I then realised my mistake. I should have checked the map for myself… day one, lesson one in fire engine driver school. I should have carried on up Parnell Road and turned left into the estate and gone to the front of the block. Thankfully I was close, but not at the right point.

This soon compounded itself as I threw out the first of the four lengths of hose, twinned to the hydrant and the dry riser, the main which carries water up through the building with outlets on every other floor for firefighting jets. The hose was just short, no more than a metre. Instead of two lengths of 23m hose, I'd have to run out four, just for the extra metre. The hydrant was slightly further away, so that meant four lengths for that as well.

"Fuck sakes," I spat. I cursed Pasty for his directions, I cursed myself for not checking the map, I cursed the Guvnor for taking Ross upstairs, I cursed Fred who had gone sick and the others on leave as we may have had both trucks and at least eight of us, not the five we now had. I also cursed Bethnal Green who should have been here by now as well. My curse fest abated momentarily, as I heard a siren from a vehicle turn into the road, but my mood soon darkened again as it was just our ADO in his car, who was on duty and in the station and had obviously followed us out.

"Do us a favour Guv," I greeted him, "Roll out a few lengths." He gladly obliged and just as we'd got all eight lengths ran out and I was shipping the hydrant, a machine pulled in.

"About fucking time," I muttered to myself, then was surprised to see it was Homerton, who still had their Green Watch night crew on board. It turns out that Bow and Bethnal Green had been at the previous fire and Homerton were standing by at Bethnal Green for fire cover. As I was driving, I hadn't checked the attendance on the call slip as I'd have done if I was riding in charge, help was in fact coming from much farther afield, it was only as Homerton were returning to base from Bethnal Green, aware of the make-up and seeing the fire at the top of this 19 floor building, they decided to add themselves to the incident. I was thankful they did.

More crews arrived, someone took over the pumping once I'd satisfied myself I had a good supply going into the building and I got rigged in my fire gear. Seeing as I was the Sub Officer, I decided I'd better go up to the bridgehead on the floor below the fire. I got out of the lift on the 16th floor and walked up to the bridgehead. The first person I saw who I knew was a bloke I'd been to school with, standing on the landing in a t-shirt and shorts his bare feet hopping from one foot to another.

"Hello mate, are you OK?" he didn't recognise me, it had been years since I'd seen him and I had all my kit on.

"Yeah, I think so. I, erm… I only went out of the room for a few minutes and I heard something smash and the whole room was alight when I went back in." He looked disconsolately at the floor and carried on hopping.

"Righto, you take care," I said as I carried on up. As I got to the top floor the smoke was thick and grey at the top of the staircase, I saw the Guvnor laying on the stairs peering beneath the smoke layer.

"Alright Glenn, have they got it?" I asked.

"They are getting there I think," he replied.

"How's their water?" I asked, fairly pointlessly; I had a grip of the 45mm hose in my left hand as I laid beside the Guvnor, it was rock solid and pulsed as the crew inside the flat ahead of us opened the nozzle again.

The fire was soon put out and the smoke began to lift, Glenn and I ventured onto the landing as Phil and Pasty emerged through the smoke. Some other crews came by us, as I told the pair of them "well done" and guided them down to the bridgehead. I joined Glenn inside the burnt out flat. Through the steam and beyond the blackened walls I looked out across Bow and Bethnal Green towards the City, it was a bright day with a good view, save for the wafts of steam that kept partially obscuring the vista. It was still oppressively hot in the flat and the heat was still radiating from the walls, I was sweating a bit anyway from running around downstairs and then getting rigged in my kit, but in seconds I was blinking sweat from my eyes and began to feel the shirt stick to my back. Tellingly, the walls were clean brickwork and there was just a layer of black carbon and plaster a few inches thick on the floor.

This had been a very hot fire that had flashed over, which I had seen with my own eyes while en route, with the flames coming out like a blowtorch before curling up into the smoke. All of the furniture in the living room had been completely consumed and most of the kitchen and hallway were burnt, with severe smoke and heat damage to the remainder of the flat and the landing outside. When my old school mate had it on his toes, he had left the front door open, as soon as the living room window failed, the fire had a nice breeze at around 200ft high, to help it on its way.

Phil and Pasty soon joined us, their helmet straps undone and tunics open. They were both bright pink from the heat and dripping. Pasty offered me a cigarette and I took one, noting a sideways glance from the Guvnor. "The fucking place had flashed over as we got up here," Pasty said to me.

"It flashed as we were on the way mate, I saw it as we were coming here," I replied.

"It was red hot wasn't it Phil? We had to open the jet from the top of the stairs, you could see the glow from there." Pasty added as Phil nodded in agreement.

Ross who was our new recruit also joined us, he was big eyed as he surveyed the flat, but he'd done very well handing BA control and everything else on his own down at the bridgehead until help arrived.

After a couple of hours, we left the scene to the Fire Investigation team, I told them I'd come back later with the pump to check the place over and hand it over to the council. We got back and de-briefed over a hastily prepared stand-easy of sausage and onion in French bread. I continued to make my case to the Guvnor and still he didn't agree; he had wanted Ross with him up top, which is standard practice, even though I was downstairs alone. He lightened it off with a big smile and stated in an exaggerated country accent, "He'd never get used to our fucking 'London ways' boi."

***

In the early spring of 1998, I had been getting on quite well with my Knowledge appearances and I knew I must be near the end. I was thankful, as my second daughter Abigail had been born in February and I was now concentrating on my Knowledge pretty much full time outside of the fire brigade, so money was tight with no part-time income. I sat nervously in the waiting room with several other Knowledge boys. Dressed smartly in our suits, all with the same ashen faces, nervously avoiding eye contact. One chap got called in and then I heard my name called. I looked up, it was one of the friendly examiners, a man in his 60s who had always been kind on my appearances.

"Sit down Mr Dudeney, make yourself comfortable," the examiner said.

"Thank you, sir," I replied.

"How are things with you?" he added.

"All OK thanks Sir, a few sleepless nights as I have a new daughter who is about a month old."

"Ahh, lovely, is she and your wife well?"

"Yes thank you sir."

"Right then Mr Dudeney, shall we go from The Chelsea Arts Club and from there take me to William Goodenough House."

"Yes Sir, Chelsea Arts Club is Old Church Street and William Goodenough House is in Mecklenburgh Square."

"Good, off we go then."

"Erm, leave on the left of Old Church Street, right into Fulham Road, forward and bear right Brompton Road…"

I took him there without any problems and made another couple of runs without any problems.

"OK, then Mr Dudeney, can we now go from Wandsworth County Court to the Flask Public House."

"Jesus," I thought, "One's near Putney, the other up in Highgate, that's miles."

I identified the points and then started to call the route road by road, working my way north across the river, up through Fulham and Kensington, through Hyde Park, then Marylebone and up around the outside of Regents Park. I can clearly remember, just as I was heading up through a complex short cut around Gospel Oak, not far from the end, he got up out of his chair and went to a tray on his window ledge where he picked up a sheet of paper and a small booklet. Seeing this made me falter and I stopped speaking, he looked around at me and stared at me over his glasses.

"Go on Mr Dudeney, try to finish it off."

"Sorry sir... yes... erm, left into Oak Village, right into Mansfield Road, forward Gordon House Road, left into Highgate Road, forward Highgate West Hill, set down on the right." I took a deep breath out.

The examiner sat down and smiled at me.

"Do you know what that was Mr Dudeney?"

"I'm not sure sir," I said with an obvious grin breaking out across my face.

"That Mr Dudeney was your last run on the Knowledge of London. Congratulations! You have met the standard required to become a licensed taxi driver."

I was speechless and a little misty eyed, I'd worked incredibly hard to attain this. On reflection it wasn't the most intellectually challenging thing I'd ever done. But for over three and a half years I'd increasingly been consumed by learning the tens of thousands of roads that make up inner London, how they all interweave, the quickest ways through them, as well as the many thousands of places of interest; pubs, clubs, theatres, hospitals, public buildings, places of worship and whatever other insignificant little place the sadistic minds of the examiners could conjure up to test us.

"Thank you Sir, thank you very much," I mustered.

"This is a list of suburban runs you will now need to learn as well as Heathrow Airport. You won't need such a detailed knowledge of these suburbs, but you will be required to demonstrate you can get from central London to any one of these suburbs. Take this sheet and book yourself an appointment for 6 weeks' time where, all being well, if you pass your 'suburbs' and taxi driving test you'll be given your licence and green badge." I thanked him profusely again and bursting with pride went to book my final appearance.

Around six weeks later on 27th May 1998 I entered the Public Carriage Office in Penton Street in Islington for the last time as a 'Knowledge boy' I had my suburban exam, which was pretty much a formality, although I did have to recall a couple of the routes in and out of Heathrow Airport, as well as the main roads from London to two or three suburbs. After this, me and several other candidates were given a talk by the senior examiner and then given our licences and the coveted green badge. I looked down at the glistening brass badge, which was painted green on one side with an unpainted band through the middle, with the number 59266 stamped into it in black. 59266 was my badge number, which identified me as a brand-new driver at that point, but like all chronologically issued items, all of these years later it identifies me as an old sweat at the 'cab game', as well as being an old sweat in the fire service.

I had a cab lined up for rent and later that evening, armed with all I needed, I went out for my first night as a proper licenced London 'Cabby'. As was the tradition, I gave my first job away… I picked two blokes up in Threadneedle Street and took them over towards Covent Garden. I explained it when I got them there and despite some protests, I drove away without taking a penny. I thanked myself it wasn't an airport job or something that would have left me out of pocket. It also changed things at home. Joanne had taken a year off after Abigail was born because she felt she had rushed back to work after a couple of months when Charlotte had been born in 1994. I was determined to work hard to get us out of the negative equity we had on our first house in Dagenham and had my sights on the more upmarket Hornchurch, where my in-laws had moved when they sold their house in Poplar.

With the Knowledge now done I decided I needed to get my career back on track with the fire brigade. I had a little spell of being all about the cab, but Tom on the Blue Watch at Bow, a father figure to the station, who I'd got to know from my earliest days in LFB when I was at Bethnal Green, straightened me out. He was a floor layer on his days off and warned me not to 'bust' myself back to the rank of firefighter, as I might get fed up with driving a taxi one day and to concentrate on my main career. He wasn't wrong and I thank him for the advice all these years later.

As my 30th birthday approached, life was a whirlwind. I seemed to be out in the cab every day when I wasn't on duty. After days, before nights, between nights as well as my days off. There was good money to be made driving a taxi back then and I was making the most of it. Whilst at work I'd study for my examinations and when I wasn't in the taxi I was spending as much time as I could at home being a husband and father.

We ticked over at Bow, picking up jobs every few weeks, but I felt a bit differently about life as a firefighter now, I guess I'd grown up as I had other responsibilities. My Dad had also been ill for a year or so and I think on reflection, I didn't really want to have to deal with that on top of everything else.

About a year after I'd got my taxi licence, for one reason or another, I wasn't particularly happy at Bow, it was a great station with four decent watches but there was still too few Sub Officers, so I'd spend a lot of my time on out duties covering other stations when their Station Officer or Sub Officer was off. This was brilliant in some respects, as I'd been all over NE Area and got to know the Red Watch at almost every station in the area. The variety had also been amazing; creeping through the back rooms at old City Banks when a fire alarm had gone off in the middle of the night, when standing by at Dowgate in the City. Working my way up into the inside of large silo's on a Fire Safety visit when I was at Silvertown for a shift, and commanding a two pump back bedroom fire whilst riding in charge at Stoke Newington.

The cab was also getting me down, or at least the routine of forever working had. I was quite well off for the first time in my life and was enjoying those benefits. However, I was like a machine and although I hadn't really thought about it, something needed to change soon. I was on an out duty at Millwall Fire Station one day and after completing the daily routines, was flicking through one of the internal bulletins when I saw an article on one of LFB's training departments. Officer Development Group was the group that had been set up in 1995 to train new Crew and Watch Commanders. They were looking for trainers, I didn't think I had a chance as I was still only a Leading Firefighter on paper, albeit I'd spent the most of the last five years as a temporary Sub Officer. I also hadn't yet passed my Sub Officers exams, although with the exam due in autumn 1999, I felt comfortable as I'd studied properly this time.

Without even thinking about it, I rang the ADO who had written the article. He was a lovely man and was interested in what I had to say. Before I knew it, he'd invited me up there for a trial detachment for a few months to see if I'd like it and them me. So in almost no time at all, before I got to change my mind, for the first time in just short of twelve years with LFB, I was going to come off station, no longer go to calls and work 9-5, five days a week as a Training Officer. I also needed the break from working so hard in the cab. I decided a couple of nights per week I'd work a few hours after finishing at training, promising myself and my family I'd spend more time with them. So, at the end of a Saturday day shift at Bow in May 1999, I packed my locker and went home anxious about my start at Southwark training centre the following Monday.

Catching Up

Despite my fears about being non-operational as a trainer, I enjoyed the fifteen months I spent in training, I used my experience to teach other firefighters who had set out on the road of promotion and during this I also learned a lot myself and a lot about myself.

The courses were around six weeks in length, a couple of weeks in the classroom at Southwark, then a week away at an outdoor centre, where candidates were taught leadership, out of the immediate fire service arena. This involved a mixture of classroom inputs, and outward bounds type tasks such as raft building and crossing a ravine, where a candidate had to take responsibility for overcoming a problem, by using his or her leadership skills to delegate tasks, all of the time motivating and controlling the group. Following this, they had another week back at Southwark to begin to understand incident command in the fire service, before their final week and assessment at the Fire Service College in Moreton-in Marsh in Gloucestershire.

I really enjoyed this part of the course, the crew commander candidates were then coupled with watch commander candidates who had been following a separate course and were set up in one of two 'fire stations' at the college. Each candidate would have their day in charge as either a crew commander in charge of one fire engine and a crew, or as the watch commander in charge of the whole station. Throughout their day, each candidate would be given a number of managerial tasks; an accident investigation, broken or missing equipment, a complaint from an enraged member of public, during which one of us instructors would put in a performance worthy of an Oscar. In between, they'd go out to small routine calls where their ability to command was assessed and at the end of the day a large incident was staged where all four appliances from the two stations would come together to deal with it.

The Fire Service College was a former RAF base, early in the 1970s a lot of investment had taken place to build several 'fire' buildings. Various reinforced concrete structures would have cribs filled with straw and pallets placed in their rooms and then set alight. Add to this the theatrics of the instructors and their macabre and dark imagination, candidates would have some very realistic scenarios to deal with. There was a house, a factory, a high rise office complex, a shopping centre and large ship at a dockside, as well as an oil rig, aircraft, stretches of motorway with wrecked cars and railway with real trains all of which came into play, to give these officers great preparation for dealing with incidents in the real world. All of this was a lot more than my generation, just a few years earlier, and all of those who came before me, had ever been given. Our preparation was the examinations, the study and interview and if successful you put on your new rank markings, went to the new station and got on with it.

On a personal note, being in a training department had allowed me to really catch up. I'd been studying, and during that time I had passed my Sub Officers written and practical exams, and had also taken the Station Officers exam, I was expecting the results of this later on in 2000. Another change was the introduction of the formal 'specialism'. LFB had suffered in recent years with a shortage of candidates wanting to go into specialist roles such as training, fire safety, command support and so on. With a view to alleviate this problem, LFB had introduced formal training and competency in these roles. As the final 'hook', anyone who wanted to go beyond the rank of Station Officer into the senior roles, now had to have demonstrated competency (usually two years) in a specialist role.

All of a sudden, I was in a very advantageous position. Me passing my Sub Officer exams enabled me to apply for the Watch Commander interviews which I passed. I stayed exactly where I was in training, now doing my specialist development as a trainer. Eventually, I'd have to do the course that I was facilitating, as a candidate myself, before going back out as an operational Sub Officer to do some additional operational units, to gain full competency as a Watch Commander specialist. In the summer of 2000, I went from gamekeeper back to poacher and was myself a candidate undertaking the course, I'd just have to wait until I completed my two years as a trainer and I'd be done.

As with all things, life got in the way. Ultimately it served to my benefit, but in late summer of 2000, my Dad's health had deteriorated so much that he was given just a short time to live. I needed to be nearer my parents and free to be able to drop everything and be there. This didn't really fit in with the strict timetables of training school, so I asked to be released back to a station.

Inevitably and somewhat understandably, my bosses in training were a little cynical. I came in to training as a Leading Firefighter and now had qualified to go out as a Sub Officer and beyond, with just the results of my Station Officers exam and the few units of the operational Sub Officer development programme standing between me and life in the senior ranks.

Sadly, they didn't deal with this at all well and one or two essentially accused me of making up the situation with my Father, which seeing him with his life ebbing away, really enraged me. I admit I did lose it in the office one day and they had to send in one of the ADO's who was an ex-Navy 'no nonsense' type to calm me down. I went to see our counselling service and once it all became clear, I was released from training. Ironically just at that time, and I swear it wasn't planned, as convenient as it all sounds, there was a vacancy back on my old watch at Poplar for a Sub Officer. So, in September 2000, I left training, under a bit of a cloud, which was a shame and I really regret that, as I enjoyed my time there, and found myself heading back to the Red Watch at F22 Poplar where I'd originally been promoted from in 1994. Sadly, my Dad went into a hospice at that time and passed away on September 12th 2000.

It was good to be back at Poplar, although things had changed. Probably half of the watch remained, but a couple of easy going officers had been through the place over the past few years and from my first night back there, a Sunday night when the Station Officer was off and I was in charge, I saw a few things that I wasn't comfortable with and my challenge of this invited the inevitable "you've changed" commentary. It was all a bit hit and miss for a while, what with my Dad passing away and then the funeral, but by the end of the month, working as 'good cop, bad cop' with the Station Officer, we got things straightened out.

I also got notice that I had passed my Station Officer exam, so I was now eligible for promotion. However, I'd missed the recent interview round before the exam results were published so wasn't able to apply. I'd be waiting a while and probably wouldn't get any acting up to Station Officer, as the results of the promotion interview panel were due, including that of my own Station Officer who was himself acting up.

We carried on through the end of 2000 and into 2001. Throughout all of this; the time in training, exams, going back to a station and my Dad passing away, we'd been trying to move to a new house. Our house was thankfully now out of negative equity and around £20,000 in profit, not a lot for ten years, but it was nice to have your property in the black. We'd sold it once and it turns out the buyer didn't even have right to remain in the UK, let alone the ability to get a mortgage. Then we sold it again to a bloke who was a few years younger than us and wanted to get onto the housing ladder, but his ability to get a mortgage and other issues here and there held the process up.

We'd found a nice house in Hornchurch that belonged to a retired police officer and his wife. They already had a house in Norfolk and wanted to make the move permanently, which they pretty much had done by the end of this ongoing farce. They had brought their family up in this house and had a lot of love and nostalgia for the place. They really liked us, a similar couple but younger, with one working in the emergency services. The lady of the house really wanted us to have it. So, bless her, she held on long after most people would have lost patience, they had the advantage of not being in a forward chain, but by that same token were just waiting for the cash, so could have sold at any time.

So, at the end of January 2001, despite having a real shit 2000, we moved from our first little house in Dagenham, into a proper three-bedroom semi, with a 100ft garden and a garage. We really felt like a couple of grown-ups now; in our 30s, two kids, proper jobs and a nice house. I vowed never to move again, I loved the new place, but it had been massively stressful. All through 2000 the pending move had numbed everything, even my Dad passing away was tinged with issues or arguments around the poxy house buying process. I wanted to punch all of the estate agents involved and even the poor solicitor who had been nothing but patient and professional, but was caught up in the whole negative episode.

When the results of the Station Officer promotion round came out, I was shocked that our own acting Station Officer hadn't got through, he was philosophical though.

"You had the best idea Steve, going for a specialism… you'll be an ADO soon, while I'm still trying to get Station Officer."

The actual moves were scheduled for April, so he used that time to consider his position and when the date came around, he moved over into one of the fire safety departments so he could carry out his specialist role to help his future prospects. We had a new Station Officer come to the Red Watch at Poplar, in fact Blue and White Watch at Poplar also got new Station Officers, as there were so many vacancies. For the first time I had a Station Officer who had joined after me, that felt a bit unusual, but Rob was a nice bloke and we got on well, working together quite a bit in the following years.

I'd had a sniff at a bit of acting up to Station Officer at Dagenham where the guvnor had gone long term sick. That would have been fantastic as Dagenham was a really busy station and was probably only 15 minutes to drive from home. However, someone equally qualified from a nearby station managed to get in just before me.

My own Station Commander at Poplar then told me that "the Station Officer on the White Watch at Bethnal Green has just transferred, you are in the borough and top of the list for 'temporary' so it's yours of you want it."

"Thanks, I'll pull your arm off for that," I replied without hesitation. Back to Bethnal Green, my first station, that would be great. I waited in excited anticipation to hear more. After a few days I got a call from the Borough Commander.

"Hello Guv, thanks for calling me," I said in anticipation.

"Steve, I think you know why I am calling, it's about the temporary Station Officer post at Bethnal Green. As you've been told, it's yours as you are top of the list," he explained.

"Yes Guv, that is great I'd like to…"

"However," he interrupted.

"Paul the Sub Officer on the Blue Watch is about to enter his last year of service. I'd like to offer him the acting up as it will help his pension."

What could I say, Paul had been my Sub Officer when I had joined back in 1987. He was a great officer and a real mentor and father figure to me. Even when I'd tried the patience of others on the watch with my youthful enthusiasm, Paul had always calmed things down and pointed me in the right direction. I didn't hesitate in my answer.

"Guvnor, that is no problem at all, I'm not sure that you are aware, but Paul was my Sub Officer when I joined, I'd happily let him have it for his last year."

"Thank you, Steve, that is really appreciated and I'll make sure Paul knows. You know I will not let you down and as soon as I hear of any other opportunities, I'll be in touch."

In the end, I didn't have to wait long, I think it was less than two weeks. The new Station Officer on the White Watch at Poplar had spent his whole career working in South London, in the old 'E' Division which then became South East Area and then Southern Command. As promotions were now done centrally, area personnel teams didn't always get their local officers to promote within. So, he'd been promoted to the Eastern Command at Poplar. These areas were like different fire brigades back then. In fact, LFB was the largest fire brigade in the country and with the exception of a handful of other large fire brigades such as West Midlands and Greater Manchester, the Area Commands, were in their own right larger than most other British county fire brigades, with the influences of their 'Area Commander' giving each its own distinct personality. Added to this chap having to sit in the hellish queue to get through Blackwall Tunnel every morning, he soon decided enough was enough, pulled a few strings back in the South, where he was obviously well thought of and managed to get posted back 'home'.

Good friends and colleagues, Steve, Rod Vitalis (centre) and Al Perez (right) at an incident in 2018.

So, another phone call from the Borough Commander, this time while I was at home off duty. Offering me the post of temporary Station Officer on the White Watch at Poplar. I of course accepted and started what would become one of the happiest periods of my time in the thirty plus years I eventually served with LFB, where I made some lifelong friends and had some incredibly unique and rewarding experiences.

The White Watch at Poplar had always been a very tight and professional watch. I think it is fair to say, they'd always viewed the Red Watch and Blue

Watch at Poplar as a bit 'quirky', although the Green Watch, like them, were very tight.

I recognised there may be some trepidation with me coming in from the Red Watch with my 'strange ways', so straight after roll call on my first shift there, which was a night duty in May 2001, I called Steve the Sub Officer, John the Leading Firefighter and Matt the senior hand on the watch into the office for a meeting. I acknowledged I'd been a firefighter, temporary/ leading firefighter and latterly the Sub Officer on the Red Watch. Matt also would have remembered me as a little kid visiting the station. But, nonetheless, I was my own man, had my own standards of professionalism and they had no worries. This went down much better than I expected. The watch had real 'old school' leadership with Matt, having been there since he was posted from training school himself as an 18-year-old in 1978. He had mentored many of the younger members of the watch and those who didn't meet his standard soon found somewhere else to ply their trade. If anyone was still sitting at the table with a cuppa after Matt had got up to get on with the routines of the day, they'd hear about it from him, without any soft edges, long before it came to the attention of the officers.

As the senior man, Matt would often be driving the pump ladder and as mess manager he didn't have to do out duties to other stations. So, most of the time he was driving me. We struck up a real friendship both professionally and personally that has lasted until this day. We'd have a good laugh while out and about, share a Marlboro with each other, I even managed to get him to change to Marlboro Lights as the Marlboro Reds that he used to smoke used to blow my lungs out. Occasionally, when we were going out on a visit I'd say, "let's have a drive Matt, you jump in my seat and take it easy" which he'd always oblige and let me have a bit of fun driving.

Me moving over to the Whites came about at the same times as 'one of those spells'. Poplar had always been busy, but generally things had gotten a bit quieter in the late 90s... in fact the last time we'd been really busy across London was back in the summer of 1995. Of course, London is a big city with millions of people. There are always going to be fires and emergencies and there had been some spectacular jobs during that time. But compared to the late 80s and early 90s, the old saying of "nine before twelve and twelve before nine", that was a general reflection of calls on a busy station on a fifteen-hour nightshift, hadn't been heard for a while. But slowly, as the summer of 2001 progressed, I noticed we were going out more and picking up some proper jobs, which as a Station

Officer were all of 'mine' to deal with in terms of command, so I was in my element.

The pump had got called out early into a Sunday night shift in my first few weeks, to smoke issuing on Barking Road, just over the border of our ground, on Plaistow's ground. I was doing a few bits of admin on the station computer so didn't really give it much thought. A few minutes later, the bells went down again, so I knew it was for us and I jumped out of the seat. I had a look at the printer 'Completion of attendance, fire in pub, Barking Road, Plaistow'. As the dutyman tore the slip off the printer and handed it to me, Matt walked into the Watchroom.

"What we got?" he asked.

"I think we've got a job, us and Silvertown have been sent as a completion of attendance to a fire in Barking Road, that is where the pump got called to with Plaistow," I replied. We jumped on the machine and headed east along East India Dock Road towards Canning Town, as I had hundreds if not thousands of times before.

"Foxtrot four five one, at Barking Road, make pumps four," came the radio message as we headed past the Blackwall Tunnel junction. This had the effect of Matt speeding up as bit, which I felt as I braced myself in the seat, zipping up my fire coat and putting my helmet on.

The Royal Oak was a famous pub in Canning Town, a large three storey pub on the corner of Barking Road and Oak Crescent, right at the western end of Barking Road. It had been known most famously as a boxing pub, with a large boxing ring on the first floor above the main bar, which among others, Frank Bruno had trained in as he was working his way up.

Although the name of the pub was not on the call slip, as soon as we came around Canning Town roundabout, I could see the smoke blowing lazily across Barking Road and I knew it had to be the Royal Oak. Matt pulled up just short of the pub and Silvertown's PL pulled past us and parked beyond the pub. I jumped down to see my pump's crew and a crew from Plaistow working feverishly, laying out hose and beginning to tackle the fire. I walked towards the pub and as I looked down Oak Crescent, a lean-to at the back of the pub was well alight. The main door was also open with smoke drifting out and smoke also percolated out of the upper windows. Plaistow's Sub Officer approached me.

"Alright Guv, I made it up because it's going well out the back but it has spread into the main pub and up the stairs, I have a crew inside dealing with the main fire but I need BA teams to get up inside the building."

"OK, thanks Lee," I said, "is there any life risk?"

"No, I'm pretty sure it's clear, it was secured when we got here, the first crew have done a quick search out the back and no one is inside," he replied.

"Is your water supply good? What about an aerial if it's going up the staircase?" I questioned him. I also noticed that Gary; Silvertown's Sub Officer was now on my right shoulder.

"Water is fine, we've set my PL in and the supply is good. I haven't really thought about an aerial at the moment."

"No worries," I said, "we'll see how it goes and call one on if we need one. I'll take it off you mate and make you sector commander one for this side of the building. Gary…" Gary from Silvertown stepped forward.

"You take the front sector for me mate. Can you put a ladder up to the top floor and ventilate to see if we can stop the fire before it gets into the roof? Set your motor in as well and get a jet up the ladder, if we need to get an aerial on, I'll use your machine as the dedicated water supply."

"OK, Steve, leave it with me," he confirmed and ran off back to Barking Road.

"Right Lee, I am now taking over, is your PL the Command Point?" I asked, Lee nodded.

"OK, get your driver to send Station Officer Dudeney is now Incident Commander and I'll get a message formulated."

"OK, I'll let you know when it's sent." Lee left me as I began to compose the message in my head, I walked the length of the pub and saw a jet working over the wall with my one of my pump's crew perched at the top of the wall looking into the yard, where I guessed my leading hand John and the other firefighter were. I also stepped inside the smoky ground floor; the crews in BA had knocked the fire down, but I could hear them working hard ahead of me and felt the heat from the fire, I guessed it had gotten ahead of them up the stairs.

I walked back into Barking Road and saw Silvertown's crew busy pitching a ladder, Matt was helping Silvertown's driver set into another hydrant on Barking Road. I looked up and noticed the smoke percolating from the upper floors was now a bit thicker. I decided to give the BA crew another few minutes to see how it went and then caught Matt on his way back to my machine.

"Matt, can you take a message from me please? From me, at The Royal Oak, Barking Road, a derelict public house of three floors… no scrub that, it steps up from the back… of one, two and three floors, erm… what do you reckon, fifteen metres by ten metres?" Matt nodded in agreement.

"Er… fifty percent of ground floor alight, fifty percent of staircase from ground to second floor alight and say ten, no twenty percent of first and second floors alight, let's get ahead of it… three jets and BA in use."

Matt was scribbling furiously in his own version of shorthand and read the message back to me. He wandered off towards Plaistow's PL to give their driver the message, as I continued to appraise the fire.

Within less than ten minutes, it had become apparent that the fire had taken hold. Dark smoke was now coming from the windows on the top floor, but the situation on the lower floors had been quelled. It was pretty certain that the fire was going to take a hold of the roof and so I decided to make the job up.

"I'm gonna make this six and get an aerial Matt, what do you reckon?" I said to Matt who was keeping a general eye on things outside.

"Yeah, I reckon that's fair enough, we are not getting hold of it are we?" he agreed.

"Lee, is your ALP in the station?" I called on the radio to Plaistow's Sub Officer, who was less than 20ft from me, but wouldn't have heard me above the noise.

I walked over to Plaistow's driver and asked him to send from me to "make pumps six, ALP required." He nodded his understanding and went to send the message.

Back inside the ground floor of the pub, I met John my leading hand, who told me they'd pretty much 'got it' out the back but the fire was going well on the top floor. He'd been up as far as the first floor behind the BA crew, but we'd need more crews to go further up and push ahead. The BA crew came down the stairs and were covered in ash and debris. They said they'd need their jet extended to reach the top floor. I looked back behind me and saw that only two lengths of hose had been used and cursed myself for not picking that up. We'd either have to lay out another jet or turn theirs off to extend it.

I walked back outside to discuss this with Lee and heard a crash of glass and some raised voices offering caution, as two of the windows on the top floor gave way and bright orange flames came mushrooming out of them. I made contact with Gary who told me there was a warren of rooms on the top floor, his crew had been inside, but after opening the door and being met by thick smoke and heat, had withdrawn to the top of the ladder. I made my decision. I was certain it would be through the roof at any moment and we had an aerial on its way, so I got on my radio and asked both sectors to withdraw their crews and move to external firefighting. I did this with a heavy heart and heard a couple of mumbles of discontent. Both Matt and John, my leading hand, offered an alternative view, but I had a feeling. It was a derelict building, there was no life risk and with this being my first decent job as a Station Officer, I didn't want to fuck it up by injuring someone or worse. I had a brief battle with the firefighter inside my head, but my decision was made.

What none of us knew, was that the roof was close boarded. So, the fire got up beyond the ceiling in the top floor, but did not break out as I suspected. Instead the close boarding on the underside of the roof was feeding a severe fire. The fire breaking through would have made my life easier, as we could have hit it from the aerial. Instead it was a slow and painful job of removing the roof tiles and then trying to extinguish the fire in the boarding underneath, which was holding up really well from the outside, despite going like Dante's inferno on the underside.

By this time, my Station Commander, who had come onto the job from his quarters at Shoreditch, had taken command and I was back in the thick of the action with my crews, having taken command of one of the sectors I'd put in place. As the evening went on, and the sun gradually set, we won the battle. Crews were back inside the pub after the aerial had done its work and the job of cutting away and damping down was well under way. My crews seemed as happy as they were dirty and despite my decision to pull them out before the aerial arrived, the feedback I got from my Station Commander and the gruff old DO, who had also come onto the job, wasn't too bad, so all in all my first job as a 'Guvnor' hadn't been a disgrace.

Matt and I jumped back onto the machine to head back to Poplar for a late supper and we shared a 'Marlboro moment' on the drive. Tired, dirty, sweaty but above all happy.

Matt was acting up for a couple of shifts and riding in charge of the pump, as John, the leading hand, was away and Steve, the Sub Officer, was standing by elsewhere on an out duty. Nonetheless, he still remained as mess manager and had cooked us a delicious lasagne for our evening meal. I was sitting at the mess table with my trouser buckle groaning, sipping a coffee whilst my dinner went down. In harmony, we all groaned as the bells went down and scraped back our chairs to head downstairs.

"Pair, fire in flat," the dutyman shouted.

I took the call slip and saw we'd been ordered to a flat fire in Furze Street, just off Devon's Road at the top of our ground. I climbed onto the machine and called across "Ready" to Moose, who was driving me that night. The pump ladder pulled out of the station with the pump right on our tail. I got rigged quickly and braced as we made the sharp turn from East India Dock Road into Upper North Street, there was urgent talk and movement in the rear cab as the Paul and Richard finished getting rigged and struggled into their BA sets.

As we rounded the sharp S-bend on Upper North Street I began to relax, it was around 9pm on a weekday evening, the radio remained silent and any decent fire, with plenty of people still being around, would have attracted multiple calls, the news of which would be coming to us over the radio by now. My stomach lurched as Moose piloted the machine over the hump back bridge at the start of Bow Common Lane and we weaved across to the right as he negotiated the traffic and made the right into Devon's Road.

"Fuck me," Moose voiced my thoughts as we turned the corner, thick smoke was blowing around the lampposts in Devon's Road, apparently coming from the roof of the flats in Furze Street. I was shocked, no further calls at all and yet there was obviously a severe fire in progress.

"Fuck me," I replied, as we swung into Furze Street, there must've been over fifty people standing in the road who all instantly turned towards us and began urgently pointing and shouting. The roof of the older flats to my left in Furze Street wasn't on fire as I thought. Instead a jet of flame was blowing from a first-floor window in the maisonettes on the right. We skidded to a halt, siren still blasting and Moose urgently blasting the road horn to clear people from the road. Somehow, I still can't remember how I became aware, whether shouting from the crowd or someone coming up to the window as I took in the shocking scene in front of me, I managed to determine that a child was trapped inside the flat. Just as Moose edged forward, I picked up the radio.

"Foxtrot two two one priority," I called urgently into the handset.

"Foxtrot two two one go ahead over," came the reply.

"Foxtrot two two one, from Station Officer Dudeney, at Furze Street, make pumps four, persons reported, over."

"Foxtrot two two one, your makes pumps four, persons reported received… further traffic."

"Fuck sakes," I said to myself, I had the door open and was half way out of the machine as the others ran by towards the fire. I could have ignored the radio but with everyone else gone, it may have been critical, so I cursed again and answered.

"Go ahead," I said.

"Foxtrot two two one, we are receiving multiple calls to this fire and information that a child is trapped," the voice said slowly and deliberately in the calm way our Control Officers always speak.

"Yeah, yeah, yeah, I know, I can see…" I said to myself trying to gather what information I could from what was in front of me.

"Received," I shouted back down the radio as I threw the handset and jumped off the machine.

I ran through the parked cars, my crews were working at a fantastic pace; the hose reel was being pulled off at speed as if it were no heavier than a long boot lace, Paul and Richard were starting their sets up and Matt had already disappeared inside the front door. I eyed the flame coming from the window, the room had obviously flashed over, but this was really being pushed out under pressure. I called back over my shoulder to get a jet laid out as well and in among the dozens of frantic people I saw a large woman who was screaming, with others trying to comfort her.

An incredibly sensible teenage girl of about 15 approached me very calmly among the crowd of excitable bystanders.

"There is a girl trapped upstairs, she was in the bath when the fire started and couldn't get out."

I looked at the flat, the BA crew were going in the door with the hose reel.

"I tried to get up the stairs with this boy." I noticed a shocked looking teenage boy behind her.

"But it was too hot and smoky, I heard her screaming though."

"Thank you, that's fantastic, well done! When was this?" I enquired.

"Just as you pulled up," she replied.

"Matt, MATT, are you receiving over?" I barked into my radio, as a blast of steam came out of the window and the flame darkened momentarily.

"Matt, she is in the bath, she was screaming and awake a few seconds ago," I said hopefully, without waiting or expecting a reply from Matt, who I knew would be doing his damnedest with the crew to get to the girl.

My dinner felt very heavy in my stomach and seemed to be stuck in my throat, the adrenalin was pumping so much I could feel my heartbeat even with all of the chaos going on around me. Time stood still and not for the first time in my life, I had incredible clarity and seemed to be absorbing every detail. Someone ran past me with a length of hose, not yet charged, the back-up jet I'd called for, people were jostling and pushing towards the maisonette but there seemed to be an invisible barrier holding them back from getting too close, thankfully, letting my boys get on with their job. Women with wet eyes holding their hands up to their mouths, kids stood there in silence, their little faces transfixed, not really knowing what to make of it all. Men pacing, almost angry at the situation.

Within what was obviously just a few moments, firefighters crowded around the door moved backwards. Matt came running out and behind him Paul and Richard half emerged from the door and half handed and dropped a human into his arms. I ran forward and Matt half carried and half dragged the girl from the door. She was quite a large girl, like the woman who I assumed to be her mother, around 12 years of age. She was soaking wet and naked, so the poor girl was as slippery as an eel. As Matt ran towards me with her, the frantic noise in the crowd reached a crescendo again, but I noticed with some relief that apart from some minor burns on her arms, she was wailing and very much alive.

Someone threw a blanket over the poor girl and her family were clambering over her as we tried to check her over and give her some oxygen. The fuss soon died down, the fire put out and back up machines, as well as the police and ambulance had all turned up and the crowd had now all but disappeared. It transpired that dad had been decorating and had stored some furniture from one of the rooms, as well as the paint and thinners, in a tiny box room at the front. The room was jam packed and an accidental fire has quickly taken hold and rapidly developed with the high fuel content in the room.

Initially the girl in the bath hadn't heard the frantic calls of 'fire' from her family and in the fuss, everyone escaped while she was blissfully unaware. By the time she realised, she panicked and just stayed in the bath, thankfully the rapid growth of the fire broke the window in the room and allowed the majority of heat and poisonous smoke to ventilate, while the flimsy bathroom door and bath water sheltered her. Paul said to me afterwards, "it was going like a train across the landing, I hit it with the hose reel to knock it back, but it flared up again so I had to hit it again. Matt told me there was a door right at the top of the stairs, so I gave the hose reel to Rich and opened the door to see the kid in the bath. I grabbed her a couple of times, but she just kept slipping out of my hands, so in the end I just got her in a bear hug and dragged her out while Rich held the fire back." The BA crew had done really well, they all had, but it was just another fire where a life that surely could've been lost, was saved by the arrival of firefighters just 'doing their job', as they do day in and day out all over the world.

***

Canary Wharf is named after the old dock the original site was built on. The middle of the three docks was to become the biggest urban regeneration in the world when bold plans were announced in 1986 to redevelop the now derelict dockland area into a financial hub to rival the City of London. After a brief spell in the early 90s where it looked like it was going to become a white elephant, by 2001 all of the large office buildings on the site were fully occupied, including The Canary Wharf Tower, at the time the tallest building in Europe. The site was expanding outwards, including several 500ft plus high rise office buildings to the east and south of the original development. This inevitably meant incidents and accidents related to construction became part of life at Poplar.

While I was still on the Red Watch at Poplar, early in 2001, we received a call one night to men trapped in a lift shaft. This was in one of the two new 700ft towers that were being built on the site. When we arrived, Colin the Station Officer and I were met by the night shift construction manager, he explained that two lift engineers were working on a platform inside one of the lift shafts and the platform had failed and fallen down the shaft. They had been there for quite some time, as no one had realised they were missing. We were guided to a bank of lifts in the near completed lobby of the building and ominously opened the doors to check the shaft. I peered, expecting the worst, into the shaft, but found it clear of everything but a bit of tell-tale debris. Using my torch to peer up hundreds of feet, I saw something many storeys above us.

We were told, in common with other very tall buildings that had several banks of lifts, that this particular lift shaft would serve the upper floors and apart from the opening on the ground floor, the next access started at the 16th floor.

We sent a crew up to the 16th to have a look in the shaft and they soon reported back that they could see the platform around 50-60ft, roughly four floors below. After quickly consulting some architects' drawings, we found out that toilets were located on the floors where the shafts did not open onto a lobby. Along with the FRU crew from East Ham, which had also joined us, we made our way up with a host of equipment. With some more deduction from the crews peering down the shaft, we estimated that the platform was around the 12th floor level.

We made our way into the corresponding toilet block, which was also nearing completion and furnished with modern sinks and expensive wall coverings. Mark, the Sub Officer in charge of East Ham's FRU, Del and myself estimated the middle of the shaft from the plans, and using hand tools furiously hacked away until we made a small hole. We shone a torch into the hole and called out to hear some groans coming from within, very close by. The hole was expanded a bit more until a head would fit in and Del looked inside. He came out to tell me that the platform was just below us and two badly injured workmen were on it. I also stuck my head in and saw, to my horror, that the platform, which was essentially a lift 'floor' without the walls and roof, used to allow lift engineers to ride up and down the shaft in the fit out stage, had indeed collapsed from a higher floor and had then wedged itself precariously at the twelfth floor, still around 180ft from the base of the building. On the platform were two barely conscious and badly injured men, who by the look of them, had some significant limb injuries.

This was like a red flag to the attending crews and soon we were working feverishly to expand the whole in the wall to enable us to get to the men. We also had the massive problem of the platform that was wedged, for how long and how well, hanging over us like the sword of Damocles. Would a person stepping on it, movement from the casualties, a breath of wind or even gravity itself play a part at any second and send the platform, casualties and rescuers to an inevitable death, 180ft further down the shaft, at any second. It was instantly decided that the FRU crew would go to the floor below and open up the walls in the toilets on the eleventh floor to do their best to support the platform. This they did, assisted by a band of enthusiastic construction workers, who moved heaven and earth to use anything at hand to make wedges and cribbing for the FRU crew to hold the platform in place, until the rescue had been completed.

As soon as the hole was big enough, which also required the cutting of metal framework holding the wall coverings onto the walls of the shaft, Del, who was

189

front and centre of the rescue effort, squeezed his way through and gingerly dropped himself onto the platform a few feet below. We all held our breath as he did this, but the platform held, he reported that there didn't appear to be any movement and the platform was stuck fast. Del made a quick assessment and reported both men had multiple injuries and severely broken limbs. The next priority was to get a paramedic in with them.

We confirmed that good progress was being made below us in shoring up the platform and next, a brave paramedic with the equipment he needed to make an assessment on the casualties and stabilise them, made his way in. We had now been joined by other medical teams, engineers and an ADO, who had been sent on after Colin had sent back an informative message from the incident. The room was now full up with people trying to help, making plans, removing debris all with the singular purpose of getting these poor men out to safety and proper medical care.

Mark, who was in charge of the FRU, had joined us again and it was essentially three or four of us working to remove the panels and framework, as well as breaking the wall of the shaft apart to make enough room to get the casualties out. This was eventually achieved with an opening probably four-foot-wide and three foot deep. Another paramedic joined the first and Mark joined Del. I turned around at one point to update Colin and the ADO on progress, they both looked ashen as the responsibility of six lives was now on them. A basket stretcher was sent in and the first and less severely injured of the casualties was removed with much cursing and shouting from all involved. As we passed him down, many hands from the emergency services and construction guys helped out, with lots of best wishes passed.

The other guy had injuries that were much worse. As well as the injuries from the fall, the 110lb motor that powered the platform had also fallen on his legs. His limbs were massively injured and he needed a lot of stabilisation and pain relief before he could even be moved, let alone rescued. I took my hat off to the paramedics who were working under extreme pressure in hot, dark and dangerous conditions. After what seemed to be an age and some more expansion of the hole to make his removal from the hole more of a gentle process, he was secured into the basket stretcher, heavily sedated and hopefully no longer aware of his awful plight. Steadily he was lifted and transferred up towards us, treating him like a tray of fragile eggs, we slowly passed him through the hole over our heads and away.

All of a sudden it was over, those of us who had been at the front of the rescue made way for others to tidy up. I was physically and mentally exhausted. As I made my way out of the toilet, I caught my reflection in a large mirror, I was dishevelled and dirty, with plaster and concrete dust stuck to my sweaty head. I gave Colin and the ADO a nod before sneaking away to chug down a bottle of water and have a crafty cigarette, despite the strict no smoking policy on the site. I think I, along with the others, had earned it. Things were soon tidied up and the site, including the wedged platform now held securely in place by a mish-mash of Heath Robinson engineering, was handed back to the construction manager. We had a debrief downstairs and then headed back to Poplar, it was now well past midnight and the mood was sombre.

We heard that thankfully both of the engineers survived. It took months of operations, over twenty for the most severely injured guy, as well as months of rehabilitation to get them mended. But I am not sure about the mental scars of falling down a dark shaft, getting seriously injured and then laying there for ages undiscovered until help arrived. A few years later, I got a call from HQ's press team asking if I'd be prepared to take part in the BBC programme '999', which wanted to do a reconstruction of the accident. I and the others involved agree, but in the end it was dropped, as the casualties, even after a few years, could not bear to relive the night. Wherever those two guys are now, I wish them the best and hope their recovery, in every sense, is now complete.

Several months before this, the Blue Watch at Poplar attended a call where three men had been killed when a crane collapsed into the road one weekend, from the adjoining 700ft tower being built near to where we'd just been. To be fair, Canary Wharf was the biggest construction site in Europe, with thousands of contractors working around the clock. The safety schemes, rules and regulations were very strict and by comparison accident numbers were relatively low. However, with such vast buildings being constructed, accidents and the subsequent rescue or recovery were much more complex than similar occurrences on a building site where a few dozen two storey houses are being built.

Back on the White Watch in the summer of 2001, I was out on the pump ladder having been to a fire inspection at the top of our ground near Bromley by Bow. We'd just turned onto the Blackwall Tunnel approach when the radio burst into life with a call for us to a 'man trapped' on one of the construction areas of Canary Wharf. With a deep sigh, I acknowledged the message and started to get rigged in my fire gear as Martin floored the throttle and I mentally prepared myself for what lie ahead. We got there within a few minutes and were directed onto the site. My pump, with Steve the Sub Officer in charge, had arrived before me as they were in the station when the call came in.

As I climbed down from the machine, I was surprised to see the head of Fire, Health and Safety from the Canary Wharf group and his entourage approaching me. I'd got to know Graham quite well over the past few months through one thing and another. He explained to me what had happened. As I made my way into the building, Steve was coming out, he looked at me, and shook his head. I knew this to mean one thing so took him to one side.

"A crowd of workers were moving some heavy machinery using a fork lift, as they were manoeuvring it, it toppled over and took one of the guys with it," Steve explained.

"Is he…?" I asked.

"Yes, decapitated, it took his head straight off as it fell unfortunately," Steve replied.

"Fucking wonderful," I said glumly, heading inside to take a look for myself. The police were already there and the paramedics obviously didn't have anything to do, so were off. We all got together for a meeting and Graham explained, they had already reported it to the Health and Safety executive, who were en route. The police said it had been deemed a crime scene for investigation purposes, so there wasn't much for us to do.

I suggested they call us back to lift the machinery when the time came and Steve volunteered himself with the pump, along with East Ham's FRU, to go back later in the day, which they did. That afternoon, I spoke with Terri, a reporter at a local newspaper, who we'd dealt with quite a bit, especially as we'd been so busy. There wasn't a great deal to discuss about this latest job, so I directed her to the police for a statement. While on the phone, I confirmed with her our plans for her to come and 'ride' with us for a four-day tour of duty in the next few weeks. As she wanted to do a centre page feature on our work in the local area and the challenges of adapting from what had previously been a run-down area, to the issues around protecting the densest commercial high-rise area in Europe. "Mid-August is always really busy," I assured her. "The kids will be off, the weather fine so we'll have all that to deal with as well."

With everything in place and all the indemnities signed, Terri turned up just before roll call on the first day of her 'tour of duty' with us. Terri, although in this role a photo-journalist, was in fact an award-winning photographer in her own right, having undertaken many projects across the world. We were excited to see what she could produce with her very expensive and professional looking cameras. After a cup of tea and all of the checks, we had a training session where members of the watch were doing their best to pose for the ultimate photo, as Terri was busy snapping away, as well as taking time to speak to all of the watch about how they enjoyed the job and the various challenges we face.

We waited for the first call of the day... and waited... and waited. The weather for August wasn't all that, it was quite cool and overcast, whereas the previous weeks had been pretty warm. I felt that alone had an impact on at least some of the calls we should be getting. Towards the end of the shift, we got our first call of the day. "At last," I thought, "here we go." I was encouraged that it was a call to a fire as well, on an estate behind Commercial Road on Shadwell's ground. We all mounted up and the pump ladder, followed by the pump, turned left out of the station and headed west towards Shadwell's ground.

When we arrived nothing much was happening, I spoke to Shadwell's Sub Officer who told me they couldn't find anything, and he was asking for a verification of the call. It was nothing, so crestfallen, we jumped back onto the trucks and headed back to Poplar for the end of the shift. The second day also brought the same, it started off well, with a call to a fire alarm in a school in Limehouse just after 9:30, but that was it. Nights didn't fare much better; a few fire alarms, rubbish fires and a car fire. All in all, two day shifts and two night shifts delivered no more than a very average day. Nonetheless, the article was a good read and the photographs were excellent, we were all given nice big copies of those we picked as our personal favourites, despite the lack of action shots.

9/11

Several burned out flats in a block in Abbott's Road Poplar.

11 September 2001 was a Red Watch first day duty and a White Watch first night duty. The summer of 2001 had been pretty average and a similar unremarkable day had dawned in London. It was a mixture of sunshine and cloud and not particularly warm, but as the afternoon rolled around it was quite pleasant as the sunny spells were more prolonged and the temperature was in the low 20s. As I was on nights later on, I was pottering around doing nothing much. My wife Joanne was at work in Canary Wharf, Charlotte was at school and little Abigail was with her nan.

People from previous generations always say they remembered exactly where they were when war was declared in 1939 and when President Kennedy was shot in 1963. My generation will always remember where they were around 2pm (London time) on that day when the news broke. I distinctly remember I was in my taxi. Joanne rang me just before 2pm and told me that her brother had rung her to say, "An aeroplane has just flown into the World Trade Centre in New York." He worked as a trader for an American bank and was actually on the phone to someone in Lower Manhattan when the first plane hit, and he overheard all of the confusion as people in nearby buildings just starting their day, reacted.

I turned the radio on to listen to the first reports and quickly stopped and got myself to a television. I'll never forget what I saw, by this time the second jet had hit the towers and my jaw dropped as I watched a loop of the second plane coming in across the harbour, at a speed incongruous with such a low altitude, and disappearing behind the Towers, where it exploded like something any of us had only ever seen in the most far-fetched Hollywood movies.

Over the next hour or so I watched aghast as the day unfolded in New York City, Washington DC and then in a field in Pennsylvania, where the last of the four hijacked jets crashed. I remember the horror and disbelief as the first and then the second tower collapsed. At some point early on, Joanne had called back, she worked in a smaller 15 storey building in Canary Wharf, right next to the 800ft Canary Wharf tower, iconic in as much as it was still at that time the tallest building in the UK. "The Tower has been evacuated," she told me.

"What for?" I asked.

"Not sure, some sort of bomb scare," she explained.

Caught up in the horror and emotion of the events unfolding… "Fuck it," I said, "who knows where this will end, just get yourself home and be with the girls." Even though this was thousands of miles away, I really felt caught up in it and unsure there wasn't going to be further attacks beyond the USA. Canary Wharf after all, was a predominantly US owned site, that had lots of American financial institutions in its many towers.

UK airspace was not closed down, but many flights were cancelled. Life as we know it effectively stopped that afternoon. It seemed everyone had stopped to find a TV somewhere or go home. In the end Canary Wharf was evacuated, along with Lloyds of London and the London Stock Exchange. Constant calls into the fire station remained unanswered and a call to Control informed me that both of Poplar's machines had been ordered to Canary Wharf as a result of the threat and evacuation. I decided to go in early and made my way to the fire station.

I was surprised that a few of my watch had had the same idea. Matt was sitting in the TV room along with a couple of others, as I bound up the stairs to catch up on what had happened. When Red Watch came back, they joined us. Hardly a word was spoken, but it was obvious thousands must have been killed and without a doubt, many of those poor firefighters that had run into the Towers were now lost too. The change of shift at 6pm came around almost unnoticed, we got up briefly to put our gear on the machines and went straight back to the TV. Matt offered a small supper, no one really felt like it, but he went off to make it anyway.

Just after 7pm, the bells went down. We were ordered to a fire in a row of garages just off Blair Street in Poplar. As we passed by on East India Dock Road, I looked down to my left onto the estate and saw a car burning inside one of a row of derelict garages. We turned left into Abbotts Road and a sharp left again into Blair Street to double back towards the fire. The pump's crews quickly made an attack on the fire, a few little Bangladeshi kids were hanging around and laughing at us putting the fire out. Feelings were running high anyway, especially among us firefighters and the link was already all over the news, with Islamic terrorists likely to be responsible.

I am not proud to say I added two and two and came up with five, thinking these kids were somehow a little too happy for my liking, with everything that had been going on. I muttered this to one or two others who nodded in angry agreement. The likelihood is, they were just kids and maybe didn't even know what had gone on, or the impact of it. But when one of the older kids said something about New York, it got quite lively for a moment, until a local police officer who was in attendance moved the kids away and out of the area before someone said something that we'd all regret.

On the way back to the station, the roads were amazingly quiet and very few people were on the usually busy streets of Poplar. Straight back to the TV, with a couple of pizza's shared around and eaten without the usual energy, we watched without a break for the rest of the evening. One of the last things was the collapse of No7 World Trade Centre around eight hours after the initial attack. Feeling sick to the pit of my stomach, drained and emotional, I dragged myself off to bed sometime after midnight when I couldn't face seeing the re-runs of the attacks any longer. As I lay in my bed, tears rolled down my face for the loss of so many people in a city just like ours, three thousand miles across the Atlantic, and firefighters who went to work just like we did and would never go home again.

"I think we should go over there," I said around the mess table, five days later when White Watch returned for their first day duty of the next week. A number of others agreed and on that morning, it was discussed, debated and decided with arrangement hastily made. I'd been in touch with a Sub Officer from New Malden, who was raising money for the families of the FDNY firefighters. 343 of them were either confirmed dead or missing presumed dead at that stage. We'd also made contact with the Red Watch at Chelsea, who had recently been to NYC, where they had run up the stairs of the World Trade Centre to raise money for charity. They had a few contacts who may be useful for us in the next few weeks.

The idea took off like a penny rocket, we hadn't even properly discussed it with our families. But the die was cast, the feelings were so strong as a watch we felt we needed to do something. The idea was we'd go to the city, hopefully help out with the recovery and do our best to find a way to raise money for the families of the firefighters. We had some money put away in an account as a watch and as soon as flights to the US were opened up again, we were going to go. That date coincided nicely with the end of our tour of duty, so on the morning of 21st September 2001, ten days after the 9/11 attacks, Beaker, Matt, Steve and I got relieved early by members of the Blue Watch and hailed a cab right outside of the fire station where the driver nearly fell off his seat when we said, "Heathrow Terminal three please mate."

Around eleven hours later, the four of us walked out of the terminal at JFK, where three of the four of us lit up a much-needed cigarette. It was a bright autumn afternoon and we squinted in the sun, having no idea who we were looking for, just knowing that a retired New York City fireman called Richie Smith, who had recently visited the London Fire Brigade, was going to meet us. Between us, we debated how we'd recognise him, where we'd end up and various other issues. Despite a lot of planning, we had essentially just got our tickets and got on an aeroplane to a city that had just suffered the most devastating terror attack in living memory.

After a short time, a slightly battered metallic blue Chevy van pulled alongside us, its V8 burbling as it drew to a halt. A grey-haired guy with glasses that made his eyes look a little bigger and a broad smile, stuck his head through the window. We all had dark blue LFB T shirts on with jeans so I guess we somehow looked semi-uniformed.

"Are you guys from London Fire Brigade?"

"Yes, yes we are mate… are you Richie?"

"Yes, I am, pleased to meet you," came the reply as Richie stepped out of the van. Naturally with suspicions so high, he asked to see our fire brigade ID, which we all produced, and then warm introductions were made.

We got into the van, it was dated but plush inside, with large crushed velvet captain style seats in a similar light blue to the outside of the van. As we made our way out of JFK towards the city, we were anxious and excited, and the story of Richie's 9/11 was told.

Richie had become a fireman in the FDNY in the late 1970s and was posted to Ladder 103, a busy 'truck' company in one of the most run-down areas of Brooklyn at that time. Straight away we felt a kin-ship, as we all knew places like Brooklyn and The Bronx were similar to inner city areas where we served like Poplar, Bethnal Green, Brixton, Hammersmith and so on.

In the late 80s Richie had been involved in a project to set up a hazardous materials response in FDNY and the result was a unit called 'Hazmat 1' based at a firehouse in Maspeth in Queens, to the north east of Manhattan. This was based with Engine Company 288, a regular fire company. In 1998, FDNY established a number of specialist squad companies. They essentially remained a local engine company for their area, but had enhanced equipment and training as a half-way house between an engine company and a heavy rescue company. Thus, Engine Company 288 had become Squad 288, which meant both were under the responsibility of 'Special Operations Command'. As such, although the firehouse in Maspeth was several miles away from the World Trade Centre, when the first call came in to Fire Alarm Box 8087, World Trade Centre, Vesey Street and Church Street Manhattan, both trucks from that firehouse were sent.

Unlike LFB, there are no dedicated watches in FDNY. Each Company has a number of firefighters and officers, each with a unique 'position number' and through a process that I never managed to figure out, different 'numbers' work with other different 'numbers' every day. Therefore, all of the firefighters and officers work together at some point. Add this to a much less formal system of how the rotas are managed, many swap shifts with each other to work 24's, by combining a day and night, allowing more time off. So, as the call came in, with much less formality around who is riding what truck at what time, and due to the obvious serious nature of the call, both oncoming and off going firefighters squeezed themselves onto the fire engines responding to the call from across the city.

In Maspeth, both Squad 288 and Hazmat 1 responded on the initial call with a total of 19 firefighters, much higher than the usual 11 or 12 that would be riding. Sadly, all of those responding firefighters from Richie's firehouse were killed when the Towers collapsed. This was the highest loss from a single firehouse in FDNY on the day.

Richie's own story was equally tragic, as we listened open mouthed on our way into the city. With amazing candour, which was inevitably due to some sort of shock, Richie explained that he had been the 'senior man' at the firehouse, with over twenty three years' service. Unbelievably, he had retired just three days before 9/11 on September 8th 2001. Since then, with a great feeling of loyalty to his former colleagues, and no doubt terrible survivor's guilt, Richie had been down to the site, which the media had now named 'Ground Zero', but to those in FDNY was simply 'the Pile', every day since. Today being the first time he hadn't been there in the ten days since the tragedy.

He told us we were going to his firehouse and that this evening was going to be the first time the families would visit since the tragedy, and there was to be a vigil with the local community. I felt my stomach somersault at the prospect, but nonetheless, I thought it appropriate we join in with this to show our respects to those at the Maspeth firehouse, as one of their former members had taken his time to meet us.

The quarters of Squad 288 and Hazmat 1 is next to the Long Island Expressway, the main highway that leads from the eastern end of Long Island out by The Hamptons, right into the outer suburbs of New York City, thorough Queens and into the Queens Midtown Tunnel, ending up on 42nd Street in Manhattan. The firehouse in Maspeth is on an avenue next to the Expressway and as this district is slightly elevated, it looks out at Manhattan roughly 5 miles away. As we left the Expressway and crossed it on 69th Street, I saw for the first time Manhattan ahead of me. Ominously to the south of the vista was a hazy cloud of white smoke still rising from the site of the World Trade Centre.

This view looked somehow familiar to me, I quickly realised it was very similar to the view towards central London as you come down onto the A12 from the Green Man roundabout in Leytonstone, the slight elevation, all of the taller buildings four of five miles into the distance and the high walls of the road where it was dug into the land. A quick left off 69th Street and we were outside the firehouse. Gingerly we got out of the van, there were a few firefighters who met us, all looking very sad. One of them, probably similar in age to myself at the time in his early thirties, came over to us, shook our hands and hugged us, breaking into tears as he did. He thanked us for coming from London and said it helped so much to know the wider world was with them. Abashed, we all dismissed his thanks as they were the ones going through hell, it was the very least we could do.

We were introduced to all of the crew and all of us felt very humbled and a little out of place, almost as if we were invading their space at such an awful time. We looked at the make shift memorial at the front of the firehouse, swollen with flowers, messages, dozens of candles and images of the nineteen firefighters from this one firehouse that had been lost, just a few days before. It was almost overwhelming as I tried to come to terms with that number alone, let alone the other 324 missing and now presumed dead. Richie told us the start time of the memorial, so awkwardly, we got our suitcases from the van and went into their locker room to change into our undress uniform.

We stood outside for near on an hour as the time for the memorial approached. Slowly, people arrived and stood with us, outside the firehouse, across the street in a small park area next to the Expressway. Retired firemen, members of the local community and saddest of all, eventually, the families. Wives, with their children, supported by other family members. Some, standing tall and proud, others absolutely shattered. I particularly remember one car pulling up, a slim woman with long blonde hair got out, she was wearing dark glasses and oversized, her husband's uniform jacket. She had several sad looking children with her and as she got out of the car and met eyes with a handful of the surviving firefighters, she half collapsed and let out a primal howl of despair.

I felt my eyes stinging with tears and tried to take a deep breath which manifested itself into more of a sob. At that moment, I could have turned my back on this horror in front of me, gone straight back to the airport and gone back to my normal life in London. I'd only left London fifteen hours previously, but now felt desperately homesick and wanted to hug my own family very tightly at that moment. That evening still ranks as one of the saddest experiences of my life.

Everyone lined up at the base of a US flag in the small park area next to the station. We made our way to the back and stood there, as the service begun with a silence, punctuated by sobs from members of the families. The thought that this would be repeated at dozens of firehouses across the city and again in the many communities where the firefighters lived in the coming days weeks and months, was numbing. I couldn't bear to think about this happening tenfold when considering the thousands that were now missing from the attack.

The service was very dignified, with local councillors, people from the community and church representatives all taking part and making speeches or giving blessings to those lost. Sadly, I doubted this would happen in such a way back in London. Afterwards, emotions calmed somewhat, the children played near the firehouse and people talked in small groups. We spoke to some of the families, who were very appreciative of our attendance, leaving us all humbled at how they were dealing with the tragedy.

After a while, Richie decided we should eat. It dawned on me I hadn't eaten for hours and my stomach was now calling urgently for some food. We jumped back into the van and drove for ten minutes or so through very 'New York' neighbourhoods, similar to what we'd seen thousands of times over the years on various TV shows. We parked up in a McDonalds car park, I didn't fancy this, but it had been a long day so I wasn't going to complain. I looked around and apparently, we were on Myrtle Avenue in Glendale, Brooklyn.

We followed Richie away from the McDonalds and across the street where we walked up to a building on a sharp corner, painted white with black beams and a sign with Fraktur lettering, bordered by US and German flags either side. I deciphered the sign to read Zum Stammtich. Obviously, we were going to a German restaurant. Richie got us a table and lots of people stopped and looked up as we walked in, wearing our British undress fire uniforms. New Yorkers being New Yorkers, questions soon started flying and Richie, as an equally unabashed New Yorker, was soon announcing that we were London firefighters in town to "help with the recovery." Again, we were left embarrassed as a number of people came up to greet us and offer us drinks. It was massively appreciated but difficult as we had done nothing apart from get on an aeroplane.

After a fantastic meal, a few beers and a healthy drink from the potentially messy 'boot full of beer', we left the restaurant amid more handshakes and back slaps, and Richie decided we should have a tour of Manhattan. It was well after 9pm by now, gone 2am London time and we'd been awake for 20 hours, but we were not going to refuse Richie's hospitality.

For the first time in my life, but under such tragic circumstances, we began a night time tour of Manhattan. Through the Queen's Midtown tunnel, emerging into 42nd Street and onto the bright lights of Times Square. It was magnificent, but we all felt a little uncomfortable. Richie seemed to be enjoying showing us around and if it was keeping his mind off the past days, then it was all good. That night, we never turned south and headed down towards Lower Manhattan and the WTC site, instead working our way gradually north.

At some point, we stopped in a small side turning, we got out of the van and there was a park in front of us with the hum of heavy traffic coming from within it. We walked behind Richie and found ourselves in a narrow stretch of park, with a main road running behind it and slightly below us. A large monument loomed and as we walked around the front of it, Richie explained it was the fireman's memorial on Riverside Drive at West 100th Street. The site of the annual FDNY firefighters memorial service. The annual service was held in October every year, each one of us pondered what it would be like at the ceremony this year, which was due in the next few weeks.

After a period of time, where we stood there lost in our thoughts again, trying to contemplate the severity of this loss if it were within London, Richie broke the silence and we walked back to the van. We jumped back in and continued our tour of Upper Manhattan. Eventually Richie piped up.

"Right, I need to get some sleep, this will do you guys, I know the boss here."

We pulled up way after midnight at a brutal slab of a structure with a large red double door, a fire station.

"Engine 37, Ladder 40... the heart of Harlem," Richie said to no one in particular and rapped on the side door.

A firefighter opened the door, Richie said a few words and the firefighter looked over Richie's shoulder at us stood by the van and the pair of them disappeared inside. Within a minute or so, Richie came back out and told us to get our stuff from the van.

"You'll be staying here."

We got our stuff and walked into the station with an engine and a ladder truck parked closely together in the bay. Like a London fire station, the place smelt of diesel, smoke and rubber. We walked to the back of the bay and into a large kitchen area where a host of firefighters, dressed variously in a range of t-shirts from fire companies in and around New York, including some from out of town, cut down shorts and boots, were assembled and greeted us warmly. It appeared the uniform in this fire station was comfortable and personal. We were met by a large middle-aged man dressed in a blue shirt and dark blue trousers.

He introduced himself as Ron, the Captain of the firehouse. We all shook his hand and introduced ourselves to his crews. We spent the next hour or so generally talking about the attacks, the losses and differences between FDNY and LFB. I got talking to one fella in his late 20s who had introduced himself as Chris Mandeville. I wasn't to know it, but Chris and I were to form a lifelong friendship and we still see each other and talk to this very day.

At around 3am, the group broke up, it was now around 8am in London, it seemed we'd been awake forever and my head was swimming trying to take it all in. Some beds were hastily assembled for us in a gym on the top floor of the station and as soon as I laid down, I fell into a deep sleep.

The fire station remained quiet overnight… at least if they did go out, I have no recollection of it. I woke around 8am after a short but deep sleep to find Matt sitting on the edge of his bed and Steve buried in his suitcase. Beaker was still an unmoving lump under his blankets. We all agreed to get up, get showered and to go downstairs as a group. When we did, a handful of the guys from earlier were still around, but the informal shift change was underway, with off duty firefighters arriving before change of shift and gradually replacing the on-duty crews one by one. We did some introductions again and were told we'd be staying here for the duration. After a quick breakfast of bagels, scrambled egg and strong coffee, we were directed to the neatest subway station, and dressed in a semi uniform of jeans and blue LFB t-shirts, we made our way to the station to get on the "four train"—the Lexington Avenue Express, down towards Canal Street, where we could walk south towards the WTC site. Somewhat worried about walking through the middle of Harlem, we raised our concerns and asked if we'd be OK. "There's four of ya's… you're bulletproof," came the reply. I guess we were reassured, but the term 'bulletproof' didn't sit easy with me.

We came up out of the station on Canal Street at the junction with Lafayette Street, where Little Italy meets Chinatown. As we arrived at street level every single image of Manhattan I had in my mind was instantly visually satisfied. I'd been here a million times, from watching everything on TV from music videos to mafia gangster movies, to episodes of Kojak. It was the first time we'd seen Lower Manhattan in daylight on foot, it did not disappoint, although it was strangely quieter than I'd imagined. As we stood there taking in the surroundings, a blip from a siren caught my attention and a fleet of three large black SUV's drove across the junction heading south.

We orientated ourselves with a fold up paper map we'd bought – Google Maps and smartphones were still a few of years away – and headed south then west, south then west, as if walking down a giant staircase on its side. Down

Lafayette, right into Franklin, left into Broadway, right into Worth Street, looking up at a strange light brown granite faced building over 500ft tall but without a single window in it. Walking down the side we discovered it was the old AT&T telephone exchange building.

We walked on down Church Street towards the WTC site but could get no further than Park Place, which had tall white hoardings up across the street. Looking at the map again, we headed east and found ourselves out on Broadway, opposite City Hall and its park, leading to a point where Broadway meets Park Row. We quickly realised this is where one of the iconic pieces of news footage from the events of the 11th was filmed, where an amateur cameraman was filming the blazing North Tower as the South Tower exploded from the left of the screen, when the second plane hit.

I felt a shudder go down my spine and a strange feeling of light-headedness, as if I wasn't really there. Matt pointed up at the buildings on Park Row, those that were, I guess, privately owned were still covered in a grey dust. But just eleven days after the attacks, the roads, pavements and public buildings had already been cleaned up. This was emphasised dramatically by the flower beds in City Hall park, that had been turned over and watered, with bright green leaves and colourful flowers on show. I wondered to myself if the same attention to detail and defiant 'life goes on' statement would have been made in London if the same terrible event had befallen our city. I'd like to think so.

Seemingly lost in a crowd of people getting on with life, we headed north up Broadway and stopped at a Duane Reede pharmacy on the corner of Duane Street and Broadway. Someone noticed a fire station just a hundred yards or so down on the left along Duane Street, so we headed towards it. It was a grand looking stone building, with three arched bay doors, all of which were open. What we did not realise at that time, is that this was the firehouse where the French filmmakers, the Naudet brothers, were making a documentary film about a probationary firefighter during the summer of 2001, and were out with the crews on a call to a gas leak in Church Street when the first plane flew loudly overhead and hit the North Tower. As the morning unfolded, they followed the firefighters to the WTC and filmed the whole event, including the collapse of the Towers which was shown on the now infamous documentary '9/11'.

We edged ourselves into the bay before a voice from the back of the bay called out in a broad New York accent, "Can I help you guys?" Before we could say much, a firefighter headed towards us and noting our t-Shirts first said, "London Fire Brigade… what the hell?"

We were ushered into a large kitchen at the back of the firehouse where we met with the Captain and the rest of the crew. Despite us not wishing to impose, we were treated like long lost brothers and plied with hot coffee, bagels and donuts.

We heard their stories of the day, amazingly everyone from this firehouse, among the first who responded to the incident, made it back from both collapses. We swapped stories of our life in LFB, how the wider world was reacting to the events of 9/11 and spoke about what help we could offer. After a couple of hours, we left them to get on with their day and resolved, although we couldn't help down at 'Ground Zero', we could coordinate the efforts of firefighters in London to raise money for the survivors and families from FDNY.

We got back onto Broadway and as the morning progressed, we worked our way further north. Through Soho towards Union Square Park where we spent half an hour or so looking at the memorials that had been set up. Brightly coloured flags from around the world, the candles and messages left, in sympathy or by people looking for loved ones missing from the day of the attack. Posters with photos of young and old in previous happier times. We continued further north, past the Flatiron building at 23rd Street and then we went off slightly right up 5th Avenue, straining our necks at the base of the Empire State Building.

We had our instructions from Richie to get ourselves to "Penn Station" where we had to catch the "Long Island Railroad to Baldwin, where I'll meet ya at five o'clock." So we stopped off at a WWE Wrestling themed restaurant in Times Square for a late lunch of burgers and a couple of bottles of beer before heading to the station.

The LIRR train pulled out of the station and spent a few minutes in a dark tunnel as it made its way out of Manhattan and under the East River. It emerged noisily from the tunnel amid a mass of tracks and railway sidings in Queens and worked its way east, getting more and more suburban as we headed through stations called Forest Hills, Kew Gardens and Jamaica, out of the city itself and into small suburban towns past Rockville Centre, and then to our stop, which the conductor announced loudly with an exaggerated "BAAALDWIN!"

Richie met us at the station, which was above and alongside a wide main road which cut the town in half. We went for a couple of beers to 'warm us up' and then made our way to his house which was a large detached white and green house on a big corner plot, set on a well-manicured green. Very typical of the types of suburban houses we'd seen on TV and in films and as an 'average' house, much larger than what we lived in back in the UK and nowhere near as expensive. The house, although one of only a few dozen on the small side street, had one of those inexplicable four figure door numbers like 1897, which gave the incorrect impression the street was several miles long.

We were ushered in and met with Richie's wife Trish and his four sons, and settled into the garden where a barbeque was glowing. We sat down and waited for Richie and Trish's neighbours who had all been invited over to meet the 'London firemen'. As each arrived, they proudly brought with them bottles of various warm English ale's which they had assumed was our staple drink. We gratefully worked our way through them, each throwing each other a sideways glance, silently begging for a few bottles of ice-cold Budweiser to wash down our food.

We had a great evening in great company, the message was the same; they felt loved and grateful that their 'old allies' from the UK were thinking of them at such an awful time and that we had made our way over to New York to support them. Although 20 miles out of Manhattan and approximately 7 miles from the NYC border between Queens and Nassau County, this was the type of town where many people who worked in the city lived. Teachers, cops, fireman, transit workers had made their homes in towns like Baldwin, so had been greatly affected by the events of 9/11.

On Sunday we attended a large organised memorial event at the Yankee Stadium. 15,000 people attended, many of whom were the families of those missing. It was hosted by Oprah Winfrey, with Mayor Rudi Giuliani making an emotional speech, followed by a very rousing speech by Admiral Robert Nutter, Commander-in-Chief of the US Navy's Atlantic fleet, who declared, "You picked on the wrong city. You picked on the wrong country."

Richie then took us down to the WTC site. Although security had been really beefed up following the desperate rescue efforts of the first few days, Richie smooth talked a cop and we managed to get into the outer cordon. We walked down towards the site and my eyes couldn't take in what I was seeing. I had seen piles of rubble before, but as we stood there on the west side highway about 100 yards from the inner cordon, the pile of rubble rose up over 100ft in height ahead of us. 100ft of twisted smouldering steel a couple of hundred yards long. I remember likening it to a pile of rubble as tall and as vast as standing outside of a great big stadium. If you stand along the road from a large football stadium, such as Wembley for example, the bulk of the structure takes up most of your vision. This is exactly what the pile of rubble was like. Almost everything within our field of view from the left to the middle of that road was a pile of rubble.

As we walked away, I remember I kept turning back every few steps to see it again as my mind couldn't take it in. It seemed the rubble pile was insurmountable, excavators digging into it and tipper trucks lining up to remove the rubble seeming like small toys next to it. We spent an hour or so talking to some of the many people down at the site. Construction workers, soldiers, Red Cross volunteers, priests and ministers, as well as many police and firefighters.

The following morning, we were back at the airport after a whirlwind and highly emotional few days in New York City. As a lover of cities and tall buildings I ached for the city and its people, as well have having a deep regret that the many times I'd promised myself a trip to New York and to the World Trade Centre in particular in my 33 years, I'd always put it off, and my first trip there was under such awful circumstances. As we boarded the British Airways Boeing 747 we were asked by a stewardess who saw our uniforms if we had been "helping out"; we replied that we didn't get to assist on the site, but that we'd been visiting fire stations and trying to get some contacts for fundraising. After a brief wait, she beckoned, "come with me." We turned left instead of turning right through the door and they very kindly gave us four wonderful business class seats for our flight back home. We were grinning like excited schoolboys at the plushness of it all, but after an exhausting few days, we welcomed the lovely seats that turned into beds and managed to catch up on some much-needed sleep.

We arrived back in London late on Monday evening and were met by Paul, one of the lads on our watch who desperately wanted to come with us, but whose wife was in the last stages of her pregnancy so couldn't risk it. We went straight to Poplar fire station, as we were due back on duty at 9am Tuesday. After a fitful sleep I got up and showered and we all met up in the office where our own watch were drifting in, and alongside the Blue watch, who were about to go off, we relayed the story of our four days over there and answered a hundred questions.

As we got back on duty, as well as dealing with everything the day brought us, we started making calls and other connections to start the fundraising efforts. It got very political very quickly; the Fire Services National Benevolent Fund were excellent and their main fundraiser made contact and gave us some great advice. But the London Fire Brigade itself not so. As Station Officer for the watch, I was summoned to area HQ at Stratford for a gentle congratulations, which subtly masked a bollocking, as a "well done… you should have asked our permission, but we'd have refused, but as it went off OK it's all good etc.…"

More and more people were trying to get involved, the foundations of future empires were being built in front of our very eyes, and off our backs. After a spirited debate around the mess table one night, we decided we'd go it alone, whilst still maintaining co-operation with the larger events, but raise our own money and donate it to the first firehouse we visited that had lost so many, Richie Smith's old place, Squad 288 and Hazmat1 in Queens.

We had Canary Wharf on our doorstep, which housed lots of American financial companies, including Cantor Fitzgerald, who's HQ was inside the North Tower and who lost over 650 members of staff in the attacks. We decided to approach Canary Wharf Management, the landlord, to ask if we could collect over there. Once again letters were written, and we got permission to collect on a couple of dates at lunchtime, when we were off duty. With some very generous donations and great local publicity, we managed to raise over £9,000 which worked out at around $14,000 for the families at the firehouse.

For one reason or another, no one else could get back to NYC before Christmas, so I decided I'd go back over there to present the cheque to the firehouse. I came up with the insane idea of taking my eldest daughter Charlotte with me for the trip, which Joanne, my wife, agreed to. I say eldest, she's an adult now, but at the time she was just seven years old. The school were only too pleased to accommodate, so a week before Christmas 2001, Charlotte and I flew to New York, where Richie Smith insisted on putting us up for the three days. There was lots of manic Christmassy sightseeing, 'Home Alone 2 – Lost in New York' kept rattling around in my head, underlined by the searing "Stephen, look after her," parting words of Joanne. But it was all good, apart from one bizarre episode at the Rockefeller Centre where Charlotte, having never ice skated before, threw a tantrum due to the fact that she couldn't make her debut right there and then, me with visions of my tiny daughter with a broken leg and "Stephen, look after her" echoing in my ears. Charlotte was an absolute angel and brought a welcome smile and lots of "Hello Sweetie" greetings wherever we went.

Most importantly Richie took me back to Squad 288 and Hazmat 1 where I was proud to handover the cheque to the two Captains and also a mounted axe from all of us at Poplar fire station.

Senior Officer

Following the decision by the Labour Government to devolve a more formal level of governance to London in the late 90s, a new 'Greater London Authority' was created to be run by an elected mayor. Ken Livingstone, the former leader of the Greater London Council, which was disbanded under the Conservative Government in 1986, was elected Mayor in 2000. He was responsible for transport, policing and fire and civil defence in London.

There was also to be more locally devolved borough accountability. So, the 31 boroughs and two City boroughs; the City of London and City of Westminster, all of which made up Greater London, also came together in a more pan London unified set up. The police lost their Divisions and the Chief Superintendents became Borough Commanders for 32 of the boroughs, the City of London historically having its own police force.

Inevitably the London Fire Brigade followed on and the same was afforded to us. But of course, we were a much smaller organisation and the setting up of 33 Borough Commands by LFB was going to be the way ahead for 2002, despite the misgivings of many. The three large area commands were to disappear overnight, a mistake that was realised and thankfully re-adopted a few years later. So overnight on 31st March 2002, these three large commands, which as I'd already said were bigger in their own right than most UK fire brigades, simply disappeared and all of the admin, training and fire safety staff were flung far and wide into 'Borough Teams'.

At the end of 2001 a promotion round for Assistant Divisional Officers (ADO) was advertised. I was more than happy with my job as Station Officer on the White Watch at Poplar, but was encouraged to go for it, especially as I was now 'qualified' because of the new rules about having done a specialism. I wasn't keen, as many experienced Station Officers, a lot of whom I'd learned from, were barred from this promotion because they hadn't done a specialism.

Nonetheless not willing to burn bridges, I put in an application and went through the process without putting in too much effort.

Unfortunately, because so many existing Station Officers could not apply, numbers were quite low and despite not putting in too much effort, I didn't do as badly as expected. I wasn't promotable but had got to a point where I was able to undertake temporary promotion to ADO if a vacancy occurred. Yet again, the numbers game played in my favour... or not as I felt. So few had been promoted that there was actually temporary promotion available from day one.

I got a phone call early in March 2002 offering me temporary ADO as Station Commander at Millwall fire station, just south of Poplar, covering the bottom half of the Isle of Dogs. As I said, I loved being at Poplar as White Watch Station Officer, but I was still in a position of not wanting to burn any bridges and wasn't really enjoying driving a taxi on my days off. The change to ADO meant I'd work a much longer shift, 72 hours on call each week, but because I lived within the LFB area, I could run from home of a night. I'd no longer be on a Watch, riding the fire engines, but based at the station and called out to larger incidents to monitor or take command, using a car fitted with blue lights a siren and radio to get to the incidents.

After much debate at home and at work I decided I'd give it ago. So, at 9am on Monday 1ˢᵗ April 2002, April Fool's Day and Easter Monday, I reported to an almost empty NE Area HQ, that had effectively been disbanded at midnight nine hours before. I was met by an older Staff Station Officer, more interested in the fact he had drawn a short straw and was working on a pleasant Easter Monday than he was me. He handed me a pager and a set of keys to an old Vauxhall Astra pool car.

I made my way through the light Easter traffic from Stratford to Millwall with a few possessions in the car and went up to my office on the third floor of the station. The Watch on duty were equally as disinterested as the Staff Station Officer, for the same reasons, so I sat glumly in my office not having a clue as to what I should be doing, willing the pager to go off to send me to a fire where I'd at least feel I had some purpose.

No calls came on the first day, the Tuesday was a bit better as everyone was back from the Easter break. I met up with my Borough Commander who outlined some of what I'd be required to do, and also took some advice from other Station Commanders in the Borough, including Glenn who'd been my Station Commander at Poplar until yesterday. Nevertheless, the sudden disappearance of the Area Commands was causing massive confusion, having been well established and efficiently run before. The new Borough Commanders, who were previously Group Commanders under the stewardship of the Area Commander and his team, were meant to find their way with a small team who had also had change forced upon them, without the support of the Mothership.

In later years as an experienced and wizened senior officer, I'd always give an analogy to new Station Commanders who came to work for me.

"Moving up to the senior ranks from Station Officer is a little like the change from primary school to secondary school. One minute, you are in a nice comfortable environment, top of the tree, king or queen of the playground with all the little kids looking up to you, everyone knows you and respects you. The next minute you are the new kid in big school. Everyone is more senior, has their position in the hierarchy and is comfortable but you are the little one in the corner trying hard not to get noticed lest someone should shout at you or worse, for not saying, doing or being in the right place at the right time."

I'd go on, "You won't have a clue what you are doing for a few weeks and then suddenly you'll think you have it sussed. You'll be in a false state of security, but after a few months the reality will hit you and you'll realise you are just tinkering at the edges and the full scope of what you need to do will horrify you. Complaints, discipline, budgets, multiple borough references and meetings of committees you didn't even know existed. But stick with it, it takes about a year, but then if you have lasted that long, you'll get to grips with it and it'll become second nature."

"Oh, one more thing. Don't piss me off or try to pull the wool over my eyes, I've read the book many times over and tried every trick in it, so I'll find out. I'll look after you and help you but if you don't pull your weight it makes my life difficult, which will come back your way in a much larger dose... good luck!"

The first call eventually came, it was a call on a Saturday afternoon to a boat alight on the River Thames at Limehouse, on Poplar's ground. I took the details from Control, ran downstairs and got into my car, put the blue light on the roof and sped off along Westferry Road towards Limehouse.

The Green Watch were on duty and my old colleague, the Green Watch Station Officer, was in charge. He was one who had fallen foul of the new promotions, in fact he'd been the Green Watch Station Officer for many years since I was a firefighter myself on the Red Watch. He was less than impressed that I'd suddenly arrived to 'monitor' him, but disguised it well with a pleasant greeting and a sarcastic "hello Guvnor" as I walked up him. In the end it was nothing, a badly running engine on the boat had kicked out a load of black smoke so we were stood down.

Over the next few weeks I'd pick up the odd shout here and there but nothing major came my way until I'd been doing the job for about 9 weeks. I'd had a few shouts from home of a night, which in those early days saw the whole family get up with the excitement. I remember looking in my mirror as I pulled off the drive and seeing Charlotte and Abigail's excited little faces as they waved at me through the window, bathed in blue light from the roof beacons.

The pager buzzed across the beside cabinet on vibrate which always woke me up with a start, just a second or two before the bleeping started. I blinked the sleep from my eyes and saw the first traces of daylight coming through the window. I concentrated my view and read the pager; Mob (for mobilise) four pump fire in scrapyard with cylinders involved, Chequers Lane, Dagenham.

I called into Control and took the details, I got dressed quickly and went out to the car, driving down the road the radio blared to life and Dagenham made pumps six. I then realised I would have to take command and this would be my first incident as an ADO, as Incident Commander. As I drove along Rainham Road in Dagenham I looked to my left and there was an ominous black angry smoke plume in the sky. There had been a number of scrap yard fires in Chequers Lane recently, all of which had escalated to quite large proportions. I had no doubt by the look of the smoke plume this would be the same.

I parked up along Chequers Lane and could see a hive of activity ahead of me. Worryingly, a couple of fire engines were being withdrawn back up the road and the smoke plume was fast moving and banking low across the road. I got rigged in my fire kit and was approached by John, Dagenham's White Watch Station Officer.

He greeted me and explained that the fire had started in one scrapyard and had already involved some volatile gas cylinders, meaning his crews were unable to approach closely, so the fire had already taken a hold. It had now spread to the scrapyard that bordered Chequers Lane, which also had lots of gas cylinders. He said his crews had removed a few of them but some 'popping and banging' had led him to decide to withdraw his crews and set up a defensive line on Chequers Lane. Effectively the second scrapyard was also going to be lost.

I wasn't overly concerned at that, after all we were talking about broken down cars and scrap metal. What did concern me though was the Excide battery factory immediately to the north, our side of the incident and an oil storage depot immediately to the south. I'd have to think of a way to get through to protect that, as Chequers Lane was a dead end with the River Thames, south of the oil storage depot.

I took command of the incident and detailed John to take command of firefighting along Chequers Lane, by getting crews rigged in BA to set up ground monitors, to hold the fire back without crews being left in the line of fire. The Command Unit from Stratford was now set up and I spoke to the Staff Station Officer in charge of it and asked he send a message that I was now in charge and that crews had been withdrawn from the scrapyard.

As if to emphasise the urgency, the air reverberated with a deep boom as a cylinder exploded, momentarily lighting up the smoke plume up ahead. I was considering my options and asked for a map to try to work out access around the back of the scrapyards to protect the tank farm. At that moment a Divisional Officer approached me. He had been sent on as my Monitoring Officer once the incident escalated to six pumps and I had to take over. I was trying to give him a briefing but the job was getting worse by the minute. I decided it would have to increase and conferred with the DO who agreed.

I called across to the Staff Station Officer, "Mark, from me make pumps eight."

"OK, Guvnor I'll get that sent."

The DO now had to take command of the incident, so much for my first job in charge, it had been all of ten minutes.

Nonetheless as part of my hand over, I explained the risk of the tank farm and my desire to get around the back to stop the fire moving south towards it. I suggested the use of Dagenham's hydraulic platform to get a monitor to work from the north to protect the factory, but the issue was still uncontrolled spread south. He gave me responsibility for the Chequers Lane end of the fire and another ADO who had just arrived was given the role of finding a way to get around to the southern end to stop the spread that way.

We settled into the job a little more and then the Senior Divisional Officer turned up, who was now going to monitor the DO. By now most things were getting put into place, but the job just wasn't running right, so everyone was getting a little irritated, I walked onto the back of the Command Unit and caught the DO and the SDO having a heated argument. This wasn't going well at all I felt and wondered if I had any part to play in the decisions I'd made in my short period of command.

One very experienced and usually mild-mannered ADO who was at the Command Unit ushered me away and then returned to the arguing DO and SDO and gave them both the benefit of his vast experience. This apparently came after he overheard the SDO threatening to take command off the DO suggesting he "had a bunch of ADO's standing around doing nothing." This really angered old Ray who'd been around years and seen and done plenty.

The job went up to 12 pumps and the SDO took over. The ADO who was sent to find a way around it did just that and took a handful of appliances and crews off back up to the A13, round into Choats Road and then into a largely unmade road called Hindman's Way, where they were able to set up a good water relay from the river and not only contain the fire from heading to the tank farm, but push forward into the scrapyard, eventually beating the majority of the fire.

I didn't have as much luck back in Chequers Lane, the continual threat from the cylinders meant we couldn't aggressively attack the fire from that side and ground monitors, although they flow vast quantities of water, were at that time fixed, unlike the oscillating monitors used today. So, after a few minutes, they were useless and required BA crews to go back in to adjust them.

There had recently been a policy change that LFB had adopted following some improvement notices issued to other fire brigades, after the deaths of firefighters when cylinders had exploded. The recommendations were sound, but the arbitrary 200m, 24-hour full exclusion zone was very clumsy and did not allow much flexibility. At other incidents around that time, including one that shut down the approach road to the busy Blackwall Tunnel and another that shut down Kings Cross Station for 24 hours, questions were being asked in high places.

As with all things, the policy was reviewed eventually and looked at with a little more finesse. Using available technology such as thermal imaging camera's and a real understanding of the difference between volatile acetylene cylinders, which can continue to decompose and heat up after they have been removed from fires, as opposed to other gas cylinders where the risk is negated as soon as they are cooled, meant that a more sensible approach to dealing with fire involving gas cylinders was soon adopted.

Back at the fire, it was approaching 11am on Sunday, we as officers had stayed to oversee the introduction of relief crews following a shift change at 9am.

I was tired, aching, wet and now bored, as I smoked a cigarette and drank from a plastic cup of coffee. Eventually I was released from the incident and made my way home feeling like my first job as Incident Commander had been a disaster and that this senior officer lark wasn't for me.

As it happens, a few weeks later I was doing a voluntary shift so someone could take leave and I was ordered to another incident up in Gidea Park, just north of where I lived, at around 5am. I was told that Hornchurch and Romford were called to a fire in a vast old Victorian railway shed and that multiple calls had been received. The incident had been made up to 6 pumps and an aerial upon the arrival of the crews, and that calls were still coming in. Following the same routine, I quickly acknowledged I was on my way and got dressed and left home. I opened the door to a brilliant clear July morning, the sun was already bright in the sky as I jumped in the car and turned left off my drive, to head up through Hornchurch to Gidea Park.

I turned left into Station Lane and the beautiful blue sky to my north was blotted with a large black plume of smoke. I headed through the empty town centre, past Hornchurch fire station, its bays empty and door open, and continued up towards Gidea Park. I was soon parking up on the scene and after getting rigged, went to find the officer in charge. Dave, who was the Station Officer for Romford Red Watch, had been around for years, I knew him from my time on the Red Watch as a junior officer and felt a little abashed as I told him I'd be taking over once he'd given me all of the details.

"That's fine Stevie, I'm retiring in a couple of months and I don't think I'll get another job as big as this, so I'm going to go and play, you are welcome to it my son."

I had a good look around the building, Dave had put a good plan in place. The building was an old railway engine shed that had been used as a storage warehouse. It was now largely empty on the inside but rubbish and other abandoned items had been ignited and quickly spread up to the dried roof timbers. The building was about 80ft wide and 150ft deep, with a similar sized building separated by a small access road about 10ft wide and connected at the upper level by a couple of rickety wooden bridges. About half of the roof was alight with the potential for spread, so I decided I'd make the job up to 8 pumps and request a second aerial, so we could attack the fire from both ends. This is where it all changed, the officers who came to support and take over from me were from a different rota group because I was covering this shift. When the DO arrived, things were much less dynamic than on the scrapyard fire, so he had time to listen to what my plan was as I handed over to him, asking questions where necessary, but letting me give him a comprehensive brief. He thanked me and said he agreed with my plan and as he took command from me, he asked me to oversee my idea of getting another aerial set up around the back.

I soon had this set up and was enjoying being in the thick of the firefighting operation when the DO approached, this time with another SDO who he was touring the fireground with. They asked me how I was progressing and seemed pleased with what I was doing, the SDO then thanked me for my quick actions upon arrival and my plan to stop the fire from both ends and protect the adjoining building.

I left a few hours later after being relived and felt very good about myself, it just goes to show how a rapidly deteriorating situation affects personalities. It can affect the dynamics of an event and those interactions have an effect on how incidents turn out. I was happy, I got on with the rest of summer 2002 happy that I'd made the right choice... for now.

***

In 1977, the UK Fire Service had its first national strike. Firemen, at the time were incredibly low paid, a fireman earned £3700 per year for a 48-hour week. During that spell, the police had received two significant pay rises, so the Fire Brigades Union put in a pay claim of 30% to bring firemen, many of whom were receiving welfare payments to boost their low pay, up to a decent standard.

The Labour Government of the time had a 10% public sector pay cap, so inevitably the pay rise was refused. Over 97% of the UK's firemen voted for strike action, so in November 1977 the nation's firemen walked out of the door on strike for a bitter 9-week dispute. It was eventually settled in mid-January 1978 when the Union agreed to a 10% rise, a reduction to a 42-hour week and a new pay agreement which would keep firemen's pay in the upper quartile of semi-skilled men's average earnings.

This dispute, which caused great hardship among those involved, most of whom were still serving in the early years of my career, was of great benefit to those in the service. During my early years in the job, I was awarded some decent pay rises as a result of the hard-won formula.

However, by the early 2000s wages had begun to stagnate again, as the earnings that the formula was set against deteriorated because the labour market had changed. Once again firefighters pay was falling behind. Although not as bad as in the 1970s, I knew of a couple of firefighters who had kids and a wife that didn't work and had become entitled to things such as free school dinners for their children. Not right for men and women who are putting their life on the line day in, day out.

At the time, the Labour Government in the UK under Tony Blair had won their second term in May 2001 with a 167-seat majority. The Fire Brigades Union once again embarked on a bold pay claim, to bring firefighters pay up to £30,000 per year, which it was thought reflected the growing professional skill set of a modern firefighter. The Government had offered a 4% rise with strings attached for further changes to the firefighters role, but this would have kept many firefighters on or around £20,000 per year, just above the average working wage, for a job with requirements that were anything but average.

There was no movement on the offer so once again the nation's firefighters were balloted for strike action. This was successful, although lots of people had doubts and many questioned how wages had managed to fall so far behind. In November 2002 the first strikes were called. It was determined that to alleviate hardship among members of the service, there would not be an all-out strike, instead a number of shorter strikes were announced. The first strike was a 48-hour strike that started on 13th November 2002. Almost immediately and typically, despite public sympathy on the ground being good, the press turned against us. The military were forced to provide fire cover using outdated 1950s equipment and were ill equipped, trained and prepared. The government friendly press also jumped on this bandwagon, with TV news crews showing how tough things were for these poor service personnel who were just following orders.

I recall this being a very bleak period in my service. All of us felt we were stuck between a rock and a hard place, no one wanting to withdraw their labour, through fear of the consequences of what might happen if a serious fire were to occur, whilst recognising that the pay of firefighters really needed addressing. These personal arguments played out on picket lines across London and the country. Although I was acting ADO, I recall joining my own watch at Poplar on the picket line at the start of one strike period, where half of us wanted to leave the appliances ready to go behind the bay doors in case an emergency arose nearby, whilst others were adamant that a strike was a strike and that they should be left out in the rear yard with the keys removed.

There is plenty written about this dispute, that went on for months and months with no agreement, and I won't comment on it here. But I found I had really fallen out of love with the fire service. Those who employed us, the media and a lot of our senior colleagues showed no support at all for what we were trying to achieve, for those who were struggling to make ends meet. Personally, my salary was pretty decent at the time. It wasn't good compared to others in similar jobs, such as a police Chief Inspector or a middle manager in outside industry, but personally I was doing OK. However, many of those who worked with me were not.

By December, feeling utterly disillusioned, I decided to throw in my temporary promotion and return to my watch as Station Officer. It felt good to be back, although I missed being at home when on call overnight and I was also back in the thick of all of the nuisance calls that came in from time to time. I recall one cold night, not long after I returned, the bells went down at Poplar at around 3am. I jumped up and emerged from the Station Officers' room to hear the duty person call out over the tannoy: "Pump only, car alight."

I about turned and went back to my room. I had just laid down again when the lights came on and the bells went down again. I made my way out to the Watchroom to see Naomi, who was the duty person, bent over the printer.

"What we got?" I enquired.

"Shut in lift, Teviot Street," Naomi replied.

"Fuck sakes," I cursed, "Who the fuck is stuck in a lift at this time of night?" Naomi rolled her eyes as she tore of the call slip and handed it to me.

"Irving House, Teviot Street," I said to Beaker who was driving me. He mumbled an acknowledgement as we turned right out of the station into the dark night. As we arrived, the block was in almost total darkness, a fox scampered away into the shadows and the world went suddenly silent, as Beaker turned off the engine on the pump ladder, apart from the 'tink tink' of the cooling exhaust.

We made our way into the entrance lobby and found the lift. I kicked the door hard at the base with my boot and shouted up, "Anyone in the lift?"

I got a distant reply from way up in the building and stuck my drop lift key into the door and looked up the shaft. The bottom of the lift was about 40ft above me, so I turned to the crew and said, "It's on about the fourth." We made our way up the stairs to the fourth-floor landing and as we entered, the light was out in the hallway and we were in complete darkness. Turning on my torch, I found the lift door and muttered a curse at the stench of piss in the hallway. I opened the outer door by torchlight and saw the lift was showing about 3ft from the top of the doorway so it appeared stuck between the fourth and fifth floors.

"Hello in the lift," I called.

"Yep, in here," came the reply.

"OK mate, we'll have you out in a minute. You two go to the lift motor room and wind it down so we can let it out," I said to Naomi and Paul without turning around to look at them. I stood there making small talk with the man inside the lift while they went up to the roof to access the motor room and start winding the lift down. There was something sticky under my feet and the smell appeared to be getting worse, almost to the point where I was trying to hold my breathe from time to time to give myself a break.

The lift was soon almost level with me and with a good push upwards on the mechanism, the inner door opened and the grateful occupant came out and side stepped me before disappearing behind me, calling, "Have a good day mate."

"Knock off make up," I shouted up the shaft and looked down towards my radio to call up Beaker to send a stop message.

Then I saw it, I had actually been standing and moving around in piss and shit. Not only that but it was very obviously human waste.

"Fucking dirty bastard," I shouted out in anguish. "What the…? Dirty, filthy bastards" and then heaved as I examined the base of my boot. I heaved again and my eyes watered as I held my breath and made a dash for the stairs.

Back out in the street, I made a dash for the back of the pump ladder, opened the gate valve and then opened a delivery outlet to let water from the tank run over my boot. Beaker soon joined me from the front cab and was delighted at the vision of me throwing swear words out like confetti, as I gave him an expletive laden rendition of my misfortune. We were soon joined by Naomi and Paul who were equally ecstatic, Naomi taking several steps back onto the kerb holding her nose in disgust.

Back at the station, the pump was in the yard having its tank refilled as I pulled on the yard hose to give my boot another going over and scrubbed it with a brush, still cursing. The story had spread and as I went up into the kitchen a number of faces were trying to stifle laughs. "It ain't fucking funny," I announced to no one in particular.

"Three weeks ago…"

"Three weeks ago, I was sleeping in my own fucking bed and only having to get out of it to go to proper fires…" I cried. "Now I'm back here, getting up in the middle of the night to get some poor fucker out of a lift and in doing so standing in a pile of human shit in the middle of some shit hole building."

Reflecting after that I actually had a point. It was great to be back with my watch, but I felt something had changed. I'd been back a couple of weeks and we'd been busy around the station and out on calls. But they had all been pretty much nothing, persons stuck in lifts, fire alarms going off in buildings, rubbish and car fires. The best was a cooking pot that had been left on in someone's kitchen over on St Paul's Way.

At the end of March, the latest ADO promotion round results came out, this had been the one that I had withdrawn from when I went back to Station Officer, so I was interested in who had got through. Glenn, our current Station Commander, had been promised a move, so he went off to a station that would improve his commute, as he lived a long way out of London. It again transpired that through lack of candidates for promotion, there hadn't been many that got through and no one was coming to take over at Poplar.

Due to the shortage over the past few months, the other three Station Officers at Poplar had in fact all been offered and accepted temporary promotion. Rob from the Red Watch had actually been promoted and was Station Commander at Silvertown, John from the Blue Watch was acting up at Barking and Kevin from the Green Watch was acting up at Dagenham. This meant I was the only substantive Station Officer at Poplar, so by default was the most senior.

With my previous, albeit short-lived, experience as a Station Commander, a lot of things fell into my lap, with the Borough Commander calling me to cover various bits and pieces. Then, when another Station Commander in the Borough moved out, he had a real problem. He had six stations and a Fire Safety team, so should have had seven ADO's, but he now had five. His PA called me one day to ask if I had anything on, and whether Nigel, the Borough Commander, could come over to see me. I said I was free, so we made an arrangement for him to pop over that afternoon.

He respected and understood my reasons for not wanting to continue at acting ADO at the end of last year, but was struggling as there was no one left on the list for temporary promotion anywhere in LFB. Instead of asking a Station Officer from out of Borough, he wondered if I would like to act up again… but this time here at Poplar.

That was a whole different proposition. Like filling out a bingo card, I had done every single rank so far at Poplar... from the 'station boy' visiting as a teenager, firefighter, acting Leading Firefighter, Sub Officer and now Station Officer. The thought of being Station Commander at my beloved Poplar was quite exciting and I was half doing the job anyway.

I agreed, just until the next promotion round, which in all probability would be a year away, I said I'd cover it until they brought someone in. I spoke to the watch and they were OK with it, they said they'd pretty much anticipated it anyway after my tantrum a couple of months back, after treading in shit at the shut-in lift call. So around May 2003 I took the keys to the Nissan Almera fleet car allocated to the station from the safe, got the pager out of the desk in the Station Commanders room and filled out my name on the nominal roll board, with a printed plate 'F22 Poplar Station Commander' at the top of it. My callsign was 'Foxtrot Two Two' and I felt a lot better about staying here doing the job.

Nigel, our Borough Commander, soon moved on to HQ and another new DO turned up to take his place. I knew Dave as he had been a firefighter on the Red Watch at Plaistow back in the early 90s, when I was on the Red Watch at Poplar. I hadn't seen him for a few years, but he had done well for himself and was destined for greater things. He popped in to see me at Poplar within a day or so of starting and we had a catch up. I explained my situation to him, and he was happy for me to stay where I was until the next promotion round.

Dave did things a lot differently to Nigel, I found that his way of doing things was quite similar to my way and with my pride in Poplar, things were going well. In fact after a couple of station inspections, which Dave did every quarter, Dave said to me, "I wish I could bring a little of the Poplar 'Magic' to all of the stations in the Borough." An endorsement, I thought, to how well things were going.

John came back from his temporary promotion at Barking and the three other watches all had good temporary Station Officers. Another Station Officer promotion round saw them confirmed in post so the station began to settle down. With Millwall being such a quiet station, I didn't get a lot of calls during the day and it was generally only nights when I was at home, or weekends when less officers were on that I'd get called out. Poplar was different, much busier anyway and my position geographically, although only a couple of miles away meant I was getting out quite a bit during the day.

As I recall, the spring of 2003 was nothing special, that all changed on May 27th. It had been a warm but overcast morning, as I found myself in the back streets of Whitechapel, dealing with a complaint related to Fire Safety in a building. I returned to Poplar, had some lunch and then disappeared into the basement to spend some time in the gym. As I was doing my workout, the bells went down and I heard noise from upstairs as the Red Watch rushed around and then both machines disappeared onto the call. About 5 minutes later, my pager went off and I was ordered to a four pump fire in a flat in Blair Street in Poplar.

I ran up the stairs, frantically trying to dry the sweat as I made the phone call, I noticed the sun had come out and the sky was clear blue. I got myself together, jumped in the car and headed out of the bay for the drive along East India Dock Road towards the fire. As I got out of the car, the sun really hit me. It had turned into a glorious and warm day, the first of many on what was to become the hottest summer we'd had since 1995.

After a few weeks of warm dry temperatures, the same pattern began to emerge as it did in 1995. Slowly but surely, every day the grass fire calls gradually increased around lunchtime and would keep the crews busy until early evening. Of course, as I was no longer riding a fire engine, most of this passed me by. But I did notice the two machines at Poplar were busier with work on other stations grounds, as well as the generous workload they already had locally. This resulted in a few afternoons at Poplar where I was alone in my office doing admin, returns or emails while the watches were out doing their bit. Occasionally another crew would be sent in to standby and I'd have a chat with them.

One afternoon, the radio had been chattering away out in the Watchroom for quite a while, it was obviously busy out there, but Poplar's two machines had been taken 'off the run' due to a pre-planned inspection and training day. I had also been unavailable but had put myself back on the run half an hour or so before. My pager went and I was ordered to a fire at Wanstead Flats. The scene of many large grass fires over the years, which were especially complex due to the peat-based soil over there. The grass fires would quickly burn underground and into the soil, making extinguishing them a slow and laborious process of digging the soil over, as well as extinguishing the visible flame on top.

Three times I tried to ring Control, once it was engaged and twice it just rang off. I know I'd been ordered to a four-pump grass fire, so decided to get in the car and make my way there, booking mobile by radio. The radio was very busy, so I didn't ask for any further detail, just jumping in when I got a break in the radio traffic with a quick "Foxtrot two two, status two to Wanstead Flats." This was quickly followed by Leytonstone coming on the radio, "Foxtrot three zero one, at Wanstead Flats, make pumps eight."

"Here we go," I thought to myself as I made my way north east out of Poplar towards Stratford, then Forest Gate to get to Wanstead Flats. Typically, I saw a large plume of greyish white smoke in the distance, which indicated they had a decent grass fire going. I also heard "Foxtrot two nine" book in attendance so relaxed a little as Leyton's Station Commander Bob was much nearer and had obviously got there sooner.

I drove down Centre Road, which as the name suggests divides Wanstead Flats in two halves, cutting through the middle of it. Flames and smoke filled the view in front of me and the fire had jumped the road. I got out of the car, got rigged and made my way up the road, calling out on my radio to "Foxtrot two nine" who I'd heard had arrived before me, so would have taken command. I got no joy, kept calling and asking various crews if they'd "seen Leyton's ADO" who was in charge.

I used the time to take in the fire scene. The tail (start of the fire) was behind me to the left. The left flank was heading north towards another junction where two roads met, I was hopeful it didn't have the energy to jump the road into the houses, so that would probably be easy to contain. The right flank however, had jumped the road and its head was now pushing north east into the larger and more wild part of Wanstead Flats.

A Station Officer I know, who was in charge at Leytonstone, came through the smoke.

"Thank fuck you're here," he said, "it's jumped the road and I've—"

"Where is Bob?" I cut him off.

"What?"

"Bob, Leyton's ADO, he's in charge, I heard him book in," I demanded.

"I dunno, I ain't seen him, you are the first officer here, I'm in charge."

"Fuck," I silently cursed, this fire was now my problem and not someone else's that I'd simply help with.

"OK Neal, start at the beginning, what and who have you got here and what have you done?"

Neal was an experienced Station Officer and had had a few jobs on 'the Flats' in his time. Seeing the fire jump the road, he had diverted a few resources he already had to the north east to try to cut off the head of the right flank. A risky strategy, but they had the road to fall back to eventually. He had then "made it eight" to help with that attack and also deal with the now smouldering areas that were behind us. I was happy with that and took his opinion on board.

"OK, you carry on trying to stop the spread of the right flank and let me know if you need any more. I'll send you help as it arrives."

I quickly walked around the middle to top part of the fire areas as best I could, a couple of additional appliances arrived, and I got them to work and headed back to my car as I'd heard the Command Unit book in attendance. It was actually the CU from our HQ at Lambeth, the local one just down the road at Stratford was obviously already out. Lewisham must have also been out, the only other one being even further away at Wembley.

I was desperate for more officers, where were all the local ADO's and a DO who should be taking this job off me? I got the CU to brief me and then it all became clear. While I had been off the run, a number of other jobs had kicked off that had emptied a lot of this part of London. My officers were still coming, mostly from Central London, although I was annoyed that a lumbering old 12-ton Command Unit had got here before them, in their faster cars. I guess a grass fire out east wasn't anything to rush to for those HQ boys.

"What about the DO?" I enquired.

"That's Foxtrot seven four."

"Where the hell is he? He's only down the road at Ilford."

In fact, the next officer on the job was the Senior Divisional Officer in charge of the 'OTPI', the performance inspectorate. A large man in character and presence who was at that time one of the longest serving LFB officers. I anxiously explained what I'd been doing and what my plan was to the SDO. As we were speaking, another couple of ADO's arrived and I gave them jobs. He seemed quite happy with where we were and although he should have taken over, he said, "We'll give the DO another five minutes."

He eventually arrived, I was still quite a new boy so didn't ask where he'd been, which I did with great joy in later years when I was one of the 'big kids'.

When he arrived and took over, the fire on the right flank had been controlled. In fact, after quite a period of time on the Command Unit trying to manage it all on my own, it looked completely different. The whole area was now bathed in a mist of white smoke, the angry plume and hot flames now long gone. I was given a job to try to organise some reliefs so had a good opportunity to walk right around the five or so hectares that had burnt. The crews were now busy digging it all over and damping it down, all of them looking exhausted from the hard work that this particular type of grass fire requires.

I caught up with Neal again. "Relief's are being sorted mate, your lot have done well, we'll have you away soon," I said to him.

"Is the Sally Army here yet?" he asked me as a reply.

"I don't think so, must be on another one of the jobs going on."

"Typical, we've worked our bollocks off here."

***

The summer continued, it got so hot as August came that I started wearing tailored black shorts around the station and on jobs. I was working a weekend shift from 8am on Saturday morning until 8am on Monday morning just before I went off on my annual leave, where I was going off on a holiday in the UK. We were looking to take the girls to Florida in 2004 so decided to keep it simple in 2003, thankfully the weather was on our side.

The Sunday was the record breaker. It was the hottest I could remember it in the UK. We'd had some very warm summers over the years, 1983, 1989, 1990, 1995. I was only eight years old in the hottest summer I'd ever know in 1976 so couldn't really compare it. I was sat in my office, shorts on and shirt undone. I had a bit to do and couldn't really head home until around 5pm where I could then be on call from home. I was writing a report on some of the arson issues we were having in Tower Hamlet's. I promised to get it done before I went on leave and was cursing myself for putting it off until the last day.

I could stand it no more, my office was in a corner of the station, there was no breeze, so I decided to get into the car and drive around for half an hour just to get some relief from the cool air conditioning in the car. I drove around the Isle of Dogs and through Canary Wharf, even though I was cool in the car the heat was still beating through the windscreen. Back in the office, I managed to finish the report and send it off to the BC and was sitting in an easy chair with my feet up.

The bells went down and I went into the Watchroom to have a look as I'd heard the cry go up from the dutyman "Pair, fire!" They'd been ordered to a fire on the Burdett Estate in Thomas Road, a notorious post war housing estate where we'd had a lot of fires and a lot of trouble with gangs. I resisted the urge to go and have a look and lazily wandered back into my office and slumped into the chair, torn between wanting it to be a job and wanting it to be nothing as it was much too hot to get dressed up in all of my kit at a fire.

Shortly after, a 'Code 2' stop came over the radio, letting me know it had been a secondary fire, probably a rubbish bin or something. I decided to wait until they got back as I'd be going on leave, then I'd be on my way home. As they pulled back in, I was irritated by the stuffiness in my office, so I put my 'out of office' on and logged off the computer. I spoke to Terry the Station Officer, "What was it Tel?"

"Nothing Steve, just a couple of pram sheds."

"That's OK then, don't forget we have that new arson reporting tool you'll have to fill out."

"Yeah," Terry replied with a sigh.

"Right," I exclaimed. "I'm off. I've just got to get tonight out of the way then I'm on annual for a couple of weeks."

"OK, are you on overnight then?" Terry asked.

"Yes mate, I'm on my duty weekend so I'll be on until eight in the morning, then leave."

"Good, well you have a quite one and we'll see you."

"Yes mate, thanks... I'm back around the end of the month sometime, see ya," I said as I walked out of the Watchroom and towards the car.

A Tragic Waste

Almost a year later and I was really happy at Poplar, having now been Station Commander there, albeit still temporary, for 14 months. July 20th 2004 was pleasant and sunny as I made my way into Poplar through the early morning traffic, the usual stop-start shuffle along the A13. I gradually edged towards the top of the Canning Town Flyover and I saw a lazy dark plume of smoke hanging in the air a couple of miles north of me towards Bow. I wasn't on duty yet for another hour or so, but reached down to turn my LFB radio on out of interest, a message was part way through being sent. What I heard was the worst thing I'd ever heard come out of a fire brigade radio: "… steady progress being made, one firefighter recovered from debris, one firefighter still missing."

I went cold, my head started buzzing and my heart racing. I don't recall the rest of the half mile journey to Poplar, but it was quick. I just heard the words repeating themselves over and over in my head. I screeched onto the forecourt and stabbed at the door entry pad to open the bay door to get in. To my horror, Plaistow's pump was parked in the bay. Both of mine were on the job… where two firefighters were missing. "One firefighter recovered, one still missing," those words repeating again.

Recovered was not rescued, no word on their condition, and a firefighter 'still missing' isn't someone who might have got lost or hadn't said where he was going. A firefighter missing almost exclusively in this business means only one outcome.

I ran into the Watchroom as Darren, my old mate from Plaistow and their Sub Officer Kevin came in from the other door.

"What the fuck is going on?" I demanded, "I've just heard a radio message one firefighter…" I couldn't finish the sentence. One of the guys on the Red Watch, Dave Andrews, was on his penultimate night duty before retiring. I had known Dave since my first visit to Poplar on that Bonfire Night twenty odd years earlier and he was a good personal friend of mine.

"There's a job in a shop at Bethnal Green," Kevin explained to me, "Not sure what happening, but it seems a BA crew went missing," he continued.

"Jesus fucking Christ," I said as I reeled back and leant on the desk. "Are my boys there? Who is it? Have you heard anything?"

"No, Poplar and Homerton are on a 'four' at an old warehouse in Bow," Darren said.

A second of relief that my lot were not there before he continued, "But the job in Bethnal Green has Bethnal Green, Bow, Whitechapel and Shoreditch on it I think... it's an eight pumper."

"Fuck me," I said again shaking my head and looking at the floor. From my years on the Red Watch I knew almost every one of the lads on the Red Watch at those stations. I couldn't take it in.

I ran into my office and rang someone I knew at Control, she had been on duty that night but as I got through to her on the formal control line, she couldn't really speak to me. A few moments later she got excused from the room and managed to ring me from her mobile phone. She was absolutely heartbroken and had been in the Control room while the whole incident had unfolded from just after 4:30 in the morning.

At 04:38 LFB Control received a call to a fire in a shop at 419 Bethnal Green Road, crews that arrived first found a small clothing shop with a 2-storey dwelling above, closed up by metal shutters, with a fire evident inside. Two persons from within the building presented themselves at roof level and a ladder was pitched to rescue them, whilst crews attempted to break into the shop.

A small portion of the shuttering was forced open and a BA crew made their way inside the shop, using a hose reel jet from the tank supply of one of the initial fire engines that attended. That initial crew found going very hard. A lot of heat and smoke had built up inside the shop and progress was very slow due to tightly packed goods stacked high inside the shop. Eventually the crew found themselves towards the rear of the shop and discovered a fire at the back coming up from the basement. This crew had soon exhausted their air, so an additional crew was sent in where they left off.

Progress was still painfully slow, so the incident was made up to six pumps. By now, both appliances from Whitechapel fire station were in attendance, along with those from Bethnal Green and Bow. Progress was still very slow, it appeared that the fire had been brought under control and a third BA team were sent in. Amazingly, the initial hose reel was still in use instead of a main jet and for some reason, the appliance hadn't been set into a fire hydrant to augment the limited tank supply.

Waiting outside in BA ready for deployment was firefighter Billy Faust. Billy had been at Whitechapel on the Red Watch since he left training centre seven years earlier. When another crew were required to enter, as the fire had been going on for a couple of hours and was believed to be under control, it was decided that Whitechapel Red Watch's new recruit, Adam Meere who had been with the watch for just two months, would go in under the watchful and experienced eye of Billy.

Not long after they had entered, they made their way into the basement to damp down what was believed to be the last remnants of the fire. The water had still not been augmented and it seems at some point around this time when hose reels were changed, one had been turned off at the pump. Critically, a command decision was taken at that time, to ventilate the building as smoke and heat were still evident. A crew were sent to the flat roof on the first floor at the rear of the building and told to ventilate it. This caused an inrush of air into the building from the first floor, down the staircase to the ground floor and into the basement, and both Billy and Adam were caught in the sudden explosive development of unburned fire gases.

The sudden eruption of fire gases from the front of the shop caused the crews outside to jump into immediate action. Despite some breath-taking command failures, the firefighters rigged in BA and made their way into the shop to rescue their colleagues. Fire had now spread throughout the entire building and the job was made up to 8 pumps. Crews battled desperately, one crew finding a hose reel that had been burned through, so had to get another main jet set up. The roller shutter door was now finally opened fully and one by one the two firefighters were recovered, but sadly it was too late.

I was still unaware of the full details sitting in my office at Poplar waiting impatiently for more detail. I was surprised when my phone rang, even more surprising was the voice of my Borough Commander Dave, with the sounds of sirens in the background. Dave had been made aware and although he had left his home in North Essex earlier upon receipt of the news, he was making his way on blue lights into London. Dave asked me to go onto the personnel system on the computer and look up the next of kin details for two names. "Adam Meere", a name I didn't know, and then, a cold shock as he said the name "Billy Faust". I'd known Billy from my time on the Red Watch when I was a Temporary Sub

Officer a few years before and had been sent to do standby duties at Whitechapel many times.

The day after the fire, flowers outside the shop in Bethnal Green Road where Billy and Adam lost their lives.

I passed the details and addresses to Dave as it was apparent that Principal Officers at Assistant Commissioner level were on their way to break the tragic news to both families. With tears in my eyes, I got up out of my chair and made my way out into the station yard to have a calming cigarette. I didn't look at the crew from Plaistow, in case I gave something away. It was not right that I should share any details when the families did not yet know the terrible fate that had befallen their loved ones.

As I was in the yard, John the Blue Watch Station Officer, who was coming on duty sped into the yard. As soon as I saw his face, the realisation dawned on me that John had been Temporary Station Officer on the Red Watch at Whitechapel before he'd been promoted to Poplar. John had already heard and was absolutely bereft.

My Red Watch crews came back from the fire they'd been at just after the 9am shift change. They knew from the radio something terrible had happened but still I couldn't confirm. I had John in the Station Officers room to give him some privacy and avoid any difficult questions for him. The atmosphere was, as you'd imagine, very subdued and everyone crept around with their heads down.

The station, usually noisy and lively in the mornings, was itself surreal. I arranged for someone to take command of the Blue Watch for the day as John was in no state to work and arranged for him to go to Whitechapel to be with them. The rest of the morning passed in a fog of nothingness until mid-afternoon when Dave rang me back and asked me to report to the pub opposite Whitechapel fire station, where the now reduced Red Watch had gathered when they returned from the fire.

Feeling sick and anxious again, I got into my car and make my way, in silence, the three miles along East India Dock Road and Commercial Road until I arrived at Whitechapel. The scene was really sad. People I know, some for a long time, others only for a couple of years, were there, along with some wives and retired members, lots of tears were being shed. I exchanged a few greetings with people, feeling massively uncomfortable to be invading this very intimate gathering. I was asked by Dave to drop a firefighter home. He was the firefighter who had travelled up from South West London with Billy the night before, now a lifechanging world away from where we were now.

With a deep sigh, I naturally accepted the request, but my anxiety was not lifted by this prospect. The journey from Whitechapel to Sutton on the far south west borders of London was not an easy one on a weekday afternoon. I let the firefighter set the pace for the journey and did not bother him with needless chat. But inevitably it came. I sat there and listened, responded and counselled as required. We went through every emotion on the journey; tear's, laughter, fond memories, anger, and most of all the unanswerable questions as to why?

I arrived home mid-evening and was met on the doorstep by Joanne who was very concerned for me. A few minutes later, the doorbell rang. Joanne opened the door and I heard some voices, into the living room walked Lynda and Pete, two neighbours who were both police officers. Holding a large bottle of Irish Whiskey, Pete spoke.

"We heard about the fire Steve and knew it was your patch. Both Lynda and I have lost colleagues in the line of duty and not many will understand how you feel right now, but we do."

I felt my eyes sting and got up to thank them both profusely.

It turns out Pete had known WPC Yvonne Fletcher, who was killed by a gunman at the Libyan Embassy back in 1984 and Lynda knew PC Jim Morrison who was killed when chasing a handbag thief not far from Covent Garden in 1991. Ironically, both of those police killings have remained unsolved.

They soon left me to get on with it, I made a decent sized dent in that bottle of Irish that night, before going to bed for a fitful sleep, with the events of the day playing over and over again.

During the day, the remaining fire had been extinguished and the area was naturally declared a crime scene. The following morning, on my way in, I got another call that I was to proceed directly to the incident at Bethnal Green Road, where all crews had been withdrawn while the Fire Investigators from LFB and the police, as well as accident investigators from LFB and The Fire Brigade's Union were beginning the formal investigation. As I arrived and got rigged in my PPE, I gave my name to a PC manning the cordon and spoke to a crew from Bethnal Green who were standing by at the scene. I knew the Fire Investigator who the Brigade had chosen for this task, as well as the Union Investigator. We were briefed and told that us, them, being the fire and accident investigators, and me as a representative of the Borough were the only ones that were being given access to the building and we worked through how the process would be undertaken.

I spent the morning inside the shop, assisting the investigators as we painstakingly picked by hand through the debris, recovering various items of equipment and other effects. This in itself was incredibly moving but at the same time a great honour. Several times throughout the day I thought back to the debris at Ground Zero and the FDNY firefighters who had been doing the same thing for months and months after the 9/11 attacks, until every last piece of debris and human remains had been cleared.

In the afternoon, we were told that the Commissioner was going to visit the scene and the families would also come to see where their loved ones had died. Shortly after, the traffic in Bethnal Green Road was stopped as the Commissioner and families arrived. It was a truly heart-breaking moment to see both families arriving at the scene where their sons, husband and boyfriend had lost their lives just over 24 hours previously. I found the raw emotion of one of the fathers particularly distressing and had to walk around the corner into a side turning to take a moment to compose myself. The crowds along the street also stood in silent respect of the scene in front of them.

On the third day, a curtain went up around the whole episode. The station, the relatives, the colleagues, the Borough Commander and the principal management of the Brigade were within that circle and the rest of us were suddenly outside. I had obviously been quite traumatised by the events of the previous days, but had steeled myself to deal with this and offer the support that should have been due as part of the local management team. All of a sudden, I was cut loose and found myself wound up tight in preparation for a difficult few weeks and then left in mid-air with nothing to do.

I never really got over that and was saddened that I wasn't even able to attend either of the funerals, them being closely stage managed by LFB. I did attend a memorial service along with over 1500 members of the UK fire service some months later, but again was tucked away at the back of Westminster Cathedral, still feeling like I had my own ghosts to lay to rest. Thankfully, in the years that followed I regularly attended the site in Bethnal Green Road with colleagues to lay flowers on the anniversary and proudly found myself as Borough Commander of the Borough at the end of 2017, when a formal plaque to remember Billy and Adam was commissioned by the Fire Brigades Union and unveiled in Museum Gardens, just next to Bethnal Green fire station.

In the enquiry that followed, a number of individuals had their actions on the night highlighted, but the fundamental issue came down to problems within LFB around training and Incident Command. Many changes were promised, but in the years that followed, austerity and further cuts to the service have led me to believe that despite some real noble efforts and some very direct and obvious improvements to procedures, that some of the big issues still exist to this day. The loss of Billy and Adam was a tragic waste of life, they became the sixth and seventh London firefighters to die at an incident whilst I was in service. I was closely associated with and really deeply affected by their loss.

Moving On

In October of 2004, I was finally promoted to substantive ADO. I had remained in the vacancy for Station Commander at Poplar, and had become very closely linked with the station, local community and some of the strategic partners such as Canary Wharf Management and those responsible for the complex roads and tunnels in the area.

I was as happy as I'd ever been and absolutely loved going to work, despite the tragedy earlier in the year and a rocky start to my life as a senior officer. However, the upper echelons of the LFB at the time seemed to be an unusual beast. To me it felt like a time of haves and have nots, in as much as those who played the game, no matter whether they had talent or not were the ones who were rewarded. And others, even if they were doing nothing wrong, or indeed making quite a success of what they were doing, found themselves often at odds with the very controlling regime that was in place. Unsurprisingly, I found myself in the latter group, not helped by the fact I was a Fire Brigades Union Officers representative at a time when the chasm between LFB management was wide and getting wider.

I wasn't surprised when Dave my Borough Commander informed me that I wouldn't be staying at Poplar. It was 'felt' that I'd be better off going somewhere else. I was disappointed and did get some support from external partners, but the word of the LFB was the rule so the die was cast. I had actually been informally offered Whitechapel, but the station was obviously still hurting after the loss of Billy and Adam and my own feelings around how I wasn't able to follow a natural healing process... not that LFB knew or particularly cared, because they were so defensive and inward facing after the fire. That made me feel that I wouldn't be a good fit for Whitechapel as I'd inevitably not be 'the LFB's man' when some potentially difficult times in the changes and investigations reported came about.

At that time, for some strange reason, Tower Hamlets that had always been part of NE area, had fallen into a 'Notional area' after the previous commands were disbanded that tied us in with Westminster and the City of London. But the Deputy Assistant Commissioner that was in charge of the remaining NE area had a number of vacancies to be filled. He rang me one day and offered me the job as Station Commander at Homerton. I accepted immediately, if I couldn't stay at Poplar, which I was fully engrossed in, I wanted nothing more to do with the past few months in Tower Hamlets. Dave was surprised I went for it but I was now back in NE area, even though these were only notional management areas, it still felt a little like the old days back before the 2002 changes.

Thankfully shortly after this, it was realised we were too small an organisation for the Borough structure to work effectively and a hybrid between the old areas and commands was re-introduced and NE area, including Tower Hamlets lived again. There were less staff and the Area Commander was now a Deputy Assistant Commissioner instead of an Assistant Commissioner, but it felt OK.

So After a leaving do at the resolute Pub in Poplar High street, with a lovely gift of a statue of two Firefighters and speeches, almost like a practice retirement do 14 years before my actual retirement, I packed my office up and bode a sad final farewell to Poplar Fire Station which had been like a second home to me. I had started off there visiting as a teenager and managed to work there in every rank up to Station Commander... the only person ever to have done that at the time as far as I could discover.

I Knew Homerton fairly well and knew enough people on each of the Watches to allow me to get settled in pretty quickly. Life in the Borough of Hackney was somewhat different with different characters, but I had a good relationship with Graham my new Borough Commander and after treading carefully with each other, all four watches and I came to a happy compromise on how things should work.

Things had quietened down for a bit but with me now going through a development programme instead of a straightforward promotion, where I had to gather and present evidence of my development as a Manager, a premises manager and of course operationally I was getting enough under my belt and making good progress. As a result of promotion, I could no longer use my pool car that was provided by the Brigade so instead of taking a lease car, I opted to use my own personal car where the Brigade paid me a monthly fee plus my business mileage. I had a siren fitted to my car along with a radio and was given a magnetic blue light to put on the roof of my car for when I had to attend calls. This wasn't as nice as a free car but saved me loads of aggravation from being flagged down by Taxi Drivers asking me to get people to move off Taxi Ranks to people randomly asking me questions, directions and in one case to break up a fight that was occurring outside of a pub.

"The International Olympic Committee has the honour of announcing the games of the 30th Olympiad in 2012 are awarded to the city of London." The British Olympic committee dressed in their beige suits in the audience of the International Olympic Committee in Singapore erupted in delight as did the crowds watching in London's Trafalgar Square as IOC president Jacques Rogge made the announcement.

It was Wednesday 6th July 2005, London had beaten off Paris in a hard-fought contest to host the games 7 years in the future. The site that had been chosen was an area of East London that sat between Stratford and Bow just south of Hackney Marshes. An area I knew well from my time at Bow attending fires in scrapyards, small factories and waste recycling dumps. Many people had their doubts the area could be transformed, but the plans were ambitious and that won the day for London.

At the same time the UK was hosting the G8 summit in the Gleneagles Hotel in Auchterarder, Scotland. World leaders including US President George W Bush and Russian President Vladimir Putin were all attending. It seemed to be a great week for the UK with the eyes of the world looking at us.

The following morning, I was driving through Dagenham from home, a little later that I should have to be fair, on my way into Homerton when I heard something on the news about a power surge on the underground which had stopped some trains in the tunnels at Liverpool street. As was typical of me, I reached over and switched my LFB radio on to see if I could find out what was going on. The news radio then talked about another problem at Edgware Road station and reports of an explosion at Aldgate. The old heart rate increased, and adrenalin started pumping. Terrorism had been at the front of everyone's mind since 9/11 four years earlier in 2001 and each of the emergency services had work and trained, both together and within our own organisations for a multitude of risks... Chemical attacks, mass casualty decontamination, Urban Search and Rescue, which is the rescue and recovery of people from collapsed buildings.

A message came across the radio from Aldgate Station stating that an explosion had occurred on a train between Liverpool Street and Aldgate Underground Stations with 'Multiple casualties' and unknown numbers of persons involved'. This was it, there had been lots of potential warnings and a few false alarms, but just over nine years since the last major terror attack in London by the IRA at Canary Wharf, we were now under attack, a day after the announcement that London had won the Olympics and with the most important World Leaders also in the Country.

I put my blue light onto the roof, tuned my siren on and started heading towards Homerton at a pace somewhat livelier than I had been. The News on the radio was now stating it appeared that two trains had been blown up, one at Edgware Road and one at Aldgate. At the same time, deep underground on the Piccadilly line between Kings Cross and Russell Square, the deadliest of the three blasts occurred killing 26.

The Aldgate and Edgware road blasts had taken place on Circle line trains, which run in large double width tunnels just below street level, so the blasts from these two devices had dissipated out and away from the trains to a degree. However, the Piccadilly line had deep surface tube trains that run in single tunnels just a fraction bigger that the train itself. For that reason, the blast was concentrated within the carriage taking a terrible toll. As it was so deep underground it also took several torturous minutes, in among the confusion already being caused by the other blasts, before the realisation that a third blast had occurred.

I arrived at Homerton shortly after and went straight into the Station office where the Blue Watch were gathered discussing unfolding events. I'd hardly caught up with what was going on when the bells went down and both the Red and Green lights for Pump Ladder and Pump lit up. Unusually, they had been ordered, to standby for fire cover at Shoreditch, which was normally a one appliance move. Additionally, they were to attend on blue lights whereas standby moves were usually undertaken at road speed.

In less than a minute, I was standing alone in the Watchroom as the two machines disappeared in a cloud of smoke and noise down the road. I recall my heart beating heavily in my chest as I stood wondering what next. I looked at my pager to check it was on, why hadn't I been called to anything. The only radio listening post in the station was in the Watchroom, so I logged onto a PC in there so I could look at the live incident system as well as listen to the messages coming from the scenes. The radio burst into life, it was an ordering for the Pump Ladder from Homerton to go to Russell Square tube station, to reports of an explosion on a train. That was the first time I realised that there had been a third blast, the details on the computer screen mirroring what I was hearing over the radio.

Unable to contain my frustration any longer I rang Control The voice that answered sounded under a lot of pressure, immediately I was aware of a lot of noise in the background from the normally efficient and calm control room.

"Hello Control, It's Foxtrot Two Eight ADO Dudeney here, are you showing me as available? I'm wondering why I haven't been called to any of the incidents."

Almost impatiently the female voice replied.

"There is a lot going on at the moment, we are still receiving lots of calls to various places, you are showing as available at Homerton…"

A silence as I heard her bashing away at a keyboard.

"We don't know where this is going to end, you are reserved at the moment in case something happens on the transport network at Stratford, we think this may be linked to the Olympic announcement yesterday and therefore we are keeping resources available for that." The phone clicked off without waiting for me to acknowledge.

A while after, Homerton's Pump was called up, they were ordered to Tavistock Street in Covent Garden, the reports of a bus that had been blown up. This was awful, I could only imagine the horror unfolding across London, where would it stop. It transpired the call to Tavistock street was actually a wrong address given by a caller. The bus that had been blown up, by a fourth terrorist was further north in Tavistock Square.

It is believed that he was due to get onto a Northern Line train at King's Cross and blow that up. But due to engineering works he was unable to get onto the train. Later CCTV would reveal he wandered around the station, with the murderous device on his back trying to contact his fellow terrorists to no avail as they had already carried out their deadly suicide missions. He left the Station and got on a bus, held up in the traffic gridlock caused by the incidents, he got off and walked before boarded another bus. A number 30 heading south from Euston Station, diverted because of the incident at Kings Cross. As it passed the headquarters of the British Medical Association on Tavistock Square, the device was detonated by the terrorist at the rear of the upper deck killing himself and 13 others.

With no desire to go over to my office to do any of the day to day work, I sat upstairs alone watching the events unfold on SKY News, occasionally getting out of the chair as an emergency vehicle passed by. The Pump came back from Tavistock street after an hour or so of sitting in traffic as an alternative attendance had been sent to the actual event in Tavistock Square. I had lunch with the remaining half of the Blue Watch until I jumped as my pager went off.

It was telling me to ring the Officer of the Watch at Control. I felt my stomach knot, thinking I'd now be getting a relief ordering. With all of the live rescues carried out, it was only the grim investigation and recovery work left to do at the four scenes.

In the event, it was an unusual request. Due to the increased workload, Control had asked a number of additional officers to come on duty. Unfortunately, quite a few of them were stuck in various places in East London trying to get to the Control Centre on the Isle of Dogs. The Watch on duty knew me, knew I was a Black Taxi driver and that I'd know a few more back routes that others may not.

I ended up spending the afternoon an evening as a 'blue light' taxi service fighting my way through the traffic to various locations to pick up staff who were required at Control that were either stranded because the entire public transport system had bene closed or were stuck in their cars unable to move.

Although disappointed, I was quietly relived that I didn't get to see the incidents and the grim aftermath. There is always a desire when on duty, or even when off duty to be at some large or complicated incident to do your bit. But in the end, all of this death and destruction takes its toll on those who have to deal with it, so calm reflection always leads me to the conclusion, I've seen enough, I don't need to add to it.

Being in the control room and seeing how they dealt with the incident was enlightening. Their cool efficiency in responding to the big events as well as maintaining fire cover for the rest of London and everything else that was going on was always something special to watch, but on a day like July 7th 2005, they along with the responders from the LFB, Police and Ambulance service, as well as the staff in the Hospitals worked magnificently to ensure many more lives were saved.

At 6:01 am in Sunday 11th December another explosion occurred. It measured 2.4 on the Richter scale and because of an inversion layer in the atmosphere, where the temperatures lower down was colder than those higher up in the atmosphere, the sound of the explosion was heard as far away as Belgium and Netherland according to reports at the time.

The devastation in the area following the Buncefield Oil terminal explosion December 2005.

I was off duty and asleep in bed at the time and remained blissfully unaware of the explosion at the Buncefield Oil terminal in Hemel Hempstead in Hertfordshire, just under 30 miles as the crow flies north west of where I lived. The explosion, the biggest in the UK since the 1974 Flixborough disaster caused incredible damage locally, flattening buildings over several hundred metres from the epicentre and windows being blown out as far as five miles away.

My first indication of it was when I got up that morning at around 8am. It was being reported on all of the news Channels. Amazingly, although it was a clear cold day, the sun was forming a weird light as the smoke, at over 9000ft in the air created an appearance of thin clouds, but black in colour instead of white. Looking over to the north west the sky grew darker, it was a sight I'd never seen before along with the faintest smell of burnt oil in the air, not dissimilar to the smell when an old car drives past.

I took little more than a passing interest in it over the next couple of days. Initially Hertfordshire Fire and Rescue Service had responded and declared a major incident with reinforcements being provided from London, Essex and other neighbouring counties. Over the coming days, with unprecedented foam supplies required to deal with the millions of gallons of blazing fuel, Groups of Firefighters from most of the UK's private petrochemical Fire Brigades based at large petrochemical and oil storage facilities across the UK worked alongside local authority Firefighters from several counties in tackling the outbreak.

London Fire Brigade had their own sector at the fire, which was to provide water for those tackling the fire, using six high volume pumps lifting water from a number of open water sources around Hemel Hempstead and pumping it over a couple of miles towards the oil terminal. That required crews from several of LFB's High Volume Pump stations and their nearby support stations working in relief's being changed several times per day. On Wednesday 14th December I was on a 24 shift. I'd had a relatively quiet day at Homerton and had not long finished dinner at home that evening when my pager started vibrating on my belt followed by the familiar beep, beep beep; Pause, beep beep beep. I was being sent to Buncefield for an overnight stint as the LFB Command Officer. Because we had our own specialist senior officers looking after the intricacies of the pumping operation and crews, my role was really only that of liaison with Hertfordshire Fire Service staff and our team back in LFB. With the prospect of a long cold night head, I put on some thicker layer of clothing, took a small 'midnight feast' to keep me going at around 8pm set off towards the M25 for the ride to Hemel Hempstead.

As I approached the junction with the M1 which was closed, I flicked the switch on the car which lit up the blue lights in the grille. A Police officer climbed out of a car and directed me north up the closed M1 to the next junction where I'd be directed to the RVP which was on a roundabout just off the motorway. I was there in short time and was directed around several lines of 5 inch hose that were snaking around the roundabout.

I climbed out of my car and noticed a slight smell of petrol fumes in the air, I wasn't aware of how far away I was, but the hose snaking around the roundabout and off into the distance along Breakspear Way suggested it wasn't too far away. I looked into the night sky but couldn't detect any of the amazing plumes of black smoke that had covered the South of the UK a few days ago.

I jumped onto Hertfordshire's Control unit parked on the roundabout and introduced myself to an Officer, he told me 'The Boss' had just done a handover and was out on the fire ground. He pointed me towards a brightly lit office building on the opposite side of the roundabout and told me to get a cuppa. I walked towards a red caravan with Bedfordshire Fire and Rescue Service written on the side and was delighted to find this wasn't the usual canteen van, but a proper Burger van owned and operated by the Fire Service in Bedfordshire.

Steve Briefing Police Officers in his Inter Agency Liaison role.

Feeling it rude not to take full advantage, I ordered myself a coffee and a bacon and egg bap. I was directed into the foyer of the brightly lit office building where I'd find some tables and chairs. As I entered, I noticed some Police tape and a flat shattered pane of glass laying beyond it. It was around 8ft by 6ft and had managed to retain its shape as it hit the floor, looking like a large jigsaw puzzle where someone had laid out all of the pieces but hadn't connected them together. I looked up and saw a large new sheet of plywood had been used to cover the gap where the glass had once been. Inside, I took a seat and nodded a greeting to a couple of groups of other Firefighters who were sat around.

After my briefing, which as expected was an update on progress and how they expected to have the last of the fires extinguished overnight I updated LFB and was pretty much left to my own devices for several more hours as the LFB crews doing the pumping were being managed by another officer. I decided to have a ride down to the oil terminal and see what was going on.

I got back in the car and picked my way back around the roundabout the wrong way and headed north up a road called Green Lane with trees on the left and open fields on the right. The hose was laid all the way along the road acting as a marker to lead me towards the fire. Outside the oil terminal, I parked my car up and became aware for the first time the absolute devastation that had been caused.

The oil terminal was to my right, a plume of black smoke rolled lazily into the sky, its underside lit by flames and large white lights from the site. It eventually merged with the night sky and could be seen no more in the gloom beyond. To my left was what appeared to have been a large distribution warehouse. Its white panelled front looking like it had been kicked inwards by a foot the size of a house with many of those panels missing along the length of the building.

I got out of my car and was immediately hit by the smell of fumes again, but this time it was really pungent. I made my way into the oil terminal and found a few badly damaged petrol tankers, abandoned at the time of the explosion sat underneath the large array of overhead pipework, all now buckled and the ground littered with large sheets of aluminium cladding that looked like bits of screwed up paper thrown from a wastepaper basket.

Having read about the power of the explosion, this didn't surprise me, but it was an amazing sight to see it up close. I spent the next hour or so wandering around the site and watched as a team of industrial Firefighters with two large foam monitors made an attack on the last of the massive burning tanks. I was up to my knees is the oily water and foam run off and noticed the fumes had given me a dull headache.

I spent the remainder of the night at a couple of meetings or sat in the office building drinking cups of coffee to keep myself awake. At one point I decided to wander along the hose lines that headed away from the roundabout to find their source. I ambled up the empty Breakspear way dual carriageway, now a car park for all of the trucks and support vehicles that had brought the high-volume pumps and hose in.

I lost interest as they disappeared into a large gap cut into some bushes, where I assumed the open water supply that they drank thirstily from was located.

Wandering back, I saw the first glimpses of daylight breaking through the clouds on this chilly December morning and decided it was time to go back to the oil terminal for a look in daylight.

This time I wandered along a lane at the left of the site. As the daylight grew my breath was taken away by what I was seeing. Over to my left was a burned out two storey office building. Soot stains covered a lot of the window openings but even where there had been no fire the windows were long gone. Patches of brickwork were also missing across the front of the building.

In a complete contradiction of physics, a number of cars were sat exactly where they had been left, their panels dented and windows missing, but other larger items were strewn around the car park like broken toys. The largest and most surprising of which was a massive rubbish container, obviously weighting much more than a car that had been blown across the car park into a corner its previously square edges rounded by the force of it being rolled around so violently.

As I continued down the lane the trees became thinner and ominously dead birds appeared on the floor as they'd either been blown out of the trees or the sky when the explosion occurred. The trees at this end of the lane were stripped off all but their thickest branches, not unlike photos I'd seen of Hiroshima and Nagasaki after the nuclear bombs had been dropped in World War II.

At around 8:30 my relief had arrived. I'd seen enough by now, I told the guy who took over from me. "Nothing left to do. We've put the fire out for you", as I winked at him and slapped his back taking my tired legs and aching head back to my car for the drive home.

The summer of 2006 followed a similar pattern, life at Homerton continued, I'd pick a few things up during the day but mostly it was weekends or nights when fewer officers were on that the fun and games would start.

There had been a few big fires in London, some of which had involved me, others I heard about when I returned to duty after a few days off. A worrying new trend started to appear, within a short space of time a handful of wooden framed building has caught fire during their construction and had completely burned to the ground, often involving other nearby buildings. One in Peckham had spread to two adjacent blocks of maisonettes a pub, which was completely burned out and several cars parked in the street.

Another trend after the devastating loss of Billy and Adam in Bethnal Green were two more Fires where Firefighters were almost lost. One was in a derelict swimming baths down in Lewisham in SE London. The old empty swimming pool had been filled with rubbish and old foam filled exercise mats. When the crews arrived, a small amount of smoke was seen coming from the building and a crew dispatched to make and entry to fight the fire. Unfortunately, instead of breaking down and opening the boarded up main doors, entry was made through a small side window into the building which was a toilet block.

Just as the crew entered the main pool area, the fire developed rapidly and the crew, now somewhat disorientated had to make a rapid exit, during this process one Firefighter got lost in the toilet block and it was only by pure chance the crew sent in to Rescue him found him exhausted and low on air in the nick of time.

Not long after this, Crews from Bow and Poplar received a call to a fire alarm going off in a large storage warehouse near Bow Locks. Ironically, this warehouse was just a few meters across the River Lea from the Gillender Street warehouse where Terry and Dave had died in 1991. Upon the arrival of the crews at this large building, the alarm was sounding but with no fire apparent crews were sent to make a search as per procedure.

A handful of guys were up in the high walkways of this warehouse when they discovered a rapidly escalating fire running through the high racking… its sounds, smoke and growth masked by the sheer volume of goods within. They called for a jet to be sent up to them to make an attack on the fire, but within seconds the built up of fire gases, superheating the goods in front of them saw the fire develop with explosive force, The crews who were high up in the building along narrow bridges running the length of the building to enable staff to access goods at a higher level had to make a run for it.

They were fast being overtaken by the burning goods and in the end had to jump over one of the bridges onto a lower level where they were thankfully able to escape. The fire soon burst through the roof of the lightweight aluminium building and because of the inevitable water supply problems the entire building was soon alight before high volume pumps could be brought to the scene and water taken from the River Lea.

I had gone to bed that night aware of a large fire that had been going on since late afternoon in Hendon next to the Metropolitan Police college involving a building under construction. It had been on the local News as the spectacular sight of several floors of timber framed blocks of flats, which had spread to the roof of an adjacent block of student accommodation as well as threatening one

245

of the Met Police communications hubs across the road which had to be evacuated, smoke could be seen across NW London.

I woke up the following day to be met with the news of not only the ongoing fire at Hendon which had attracted 20 pumps, but also this outbreak nearer to me in the warehouse that had also attracted 20 pumps. I fully expected to be called onto a relief to the warehouse fire and ate a hearty breakfast and dressed in a LFB T-shirt instead of the usual shirt and tie ensemble.

As expected, my pager went off just after 8am, what was unexpected was that my ordering was to the fire at Hendon and it was an 'immediate relief' meaning I was to treat it like a fire call and attend on blue lights. I made my way into London and turned right up the A12 when it met with the A13 at Blackwall tunnel to trace my way north. I passed by the burning warehouse just beyond the building on my right had side and cursed at it was still well alight with bright flames and thick black smoke rising into the sky.

I eventually arrived at Hendon, a little exhausted after the concentration of such a long blue light drive right through London in the rush hour. Things were much more sedate here, the battle overnight had been won and there were just a few sorry smouldering corners of the building that the day before had spread 200m or more across the site. Nevertheless, I got on with my job which was nursing a couple of crews on jets and an aerial platform dousing one of those remaining corners. What was apparent as the aerial crew were from SE London, the furthest aerial from this part of London in fact, that all of LFB's aerial fleet, which had been depleted down to just eleven trucks from the 35 that were in service when LFB took on its current size in 1965 were in use. Either at this fire, the fire in Bow or another fire, in a car spares warehouse in Plumstead that had also happened overnight, but I wasn't aware of.

Each of the aerials from Hayes right out west, to Dagenham in the east. From Wimbledon in SW London up to Wembley in NW London and all of those in between had either been at the fires or were on the road to or from a relief. The crew from Greenwich with me, now well past the shift change at 9am and desperately awaiting a relief, from a fresh crew who's own appliance will still trying to get back to Station, informed me they'd been on the make up at Bow from early in the incident which was about 10:30pm the night before. They had just missed the fire at Plumstead which wasn't far from their station and after a brief rest, they'd been ordered all the way over here to Hendon at around 6am. I tried my best to sympathise with them, but imagined they'd be here a couple of hours more before we got them away.

The same happened with the handful of Senior officers who had been on duty overnight. Everyone had been to one of the three fires, some of who had been relived in the early hours, finding themselves sent out again. Word on the grapevine was that quite a few officers who were on a 9 shift that day had volunteered to convert their shifts to 24's to give wider cover the coming evening. I added my name to the list, but in the event wasn't required.

I needn't have worried about missing the fire at Bow. Early the following morning I was ordered there for a relief and spent most of the day there. The fire was largely under control by now, but with so much stock in the warehouse over such a large area, there was still a decent amount of work to do and as always, I enjoyed getting myself dirty and getting involved in the thick of it. The fire actually carried on for over a week as demolition crews gradually ate into the building and uncovered more of the deep burning piled before it was finally extinguished. I found myself back there another three times, getting less and less interested each time I went back until the job was finally closed down two weekends after the fire.

A Quieter Life

Life was moving on for me and by the spring of 2007, I'd been moved from Homerton to Shoreditch, still within the Borough of Hackney. Shoreditch was one of the biggest stations in LFB, five floors in height with six bays having been built in 1964 as the new HQ for the C-Division.

At home, 2005 had seen the arrival of my youngest Daughter Imogen. My middle one Abigail was in Junior School and my eldest had just gone to Secondary school. Joanne was stilling holding down her job in Canary Wharf three days each week and without the help of her parents we'd have been in a mess. Having considered it through 2006 I put in a transfer request to move out to the Borough of Havering. This was where I lived, the Borough had three Fire Stations, Hornchurch, Romford and Wennington.

When I was moved to Shoreditch in April 2007, I did remind my boss that I was due a move nearer home and that I expected it as the result of a retirement in September of that year. He said, he'd deal with that nearer the time and to carry on with my move to Shoreditch. In the event, one of the Station Commanders in Havering decided to retire earlier than expected.

So when the phone rang in my car as I was driving back from a meeting at Hackney Town hall one afternoon in late June, I was surprised with the voice on the other end of the telephone offering me a transfer to Havering where I'd be based at Wennington as Station Commander. I accepted in a heartbeat and soon found myself packing up my office again for a move. I was just coming up to 20 years' service with LFB and for the first time, since my early days at Bethnal Green and Poplar, would no longer have to face the challenges of an hour or more in rush hour at each end of the day.

Wennington Fire Station had been built in the early 1960s by Essex Fire Brigade. It covered the small village of Wennington, Rainham, Aveley and parts of Purfleet. However, not long after it opened in 1965 the Greater London Council was established and London, including its Fire Brigade expanded.

London took in lots of new Stations, almost all of the County of Middlesex to the north and west of London. The entire county Boroughs of Croydon, East Ham and West Ham as well as quite a few stations from Essex, Kent and Surrey.

For its part, Wennington found itself in an unusual position. The new county line between London and Essex was just a few hundred yards east of the station. So Wennington lost all of the ground to the east including Aveley and Purfleet and unlike most fire stations, which are more or less in the middle of the area they cover, it was abandoned in a small village surrounded by fields at the very eastern edge of the newly formed Greater London.

As a result, Wennington was a very quiet Fire Station. With just one fire engine and seven Firefighters on a Watch it only attended several hundred call per year. In many other parts of the UK, it may well have found itself as a 'retained' station where crews live and work in the local area and only respond to the station when a call comes in or for training. Although it was quiet, it did have an unusual honour of having one of the highest 'call to working job' ratios of any fire station. In short, they didn't get much, but when they did… Large industrial fires in the many riverside industrial estates that ran along this part of the River Thames, lots of very nasty road crashes on the fast roads that ran through the area or twisty back lanes and plenty of fires in fields and the large country parks during long hot summers.

I knew a handful of people across the Watches, mainly older Firefighters who had 'done their time' in the 80s and 90s in the East End and were seeing out their careers at a quieter Fire Station nearer home. These Firefighters were great assets, very experienced and not phased on the occasions they did turn out to something spectacular and have to work very alone and alone for the vital minutes until back up arrived.

The Borough Commander, Trevor, was also a brilliant and well-respected Officer. He had also done his time at busy inner London Stations such as Kingsland, Stoke Newington and Stratford as well as having built a formidable reputation as a senior officer in the past decade working as part of the LFB's Performance Review team and part of the specialist Inter-Agency Liaison team, which I longed to be part of. Given specialist training to respond to terrorism, public order and other critical incidents.

Even the Commissioner himself often sought Trevor's Counsel and his ability to 'tell it like it is' without fear of repercussion. I had a lot of good bosses over the years, but no one taught me as much as Trevor did which went on to serve me well and cement my reputation in my last decade with LFB.

Although Trevor had known me for a few years as one of the NE area officers, he had never worked closely with me and in my first months at Wennington, he put me to the test. Thankfully my first two station performance audits went well as did my planning of a large-scale multi-agency exercise at a large high risk compressed gas plant on Wennington's ground.

Operationally, as expected, Wennington didn't provide many challenges, although I kept myself busy as I'd changed to a different officer rota group and was often one of just a few 'out east' during the day, at the weekend and overnight. This allowed me to pick up some decent job around Dagenham and Ilford during my time there.

Having gone to Wennington in July, I also expected to really earn my spurs with large grass and wildland fires. The previous two summers had been very dry during the spring and early summer, meaning a lot of crews out this way had a version of what we'd seen in the dry summers of 1976, 1983, 1990 and 1995. However, typically of my luck, the spring wasn't up to much and the long-awaited summer never really arrived. July 2007 was awful with a lot of floods across the UK and London's worst day being the 20th where almost five inches of rain fell.

My work in the Borough also changed. Most of my time working with the Local Authority in Hackney and Tower Hamlets dealt with issues around crime and disorder, social housing, arson reduction and all of those other inner duty issues. Here, a few miles east in a borough that was primarily suburban with some heavy industry and rural risk it was all different.

I was meeting with regeneration people at the local Business improvement district meeting as well as the Environment agency and park rangers looking after a lot of the common land, Country parks and Rainham Marshes which is a 'Site of special scientific interest' or 'SSSI'. Often meaning even a small fire in the marshland would have my phone ringing red hot with people 'taking an interest.'

Life at home was great in terms of my newly found work life balance. The senior officer shift system in London Fire Brigade, was an average of 72 hours per week. Half of that time was standby hours or 'negative' hours as they were known, when on call from home overnight, with regular office hours during the day, whether that be weekday or weekend. Add a couple of hours commuting to that each day and it could mean quite a bit of time away from home. Now, I could leave the house I lived in at the time and get to Wennington in about 12 minutes without even seeing a set of traffic lights if I went to work through the lanes. I'd also drop my eldest Charlotte at school and still get there in under 20 minutes. I could pop home for lunch if required, although I'd often eat with the Watch in the small mess at Wennington which was more like a home dining room that some of the large mess decks at the bigger stations.

Encouraged by Trevor, in 2008 I applied to join LFB Inter-Agency Liaison officer cadre. They had come about following a large-scale exercise at Bank Junction back in 2000 where all of London's emergency services, the military, security services and others had come together to practice a large scale terror attack on the transport network. One of the main lessons learned was how each of the organisation worked within their own organisational silo's with little regard or information related to what the others were doing or had to do.

The ILO's were a team of around a dozen or so Officers who had high level security clearance and training alongside specialist Police teams, the Military, Health services, Security Services and other Government departments. Their role was to represent the London Fire Brigade and decide which specialist LFB assets or regular crews should be deployed in the event of a terror attack, large scale public order events and other critical events or incidents from armed sieges, to chemical attacks or presidential visits.

The selection process was tough and I got through it, but didn't make the initial cut, instead getting put onto a reserve list. In the spring of 2009, I had got the call and was soon to start my training for the role of ILO. Unfortunately for me, this coincided with the G20 summit being held in Docklands in East London with world leaders including US president Barack Obama in town for the April 2nd event. As part of the response from London, LFB crews were tasked to standby at various locations for the day to ensure an immediate response was ready should the worse happen.

It's funny how the smallest of things can turn into potentially career defining moments. Wennington was one of a number of Fire Stations in LFB that house large Mass decontamination units. A series of tented structures with showers, disrobing facilities and other items that could be used to decontaminate large numbers of people in the event of a chemical attack.

On the day of the Summit, Wennington's crew took their fire engine and de-con unit to the Docklands area to set up and standby. Unloading the large truck and setting it up was thirsty work, so after everything was in place, the crew, remote from some of the large gatherings approached a Police canteen van and tried to get some drinks. An officious operative on that unit dismissed the LFB crews stating the drinks were "For Police only". They went away, somewhat annoyed and still very thirsty and managed to get some water elsewhere.

The following day, they reported this to me, much aggrieved and I, being a reasonable boss, agreed and fired off an email to the planners of the event. I simply asked that in future, the needs of crews who cannot leave their posts for hours on end should be considered. I thought it was a reasonable email, raising a genuine welfare concern and only sought to make some constructive criticisms.

At the time I was also a Fire Brigades Union officers section representative, which I knew, in that climate of a very aggressive Conservative majority running things at City Hall, was not seen as exactly career defining. But with my progress onto the ILO group as yet unhindered, I thought no more of it when I was summoned to see the Deputy Assistant Commissioner in Special Operations, who was responsible for the ILO group.

What I was not expecting, but what should of become obvious with all of the faces who looked away or down at the floor as I arrived at the office at Headquarters was the sudden onslaught of badly constructed argument that was thrown at me, using a printed out copy of my email with various lines highlighted.

I was accused of undermining the group, causing bad feeling, embarrassing the LFB among other things that had been spun completely out of hand from my own words. I tried to explain and then it got a bit heated when I was being spoken over and told what my own words from my own mind actually meant. Fifteen minutes later, I walked out of there, being told I was not suitable for the group and that I had been removed from the programme.

I am a fairly robust person who gives and good as he gets and many will testify I enjoy a good spirited debate. However, I felt attacked and almost abused by the powers that be with no means or form of redress. I remember getting back in my car and spending a couple of hours just driving around Central London in an angry daze. I went home from there, being unable or unwilling to go back to Wennington.

The following day, I met Trevor at Wennington along with Tony, the area Commander who was our DAC and told them what had happened. Trevor, as I said previously, not being shy to tell it like it is, rang the DAC at HQ and the row they had was blinding. Trevor, as one of the senior ILO's actually threatening to withdraw himself from the group as they "Had no integrity". Before this loud exchange from the office next door concluded, I did hear Trevor say, "That is out of order and I am going to tell him."

When he got back, it transpired that someone 'at the top' had been shown my email and in that instant, without review, reflection or explanation my career as an ILO had ended before it had begun. The DAC who had been told to call me in to tell me so had to make it happen, so I pitied him having to find a reason, which he did I guess on reflection, by pulling apart my email and reading what they wanted from it.

Trevor told me that the decision stood and that I'd be allowed to apply again next time, so clearly this was a summary punishment, but I took some satisfaction from the fact Trevor had unearthed the truth of how it had come about and I now knew that and they knew that I knew.

It was during this time at Wennington that I had one of those spells when I felt like Doctor Death. It seemed week after week no matter what I was called to I'd bear witness to a loss of life. Sitting in my office one pleasant afternoon my pager went off and informed me rather cryptically of a 'car on fire, person involved. The address was the main road just at the top of Wennington Road where the fire station was.

Ringing control, they told me they'd had several calls to a car alight and that a person was in the car, Wennington, who were out of the station doing a fire safety visit had been called along with the Pump from Dagenham. Walking out to my car, I looked across the fields and sure enough, maybe 500 yards away I could see the tell-tale pall of smoke. I took my time getting into the car, not wishing to be the first to arrive as I'd be able to do very little without a fire engine and water. Nevertheless, I made my way, turning into the main road, I could see the car alight ahead of me and was horrified that no fire engine was present.

However, I was now committed and had to make my way along the short distance. Stopping ahead of the burning car, I was relieved to see the bright headlights and blue beacons of Wennington approaching. A crowd from passing vehicles was stopped and I saw some people surrounding someone on the floor. I jumped put and made my way towards the crowd, looking into the burning car, from what I could see, no one was inside, but on the floor was a man very severely burned being comforted.

A familiar face looked up at me, an off-duty Firefighter from Dagenham had seen what was going on as he passed by and bravely dragged the man out of his burning car and was attempting to treat him. Thankfully Wennington's machine was now here and with a couple of the crew attacking the car fire, they started to treat his burns. The Ambulance soon turned up and minutes later the familiar sound of the London HEM's medical helicopter was heard overhead with an increasing crescendo of noise as its pilot skilfully landed it just a few yards away. The car fire was put out and the medic on the helicopter treated the casualty and mercifully placed him into induced unconsciousness before transporting him away.

It transpired from my conversation with the off-duty Firefighter that the driver of the car had been to fill up some containers with petrol, that although liquid tight, still allowed the vapour to escape and fill the car. For an unfathomable reason, the driver then lit a cigarette and was instantly engulfed as the petrol vapour exploded into ignition within the car.

Cars were the cause of many other fatal incidents I attended. The number of late-night traffic accidents where young boy racers caused or were involved in accidents was an all too regular occurrence. It always seems that as they lost control, their natural evasive action led them to avoid the worst of the injuries and their poor passengers, often teenage girlfriends, take the full impact.

It affected me in a strange way, having Daughters approaching that age, I had an irrational fear of young boys in cars. Not only did it make me hyper vigilant and quite reactive when I was being tailgated or passed by a young kid in a car, I was also absolutely determined my own Daughters would never get into a car driven by a young inexperienced driver with a testosterone filled belief in his driving that didn't match his actual skill.

The two eldest ones have missed out more than once because a 'lift' somewhere involved a journey in a car with a young lad, but they were very good about it and never moaned, understanding my worries which was good of them.

I was such an issue in the outer Boroughs, where roads are faster and more affluent families were able to buy their sons cars, without considering the consequence of how fast the cars went, that we run a project alongside the other emergency services in the Borough and Havering Council called Safe Drive stay alive.

It was a very hard hitting programme, run in a number of places across England where during one week of the year, all of the year eleven kids aged

15/16 from every school in the area were taken to a local theatre where they'd be shown video's and members of the emergency services would take to the stage to tell their particular story alongside 'survivors' such as Carol, the Mum who had lost a teenage son and Mick a promising young semi-pro footballer who was now confined to a wheelchair and brain damaged after attempting to overtake someone and crashing head-on into a truck.

Mick really hit hard, he was crafty, he used to play up, but genuinely had trouble forming words and used to drag himself slowly on stage in his wheelchair after photographs of him playing football had been shown. The poor lad used to dribble as he spoke, so would have to stop and wipe his mouth as well as dab tear away. The girls and some of the boys would be heartbroken. It was tough, but I know from the experience of my daughters, the eldest of which still has the 'Safe Drive Stay Alive' keyring on her car keys many years later, it was a lesson they'll never forget.

I also had two other very unusual incidents around a similar time. The first was early one weekday morning. It was in August and already light when my pager went off just before 6am. Blinking as I woke and focussed on the message, I sighed deep at the first letters 'A1F' A1 meaning it was a primary fire, F meaning it was a fatal incident so a fire where someone had died. What came next as the incident description and address was a little more unusual. 'Car alight' garages rear of a main road in Romford.

Arriving at the scene having prepared myself mentally, I made a silent promise to myself that I'd do what I had to do without getting too close, knowing full well from others experiences that the 'tank' gradually gets filled with ghastly sights over the years until one day, without notice it overflows. I didn't want to be one of those poor souls. Speaking with Dagenham's crew manager, he explained they'd been called to a car fire and as they were putting it out and the smoke cleared a body was found in the passenger seat. I kept my distance and noted what I needed to as we waited for the Fire Investigator to arrive and start his investigation alongside local Detectives.

The FI was a guy called Ian I'd known for many years, he started his worked and called me over.

"Have a look at this Steve."

"He appears to have unusual injuries and it looks like something is around his neck."

Before I could have another thought and despite my promise to myself, seconds later both Ian and I had our heads right inside the car examining the burned corpse of this poor soul trying to work out what had happened. It transpired that this poor fella had taken his car to a nearby address to sell it. An argument had broken out that turned into a fight and he was seriously injured. As if that wasn't bad enough, the perpetrators then bundled his body back into his own car and drove him to the garages where they set the car alight to cover their crime. I'm at least pleased to say this became evident very quickly and the perpetrators were brought to justice quickly.

Not long after this another incident didn't have such an outcome with justice served. In the early hours of the morning when I was on duty I'd stayed up late and was just about to turn in when I was ordered to the usual 'Four pump fire, persons reported' at an address in Dagenham. I arrived and was met by Jason the Watch Manager from Barking who was incident Commander. I'd heard a message en route that had informed me that a number of people had been rescued by crews but that one person had been found 'apparently dead' within the property.

Steeling myself again as I'd done on so many other occasions, by this time in my career now sadly countless with more forgotten than remembered, I let Jason speak.

"Bit of a weird one this Guvnor, we've rescued the Dad and two kids from an upstairs bedroom by ladder, but the BA crew found the Mum on the sofa downstairs dead."

"OK, go on, I said rather puzzled with the way he finished his sentence as if there was more."

"Well, she isn't badly burned at all, the fire in the sofa she is on didn't get going that much, but it appears her head has been caved in."

"Jesus Christ," I sighed whilst thinking, "Why me" lately.

Jason was right, inside the little house the fire damage wasn't too bad at all, but this poor young woman was sprawled unnaturally on the sofa with very severe head wounds that were not consistent with her falling, nor was she particularly burned. The Police had questioned the partner, who happened to be the stepdad to the two boys, and he insisted he went to bed and left her downstairs watching TV. He woke up with the smell of smoke, was unable to get downstairs so woke the kids and called for help from the window where they were then rescued by LFB.

There was no sign of a break in and no sign of any weapon, so it was all very odd. Especially as the partner was fully clothed when rescued and even had his shoelaces tied, which isn't a common situation when rescuing people from fires late at night. Following a thorough investigation by the Police, the partner was arrested, charged with murder but following two trials was not convicted so that poor girl and her children never got the justice they deserved.

One of the things that came out of the industrial dispute of the early 2000s and the new Fire and Rescue Act of 2004 were the loss of National Standards of fire cover, from the requirement to get several fire engines to any given point in a city centre within a few minutes, to just one to a rural location within 20 minutes. Instead each Brigade had to carry out regular reviews of their fire cover called Integrated Risk Management Plans… why use a simple term when a great new 'dolphin speak' title can be used to confuse people and cover a litany of cuts and reductions in service.

LFB had already been through a couple of these that had seen lots of pumps removed from stations and a handful of station closures. However, to give it its due, in Havering it actually identified that the Harold Hill area of the Borough, a swarming housing estate of almost 8000 homes that had been built in the 1950s in response to the post World War II housing shortages in London, did not have sufficient fire cover. The nearest Fire Station in Romford and the next nearest in Hornchurch could not meet the standard identified in the most recent IRMP.

The risk map, working from various topographical and demographic computer programmes actually identified that the precise are for a new Fire Station was smack bang in the middle of an industrial area between a very large BMW car dealership and a B&Q warehouse. Neither of which were likely to give up their prime spot for a new Fire Station. However, just a few hundred yards along the road, a new industrial estate with a dozen or so small industrial units was being built.

It was decided, to save on the large Capital costs of purchasing land and designing and building a new fire station that an industrial unit would be purchased on the site and for the first time in the UK as far as we knew, turned into a Fire Station.

Trevor gave me the role as the 'local' representative and I was placed on the project team alongside staff from our property services department and central operations. I gave up my role at Wennington as Trevor had managed to secure an additional station Commander post, so found myself driving just a mile or so to Hornchurch Fire Station every day while the station took shape.

Building a replacement fire station is one thing but setting up a whole new station with new personnel, equipment and a fire engine was more of a challenge. I also had to consider the are the new station was going to cover and transfer all of the risk records from Hornchurch and Romford to what was to be the new Harold Hill fire station.

Gradually, the empty industrial unit took shape with accommodation, offices, lecture facilities a kitchen and rest areas as well as a unique training area that was actually built inside the structure including a training tower. There was again political controversy. The Political leader of the Fire Authority decided there was to be no proper resting facilities at the station, the only one of London's then 113 stations without it and instead 'reclining chairs, which were not fit for purpose were procured. This caused merry hell with both the Union and LFB's own Health and Safety department which also had a responsibility to Health and Safety legislation as well as the LFB who were their employee's.

Eventually a crude informal solution was agreed. Proper sleeping facilities were brought in 'under the radar' while the political leader got his wish of having several unused and pretty much unusable reclining chairs in place. Thankfully, following the next Mayoral election where Boris Johnson secured his second term as Mayor of London the chair of the authority was changed and a new one appointed. And then the awful chairs were removed, and proper fire station beds installed.

There are of course plenty, especially others working shift work who question the fact that Firefighters are paid to 'sleep on duty'. In essence this is the way it us all around the World due to the longer shifts Firefighters carry out overnight, sometime 24-hour shifts and is all based on the fact that historically Firefighters would live on fire stations with their families on an almost continual duty system.

Improvements to working arrangements and hard-won union battles to improve terms and conditions and reduce working hours over many decades has led to a situation where Firefighters now work in a four shift or 'Watch' as we call it, rota pattern. Yet the original model of Firefighters being available to respond at a moment's notice from a centralised location across the World has remained unchained. Unlike Police who patrol their area and provide a visible presence, no one internationally has come up with a better system than having a group of Firefighters 'housed' is a building with their fire engines and equipment ready to respond to a call for help.

Thus, to this day we still have Firefighters who live at their fire stations for their period of duty, notwithstanding all of the inspection, training and community work they do in the area they serve.

So, on a cold snowy morning in early January 2010, the new Fire Station F57 Harold Hill went live at 9am. I took on the role of Station Commander with a lovely well-appointed office overlooking the internal training area as well as the comings and goings on the industrial estate. Incidentally, the first call for the new Station came in around two hours into the first day and was a call to a fire in a bedroom in a house in Gidea Park, the edge of the new ground which had previously been on Hornchurch's ground. The crew from Harold Hill arrived half a minute before Hornchurch vindicating the work we had done carefully redrawing the station boundaries.

The Big House

During the last month or so of the project to bring Harold Hill online, I had applied for the next round of promotion. Without a doubt, I should have applied years earlier as I had now been in the rank of Assistant Divisional Officer, now called Station Manager, for almost seven years... some of those who had joined me in the rank in the years after me had already gone on to a higher rank but I thoroughly enjoyed the role, recognised that I had blotted my copybook on more than one occasion and also firmly believed you didn't have to just achieve a job before moving up, you need to do the job and become very experienced at it.

Fortunately, although it was felt at the time people had to be based at headquarters to 'get on' the unique work I did based on the new station, some great mentoring by Trevor and my operational experience having been in this role now for several years paid well and I got a telephone call whilst sat in a Borough Management meeting late in February 2010 that I had been successfully promoted to Group Manager... or the much fabled Divisional Officer or 'DO' in old money.

Most people got their posting straight away, but I had an additional wait of an hour or so, probably while they all fought over who *didn't* want me, until one of the DAC's in training rang me. I was offered the role of 'Curriculum Manager' in one of LFB's training departments. I was to be head of the Leadership, Management and Development team, a group of around 30 uniformed and non-uniformed trainers who had the responsibility for the leadership and management side of training as well as equality and diversity training right across the organisation.

I was to be based in a building at the Headquarters complex and for the first time, apart from my spell in training a decade or so before was going to be working away from a Fire Station up at The Big House.

I was sad to leave Harold Hill, I'd only actually been their three months by the time I left at the end of March 2010, but because I'd had a hand in getting the station up and running and we'd pretty much been able to hand pick most of the personnel there, I really felt a big part of it. Nevertheless, the die was cast and after almost three years of not having to worry about the rush hour and traffic jams, I loaded my car to its roof with my belongings and set off very early for the drive to HQ. Instead of parking easily as I had at the fire station, I was allocated a space in a nearby car park that LFB leased and given a desk in a management office shared with half a dozen others instead of my own space and a personal locker in a locker room at the old Southwark Training centre several streets away from the building I was based in.

The team I was going to be working with made me very welcome. I knew a few of them from being around, but I had two uniformed Station Managers and four lovely non uniformed managers, Angie, Angela, Tracey and Clare who really knew their stuff. I was told early on, "leave it to the girls, they know this inside out." That was not wrong and in fact I found my predecessor had been much more thorough than was required and soon relinquished a lot more of the responsibility to these brilliant ladies who simply just pointed me in the right direction, told me what to say, sign and do while I dealt with all of the strategic stuff coming down from above.

Sadly, once again the Political leader, of the Authority had made some decisions around cost cutting. It had been suggested that due to the age and condition of our dilapidated main training centre at Southwark, a wonderful but sadly neglected facility that was an integral part of LFB legend over the past century and a half, along with the fact that the budget and resources required to train and maintain the competency of thousands of LFB staff was too expensive.

LFB could not afford to the regeneration of Southwark Training centre and keeping the training where it needed to be was also more than our political masters were willing to write a cheque for. The head of training at that time, a brilliant Officer who had been at the forefront of the LFB's strategic response to the lessons learned from the 7/7 attacks and the recent Lakenhal House fire was charged with writing a detailed report into the 'Future options for Training' This well balanced and detailed report looked at a number of options, but decided in the end that the status quo should prevail and whatever the cost LFB training should remain in house.

However, the powers that be, were not that impressed with the outcome so this officer was moved sideways and another officer brought in. This time with a tighter rein on how the report should look. Second time around, the desired outcome was achieved, that was to outsource all of LFB's training to an external company. Over the next year or so, I was in the thick of this as tenders were put out and negotiations took place. I along with all of my fellow curriculum leads from the many training disciplines had to provide reems of information, data and detail that was chewed up and analysed by those doing the negotiating.

By the end of 2011, there was a clear winner and Babcock International were going to take over all LFB training; lock, stock and barrel. It was a sad time for all of us, despite the clear proven excellence Babcock had across multiple disciplines including Military, logistics, engineering and transport. It still felt that we had sold the family silver with our 150th anniversary just a few years away and the excellence in which we had proudly trained our own people through war and peacetime, feast and famine.

Of the 30 or so staff I had, the uniformed ones either went back to an Operational station post or continued in training for a defined period detached from LFB. But all of the non-uniformed staff including Angie, Clare and Tracey were moved over to Babcock on under the TUPE process. I felt really sad that we were letting so many of the dedicated and professional non-uniformed members of the LFB family go and still regret that to this day.

So, in April 2012 after two years as the head of Leadership and Management training for LFB, with so many of my brilliant team now working for someone else, I found myself along with most of the other uniformed senior training department staff without a job. But with the Olympics now underway and my previous upset with the ILO group now water under the bridge I found myself sat at a desk in LFB's Special Operations Group with a bit of a 'roving role' I think that is the polite term they use for someone they have to find a position for.

Operationally, I accepted that things would be quieter in my role as Group Manager. As a SM, I'd be sent out on any fire that was receiving multiple calls, if persons were reported involved or once the crews had made the initial fire up to four pumps. In addition, any incident with persons confirmed trapped on a confirmed incident involving hazardous material would also get me out on the road.

Over the course of the six plus years I'd been a SM, I had attended lots of incidents and because of the seriousness of their nature, this is where my belief that the role of ADO/SM is the best in the fire Brigade when it comes to getting not only good fire ground experience but also valuable command experience. By virtue of the incidents attended in that role, generally all serious, the exposure is much greater to Firefighters and Officers at stations who may attend many dozens of small or routine incidents between the more serious ones.

Now, as a GM, I'd only be getting paged just to let me know when a SM had been sent out. Potentially and from bitter experience, ask my wife, the pager would often jump into life at all hours as I might be the only GM on duty over a large area covered by several SM's. Every time one of them was sent out to a road traffic collision, a person's reported fire or multiple calls to a fire, I'd get woken up, have to tramp downstairs, phone control to get the details and then listen to the messages coming back on the radio.

I would now only be required to attend if the incident went beyond four pumps and the SM had taken command or for some other reason that required the higher level of monitoring or command. 2010 was actually pretty quiet operationally, nothing major jumps out of the memory banks that greatly affected me. I did have the occasional ride down the road to a job, especially hazardous material incidents as a change in policy, that only lasted for a short period required a SM to take command of these incidents meaning the GM then had to attend. A handful of those and one six pump fire at a works unit attached to a large municipal park in Enfield was about it for me for the first six months. I was beginning to get itchy feet.

The latter part of 2010 saw another masterpiece from the Political leader that caused industrial unrest among the crews and effectively caused a number of actions where they were working to rule in some aspects of their duties, which included acting up to a higher rank.

Still tied to the bed issue no doubt, a proposal for new shifts was put forward. The desire was two 12 hours shifts, which on the face of it doesn't look too bad. But two 12 hour shifts mean equal shifts between days and nights. Once this is in, then the LFB could if they want shut certain stations of a night or move appliances to different areas and personnel could be deployed anywhere. Other shift based organisations had been put through this and the terms and conditions of those doing the shifts were worsened as a result, notwithstanding the risk to the public with closing station at certain times and playing Russian Roulette with where your fire engines might be versus where the fires might occur.

As big organisations often rely on people acting into higher positions, this ended up with a shortage of junior officers and meant some appliances were off the run for parts of a shift. The key rank in all of this was the poor old Leading Firefighter or Crew Manager as they had been renamed in 2005. Essentially a

Firefighter with additional responsibility who took charge of a crew and an appliance as well as the day to day running of the station this rank was key to keeping the wheels of the Brigaded well oiled.

The acting up ban didn't really affect the organisation too badly, apart from the general voluntary rule that the CM would deputise for the Officer in charge if they were on leave and thus became the rank that would keep stations and appliances available. Firefighters couldn't undertake this role, so the poor old CM and some Watch Managers had the weight of the whole dispute pivoting on them.

In line with the perfectly legal industrial disputes process, that had been properly balloted, CM's were refusing to undertake any acting up. So, at change of shift, while other officers were found to fill in when the OIC was on leave, the CM's exercising their right didn't want to cover. The way the Brigade handled this, encouraged no doubt by the usual protagonist, led to the worse period of low morale and industrial unrest I saw in my 31 years with LFB.

Officers and Firefighters were divided like no time previously, not assisted by a real 'push' by the LFB to encourage… to use the term in its widest sense… Senior Officers at SM and GM level to leave the Fire Brigades Union. Many Officers did leave the Union which strained things further. I retained my Union Membership during that time and thankfully, due mainly to an understanding by other colleagues of my personal views, was spared involvement in the worst of the dispute.

The poor old CM's were being rung up at the change of watch and asked if they would act up to keep an appliance on the run. They obviously said no, to which point they'd be read a statement where they were informed they'd be deducted 20% of their pay for what was termed 'partial performance'. Many of those Junior Officers had to face this several times over and, in some cases, had multiple deductions.

It was a disgusting way to treat valuable staff and for the first time I began to think about my time in the Fire Service and started looking forward to the time I could take my pension and put this job behind me. The dispute was eventually ended with a completely ridiculous solution that each side declared a victory but was in fact comical.

The previous nine-hour day shifts from 9am to 6pm and 15-hour night shifts from 6pm to 9am changed to an incongruous 9:30am to 8pm day shift and 8pm to 9:30am night shift. The case for the reduction of pay went to court and thankfully it was deemed an illegal stoppage of pay and all personnel got their money back. But the industrial relations in LFB were now badly damaged and pretty much did not recover until a new Commissioner and Deputies were appointed in 2017.

During this dispute, as I said I'd been spared the dreaded 'phone call' duty. But I was occasionally required to report to a nerve centre that had been set up at NE area HQ at Stratford Fire Station when I was on 24 duties. I was mostly used to drive to stations to take care of the station keys once the off going officer in charge went home. One evening I was just leaving Stratford when my pager went off. I was being informed that a SM had been sent to a call to a fire at a 31-storey apartment block and hotel near Canary Wharf on Poplar's ground.

By the time I got through on the phone, I was informed that several calls had been received some with some residents in the flats above the hotel stating they were trapped. I recognised this was a significant incident and told control I was on my way. I quickly raced through the dark streets from Stratford to Canary Wharf, all of the time listening to the radio where poor old Poplar were being inundated with Fire Survival calls from Control of people trapped on multiple floors. They had managed to get one message back making pumps six and persons reported but I had no idea still of what I felt sure was a disaster unfolding.

A year before in July 2009, the tragic Lakenhal House fire had occurred where a fire in a 14-storey block of flats spread irregularly up, down and inside of the building. Crews were chasing the fire everywhere and were struggling to get onto the floors where people were trapped. Sadly, six people were killed, some of those died whilst still on the phone to control having dialled 999 to report they were trapped as crews just could not get to them because of the layout of the building and spread of fire through the common hallways which despite being designed as escape routes had failed catastrophically and were now filled with flames and smoke.

As I approached, I was absolutely certain this was happening again as all of the calls stated people were trapped in their apartments. Pulling off Aspen Way into Hertsmere Road I drove straight through a piece of police tape that had been placed across the junction. I pulled my car up outside the Marriot hotel and jumped out. There was frenzied activity with Firefighters running everywhere and as I looked up I was stunned to see no sign of smoke or fire at all, but really worryingly a person waving a white T-shirt or similar item from a window on one of the upper floors.

Someone called from behind me and I tuned round to see a man in civilian clothing with a Police vest on.

"You nearly killed me," He shouted at me.

"Do what?" I replied.

"You came around that corner so fast you nearly hit me."

"No I didn't. You were on the kerb," I said back to him now becoming irritated.

"You did, you took that corner…" he started his reply.

"ENOUGH!" I shouted at him. "I've potentially got dozens of people trapped and I'm here in charge of this incident, I haven't got time to argue with you, go away."

To be fair that had the desired effect as I turned away to get rigged in my kit I was aware that he was walking away grumbling. I was unable to book in attendance as the radio was frantic by now and the driver of Poplar's Pump Ladder was becoming buried under slips of paper with details being written on them. I was approached by Poplar's Station officer looking exhausted.

"What have we got, Shaun?" I demanded.

"I've no idea Guvnor, we can't see a fire anywhere but people from the flats are coming down stating there is smoke everywhere on the upper floors. The hotel runs from ground to the 13th and they have no issues although the hotel and restaurant have evacuated as a precaution, which isn't helping us as we've got people everywhere. I've got Dave my CM up on the 14th setting up a bridgehead and I'm sending him more crews but we've got FSG calls on multiple floors," Came his breathless briefing.

"OK Shaun, I'm going to take over, I'm gonna make it ten and try to get a grip on it, get your driver to interrupt Control and make it ten and show me as Incident Commander, you stay down here with me for now as I'll need to go through exactly who and what you have sent inside."

At that point I was glad to see Jim walking towards me. Jim was a SM on my rota group and we'd worked well together over the past few years, I'd known him for many years and he was an exceptional Fireground Officer.

"Jim, I've no idea what we've got. The fire hasn't been located, there is nothing showing from anywhere but you've heard we've got FSG's going on all over the place I've nothing more to tell you but I've made it ten and taken over. I need you to go to the 14th where the Bridgehead has been set up and manage it for me. I'll send you crews as they come on and for the time being everything upstairs including firefighting and rescue is yours... OK?"

"No problem Steve, leave it with me," Jim said with his customary calm and ability. "What have I got up there?"

Poplar's Station officer chipped in, "You've got my CM and my PL's crew, I also sent Millwall and Shadwell up there, I've got no one else at the moment.

"Thanks, I'll sort it," Jim said to me with a determined smile and off he went into the building.

The next ten minutes or so were a hive of activity. The calls continued, the fire still hadn't been found and as Officers in charge of appliances turned up I spoke to each of them directly.

"We don't know where the fire is but we've got multiple FSG's. Get yourself and your whole crew rigged in BA and take full High-rise kit up with you as we don't yet know if you'll come across the fire, report to the SM at the Bridgehead on the 14th." Luckily, the Blue Watch who had come on at 6pm that evening had some excellent Station officers on duty and I was becoming more confident as I saw faces like Mark from East Ham and Martin from Bethnal Green among others report to me.

I was beginning to overload with information, so I said to 'Boiler' the Command Unit Officer who was now with me frantically trying to get some proper command support set up. "Boiler, come over to the edge of the dockside, I need to get away from everyone for a minute and run through everything we've done so far," he followed me away from the building and the hive of Firefighters and evacuees towards the dockside. As we turned around, I was now at the back of the building looking into the glass fronted ground floor restaurant which overlooked the water and Canary Wharf beyond it.

Then I saw it, inside the restaurant was an open cooking range. From the middle of that range danced a bright orange flame that was roaring up into an unseen overhead canopy.

"What the fu..."

I turned to Boiler who had also seen the same.

"There it is, there's the fucking fire... It's a cooking range on fire, it must be going right up into the ducting throughout the building, get me a BA crew and get them in there to put that out."

He didn't have to, I saw another Station officer and called him over.

"Matt, I think we've found the fire, get a couple of your crew rigged, take a jet and put it out, I need to know how far up inside this is going."

With that, a chef who had been standing in the crowd, seeing us all pointing towards his burning range came over to us. His English was not brilliant and between me being stupefied he hadn't approached us earlier and allowing him a minute to talk we worked out he'd evacuated when the fire started which instantaneously set the alarm off. He assumed by the arrival of crews that we were aware of his fire through the alarm system and had wondered why so many Firefighters were going into the building and not putting his range out.

The message soon filtered up to Jim, who also calmed me immensely by telling me that a couple of crews that he had committed to go to those trapped had found just a very light smoke haze and nothing to worry about. The fire was soon put out, it did extend but only a floor or so into the hidden vent system which we soon had broken open and extinguished.

The panic was just perception. Once we got all of the evacuees moved into a large conference room, we worked out who was from the hotel and established a number of people from the apartments had smelt the smoke, opened their doors, seen it was just light smoke and walked completely unaided through it. Those who had rung up had done the same but as soon as they caught a whiff or sight of the smoke immediately assumed, they were trapped with nowhere to go.

Once we got everything settled, with the aid of the Fire Investigation team and a Senior Fire Safety Officer, we established the ducting went right up through the service shaft of the 31-storey building. There was a difference in the way the compartmentation was laid out in the hotel, so the fault, poor smoke stopping in the ducting hadn't affected them. But it had seeped out of the service shaft up on the floors above which housed the private apartments. This was a Fire Engineering and building regulation issue that would need further investigation, especially as the building was only a few years old. Thankfully, it all calmed down very quickly and apart from a two-week old baby that had some unrelated breathing difficulties everyone was fine.

As everyone gathered about making gear up and getting a breather, the public from the hotel, restaurant and flats made their way back in. Football Manager Harry Redknapp had been caught up in it all and I was glad to see he took time out to have a bit of banter and some photographs with the crews.

Riot

Several months after my promotion in 2010, there had been a number of changes in the Special Operations Group at HQ, not least within the ILO group that I had fallen so spectacularly foul of. The Officers now running it felt that I'd had a bit of a rough ride and one afternoon, while off duty at home I got a telephone call.

Daryll was the SM in the ILO team and a good mate of mine. He told me that the ILO process was out again and that I should apply. I thanked him and asked him did I really need to go through the process again as I'd already passed once and didn't feel it fair to have to apply again. He wasn't the decision maker in all of this so simply passed me the message, where I thanked him but my pride (and my stubbornness) wouldn't allow me to go through it all again.

Not long after that, Graham who was the head of the ILO group, also a good friend and a formidable character rang me back.

"Steve, you need to apply for the ILO round, me and Daryll want to make it right, we want you in the group, so you need to apply."

"Graham, I'm sorry mate, I applied once and passed so don't see why…"

"STEVE! Shut up and listen to me," Graham cut me off in a way that someone with his ability could.

"Do me a favour… I'm asking you to apply for the ILO round. OK? Just apply for it and let the process play out. I expect to see your application coming in soon."

And that was it, I had been told, so with my stubbornness now retreated well back into its box, I did as I was told. I went through the process of application, an interview with Graham and a senior non-uniformed member of staff, after successfully getting through that was accepted into the group and was soon reporting to the old HQ at Lambeth to carry out my initial five day intensive training.

As I'd already mentioned, this was a specialist group… Often mocked by others in LFB as the 'secret squirrel' gang. But it did require an elevated level of security clearance to "Secret and occasional Top Secret" level due to the type of information we'd be handling and those we'd be discussing it with.

In that initial five days, we met with some amazing people from many of the Police specialist departments, Military and the Security Services as well as experts in International terrorism, lawyers and criminal psychologists. I'd done 23 years with LFB by this time, but this was a real eye opener. Once we'd finished the initial training, we were back to the day job where we'd shadow the duty ILO on our own rota group to gain more experience and once our security clearance had been completed, we'd be allowed even more information.

Initially, I was speaking with the duty ILO on a daily basis to discuss what had been going on, a few weeks in and they'd ask me what I would have done with various calls and towards the end of the shadowing process, with the Officer of the Watch at Control aware of my role as a 'trainee' ILO, I'd be passed certain ILO calls to deal with on my own.

Once it was decided I was ready, I attended another two week 'National' ILO course down at the Fire Service college at Moreton in Marsh with a detailed time critical assessment based on a real incident at the end and then back to London where Daryll and Graham, both of them over 6ft tall, grilled me across a desk.

The pair of them took it in turns to ask me procedural and scenario-based questions as well as taking it in turns to play 'Good ILO' and 'Bad ILO' I sweated through it, but the beaming smile that broke across Graham's face as we finished and he offered me his hand, indicated that I had passed and was now one of the LFB's ILO cadre.

I was issued with an additional radio and all sorts of other interesting clothing, books and guides including some other information and records that I can't talk about lest I get a knock on my door from some men in suits. The following Saturday was my first shift as duty ILO. It was what was known as an 'exclusive duty' meaning no matter what happened I would only be dealing with ILO calls while the other ILO's on duty went about their usual role unless I needed them. Nothing out of the ordinary happened for a few months until one night in August 2011.

On the evening of Thursday 4th August 2011, a team of Armed Police stopped a Mini-Cab in Monument way in Tottenham. The passenger in the mini-cab, Mark Duggan who was known to Police jumped out of the mini-cab and allegedly reached into his waistband to pull out a gun. An Officer shot Duggan and he died on the scene from his injuries. The relationship between the Police and local community in Tottenham had always been fraught going back to before the previous Tottenham riots in 1985 where PC Keith Blakelock was killed following the death of Cynthia Jarrett when police raided her home the day before the riot.

Blitz like scenes, A burned out building, in the hours following the Tottenham Riot in 2011.

News of Duggan's death spread rapidly around the area, including unconfirmed reports of police standing over Duggan and shooting him. Protesters were planned for the following evening, the Friday night, centred around a nearby community centre. LFB were aware of the threat and a number of us within the ILO group were told to standby to be recalled to duty should trouble break out.

In the event the Friday evening was quiet, the following afternoon the Local Police Borough Commander was alleged to have reassured interested parties that there was no intelligence of any likely trouble. A deputy, a Chief Inspector was left in charge of Haringey Borough Police and was on duty at Tottenham Police Station.

That evening, members of the Duggan family and supporters made their way to Tottenham Police Station and demonstrated outside. Members of the community spoke to the Chief Inspector but demanded to see a more senior Officer. No one else was available. At some point after this, a group of youths, which it is said had nothing to do with the protest attacked a couple of police cars along Tottenham high road and set them alight. The crowd grew, a bus was set alight and several shops were looted. The 2011 Riots had started.

I was off duty, my standby shift having ended at 8am on Saturday morning after nothing materialised the previous evening. I decided to have one of my days out in the Taxi, which I still drove from time to time to 'keep my hand in'.

I had a usual Saturday afternoon in the cab, ferrying people to and from stations, dropping tourists and shoppers off and at around 9pm I headed back to Poplar Fire Station where I dropped the cab off and picked my car up. I had a half share in a cab with Beaker one of my old White Watch colleagues at Poplar.

I noticed the bays were empty and with my usual curiosity, had to go and have a look at where they had gone. I walked into the Watchroom and picked up the teleprinter slip and noted without much interest they'd been called to a fire alarm in a nearby office block, just as I walked out of the Watchroom two things happened.

Since I'd been an ILO, before formal recall arrangement had been put in place, there was an unwritten rule that all ILO's carried their pagers with them 24/7. I was quite surprised as I felt the pager start to vibrate on my belt whilst off duty, then the teleprinter went off behind me in the Watchroom. I pulled my pager off my belt and saw a cryptic message that all ILO's should call Bob, the ILO support officer if they were available, I picked up the teleprinter slip to notice a message to All Stations sent by control that a 'Civil disturbance' was taking place on A33 Tottenham's ground and that Civil disturbance procedure had been implemented in the following route card areas... it went on to detail other operational specific information.

With a surge of adrenalin running through me I fumbled for my phone and rang Bob. I managed to get through straight way.

"Bob, what have we got mate?" I asked urgently.

"Hello young Stephen, are you available?" Came Bob's usual calm reply.

"Yeah, er, yea, well I will be. I'm about half an hour from home but as soon as I get there and get my kit on I'm ready."

"OK Steve, I'll show you on duty, get yourself ready and let me know on 'ILO2' when you are ready to go." He said indicating what one of the encrypted radio channels we were using.

I sprinted over to my car, opening the bay door as I went, placed my blue light on the roof of my car and pulled out of the bay at Poplar heading home and then God knows...

I heard a number of people on the radio whilst on my way home. Trevor my old boss had booked on scene in Tottenham and had met up with the initial local crews. Tony called up to say he was mobile to the Police Special Ops room at Lambeth, Bob and the duty ILO were co-ordinating. I rang Joanne and told her what was happening and that I was on my way home to head out again. I asked her to get my 'black kit' comprising a black LFB ILO polo shirt, black cargo pants and black tactical boots ready as I briefly explained what was going on.

We had just moved into a new house a month before, so I was lucky enough to have my own study now. I kept an ILO grab bag in there just in case something like this happened. I pulled onto the drive in a cloud of dust and one of the girls opened the door looking concerned. As I came into the passage, already undoing my shirt, I looked into the living room and saw images on the TV that was on live on Sky News showing a blazing bus and angry crowds throwing missiles.

I called Bob up on the radio and told him I was ready to go, He told me to report to Edmonton Fire Station which was the Forward mobilising point where I'd be the ILO liaising with another GM from the rota group on duty who would be acting as Mobilising officer. I acknowledged Bob, got changed quickly and wolfed down a sandwich Joanne had kindly made me. With demands that I "Be careful" from Joanne and the girls behind me I jumped back in the car, reversed off the drive and headed towards Edmonton fire station.

The drive took me around 30 minutes, as I drove along the A406 North Circular Road, heading towards the A10 where I'd turn north towards Edmonton, I looked over to the left towards Tottenham as I got to the top of an elevated part of the road. Ominously there were several large palls of smoke coming up from the area and a Police Helicopter, its bright 'Night sun' light shining down onto the streets below.

As I drove through the main part of Edmonton, there were lots of huddles of young people hanging around. Too many for my liking, I turned left into Church street and shortly after drew up outside of the Fire Station. There were a number of Fire Engines parked in the street and others being backed into the four large bays of the station. I looked left and right and decided to park my car outside among some other Officers cars... I thought back to the crowds gathering up on the high road and wondered if my car would become a victim should things turn nasty at this end.

In the yard, I approached the Command unit. I met up with Steve, another Group Manager who was allocated the 'mobilising officer' role. Essentially, as a Forward Command Point, once we were up and running, all calls to a predesignated area within Tottenham would be passed through to us for assessment and then a decision made as to whether we should attend. Calls to bins alight or cars burning would be left. But more serious fires, would require an assessment from the mobilising officer and me as the ILO, I'd gather Police intelligence from the ILO at the Police control room and then we'd make a decision on whether to attend. A big call when it could be someone's home or business burning, but we couldn't send Firefighters unprotected into a dangerous area.

When we were satisfied, we had everything in place, we let our control room know and then started to take calls for the designated area, these were being passed by telephone to the command unit staff. We had a few car and rubbish fires that we left and then some building fires came in.

We actually didn't do too bad. Trevor and another couple of Officers on the ground had around half a dozen crews with them who were following the Police down the high road as the rioters moved further north. Between me Trevor and Tony in the Police control room, we managed to work out that most property fires were being fought... albeit not in their usual way. A whole supermarket alight, probably 10 or 15 pumps usually, with just a couple of crews doing what they could to protect the exposures. We manged to get a few appliances sent down there to help out as the area affected grew.

At some point in the early hours, we began to take multiple calls to a large carpet shop on fire at a major crossroads. Picturing a single storey industrial unit in my mind, I couldn't understand when we were getting calls that flats above it were alight. I quickly had a look on google maps on my mobile phone and was horrified to see this was a big old corner department store with a couple of floors of flats above.

Steve and I looked at each other and began to think about getting some crews down there. At that point Trevor had got that far and informed us that he had made it as far forward as the junction and Firefighters were making ladders rescues from adjacent buildings. The radiated heat from the fire was so bad, people opposite could not get out so had to be rescued. Trevor said he could cover the rescues but would need at least 6 more Pumps for this fire.

Events moved quickly after this. A more senior officer turned up to take over the role of Mobilising officer and an ILO support officer arrived with him. Then Trevor came on and said he was now covering about a mile of the high road with many burning properties and needed more assistance. Steve and I looked at each other and quickly agreed that we would be better down at the scene.

We both got rigged in our fire kit and each jumped on the back of a couple of the six fire engines that were about to leave for the fire. The route was torturous. Usually, it would be a left out of Edmonton Fire Station, right into the high road and continue down for a mile of so until we reached Tottenham High road all of which was part of the same long road out of Central London.

But because the riot was moving north, we had to take a long route. Initially I recommended going south down the adjacent dual carriageway part of the A10 and left into Lordship Lane which would have brought us directly and quickly to the junction where the carpet store fire was. However, the riot had reached its peak by now and numbers the Police were trying to control were beginning to stretch them. Trevor was happy we could get to the junction, as he was there, but we couldn't get the vital clearance from Police control, so had to take a torturous route back down to the A406, then turn east for a mile or so and south again down Monument way to bypass the riot and come back in from the south where it had all started several hours earlier.

As we slowed to a halt just past the Police Station where it had all began, I got off the appliance as I knew Trevor was at the north end a mile or so ahead of me. I contacted him to tell him help was now with him, although it would take more than 10 minutes for the 6 appliances to slowly pick their was over debris and manoeuvre around the other appliances already Firefighting. My intention was to make an assessment of all of the fires, who was dealing with them, did they need any more help and finally come to an assessment with my colleagues when or if I got to the front.

I looked ahead of me and was awestruck by what I faced. Tottenham High road is pretty much a straight road as it runs north. I could see what I estimated was a mile ahead of me, but it was in fact a mile of fire. I was instantly reminded of photographs and film that I'd seen of the London Blitz in World War II. In front of me various buildings to the right and left were ablaze with flames and thick smoke rolling out of them and up into the night sky. Solitary Firefighters were standing there in small groups playing water on the burning structures towering above them. I started to walk forward… uneasy at first as the road was literally littered with bricks and other debris which made progress really slow.

I soon picked up some sort of shuffle which cleared the smaller debris in front of me and hopped over larger bits. To step on it would've meant a very quick end of the night with a sprained ankle otherwise. In places there was hardly any debris by comparison, it was strange, but I guessed these were the places where the rioters had stopped from time to time and barrages launched at Police before they moved on again.

I walked past a burned-out bus, marvelling at how its aluminium bodywork had melted like a candle with bright pools of now cooled molten metal on the road. Other parts of the bus had been made of fibreglass and this gave an effect of looking like it was covered in white and grey hairs. A couple of burned out shops were still smouldering, but after a quick trip inside I satisfied myself they'd need some attention but were fine for the time being.

I came across the first crew, a male and a female firefighter using a large jet to control a fire that had completely consumed a row of about four shops with two floors of dwelling above. I think they were from Chingford, I enquired how they were and with broad grins both of the youngsters proudly told me they were fine. I asked where their guvnor was and they pointed towards a smoky shop on the other side of the road.

I smiled at the driver who was looking after his pump controls at the back of his truck ensuring they maintained a decent supply of water whilst using his foot to kick minor adjustments to a ground monitor that was also pouring hundreds of gallons onto the burning shops. Creeping into the smoky shop by the light of my torch, the reflective stripes of the fire coat that the officer wore jumped back at me, he looked up.

"Hello mate, how's it going?" I asked almost incongruously in our surroundings.

"Morning Guvnor, we are all OK thanks. Someone had given this shop a drink earlier on but it's starting to get smoky again. It's alight out the back…"

"OK, great job, keep an eye on it and your crews, we'll try to get some more help for you as soon as we can," I said with more confidence than I felt. I patted him on the back and made my way out of the shop heading towards the next pocket of smoke and flames.

This was the Aldi supermarket and a gym that would normally have had dozens of firefighters attending it. There were four fire engines and a few small groups of Firefighters around the building, it's roof now buckled and scorched with grey smoke rolling lazily across the car park as they got to grips with the fire inside.

I approached Tim, Enfield's Guvnor who I had worked with years before at Poplar…

"Alright Tim, just like a Friday night at Poplar back in the day," I called out to him as I approached and shook his hand.

"Jesus, this is unbelievable, we've been here ages trying to get to grips with it but we are winning," he replied.

"Are you all OK? We'll try and get some fresh crews in when we can and give you all a breather."

"Yeah, we are OK, we managed to get hold of a few cases of water, I'm revolving the crews to make sure they are rested."

We had a bit of a chat and a laugh about the old days and I bid Tim farewell as I kept heading north. The light from the fire in the carpet store was now looming large ahead of me. There was further smoke and flames just beyond that, so it had spread in the hour or so since I left Edmonton Fire Station. As I got closer, I could see this was now where the majority of the LFB response was. A couple of groups of white hatted senior officer stood in huddles. I went over to one where Pete and Gary were standing discussing pumping water from one pump to the next to secure a better supply. Again a handful of exchanges and light hearted comments underlining the way we had always dealt with being right at the coal face of adversity with the pressure on.

Walking to the junction I met up with Trevor, without really looking at each other, both of us transfixed by the burning carpet store… bright flames evident throughout including in and around the clock tower that was built at the very top of the building on the corner. Between us we went over how many buildings were on fire. We estimated each of these as a fire on their own would add up to around 80 Pumps worth. And several aerial trucks set up to deliver water from above to the heart.

I mentally calculated those I had passed on the way up here as well as those we now at here and it came to 19 Pumps… No aerials, no other support vehicles. "It shows what can be done," Trevor said to me. "Just don't tell the politicians," I replied. More water came through, but the fire was also beginning to darken down anyway now as all of the fuel was consumed. The carpet store was essentially just the outside walls now, so we checked the crews were at a safe distance should part of the building collapse, which it did a few hours later.

Probably a hundred yard ahead of us was the front line of the riot. Distant shouting and jeering in a continuous angry hum, the noise of the helicopter overhead and the deep cracks and rumbles of the fires in front of us. One building fire had been dealt with successfully, but another tall detached shop still had angry grey smoke coming out of it.

In any other circumstance, crews wearing BA would be fighting their way to the heart of the fire blindly feeling their way forward until they could attack the seat of the blaze. But with an angry riotous mob of several hundred just ahead and none of the usual safety and support systems in place, this was a frustrating defensive bit of firefighting, having to wait as more and more of the building was slowly consumed before it broke out and allow them to attack it.

Between the clouds of grey smoke and the bluer broken clouds in the sky I noticed a watery blue sky beginning to appear. It must have been getting on for 5am and happy we now had everything in place I started to work my way gradually back down the high road towards the Police Station to try to get a conversation going around opening things back up with a view to getting more crews and appliances in.

I took my time getting back stopping in various buildings to check them out. I also passed an orange painted and brightly lit Turkish grocers... The owners were outside sweeping glass but the store was untouched, the bright neon lights inside making the glass outside twinkle. There was quiet a large Turkish Community in this part of London and also a lot of Turkish and Kurdish gangs. It seems the rioters had picked their targets on the basis of not wanting to bring an unwanted and potentially very violent response onto the nights proceedings.

"Are you open mate?" In enquired to one of the two shopkeepers.

"Yes, yes, what do you want?"

I was starving, thirsty and despite being only a social smoker by this point I was desperate for a cigarette. I bought myself a Yorkie Bar, an ice-cold bottle of water and ten Marlboro lights and a box of matches. I walked away from the shop and propped myself up against a traffic signal cabinet and took off my helmet and fire coat. After the chocolate and a drink, I smoked two cigarettes one after the other and felt the nicotine surge through me and settle me down.

Another strange thing happened. One by one, then in twos and then slightly larger groups, young men started walking back down the high road. They hadn't appeared out of nowhere at 5:30am so I assumed they must have something to do with the rioters. I radioed Trevor. "What's happening up by you mate with the riot?"

"It all just sort of fizzled out about a quarter of an hour ago…" Came his reply.

Then the Police came… A few on horses, others walking, a few in vans. They were walking, or driving, exhausted along the same road as those who they had been fighting against in the hours earlier… it was the strangest thing. Almost as if they'd all exhausted themselves as daylight began to break and the need to rest from the madness had become the overriding human desire. As if a whistle had been blown at the end of a long game and the players were now wearily heading back into the changing rooms.

I managed to cadge a lift back to Edmonton and happily scoffed down a couple of rolls and a hot coffee, plus a couple more cigarettes at the canteen van that had set up outside the Fire Station. There was talk of de-briefs from one or two officers at Edmonton, but the looks they got from the crews as well as encouragement from those of us who had been down at the High Road pretty much put paid to that… I assume, because I jumped up onto the Command Unit and announced I was leaving and wearily headed back through the bay and into my car before anyone could convince me otherwise.

I got home at some time after 9am and after a quick chat with the family fell into bed after a hot shower and slept like a baby. I was woken mid-afternoon by my phone and felt dizzy as it rose me from the deepest of sleeps. It was Bob, asking if I was still available for duty. I told him I was and he said that there was intelligence that things may liven up again later and to be ready. I laid my head back on the pillow, but my mind was racing now, replaying the events of the night before. So I got up and went downstairs to watch it all again on TV.

By Sunday evening, the great and the good of London's emergency services were all now in the game, without a doubt the unexpected Saturday riot had taken everyone by surprise. Other Officers as well as ILO's had come back so with me already having earned my spurs on the ground, I was asked to cover an overnight shift at the Police Control room. I accepted of course but felt like I'd rather be out on the street.

I took over from another Officer at 8pm and was soon joined by Natalie one of the Control Room supervisory officers. We got ourselves settled and watched various news footage, CCTV feeds as well as live footage from the Police helicopter on the massive bank of screens that lined one end of the room which was probably about the size of a school hall, filled with dozens of screened pods for the various and numerous departments of the police as well as British Transport Police, London Ambulance and us. To one side of the room were a number of pods containing offices where the Police 'Silver' and 'Gold' Commanders held their briefings. I was the LFB rep for both Silver and Gold level that night so occasionally got a change of scenery to dart into a meeting every couple of hours.

Tottenham was flooded with Police and things were pretty quiet, it had a few gatherings of people, which history tells us usually leads to some more trouble but it all seemed OK. Enfield, which was further north, was a different matter. Straight up the road from Tottenham, past Edmonton you came to Enfield, a fairly nice suburban town just within the London boundary.

The gathering there had got quite lively and the Police had arrived, we watched with interest as it flared up and calmed down a couple of times as darkness fell. LFB had managed to get some better arrangement in place. They had set up a number of 'hubs' at Various Fire Stations across the Capital each with Pumps, Rescue Units, Aerials and Officers all ready to respond to whatever else might break out.

Brixton, the scene of the first major riots in the early 1980s had been getting warmed up as darkness fell. Initially with crowds gathering, then a bit of disorder, as life carried on around them… buses still coming and going, people in and out of the tube station. But it began to grow and go until a point where I guess you'd say the disorder became a riot.

I'd been dealing with a telephone call when a headset wearing Police Officer came over to me and pointed to the screen… "Looks like we may have a fire, crews on the ground are asking for LFB as they've looted the Footlocker on the high street at the junction with Atlantic Road and torched it." I nodded an acknowledgement and looked at Natalie as she reached for the phone to call control in anticipation of the calls they'd be getting soon. The CCTV camera wasn't clear as there was tree between the camera and the shop, but I did see a few tell-tale wisps of smoke.

I got on the radio to the ILO who was at Lambeth Fire Station, the old HQ building which was the nearest LFB hub to Brixton. I let him know that we'd likely need a few crews but to hold on while I got a safe route and even more critical got them a safe cordon to work in.

Natalie briefed me that Control already had Forward mobilising in place for Brixton and they wouldn't send anyone until I gave the say so. Springing out of my chair I went over to the desk containing the team I'd be liaising with and asked the situation in terms of protection of crews. I was informed the riot had generally moved south and was more based on looting than anything else. They'd pretty much had what they wanted from the shops in Brixton Road and had now turned their attention to the larger retail parks on Acre Lane and Effra Road to the south.

I also quickly spoke to the pod dealing with traffic movement who confirmed our crews would be safe to approach from the north out the back of Lambeth to Kennington Road then into Brixton Road. With all this clear, I looked back up at the CCTV to see the fire was developing nicely now so spoke to the hub at Lambeth and recommended they sent four machines on it.

Within a short time they'd arrived and although it was going pretty well, unlike the night before where one crew may have been tacking a couple of buildings on fire, they were able to request back up. It ended up with 6 pumps attending the fire. It started to rain quiet heavily so that seemed to calm things down across London and that was pretty much the only serious fire related to the riots that night. LFB got away lightly, although one officer heading towards the fire at Brixton from South West London got his car attacked in Acre Lane as he drove through, thankfully he was able to keep going and was unharmed although his car had a few dents in it.

As the night drifted on, I was popping in and out of meetings, I was talking to one plain clothed Officer in the intelligence cell about the messaging that was coming across on the Blackberry Messenger app, Blackberry's being a very popular phone back in 2011 when the iPhone were still a bit of a luxury. As we were talking, I found him staring at me and I also recognised him. We quickly sussed it, he had grown up near me in Poplar and although he was around three years younger, I remember him and his family. I did recall that he had been very badly injured on duty after being attacked in the mid-90s so had assumed he'd left the Police. I was glad to see he was doing well and still serving.

Although you'd never know it in the police control room that was deep underground, Monday had dawned a pleasant day and our reliefs had arrived early. Not thinking it fair that Natalie should have to battle with Monday morning rush hour I offered her a lift home as she didn't live a million miles away from me. I was home again before long and followed the same routine, eat, quick shower then some sleep while I could.

Joanne woke me up mid-afternoon. "Are you hungry? They've started again by the way... Hackney this time."

"What, really? It's still early isn't it?" I confirmed by turning and looking at the clock on the bedside cabinet.

I went downstairs and there it was... more rioting, two spots, as usual, right in the middle of the district, the 'high road' or in Hackney's case Mare Street the main road running right through the centre of the borough. The other area was a little further north on Clarence Road next to the notorious Pembury Estate which I knew well from my time at Homerton.

A little later on the rolling live News then cut across to Peckham in South East London. Another outbreak of trouble in the high street. It was simply looting and greed now. I really doubted any of these young people, boys and girls, black and white cared anything about Mark Duggan's loss.

A shop was soon ablaze and we watched from TV helicopters as the road was cleared and fire crews came in to deal with the blaze. What happened over the next few hours was really quite frightening. Almost every corner of inner London and some of the suburbs broke into violence. Buses were attacked, Police were really being hard pushed but thankfully reinforcements had arrived from across the UK by now with Riot teams from as far away as Yorkshire dealing with events as they unfolded.

As darkness fell so did my mood, what was going on, what is happening in my country and where would it end. I was still on standby and inevitably would be called out again. In Croydon we watched on TV as rioting spread down London Road with many shops being looted and randomly set on fire. The camera then panned to another crowd not too far away who were looting a large furniture store called Reeves on an island site surrounded by a circular road. The store had been there for almost 150 years and soon the tell take wisps of smoke appeared. I watched transfixed as the whole store went up the radiated heat setting fire to buildings on the other side of the road encircling the site.

My pager went off and I was being sent out. I was headed to East Greenwich as an ILO where a hub had been set up. I made my way thought Hornchurch down towards the A13 and then in towards Blackwall tunnel. The radio was alive with reports of fires all over London, Clapham Common had now joined Croydon as a hot spot for larger fires along with Woolwich.

I was called up on the radio and it was explained to me I'd been ordered in error as there was already an ILO at Greenwich. Somewhat crestfallen, I slowed the car down, switched off the blue lights and turned around at the next intersection. As I approached Barking I was passed by a fast moving convoy of around 10 Police riot vans, approaching Barking Fire Station I was looking ahead as the vans turned off in towards Barking Town centre and my eyes saw something down to the left… it went in a flash as I was driving at around 50mph but I found myself braking as I passed the fire station and indicating left to pull off the A13 and turn towards the Town centre. As I passed the park and made a left onto Movers Lane, I ducked and bobbed my head trying to see through the trees in the park but nothing.

But I had seen something, something bright out of the corner of my eye. I got to the end of Movers Lane and turned left onto Ripple Road, all of the Police vans had come to a halt and beyond them at the junction with King Edward Road a derelict Pub was burning right up through the roof. Most surprisingly was the fact no one from the LFB had arrived yet. I pulled the car up and jumped out approaching the lines of Police and the burning building. Struggling to remember which road I was on I called a priority into the Radio.

"FE from Foxtrot one, one, zero priority, running call over," I called into the radio as I eyed the building.

"Foxtrot one, one, zero from FE go ahead over," Came the metallic reply.

"FE Foxtrot one, one, zero… called by running call to a derelict public house alight… Ripple Road… Barking… Junction with… Erm… King Edward Road… Request…"

Control cut across me.

"Foxtrot one, one, zero. We are already receiving multiple calls to this fire, appliances are on route."

"Foxtrot one, one, zero received, further traffic over." I was going to make the job up, but by doing that I would then be in command of the incident and noticed that Barking's pair were just pulling up on the King Edward Road side of the fire.

"Er… Foxtrot one, one zero to FE… for your information a Police Serial Unit are already in attendance and can you show me status three as ILO please."

"Foxtrot one, one zero all received." I pocketed my radio and met with the guy in charge of Barking that night.

"Hello Guv, how did you get here so quick?" he enquired.

"Hello Tony, I was passing on the A13 and saw it so doubled back, it must have been just as you were getting the call, it's going well, I was about to make it six and ask for an aerial as I saw you pull up."

"Yes… OK Guv, I agree, I'll make it six, shall I send it in your name?"

"No mate, you have it, I'm here as ILO as we are in the middle of a disturbance but I'm here for you… I'm just gonna have a chat with Plod and get rigged."

I walked over to the Police Inspector in charge of the serial, he was identifiable by his bright red shoulder markings on his protective suit. I introduced myself and explained what was happing with the fire and asked what the situation was locally. He said that there had been some trouble in the Town centre and they were headed there when they saw the fire. The issue in the town centre was now contained but they'd stay and protect us for as long as they could. Happy with that, I returned to my car and got rigged.

The Station Manager from Dagenham Paul was soon on the scene and took command. He was joined shortly after by Steve who I'd been at Tottenham with on Saturday night as Group Manager. I let them know the situation with the Police and just stood back as a casual observer listening in to reports from other ILO's out on the ground. I had both radios with me, but with the main-scheme radio being so busy I switched it off as it had become a constant annoying background noise.

Steve and Paul came off the command unit and approached me, they explained that they were letting two pumps go as a massive Sony distribution warehouse up in Enfield next to the M25 had been torched. Hertfordshire Fire Brigade were attending with LFB crews but the job which would normally attract a 20 plus pump attendance only had eight on it as we were running low on appliances due to the amount of fires across London.

Not long after that, the PSU Inspector made my night even more interesting. He told me they'd been called to Ealing as rioting had broken out there. Ealing is in West London and about 15 miles from where we were stood in Barking. 15

miles down a motorway is not far at all. But 15 miles across one of the world's biggest cities is a long way. I was astounded...

"Do they know where you are?" I enquired.

"Yeah, they do, but there is no one else and its looking quite nasty there. Apparently, a member of the public has been attacked by the rioters and it doesn't look good for him."

"Jesus," I replied, not knowing what else to say.

"I can leave half of my PSU with you for about 20 minutes, will that do you?" He asked.

"I guess it'll have to I replied, we'll drown the fire and have to leave it, it's pretty much on its own with no exposures so should be OK."

I called Steve and Paul over and explained the situation. They both looked at me then over towards the pub. We all agreed the ALP was now doing a good job in knocking the fire down and 20 minutes would allow us to have it well under control, if not completely extinguished. But the last few nights had been a new reality, so we just got on with it.

True to their word, the Police stayed and we'd pretty much made all of the gear up as they withdrew leaving two local WPC's on the scene in regular uniform in a panda car. The pub was by no means out, there were no more flames but lots of steam still rising through the roof. We withdrew from the area and Barking said they'd do a ride by every couple of hours and order a relief when daylight came. I left them to it and went home actually managing to get into bed, albeit in the early hours for the first time since Friday night. I drifted off, half expecting to be called again at any moment, but the call never came.

When I got up on Tuesday morning I was now back on a regular day shift. I rang control and booked myself off for a few hours and contacted the ILO group and let them know. London had never seen a night like it and I shook my head in disbelief as the news went from one burned out and pillaged area of London to another.

I was ready to go on Tuesday evening. Not fully on duty but on recall should I be required. But London was now swamped with Police from across the UK, I think the rioters, who were by now just crowds of opportunists looking to loot what they could, realised that the game was up. Instead it was the turn of other Cities, While London was now quiet, Manchester, Birmingham and Liverpool had their turn with copycat looting-based riots, all of which had nothing to do with the death of Mark Duggan in the previous week.

London Fire Brigade tackled over 100 serious fires on the three night of rioting on the 6th, 7th and 8th August. Several Firefighters were injured and 8 fire engines and two Officers cars were damaged. The cost of the riots was put at over £100 million.

I was on my Thursday/Friday double 24 shift at the start of February 2012. The Friday night had been pretty quiet, which I wasn't at all sorry about as it was bitterly cold and snow was forecast for the Saturday evening. I was paged to monitor a job in the early hours and while I was on to control, they informed me, just out of interest that they were also dealing with a fire in a KFC Restaurant in Leicester Square in London's West End that had just been made up requesting more appliances.

I monitored my job, which was over and done with within the hour and went back to sleep. Again, the buzzing of the pager as it vibrated across my bedside table woke me before it started bleeping and I was surprised to see a 'Mobilise' instead of Information. I gathered my thoughts and once I'd realised where I was, I noticed it was 07:48. Just 10 minutes before the end of my Shift. What was even more unusual was that I had been mobilised to a fifteen pump fire in the heart of London's upmarket Mayfair district. I spoke to control again, they apologised as they knew it was just before I went off duty, but went on to explain that the fire in the KFC had gone up to 10 pumps after I had last spoke to them and then at around 5am they'd been called to a fire in a large house in Mayfair that had been a six pump fire for a while, but had then gone to 10 then just now 15 pumps. So, within a mile of each other in the West End, we had two large fires on A24 Soho's ground that had now pretty much called all of the available senior officers who had been on duty overnight.

I quickly got dressed, brushed my teeth, grabbed a cereal bar and a handful of biscuits to stave of the cries of 'breakfast' coming from my stomach and got in the car. By the time I was heading down towards the A13 and the fast road into London it had already gone 8am when I should have been off duty. But I wasn't worried as it sounded like this was an interesting fire.

As I approached one of the few sets of traffic lights on the A13 at Barking, I noticed ahead of me as I pushed through the line of cars heading into central London, one of my colleagues on another rota group, who had just come on duty and was heading in to his office. As I approached with the siren blaring I could see his head bobbing around looking in the mirror and over his shoulder. As I passed him, I smiled and shrugged my shoulders while he just stared back and me with his mouth open.

His Rota group were now on duty and mine should have been off, so he must've thought What the hell is Dudeney doing driving into London on blue lights off duty and I'm sat here oblivious? He did tell me later that he actually rang control to ask what on earth was going on and then had it explained to him that the most recent call for reinforcements had come in just before the change of shift.

With traffic pretty quiet on a Saturday morning I soon flew along the A13, through the Limehouse link tunnel, along the Highway and into Lower Thames street before heading along the Embankment and turning up towards Trafalgar Square. I few more lefts and rights and I was at the scene and found a parking spot outside of a posh hotel in Albemarle Street, where I got rigged and walked round the corner into Grafton Street. Ahead of me beyond the Command unit was a very large four storey Georgian Terraced house with dark grey smoke rolling lazily from its upper windows and roof. A hydraulic platform was set up outside the property with crews appearing on the roof as the smoke parted.

I jumped onto the back of the Command unit and was surprised to be met by the Duty Assistant Commissioner who was now in charge of the incident and one of the Deputy Commissioners, the other 'Dep' at that time being a non-uniformed Director. They both greeted me and the Dep followed up.

"Give us a few minutes Steve, we have a situation here that will require your skills as an ILO." Intrigued, I acknowledged him and jump back down from the unit to get an idea of how the fire was progressing.

The way this incident had been a slow-burn, if you pardon the pun, the fact that not a lot of visible fire was showing and all over the street were hot and sweaty Firefighters with their BA sets at their feet, indicated to me that this fire, wherever it had started had now got into enclosed voids and was burning unseen inside of walls, requiring lots of crews in BA labouring away, cutting into these voids to access the hidden fire. In fact, had the whole lot gone up with flames out of every window it would have been a 'surround and drown' firefighting strategy that would have required less resources. Playing into the old adage that the size of the fire doesn't always equate to the size of the incident in terms of resources required to deal with it.

The Dep called me back into the Command Unit. "The problem we have Steve is that pretty early on, the crews broke into the premises next door to check for fire spread…"

"OK…" I replied a little confused.

"That building is the Hong Kong Economic and Trade Office, so effectively it's Chinese Diplomatic property."

I now got the gist of the issue.

He continued, "We've spoken to the Diplomatic Police, they are going to speak to the Chinese, but we need to have a look inside the building, see what the situation is in terms of any damage and then explain why we acted a little early with a view to selling it as we have saved them a lot of damage."

I got the message and got about finding someone from the Diplomatic Police to try to stave off an 'International incident'.

As with all diplomatic properties, they are effectively a small piece of foreign land in another Country. We all know that from people in far flung places going to their Embassy in the midst of an emergency to seek protection, or the more dubious practice of those who have played hard and fast with local laws hiding in their embassy and then claiming diplomatic immunity.

Obviously LFB crews, especially in that part of London are well versed in attending incidents in Embassies and High Commissions, where even if the building is burning down behind them, still have to have 'permission' to start Firefighting. However, this wasn't an embassy but offices belong to the Government of Hong Kong, which since it had been handed back to the Chinese in 1997, was now Chinese Sovereign property and as such we should have asked their permission before breaking into the building as we are entitled to do for other properties under the Fire and Rescue act in pursuance of our duties.

I located a Police officer from the Diplomatic Protection group. He was well aware of the situation and informed me that the Chinese were aware and did not have a particular problem but wanted a clear update and explanation very soon. I told him I'd have a look round the building and get back to him. It became obvious to me that the Chinese had very little of interest in the building or else we'd be in a much more precarious situation.

I walked in through the broken front door of the building and heard the burglar alarm panel chirping angrily at me, there were a few splinters of wood on the floor, but all looked well. Walking up through the building, I was reassured that all of the offices remained locked and had not been disturbed by us. I eventually got to the top floor where I noted an open hatch and a pull down ladder leading to the loft. Climbing up it, I found myself in a service area at roof level with a door open to the roof, as I walked through it, I noted the door was hanging off its hinges and the lock was on the floor.

I was now stood outside right next to the house that was on fire and found a crew of Firefighters with a jet that had been hauled up from the mews road behind. They had been dousing the fire that had now spread to a covered roof terrace and had in fact prevented the fire from jumping across to the Hong Kong trade building and spreading.

"Morning Guvnor," one Firefighter called to me.

"They are setting up a TL in the road behind to work on this roof area, so we are pretty much done here." He volunteered before I could ask.

"Lovely, I replied, so you think we are OK in here?"

"Yeah, another few minutes and we are going down to get a breather, it's a bit better now, but it was quite smoky earlier. They really need to get onto that roof terrace and start cutting away to expose it, we can't do much more from here apart from flood it."

"Well done, I'll go back down and let the Diplomatic Police know when we are finished..." I was going to let them know about the whole situation but thought better of it.

Back with the Police Officer, I explained the limited damage and asked him to speak to get his Control to speak with the Chinese and let them know that had we not have taken such 'positive' action, we may now have been dealing with a fire in their property. I said I'd be happy to walk one of their representatives around the building, but the message came back they were happy to leave it with the Police if we had finished inside the building and they'd deal with it later.

I went back to the Dep and told him, it was all taken care of and the Commissioner wouldn't be called into the Foreign Office to explain himself to an unhappy Foreign Secretary. That was me pretty much done he declared, but seeing as this was quite an interesting job, I 'volunteered' to 'hang around' just in case... Which pretty much gave me a chance to have a good look around the fire and get involved. With a knowing smile and wink, he agreed.

As the reliefs arrived through the morning, some of the crews from my side of London were there, so I joined a few of them inside the building. Owned by an Iranian billionaire the inside of the house was unimaginably opulent. His staff had been on scene for several hours and were concerned about his art collection, valued at several million pounds and bizarrely, some of his shoes? We managed to get them inside on the lower floors for a look and they were happy when a team of Firefighters managed to retrieve all of the artwork and carry it down to a waiting van where it was removed for safe keeping.

The building had been altered massively from its Georgian origins. A long enclosed spiral staircase leading from the basement to the upper floors, enclosed on all sides had been the main culprit for the hidden spread of fire from its origins on the third floor, as a result of an electrical fault, right up to the roof. The damage was shocking, room after expensively decorated and furnished room had been burned out or covered with wet fallen plaster. Even after all of these years of Firefighting in everything from back street slums, to large office complexes to these multi-million pound houses, the damage caused by fire was always sobering.

By late afternoon, the sun had gone behind threatening clouds, it was raw as the wind picked up ahead of the predicted snow, I was tired and needed more than the sandwiches, crisps and chocolate bars available on the Salvation Army canteen van, as much as we love and cherish the service they provide for us.

Another officer relief had arrived so that was my cue to head off. I said my goodbyes, and headed back to my car, stripped out of my wet kit and suddenly felt very tired as I sank heavily into the driver's seat, where I reversed my journey from several hours earlier at a much more sedate pace.

In my new job after I left training when it was outsourced to Babcock in April 2012, I didn't have a lot to do. The 2012 Olympic games was fast approaching but LFB had a whole dedicated team working on that Firefighters and Officers from across LFB were going to be detached into two temporary fire stations within the Olympic park at Stratford where they'd respond to any incidents in a four Mini Countryman cars that had been donated by BMW or if required one regular Fire Engine.

As an ILO, we had some involvement in the security side of the operation, liaising with the Police and Military who would be working to ensure the games could be delivered safely. After a run of decent summer in the early 2000s the past few summers had been pretty average in terms of weather. 2012 was no difference. I recall a Saturday morning in May when me Chris and Richard, two other ILO's I worked with had to visit a number of sites where the Military were going to establish Ground to Air missile sites to protect the Olympic park from any airborne terror threat from rogue hostile aircraft.

We had visited a couple of sites, at the top of tall buildings not far from the park, to carry out an assessment of the risks related to fire from having the missile battery installed and had moved on to a site on the very edge of NE London. When it should have been a warm sunny day, we were dressed in our wet weather gear, and freezing cold as we held a meeting on top of a hill overlooking London. We met with specialist Police Officers and Military advisers, but to be fair at this open site, the measures they had in place for emergencies were more than adequate. The real details were arranging for access for fire crews should something happen. As we were very close to the border where London, Essex and Hertfordshire meet, confusing calls to an incident, especially if it involved an explosion, could easily see crews from three different services mobilised which would be a security nightmare. Trying to explain we couldn't provide registration numbers for Fire Appliances as those supplied could be on a call elsewhere or even away for servicing with spare appliances in service was a challenge but we eventually got there.

Summer 2012 continued in the same vein, with some really good summer weather in the early 2000s and in more recent years, the period around 2007 to 2012 was grim. Even the opening night of the Olympic games was embarrassingly showery, but the weather played nicely in the following weeks. On reflection, the UK had a fantastic Olympic games, one of the best ever in terms of the quality of the experience, which was acknowledged by commentators from across the globe.

From an LFB point of view, it went really well. No major disasters and the little Mini's with their 'welcome' messages in various languages plastered over them became an essential part of the visitors must have photographs. Because of the special reserved traffic lanes from Central London out to the park those of us who lived east but worked at HQ had to opportunity to work locally, I spent my time working from the NE area HQ close to the Olympic park at Stratford or my local Station Hornchurch.

On the very last day of the games with the closing ceremony due, I was the ILO assigned to the Police Control room deep underground in Lambeth. I was in the LFB pod in a far corner of the room watching various goings on across London on the large wall of screens. I became aware of multiple calls to a fire on an industrial estate in Dagenham, no big deal there, I've been to plenty myself that way. Upon the arrival of the crews the job was made up to 6 pumps, which got me a little interested. I asked one of the support officers to pop over to the Police 'Silver' for the day just to give them a heads up.

The fire was in a recycling yard and large rolls of baled mix refuse were burning causing quite a bit of smoke. All of a sudden, while looking up at the screen for one of the Police Helicopters circling the Olympic park at Stratford, their camera picked up the plume of smoke six miles to the east, the camera zoomed in and soon enough it appeared the Helicopter was headed that way. In the few seconds the operator at the Helicopter desk in the control room took a radio message from "India 99" that particular Police Helicopter and made his was over to my desk, the helicopter was overheard and zooming in on a fire that was spreading across the yard with great enthusiasm.

"Hello sir, just had a call from '99 they are going to have a look at this fire, is it bad." The operator said to me.

"Well they have just requested assistance, but looking at it, I think it has legs and will likely increase in size," I replied, "But big fires in that industrial area of Dagenham are quite regular."

What I did notice was that we had a decent warm breeze across London which was blowing from the south east, meaning the smoke was heading in a north westerly direction… Straight towards the Olympic park. More and more people were getting interested and suddenly my little corner of the control room was very busy, including a visit from the Commander who was the Police Silver for the day and his entourage of staff officers and analysts.

"What do you reckon?" He asked. The job had been made up to a 15-pump fire, so it had now become significant.

"Fifteen Pump fires, particularly in industrial areas like Dagenham are not that unusual, we probably have 7 or 8 of them across London in a year, it's a fairly typical response for that type of area when you consider the volume of fire and the logistics of getting enough water into the area," Came my reassuring reply.

I noticed, I had now been graced with the presence of the Police Gold, the Assistant Commissioner who had overall Police Control for London that day. I delved into a little more detail in an attempt to provide further reassurance and glancing down at my screen I told them that one of our Assistant Commissioners Dany had been mobilised to the incident and she would probably take charge of the operation.

One of the entourage whispered into the ear of the Police Gold, he nodded and interjected. "I think we should organise an extraordinary Gold meeting, can you get your Gold in here for say thirty minutes time, meanwhile if you could have a quick Silver meeting Bob." Turning towards the Police Silver, "Where we can record everything LFB have just told us."

I made a few calls to some of the 'grown ups' in LFB and got the duty Assistant Commissioner into his car and on his way. I left my support team to tidy up around the edges and let everyone know I was now in a silver meeting as I made my way through the maze of desks in this vast room towards the Silver Commanders offices.

Within the thirty minutes, I was joined by Jim, one of our AC's and quickly briefed him as to what was happening here. "Although it's a routine fire, they are quite excited over it, especially with the closing ceremony due and the smoke generally moving in that direction. However, I've been keeping an eye on the screens and although it is a smoky old job, I can't see any evidence of the smoke plume being detectable as far away as Stratford."

"Hmmm, OK," he replied, "thanks Steve anything else?"

"Not that I can think of Guvnor," I said.

We sat down in the large conference room the meeting was chaired by the Silver with the Gold and a couple of others sat beside him on the top table. The room had everyone in there, Transport and Ambulance service reps, Emergency Planners, local authority staff and military staff. The meeting got underway and just as the scene was being set by the Police, moments before the whole room turned towards Jim our AC for a reassuring solution I saw one of the Officers who was with me that day waving franticly at me.

I stood up and crept past people and headed to the door.

"It's gone 40," Gary said to me in a 'shouted' whisper.

"Wha...?"

"Dany has just made Pumps 40 down at Dagenham."

"Are you serious? We haven't had a 40 Pumper since... maybe the 70s, the last one I can think of is the Gardeners Corner fire in Whitechapel... 1972."

"Yup, well not anymore, we've got one now."

"Jesus, that changes the whole 'regular fire' thing don't it? OK, thanks Gary." I turned and walked back through the lines of people towards the boss who was looking questioningly at me.

"It's gone to 40," I whispered to him.

The same "What" reply.

"Yep, Dany has made it 40... No idea why at the moment."

"Christ, that's unusual and changes things a bit," He said.

Within seconds the Police Silver turned to Jim, "We'll get an update from LFB now, Assistant Commissioner?"

Jim managed to brief the room telling them it was now a 40 pump fire but without getting everyone alarmed. The real concern which us and a number of people were trying to get across was that the smoke plume by the time it reached Stratford was going to be so high and so diluted it wouldn't even be perceptible. Nonetheless, with the eyes of the World on the Olympic closing ceremony, a 'belt and braces' approach was agreed on and that STAC, (Science and technical advice cell) would be set up to carry out a smoke plume analysis and to monitor air quality.

Once all that was settled, I went back to my quiet corner of the control room, although the twelve-hour stint down there went quicker than it usually did that day. The fire at Dagenham wasn't done with me yet. Early the next morning my pager went off and I was ordered onto a 'relief' to the job which was still burning. I spent another six hours traipsing around there as incident commander.

Borough Commander

I'd had about a year in Special Operations without a great deal of work on my plate and it had always been my ambition to get a Borough Commanders role. I'd wanted that as I came out of training in 2012, but for lots of reasons that they explained to me, which of course I never agreed with, it wasn't to be just yet. "Steve, don't worry about being a Borough Commander, we've got a fantastic job for you in Special Operations, right up your street." Yeah, right, a nothing job as I predicted and as it turned out.

Anyway, in late spring 2013 I'd been making some noises, I was getting under the feet of my boss at the time who had a lot on but had all of the people in the right places to manage that. I was asked to go and see Dave, who had been my Borough Commander back in 2003 when I was Station Commander at Poplar, He was now the Third Officer and responsible for London's 113 Fire Stations and the Boroughs in which they sat.

I know that another one of my previous Borough Commanders had put in his retirement papers, but so had a few others. So in the informal interview we went through the requirements of the job and if I'd be suited to it, although we both knew It would be an ideal fit, I knew Dave thought I was still a Firefighter at heart and could be deemed to be a bit too friendly with the troops. He wasn't wrong, but although I wasn't one to jump quickly into formal discipline, I wasn't shy of reading people their fortunes and much preferred that as my management style as in my opinion, it showed real leadership.

We then went through 'Borough Poker' Where he mentioned two of the boroughs where vacancies were about to arise, Wandsworth in South West London and Westminster, but not mentioning the one that suited me. I am sure this was a test of my reaction and I sat there, poker faced agreeing any opportunity would be fantastic. In the event, Westminster would be great, especially as ILO because of the Government security zone and the kudos of being BC in one of the most high-profile areas of the UK. But the office was at

Paddington, which would be quite a journey for me every day. Wandsworth would have been horrific. It would mean an hour and a half to two hours of travelling each way to get there, but I nodded enthusiastically anyway.

A week or so later, Dave's Staff Officer bade me to come up and see him again. Sitting me down in his office, he cut to the chase.

"Steve, with regard to your request to take on a Borough Commander role, I've given it some thought and I think it's time you had a go. You may know that Graham has put his papers in, so I'd like to offer you Borough Commander for Hackney starting from August 1st."

I couldn't keep the smile off my face. I was absolutely delighted. I'd worked in Hackney before, when I was Station Commander at Homerton, and it was a fantastic Borough that runs north and east of the City of London. It had Tower Hamlets to its south east, Haringey to the north and Islington to the west. It was 'inner city' Firefighting at its best and all four stations were lively. Three of them, Homerton, Kingsland and Stoke Newington were noted back in the 70s, 80s and 90s as being part of the 'Hackney Triangle' where there never seemed to be a day that went by when one or the other stations was not out dealing with a significant fire. That was the time Hackney also got the title of the 'Borough of fire'.

The remaining Station, Shoreditch was a large 1960's Divisional Station that had been the C-Division Headquarters up until 1986 when the old Divisions were amalgamated. It was one of the biggest Fire Station in London with the station, offices and accommodation over 5 floors. The Borough Commanders office was one of four large four-bedroom maisonettes that had previously been the accommodation for the Divisional Commander and his staff back in the early days of the Divisions when accommodation was provided. It was a fantastic large office which led out to a spacious terrace balcony, it had a conference room with kitchen facilities and the bedrooms and bathroom upstairs occasionally used by officers on duty overnight. I absolutely loved the place and to this day it's one of the things I really miss.

Since the early days of Borough Commanders back in 2001, there had been a series of rationalisations. The Admin staff had all been centralised for the area and were temporarily located at East Ham, the Fire Safety team were still downstairs for me, but were now a joint City of London, Hackney and Islington team so I'd no longer have them. It would be me, the four station Commanders and the 192 Officers and Firefighters at the four stations.

In late June, I'd pretty much been released from Special Operations, so I plotted myself up at Shoreditch in an empty office next door to my soon to be BC's office. Graham was winding down towards retirement and getting some leave used up so wasn't about a lot. I took that opportunity to pay a few visits to a couple of the stations but didn't want to step into what was still Graham's domain.

Throughout July we gradually handed over, I knew the four Station Commanders and joined them for a couple of management meetings and other events in the Borough. Graham took me along to some of the strategic meetings in Hackney so I could get to know people such as the Chief executive of the Council, the Mayor, the Police Borough Commander and other lead officers. It was a busy Borough with lots going on and I couldn't wait to get started.

I arrived early on July 31st. It was Graham's last day and he was already in the office packing up his last few things. We went for Breakfast and without any ceremony we walked out of the office and he closed the door handing me the key and saying, "There you go, all yours."

I followed him to LFB's lease car contractor in Lambeth where he handed back his car and dropped him to HQ where Dave was going to take him for lunch once he'd handed all his kit back. I said goodbye, and that I'd seen him at his retirement party later in the week. So I was off, back to Shoreditch to take up my place in my new office.

I spent the rest of the afternoon getting it as I like it. I'd already contacted a well-known local fire photographer and ordered a few prints for the wall of jobs in Hackney over the years. I was absolutely over the moon and looking forward to the challenges ahead.

August 1st was my first proper day in the office. I'd already emailed each of the 16 watches at the four stations and planned to visit all of them in the first week. I'd been downstairs to see Shoreditch White Watch and planned to do the other three White Watches at the other stations after lunch. That all changed, I didn't really take much notice as both of Shoreditch's trucks went out on a call, but a few minutes later my pager went off. I rang Control, "Hello Control, Foxtrot one, one, zero here. I've just been paged to multiple calls."

"Hello, yes, we've had multiple... ok, hold on a second..." The Control officer replied.

"No, it was to inform you, but they've just made it six, you are now going. Have you go the details, we'll send them through again anyway." She added with a sense of urgency.

"Erm, let me look, Fire in Flat... Menard Court, Galway Street EC1..." I said, trying to scroll through the message on the pager.

"Yep, that's the one, shall I show you status two?"

"Yes, please, Thanks, bye." I clicked the phone off and reached for my radio.

I ran down to the bays and stabbed the bay door button, bright sunlight filled the bay and I open the car and placed my blue light on the roof. I pulled out into Old Street and turned right, noticing a mist of thin grey smoke in the air. I headed straight across Old street roundabout and made the first right into Bath Street, the smoke was clearer now blowing between the taller buildings on the left. I quickly booked in attendance on the radio and pulled into Galway Street, halting as I saw flames and dark smoke coming from the first floor of a block of flats up on the right. I noticed only two pumps were in attendance, thinking of the others still on their way, I backed the car out onto Bath Street and parked up on the pavement. Deciding the appliances would need to be nearer the fire than me and I'd also not be blocked in when I left.

As I got rigged in my fire gear the remaining appliances arrived and pulled into the street with one or two others waiting out on the larger street. I called Stuart, the guvnor from Shoreditch up on my hand held to let him know I was there. Shoreditch's Station Commander was off duty as was Clerkenwell's, so I'd actually arrived first. Soho was where the nearest Station Commander was on the day, so he was still making his way.

This is exactly what I imagined life as a Borough Commander to be. Unlike being stuck with dozens of other Officers at HQ, where the chances of a call during the day are very slim, I was back in the thick of it on day one. Although this was very much Shoreditch's stations ground, the Borough boundary between Hackney Islington and The City of London was pretty close to the station so this was actually within Islington Borough. I rang Rhys, the BC for Islington, based down the road at Clerkenwell and informed him I was attending a fire on my ground but in his Borough. He laughed and accused me of nicking his work already, but asked me to let him know if there were any issues that he would need to raise with Islington Council.

The Station Commander from Soho arrived and took over the incident as required at a 6-pump fire and I was designated Monitoring officer overseeing him. It had been a good hot job, the BA crews had done an excellent job, although the fire was fierce they'd pushed in through the front door and hit it quickly. It was all over in half an hour or so and a stop message was sent, that was my cue to head off after a perfect start to my first day as a Borough Commander.

Over the coming months I'd settled in quite well, I began to get to grips with all of the various committees and boards I sat on at the Council and the Politics that played out. Hackney had one of the largest Orthodox Jewish Communities in Europe at the top of the Borough in Stamford Hill. They were very courteous and generous people who would invite me to so many different events I often felt I was being ungrateful. But a lot of these were late at night or over weekends when I wasn't on duty so I had to draw a line or else I'd have trouble on the home front.

However, as always happens in life, storm clouds were brewing on the horizon. Following the election of David Cameron's Government in 2010 after the 2008 financial crash, Austerity was the word of the day and as always Public services were an easy target. Fire Services along with colleagues in other services were getting their budgets slashed.

The mayor of London at the time, who now holds the Prime Minister's job himself at the time of writing had insisted when he took over as Mayor of London is 2008 there would be no cuts to front line services. However, five year later all that had changed. London Fire Brigade had to save £35 million and that wasn't going to be done without some significant reductions to front line services.

The initial proposals for the fifth London Safety Plan, known as LSP5 were shocking. It proposed shutting several stations and removing the pumps from many of the two pump stations with the subsequent loss of positions that would be achieved through natural wastage. Among the changes were the loss of the Pump from Shoreditch, which had already been temporarily removed just two weeks after I took command of the Borough and the complete closure of Kingsland Fire Station, once one of the regulars in the Top ten of busy stations in London. That really caused a lot of upset locally, among the crews and of course with Hackney Council who represented the Community.

Of course as Borough Commander, I was the representative of the LFB and despite personally thinking it was abhorrent I was bound by the job to be the representative of the official LFB line. There was a very vocal and often angry campaign across the areas of London affected by the proposed cuts. But in the end, with the deciding vote of a Mayoral appointee the decision to implement LSP5 was carried by one vote.

So then the final plan was set in stone, the biggest cuts ever made to the London Fire Brigade that would also see the day it fell from the third biggest Fire Service in the World after Tokyo and New York City to fourth, with Los Angeles City Fire Department now rising above us in terms of stations and personnel.

The stations that were due to close were Belsize, Bow, which was one of my old stations, Clerkenwell, a very busy station and with the original building dating back to the 1870s, the oldest working fire station in the World. Downham, Kingsland, Knightsbridge, Silvertown, Southwark, Westminster and Woolwich. On top of that the second pump was to be removed from 7 other stations, but they wasn't done yet as 11 of the pumps that had been temporarily removed were also unlikely to return to make more savings. That included Shoreditch, with a total loss to Hackney of one Fire Station, three fire engines and 72 Firefighters and Officers. My beloved Poplar was also going to lose its Pump which upset me personally.

So on a very cold and wet morning in January 2014, I arrived at Kingsland to oversee the closure of a fire station that had served the area, albeit from two different buildings for over 100 years. It was and remains one of the few duties in my years as a Firefighter that I look back on with great sorrow and regret. The station was already looking half derelict as all of the other watches had finished their last shifts and had left. The Green Watch were the ones going on duty across London as the shift came to an end and the lights went out at ten London fire stations forever.

There was a crowd of protesters outside including the local MP and some of the personnel went out to engage with them. Although the TV media were at Clerkenwell and Westminster for their closures due to the significance of the stations and the large protests, The General secretary of the Fire Brigades Union was with us at Kingsland as it had once been where he served. At some point I received a call at the station, answered by the dutyman who handed the phone over to me with a sad look on his face. It was someone at HQ who were part of the so called 'implementation team'

"Steve, some of the crews there are outside the station, mixing with the protesters, can you get them in," Said a familiar voice from a colleague at HQ.

"What... How?" I spluttered.

"We've got CCTV feeds from all of the stations that are within range of local CCTV so we can keep an eye on things."

I was outraged... Talk about big brother is watching. I was the Borough Commander quiet capable of doing my job, but the typical micro-managing from HQ wanted to be all over this.

"Are you fucking kidding me?" I spat down the phone.

"Whaaaa, er..."

"Who the fuck told you to ring me and tell me to get the crews in, don't you think I'm capable of looking after things down here? Tell them I said bollocks, I'll manage this my way," I shouted and slammed the phone back in its holder without waiting for a reply.

The station was teeming with people from HQ getting ready to shut of services, agency driver waiting to take the fire engines and then a team of security guards arrived who were going to take responsibility for the station after it closed at 09:30.

Matt, the union general secretary rounded on me as everyone was getting quite angry and emotional. As the representative of Management, I was fair game. "Get a grip on this Steve for Christ sake, you are meant to be a people person, this is a fucking disgrace, the watch is upset and these people are taking over and they haven't even closed yet." I looked at him and then looked around at all of the strangers in the Station.

Nick the Station Commander came to my defence bless him.

"Hold on Matt, Steve has been really good through this, he's been to see all of the watches and worked really hard to get everyone the postings they want." I raised my had to Nick, but he wanted to have his say, Matt looked at us both and walked out into the bay.

"Do you lot have to fucking be here now?" I said to all of those massed in the office.

"Can't you wait over in the fucking café till half past nine then come back?" A couple of people shuffled out of the Watchroom and left the station via the front door. The two people from property services looked at me and offered the beginnings of an explanation as to why they had to stay and the two suited security guards, who looked like ex-Ghurkhas either didn't understand me or had their instructions and were not leaving now they were in the door.

Soon Nine thirty arrived and the tannoy announced the change of shift, except there wouldn't be a change of shift here at Kingsland or any other of the ten Fire Stations that closed that morning. Slowly and sadly the crew removed their gear from the appliances and finished emptying their lockers. They were going for a goodbye breakfast, I wished them all well at their new stations and for the future. Then after a while one, then the other appliances were driven away from Kingsland for the last time. Nick closed the door behind them and all of a sudden everyone was gone apart from a couple of property service people and the guards. As he turned around his eyes were full of tears and he broke down. I ushered him into his office on the other side of the bay and comforted him before giving him a moment.

I told him to go home and decided it Fuck it, Fuck the London Fire Brigade. I was going to take the rest of the day off as well. After a last look around the Station that I'd known for about 27 years since I did standby duties there early in my career. I jumped into my car and drove out of Kingsland's bay for the last time not looking back. Another bit of the Firefighter in me died that day and in the latter part of my career, I was beginning to get tired of the politics and bullshit.

Things in Hackney soon got back to normal, the council eventually 'forgave' me and I got used to only have three Fire Stations to worry about. Shoreditch had now become one appliance but with the closure of Kingsland and Clerkenwell as well as a Pump going from Whitechapel it actually got very busy... One of the busiest in the Brigade actually constantly jockeying for top spot with Euston's Pump Ladder.

The fires still came along pretty regularly, and by early 2015 was beginning to think about life beyond the LFB and took some fire safety qualifications that were recognised outside of the Brigade as well as being useful for my work within. By the end of the year I'd done the courses and assessments and passed one final assessment and I was now on the Brigades 'Senior Fire Safety officer' rota as well as being an ILO and of course a general command officer. Fire Safety officers would be called out to make an assessment of a building that was on fire in terms of its stability and what fixed installations were available, used post fire to assess the general fire precaution measures and if they'd contributed or not as was most likely the case in preventing the spread of fire. I'd also get called out by crews or other people for alleged fire risks, often at the far side of London from where I happened to be and always seemingly at an unholy hour.

People having raves in buildings with no staircases, let alone fire escapes, take away restaurants with bedrooms in a basement under the kitchen, hotels or hostels with no fire alarms and fire exits fixed shut. You name it, I saw it. I'd also been to some fantastic fires as a SFSO that I'd probably not have attended otherwise and when I got there was used in a command role due to the urgency of the fire and some other poor sod had to be ordered to deal with the Fire Safety issues.

In 2015, the old Taxi I shared with Beaker at Poplar finally hit the 15-year mark and was no longer able to be used, so that was pretty much in in terms of driving a Taxi. I hadn't worked long hours for many years but had kept my hand in doing the odd weekend. But now it was just a matter of hiring a cab for a week or so every now and again to keep my 'knowledge' up and to maintain the requirements of my licence.

At home, life was great, by 2016 my eldest Charlotte had graduated from University and had a good job, my middle one Abigail had left school and gone to University and the little one Imogen was now in Secondary school. Joanne was still working hard at her job and generally stewarding us all into what we should be doing and where we should be doing it.

I'd also made a decision. Back in 2012, as part of a package of measures to save money and reform public sector pensions the Firefighters pension scheme was going to be altered. Those commentators who were against so called 'gold-plated' final salary schemes were whipping up the frenzy and everyone across the public sector faced changes.

On our part, the scheme had already changed for new entrants back in 2006, so as each year went by there were less and less of us on the old 30-year scheme. Our change had already happened, and it wouldn't be the end of the World to leave people alone on the pension they had joined and paid into. But no, the narrative was set and Austerity was the byword for every single thing we had to do in the public sector.

The new scheme meant that after April 2015, everyone that was over 43 year of age at that time had full protection, no matter how long they had served. So a Firefighter who had joined in 2000 aged 35 who had served for fifteen years could remain on the old 1992 pension scheme. Yet someone who had joined at 18 in 1990, having now served 25 years was destined through age to work on another 10 years from what they had signed up to. Age discrimination if ever I saw it.

The pension, to be honest was very good on paper. Along with the Police is was one of the best public sector schemes and hands down beat anything out on the open market. With many private final salary schemes now ended, we were looking more and more vulnerable out on our own.

But it wasn't all as 'gold plated' as it seemed. First of all, at the time we were contributing 11% of our salary to the scheme and our pay reflected the cost of the pension paid by the employer. At the time, my salary was around £65,000 per year. My unit cost, that being my cost to the Taxpayer for my salary, pension, uniform and other costs was around £89,000. However, someone in an equally skilled sector outside, with similar management responsibilities of several premises and around 150 staff could easily command a salary of over £100,000. So the 'gold plated' rewards we were to expect were relative and simply cut a different way to other people.

That didn't suit the mainstream narrative though, so we all just got on with it. The Fire Brigades Union went into dispute with the Government over the unfair changes to the pension and unsurprisingly in later years when it went to court, it was deemed discriminatory and the Government had to quietly back track with none of the fanfare of the original announcements.

From my point of view, I'd always aimed to serve until I was 55. But with the changes hanging over me I initially thought I'd be staying until I was 60, 42 years of service. But once the details had been released, it became apparent that although I had missed out on full protection by a matter of months, I'd actually be given a form of 'tapered' protection, which would been I could remain on the old scheme until February 2020, which was a year and several months past my 50th Birthday which is the youngest I could retire. With that in mind, I made the decision that in July 2018, on my 50th Birthday, with 31 years and two weeks service I'd retire.

This was a real shame as I never wanted to go, one minute I was thinking I had another seven years left, the next I was looking at leaving it all behind in just over two years.

Early in 2016, the LFB's press department contacted me as they knew that I was a bit of a history buff and asked if I'd like to take part in a BBC TV Documentary about the history of the fire service in the UK. I was an ideal candidate as I was a long serving officer who remembers some of the old ways but had lived through great change. The producer had actually read a blog I'd written titled "The 80's Firefighter" in which I made just that point that we'd been the generation to see the greatest change.

I was interviewed at Shoreditch, strangely squeezed into the smelly store where the uniforms were hung instead of my comfortable office as the producer thought it more atmospheric. Nonetheless the end product was pretty good and I'd had my five minutes of fame and hadn't embarrassed myself or anyone else. The documentary was part of the 'timeshift' series and titled Blazes and Brigades the story of the Fire Service.

As a result of that, around a similar time the Brigade had finally allowed the cameras back in for a fly on the wall documentary. We'd done that once before, in 1991, ironically a large part of that series was filmed at Kingsland, my recently closed station. It didn't go well, although a great representation of the work LFB did in the early 90s a little too much of the antics around station, where Firefighters playing up for the cameras ended up on the small screen instead of the cutting room floor.

A lot of years had passed, and a production company wanted to give it a shot. The outgoing Commissioner agreed, and film crews were sat alongside Firefighters for shifts at various stations, with small heat proof cameras worn by Firefighters for added reality. Some of the other members of the TV crew also given Officers who would chaperone them to other serious incidents across London should they break out. I'd been asked to be part of that and jumped at the chance.

It was a free ticket to go to any call we wanted if I felt it had legs as well as being a beneficiary of the very decent expense account when it came to ordering lunch and dinner. I started at Brixton for the first day but managed to convince the LFB representative looking after the whole thing as well as the TV crew that my opulent and spacious offices, with four decent bedrooms and the location right in the middle of London were fantastic.

There were essentially three crews, the first day the crew I was with wanted to go from Brixton all the way to Harrow, where they had been the day before at a fire, to see the Fire Investigation team at work. That wasn't very exciting, and I began to think I'd been sold a pup. It was painstakingly boring as it was all slow pace so they could retake to their hearts content to get the perfect shot as the FI guys were in no rush. What annoyed me more was that they'd missed a pretty spectacular fire in a derelict office block in Stratford. It was only a six-pump fire, but the 20 odd calls received to it indicated to me that it would have looked good for the cameras.

Once we'd done there, we made our way back to Brixton where nothing else happened. The next shift we had planned was an overnight shift, with one of the other crews and was going to be run from Shoreditch. The Crew, Miles, Jasmyn and Sam arrived at Shoreditch late in the afternoon and seemed much more enthusiastic. We had a few decent runs to bits and pieces, they got some footage but not a great deal happened for a while. I then noticed a fire call that was received to a fire in a house under construction in NW London. I had a feeling in my water about and said to them that we should go. It was quiet a way, but late at night I figured we'd get there in a decent time. The radio remained stubbornly quiet as we approached and I thought I'd called it wrong. However, after an age the silence was broken and a massage came back confirming it was a job.

They got some great footage that eventually made episode two. they were a great crew who I had a really good shift with. On other Days Jasmyn would be teamed up with Leanne and someone else, or Miles and Sam would be with me with yet another member of the team. I'd got lucky with them quite a bit, so I was seen as one of their lucky charms. I travelled far and wide with them to some decent fires and accidents, between the stations, chaperone officers and the three film crews they must have got hours and hours of footage, of which the vast majority has never been seen.

This took place in the last few months of 2016 and apart from a few extra days filming in early January was pretty much done early in the New Year as they went away to edit it into the three one-hour episodes. Little did they know what they were about to miss.

2017

I'd had a pretty quiet Christmas and New year at the end of 2016, I wasn't on duty much over the period and what shifts I did pick up were quiet apart from a serious fire in a flat in Stratford in between Christmas and the New year, I don't recall many Christmases in my entire service when I didn't attend some sort of fire in a residential property, made all the worse to bear by the time of year. I was back on duty on Monday 2nd January and had a late start at 11am for a 9 plus shift until 8pm that evening. I took my time getting ready and was about to leave home for the office when my pager went off.

I thought it odd, I'd just come on duty for the first shift of the year and my pager went off within minutes… that should have told me something about the year I was about to have. I'd been ordered to a 10 pump fire on an industrial estate in South Tottenham. Pat was the Borough Commander for Islington and had his office next to me at Shoreditch, where the Islington BC was based since the closure of Clerkenwell. He was in charge and I gave him some stick about getting me out so early on my first shift back well as wishing him happy New year when I arrived.

Things were pretty under control, but he asked me to keep an eye on things as he had two sectors working either side of the building. I was there most of the afternoon and was pleased that everyone had done a good job in keeping the fire within the main units where the fire had stared without spreading elsewhere.

Within days I was off again as a Fire Safety officer this time at a fire in a big detached house in Barking, then later that evening all the way down to New Malden, pretty close to the Surrey border for a fire in the roof of a row of shops. Again a few days or so later in the middle of the night to a fire in a Restaurant in Islington that had started after closing to then break out for all to see in the early hours of the morning.

A week after that, I found myself on my way to Wembley one evening to an 8-pump fire in a warehouse that was proving very stubborn. By the time I got there, the crews had been dealing with it for over an hour. As Fire safety Officer, there wasn't much to go on as it was a very long brick and concrete warehouse that had been subdivide into lots of small businesses, so no central plans, alarm systems or other things to make a determination on. From what I saw, the fire had remained within a small unit that had entrances on both sides of the long building. Part of my role as a Fire Safety Officer was to determine the integrity of the building. It was a substantial building on the face of it due to its construction so didn't overly concern me. What was of slight concern though was the white smoke drifting lazily from the three peaked ridges of the roof of the building. Although the fire seemed contained in the unit of origin as I'd been into the units each side of it, I wasn't happy about the smoke.

Walking back down to the main seat of fire, I walked up to a Watch Manager who was overseeing the crews. He was holding a Thermal image camera. "Hello mate, can I borrow that for a minute?" I said to him cheerfully.

"Yer, no problem Guvnor, be my guest," He replied.

I took the camera and walked back to the end of the building. I held it up and pointed it at one of the peaks, it read 36° Celsius, I pointed it away to take the ambient temperature and on this cold night it was 4° Celsius, so the camera wasn't misreading. I pointed it again at the middle peak of the roof this time and it read 74° Celsius, now that was very warm, and an indication all was not well. To have smoke coming from a roof quite a way from the seat of the fire at that temperature was a big problem.

I called up the Incident Commander and Monitoring officer and asked them to meet me. As they approached, I said, "Have a look at the temperature of that smoke, its 74 degrees in the middle, you have a problem, the fire is spreading." They looked at me for more information.

"Has anyone been up to the first floor of this building?" I asked.

"Yes, earlier," came the reply of Richard who was in charge while Andy who was the DAC Monitoring nodded in agreement.

"Do you think we need to have another look?" I suggested, and they agreed. Andy went back to the Command Unit and Richard and I made our way into a door that had previously been opened and led up a set of stairs. All was clear and we used a step ladder to push open a ceiling tile to shine into the roof space, our torches met with smoke and again the thermal image camera detected significant heat.

Moving on we came across a locked door which took us further into the building, with a bit of effort we broke to door open to be met my smoke and the sounds of distant burning.

"Fuck," Richard said, as he dropped to the floor and scuttled along the corridor towards the sound of burning.

"I told you something wasn't right," I called after him. I also got down and crawled off in another direction towards the front of the building, but the smoke was quite pungent and was getting more productive. We made our way back outside and met up with Andy and walked back to the Control Unit.

"What do you reckon?" he said to me.

"It into the roof space and spreading along the first floor, it's going to break out and will likely take the whole building so for me you need to go to twenty pumps with four aerials."

His eyes flared at that suggestion and he asked one of the CU officers to make a calculation of what was required. Somewhat affronted by this, I said, "Andy, I've seen it dozens of times over the years, a large commercial warehouse of this size is a twenty pumper all day long with an aerial on each side."

Before he could reply, the CU Officer said to him, "With what we have now and what you'll need that'll be fourteen pumps."

"OK," Andy replied, "make pumps fifteen for me please and I'll now take over from Richard."

I shook my head lightly and shrugged.

"OK, do you need me to do anything now it's going to change."

"Well, I'll make Richard Ops Commander, you OK with that Rich?"

"And you Steve, can you sort out the water, we are going to need a lot more, the water board are here, go and find him and see what you can do, let me know what you need."

"No worries, but don't you have a BMA here already." A BMA is a bulk media adviser, essentially an officer who has had additional training in moving large amounts of water, either towards the fire in this case, or away from areas in the case of large floods such as when Rivers break their banks as we've all seen on the media in recent years.

"No, the BMA isn't here yet so can you make a start."

"Yep, no problem, oh and you'll need to order another Fire Safety officer now I'm doing water." I replied as I jumped down off the unit in search of the Thames Water turncock's van to see what I could do.

309

More and more machines arrived along with the BMA who found me out in East Lane, the road which served the entrance to the industrial estate talking to the Water Board official outside North Wembley Tube Station. He'd outlined a plan to bring water in and I'd requested a high-volume pump with an additional hose box to cover the distance. The BMA was happy with what had been agreed so I left them to that while I began to make my way back towards the fire to try to organise how many pumps we'd need in the water relay. As I came past the control unit, I saw that Dan one of the AC's had turned up and was about to take over. "Alright Dan," I called to him.

"Alright Steve," came his reply and a face that said more.

"This is more than a fifteen he said."

I exaggeratedly shrugged my shoulders and lifted my arms.

"I did say it was a twenty with four aerials, but hey?"

"Well that's what I'm gonna make it anyway," he said.

"What are you doing?" he asked a further question.

"Just sorting your water out, the BMA is getting it all in place I'm just counting relay pumps," I answered.

"OK, I won't hold you up," then he said with a smile and jumped back on the Command Unit.

Dan was junior to me in age and time served. He had actually taken over form me at Homerton in 2007 as temporary Station Commander and had made Group Manager at the same times as me back in 2010. Now in 2017 he was one of the Assistant Commissioners, A very bright bloke and a good old East End boy like me. I had a lot of time for his no nonsense attitude and his quick witted often sharp replies to people.

As predicted the fire had spread across the building, although the lightweight metal roof, that had obviously replaced the original roof was not burning through very well so was causing more lateral spread. Although we could get aerials up to ventilate the edges if we needed to, the building was too deep for the middle roof to be reach by any aerial device and sending people onto a weakened roof with an inferno below was an invitation to a Firefighters funeral and some very long and painful days in court.

Back in the office after a torturous journey across London's rush hour I had a hot shower, I was exhausted and with nothing much in my diary for the day, I decide to make use of one of those bedrooms upstairs from my office to get some much-needed sleep. I'd be 49 in six months and although I was healthy and relatively fit still, I was beginning to feel it after long night out of bed more and more these days. As I lay in bed trying to settle my mind after the activity of the night at the fire and the hard slog through the traffic, I mused that it was only the third week of January and it had been very busy. Not just for me, others seemed to be out and about when they were on duty.

The threat from Terrorism had changed, no longer were we expecting terror to come from the sky as it had in NYC on 9/11. There was still a risk from explosive devices and suicide bombers, but following the Mumbai attacks back in 2008, a lot of what we'd been preparing for over the years was around a marauding terror attack with people moving from one place to another before strong holding in a building as they had in Mumbai.

It is of course inappropriate for me to discuss that preparation, but we trained in many different places across London and beyond with Police and Ambulance colleagues as well as with branches of the military and security services. Time and time again different scenarios were played out and our response was tested and tested almost to destruction.

I was in my car heading to Headquarters when I became aware something wasn't right. I quickly switched on my blue grille lights and siren and pulled out from behind the line of traffic and sped my way the last mile or so to HQ. Pulling up outside without parking properly I jumped out of the car and ran across the street still in conversation with another ILO who had also parked up nearby to await further instructions as events unfolded.

From what we knew, there had been a terror attack on Westminster Bridge, information was sketchy, but so far it appeared a car had been driven through crowds of people on the bridge and then an assailant had run into the Palace of Westminster to continue the attack. LFB were already attending as the initial calls had come in reporting a road accident, my mate Daryll was the ILO nearest to the scene and was already on his way.

I passed through the barrier and ran down the stairs to the Special Operations office, using my swipe card to gain entry, I walked in the room to find it a hive of urgent but calm activity. Already one of the Assistant Commissioners and a Deputy Assistant Commissioner were in the room setting up as we'd planned should this day ever come.

I made eye contact with Matty who was the duty ILO that day, he was talking on his radio with a mobile phone to his ear. I caught Bob, the ILO support Officer and asked him, "Daryll is on scene as ILO one, who will be two and three?"

"I don't know if he has got that far yet," Came Bob's reply. Waiting to jump on Matty, I looked up at the large TV screen and already live helicopter footage was playing of what was now looking like a terror attack on the home of the British Government.

Matty was off the phone. "Matt," I called forcefully.

"Who have you got as ILO two and three?"

"I'm just about to…"

"I can go as ILO two and Ronnie is standing by just near Dowgate, he is happy to go as three… do you want me to organise?"

"Yep, yes please can you do that for me?"

"Consider it done, I'll let the Officer of the watch at Control know as well."

And with that I was on my way, back up the stairs swerving impatiently through the barrier and out to my car, surprisingly I got through to the Officer of the Watch after a couple of rings and I let her know what was going on with me and Ronnie.

Back in the car I called up Ronnie and told him his role and confirmed it with Daryll who was now on scene.

"You need to come in on the north side if you are coming from HQ, don't try to get over Westminster Bridge as its completely blocked, I've just had to walk over, FCP is at P Square, and I'm gonna change our RVP to here as well, we are considering P square as 'Cold' acknowledge."

Confirming that I headed along Union street, I thought about taking Blackfriars bridge and then thought better to take Waterloo Bridge. I was literally pointing towards Westminster bridge from where I was but didn't want to be the wrong side of things. Traffic had already pretty much gridlocked and despite the blue lights and noise progress was painfully slow.

I got onto Waterloo bridge which is a dual carriageway and ground to a halt, trying to bump up onto the central reservation and squeeze through. A marked Police car came up the wrong side from behind me and slowed next to me, the officer in the passenger seat gestured to me to follow so I pulled across the central reservation, feeling a lot more confident with a marked Police car forging ahead of me.

To my despair, as soon as we got the other end of Waterloo bridge on the north side and I aimed the car left into The Strand, the Police car in front carried on ahead of me heading further north. I was stranded again and this time nothing was moving. I paused briefly, then decided to slowly take on the traffic heading towards me coming east down The Strand, another road, like Waterloo bridge divided by a central reservation. I edged across into the wrong lane and immediately caused chaos with the oncoming traffic.

I cursed, but I was committed now with nowhere to go apart from straight on, so I pressed ahead. Daryll came back on the radio giving us a brief update.

"Several killed and injured on the bridge, suspected IED in the car, Police Officer killed by suspect, suspect neutralised by Firearms Police, unknown at this time if others are involved, SFO's carrying out an emergency search of Palace of Westminster... Dudes and Ronnie, enter via Victoria Street, confirm Victoria Street."

Again we acknowledged, with this information I wish I'd have taken Lambeth Bridge, I eventually cleared the longest stretch of The Strand and just had the last hundred or so yards which is bus lane before I hit Trafalgar Square. My intention to go straight down Whitehall land into Parliament Square no longer an option, I headed straight across into the Mall and then took a left down Horseguards Road, a few hundred yards of free movement then I was stuck again at the junction with Birdcage Walk.

A policeman on foot came running over to me.

"Fire Brigade, I need to get to the FCP at Parliament Square, I've been told to enter via Victoria Street," I said to him sticking my head out of the window. Without another word he started waving at the gridlocked cars to back up and made space for me to do the dog leg cross over into Storey's Gate. Up the side of the Queen Elizabeth conference centre and I was in Victoria Street, now free of traffic. I turned left as it changed to Broad Sanctuary outside Westminster Abbey and I stopped at a Police roadblock where I identified myself once again.

I was let through the tape and immediately pulled up behind Ronnie's car, somehow, he'd got ahead of me.

"Alright me son," he greeted me with his usual cockney lilt and beaming smile. "Some cabby you are, I got here before you," he continued.

"Bollocks," I said with a smile before we got down to the serious business of what was going on.

I got rigged in my fire kit and then put my ballistic protection on over the top. I also picked up my ballistic helmet, in case, but we'd both noted Daryll had informed us this was now considered 'Cold' so any ballistic threat was deemed unlikely.

We walked across Parliament Square together where we confirmed our roles with each other before we jumped onto the back of the Command unit which was set up opposite the side of St Margret's church facing Westminster Palace ahead of us.

Booking in with the CU crew and trying to gather as much information as I could from the scant detail that had so far been written up on the whiteboards, I called Daryll up on the Radio.

"D, it's Dudes, me and Ronnie are here we are on the back of the CU." Nothing came back, I waited a few seconds and was going to call again when he replied.

"OK mate, stay there I'm on my way back over to you now."

Within a minute Daryll's huge frame filled the small doorway of the CU, he gestured us outside where we were joined on the Pavement by John, one of the team of responders trained to assist with casualties in events like these.

"OK, so the situation is as I have told you. The perp, believed but not confirmed as a single operator has been taken down by armed Police in the gardens in front of parliament just through the gates over there to the left. Sadly, a Police Officer was stabbed to death by him before he was neutralised. SFO's are now carrying out a full search of the Palace, but we have 1500 people still inside including several parties of visiting school children."

"The priority after the search is to move everyone from within the buildings over to the Abbey where they can be logged, checked and then released, obviously the kids are a priority."

I thought to myself the horror going through the minds of parents across the Country, knowing their children were on a school trip to the Houses of Parliament who were now aware it had been involved in a terror attack. I nodded in approval of Daryll's words as he continued.

"Things on the bridge are pretty static now, there are multiple casualties and fatalities. Including someone trapped under a bus and someone in the water, the Fireboat is taking care of that, they have the casualty on the boat and are transferring them to land. The Fireboat was just passing by as this unfolded and as it happens Tony was on board, so we've got an ILO river-side which is useful for updates."

"All injured casualties have been removed, the deceased have been left in situ, and all crews have been withdrawn from the bridge for the time being. Lambeth and Euston's FRU are south side, Soho are back here with us as you can see. The IED threat from the car was just a precaution and not based on any specific intel, that has been cleared by EOD now."

"So going forward, we need to set up here alongside London Ambulance Service as a joint RVP and the priority will be our MCR teams assisting LAS and the Police to get the people cleared from the buildings, all OK with that?"

"I'm first on scene from MCR, so I'll be team leader as per," Said John, before Ronnie took the words out of my mouth.

"What do you want from us Daryll, we've informally agreed Dudes will be ILO two and I'll be ILO three?"

"Well, I'll need you both, but as it looks at this time, we are entering a settled phase, we don't really need to work within the Joint Ops procedures. I'm going to keep the nominal ILO one role as I'm established now with the Police and LAS commanders, but you two need to pick up all of the other stuff such as briefings recording, organising and such like."

The meeting continued for another few minutes as we worked out who would be responsible for what, meanwhile more and more of our responders arrived in the square so briefing and corralling them became an immediate priority that fell to me. Stood on the slightly raised grass area of Parliament Square, I briefed the sombre looking faces of the LFB responders. They were about to be deployed in the Palace of Westminster to assist in the operation to move people across the road into the abbey.

Out of the chaos came organisation, I was working with the LAS team and our own casualty clearance teams in coordinating the evacuation of the palace into the abbey. I was in the middle of a discussion with a lady from LAS when I was distracted by two armed Police Officers running across the square towards the roadblock in Broad Sanctuary followed immediately by two powerful BMW X5 Police cars which screeched off in the same direction and sped off down Victoria Street with their sirens blaring.

The LAS officer turned her ear towards her radio and was taking a message, suddenly Daryll was on our radio. About a quarter of a mile away along Victoria Street, outside of Westminster City Hall, a person wearing a rucksack had collapsed on the floor and had smoke coming from the rucksack. As I took this information in I felt my adrenalin rise and by heart beating in my chest.

This attack appeared to be developing and did now look like it was a multi-sited attack after all. The two armed cops who had sprinted past us were now acting as Sentry's at the roadblock on Broad Sanctuary, their eyes everywhere looking for the potential for a further incoming attack. All services were rapidly taking stock of who was where trying to ensure they knew the whereabouts of their teams with the ultimate aim of protecting the public, MP's, Lords and other officials who were now under our joint protection.

I first heard the shout from a Police Officer who was stood just behind me.

"Stand down, stand down." Again, people looked to their own colleagues for an update. Within seconds Daryll came on the radio. I looked over towards the gates where he was stood among a crowd of Police and Ambulance Officers, he was looking right back at me as he spoke into his radio.

The Police who had rushed to the scene had found the person on the floor, but after a rapid assessment, they actually found out that a chap who was walking along, with a rucksack in his back smoking one of the really powerful vape pens that produce large clouds of smoke had suddenly fallen ill with an epileptic fit. For those who witnessed him on the floor, he was fitting and foaming at the mouth with his last exhaled cloud of smoke still hanging over him. It was quite understandable that people in the area, already heightened by what was going on came to a worrying conclusion.

Within the next hour or so, we collectively managed to get all of the children and non-essential visitors to the Palace of Westminster that day released and free to get home or go about their business. That must have been a relief for their worried families and it certainly bought us some time and felt like things were now falling into place.

However, like some sick incident command exercise where every time a problem is solved a grinning facilitator chucks something else into the mix, we were then approached with another problem.

We met with an anxious Police Commander, "I think we may have an issue inside the Abbey. Officers are searching people and we've discovered an unknown white Powder inside someone's belongings, and we are concerned about what it is. The thing is, tensions are quite high anyway over there and we've spoken to some of your guys who said you may be able to help us discreetly. There are a number of MP's and Lord's over there so we need to be delicate."

Discussing the issue, we decided to place a call to Tony who was now back at the old HQ at Lambeth. He was one of the UK Fire Service leads on Chemical, Biological, Radiological and Nuclear attacks, known as CBRN and the specialist team that deal with this were sat at Lambeth along with their boss Paul, another of our ILO's.

It was agreed they'd pop over to the scene, just a short trip from Lambeth with a few small items of detection and monitoring equipment and as far as possible dress down to appear discreet when making an assessment of the powder. One of the team already over there was part of our cadre of Hazardous Material Officers, so we were gathering additional information from him. Soon enough Tony, Paul and a couple of the CBRN rapid response team were with us and suitably dressed down, they were taken across to the abbey.

As a Command team along with Ambulance and Police, we discussed our strategy for mass decontamination if, God forbid, it might be required and how quickly and where our mass decontamination assets could be deployed. The prospect of first responders clad in full chemical suits leading hundreds of people through mass decontamination showers didn't play out well whatever way you cut it.

Thankfully, once again, it turned out to be nothing more than someone reacting, quite correctly against the background of the day so far, to a perfectly safe and legal food additive, which seemed incongruous to how it was being carried.

We were now into the evening and the pace was much more settled. The Police Counter-terrorism teams along with the security services had been doing their usual wizardry and our Officer embedded with them updated us that a lot of the key details about the terrorist, his recent movements and associates had already been established. The CT Police were about to go off and do some 'door knocking'. Each of those sites had potential so we now had to unpick a lot of our assets from the scene and other parts of Central London and get them away from the gridlock and ready to respond again if required.

Daryll and Ronnie, along with Chris who was in with the CT Police at a nearby location managed that while I had to figure a way working with a request from the Senior Investigating Officer from the Police to manage to keep the entire scene lit overnight while they carried out detailed forensic work. I managed to secure use of our contractor who provided bulk lighting units to us at any given scene with a very quick turnaround. The Police were delighted as the big flatbed truck rolled into the square with several large self-generating floodlight sets on the back.

Once that was done, I realised I hadn't been to the toilet for hours so I took the opportunity to rattle on a few closed doors to office buildings until I was faced with a security guard who had ventured out from his desk. He willingly obliged and now, very hungry with a post adrenalin tiredness in every bone of my body, we were relieved by another ILO who was going to man the fort overnight. The attack itself only lasted for 82 seconds. 6 were killed including PC Keith Palmer and the perpetrator and of the 49 injured 12 of those had life changing injuries.

In the following weeks we held our own post-mortem of the LFB's response from a Command point of view as well as from the ILO group and our key role on the front line of these events. By and large it had gone to plan and where it hadn't, we quickly realised that and made amendments on the ground at the time. Nonetheless, a number of redrafts of our procedures and action plans took place with the benefit of hindsight and lots of debate, we felt we were now better prepared should it ever happen again. We didn't have to wait long.

I was sitting in my study one Saturday night quite late reading something on the computer. I was off duty and even though we now had a formal recall to duty policy, it had been agreed in any case that a less formal arrangement of availability would sit over the new policy just in case.

Charlotte and Abigail my two eldest Daughters came into the room, "Daddy, what's happening at London Bridge?"

"I don't know, what do you mean?" I asked, feeling a tingling burst of adrenalin run through me as I stood up.

"Put Sky News on," I said as I reached into by bag and pulled my two handheld radio's out and turned them on. They bleeped into life and most surprisingly I was immediately confronted by the familiar voice of Pat, the duty ILO that night mid-conversation. This particular channel was only used by ILO's if something was going on so the chances of hearing someone talking at any other time were absolutely minimal.

I got the gist of the back end of a message where Pat was ordering Tony and Matty to Southwark Police Station to a FCP. The initials FCP meant everything to me in terms of a terrorist attack. One of the girls gasped as the live Sky News footage confirmed that yet again, a marauding terror attack was underway in London.

Thinking about the recall policy I paused, but then thought what the hell. Pat finished his message, so I pushed the transmit button on the Radio.

"Pat, It's Steve, I can see something is going on at London Bridge, I'm available and standing by here on channel two if required." I wasn't expecting the reply that came back.

"Steve, thanks... Get yourself ready to go, I'm going to need you down at London Bridge, just give me a minute."

"Standing by," I replied. I'd been aware of this for a matter of minutes. At best I'd expect to be held in reserve as the recall officers were used, with possibly a deployment to the Police CT hub or their control room. But now it looked as if I was going to the scene.

"Go and tell Mummy what's going on and that I'm going out to it," I said to the girls. Although they were both adults now, their big-eyed shocked stares and the wordless nods as they turned and left the room made me think that they were 8 and 5 years old again.

Minutes later they were back with Joanne in tow then followed by Imogen who had been asleep and came down the stairs to find out who had dared interrupt her.

"What's going on?" She slurred her eyes blinking in the light.

"Nothing Baby, there has been another terror attack, Daddy might have to go there, you go back to sleep," Joanne soothingly replied.

"What... Where?" She said.

"London Bridge, in in the City," I said while trying to log onto my remote access to the LFB system.

"Oh, OK then, be careful..." And with that she was gone, the dog, also losing interest following her out of the room.

Pat came back on the Radio. "Steve are you ready to go?"

"Yes mate, go ahead."

"I need you as ILO three, Matty is ILO one and Tony is ILO two. The RVP for you is Borough High street and they are at the FCP which has just been moved to... Hold on... Borough High Street at St Thomas' street, do you know it."

"Yep, know it, I'm on my way, anything else."

"Not at the moment, keep channel two on as I'm going to brief everyone in a minute."

I sprinted upstairs and changing out of the shorts and T-shirt I'd been lounging around in pulled on an ILO Black polo shirt, a pair of tactical black trousers and running back downstairs put on my Magnum boots. I picked up my grab bag and radios and with a handful of snatched kisses left behind a chorus of concerned "Be careful's".

I'd long accepted and pretty much no longer considered the risks of the job. By this point I was relatively well paid for what I did, I knew the job well and most of the risk I took was in the decisions I made that affected others opposed to my own safety. However, leaving behind those three worried faces, made me consider how it must be for them. Joanne had been used to it for years, spending nights alone in those early years when I was still on the back of a Fire Engine, fires were more frequent and the equipment less advanced as it is today.

The Girls had by and large been sheltered, by age early in their lives and by rank later on as although I attended serious incidents much more often than I ever did, my role was generally a command role and, despite my irritating insistence of often getting in the thick of things, was quiet safe by comparison. Yet within minutes of them becoming aware of something out of the ordinary happening in central London, their Dad had now left them to attend that incident, the scope of which was as yet unknown and uncontrolled. I felt pretty safe and unconcerned myself as I headed mile by mile ever nearer to the scene as I was in control to some extent. But suddenly, knew the time had to come soon where I gave them a break from all of this.

Arriving at the scene after a quick high speed journey through East London and across the River, I parked up behind a line of emergency vehicles in Borough High street. Something about this felt very different from Westminster bridge, there was an edge in the air that I could almost feel, heightened voices, Police Officer running, shouted orders and small groups of people being hustled along the road to safety. I was incredibly familiar with Borough High Street having walked or driven along it thousands of times.

As familiar as I was with it, it all felt a little dream like. Pat had given a comprehensive briefing over the radio as I'd been driving to the scene and I was struggling to comprehend what had happened all the time knowing that it was real. Once again, for the second time in a few months I rigged I my full ballistic protective equipment, locked the car and walked towards the scene.

Turning the corner from Borough High street into St Thomas's Street, I took in a scene of multiple Emergency Service responders all very busy in a crowd of around 50, organised chaos was a thought that briefly swept across my mind as I took it in and tried to identify a familiar face. I saw several, from the Police and Ambulance service, those who we had trained alongside over recent years.

In among the crowd I saw Tony, determinedly briefing a small crowd. I tried to make eye contact with him, he saw me and gestured with his head to a pub behind. Smart black paint with gold etched windows and golden lettering above the open central doors read Bunch of Grapes, a number of tables made from large wooden casks were littered with abandoned drinks by those who had fled in panic a short time before.

Looking into the pub, there were a handful of armed Police Officers in full protective equipment standing in small groups with their Heckler and Koch semi-automatic rifles at their side. Beyond was a large table with a big light hanging down providing a lazy off-white light over the table. Around that were the joint command team and their various logistics and comms officers from all three services. Alone in the middle of the group was Matty who was obviously carrying out the ILO one role.

A loud shout, I spun around and looked back towards Borough High Street, an armed cop stood in the middle of the road was shouting at someone unseen from my position to "Get Back, clear the area." Walking into the pub, eyed casually by some of the Police standing there I sidled up to Matty and whispered to get his attention.

"Alright Matt, I'm you ILO three, what do you need."

A raised hand as he concentrated on what was being said by the Police Tactical Firearms Commander, all the while furiously making notes in his log. Up until recently we'd had an ILO Support Officer, one always being available to carry out a role like this. A decision had been taken to remove that role, I bet Matty wished he had one with him now.

The conversation ended and Matty turned to me and outlined a number of issues he had pending. Tony was doing the briefing and he also updated me on the next steps. 'Fire as a weapon' was a distinct possibility here, a number of the terrorists, three so far had been shot and killed by armed Police within minutes of their rampage starting but it was though more were outstanding and still in the area.

We needed to bring a couple of Fire Engines and their equipment forward into this area from the RVP and get hose lines and other equipment laid out should a fire start. Some of our specialist responders were arriving and being briefed by Tony should that be required. My role was to make that happen, the Police had also requested detailed plans of the Borough Market area and the Deputy Assistant Commissioner who had been mobilised with the balance of the regular LFB attendance to an RVP some distance away also needed bringing up to date with everything that had happened so far.

I took all of that in and patted young Matty on the back. "Well done, Matt, leave it to me."

Matt was quite new to the ILO group but had been the duty ILO for the Westminster Bridge attack and was now ILO one on scene tonight. I'd known him when he first joined in the late 1990s and he was also one of my Station Commanders when I took over Hackney in 2014. I was very fond of him and proud he was doing such a brilliant job.

I called up the DAC and asked was he in a position to be briefed. He replied he was just getting out of his car and would be with me soon. That wasn't expected, he should have been at the RVP, but it was what it was. A couple of minutes later whilst I was trying to organise a safe route in for the two fire engines we required, I heard a familiar and raised voice. Tony had seen the DAC arrive and had taken issue with the fact he had come forward into a 'warm zone' that wasn't yet risk free and that he'd come in through a higher risk area, potentially a 'hot zone' to add to his frustration.

I walked over and pulled the DAC away before it went any further and briefed him on all we knew so far.

"A van was driven across London Bridge where it mounted the pavement and hit multiple persons. Some were severely injured and a couple killed, number yet to be confirmed. The van then crossed the carriageway and hit the railings overlooking Southwark Cathedral where it is still in situ. They left the van and ran down the stairs and started attacking people on foot within Borough Market, all of which lies beyond us across the road." I pointed over my shoulder to the buildings behind.

"Again, there have been injuries and fatalities, numbers unconfirmed with casualties still being treated by LAS and our Casualty teams within the market. Three terrorists were met by armed Police in Stoney Street and have been killed, we can't confirm as yet whether or not there are more and their whereabouts. Fire as a weapon is a possibility due to the some of the contents of the van that were identified following an emergency search.

"Going forward, we need to continue to assist LAS and I'm getting some of our trucks moved down from the RVP to get equipment prepped should we need to use the Firefighting teams. I've also asked for one of the CU's to come down as Police would like detailed plans for the market and buildings."

The DAC had a few questions but was pretty happy with our plans so far and stepped away from me to make a phone call, no doubt updating one of the Staff Officers to the Commissioner's group who were probably all heading into HQ through the darkened streets as we spoke.

Out on Borough High street, I was under the railway bridge making an assessment of distances for possible hose runs. Once again, the incongruity of the warm June night hit me as the familiar surrounding were eerily empty of partying crowds but instead the bridge beyond was lined with dozens of abandoned cars and buses and a couple of victims were laid on the floor where they had been ruthlessly killed no more than an hour or so ago. Sadly I said a silent prayer for them and carried on with what I was doing.

Everything was now coming together, and I desperately needed the plans. The mapping system on the Command unit was good enough, the printers however were notoriously poor. Like watching paint dry I lost patience as a highly detailed plan was edging millimetre by millimetre out of the printer.

"Bollocks to this," I said to no one in particular.

"Can you download those to a memory stick?" I asked the Command Unit Officer.

"Yes Guvnor, we can plug it in there," he replied pointing to a bank of ports below the screen. I felt for my keys in my pocket that had my 'Ironkey' memory stick attached by a key ring and offered it to the officer.

"Stick'em on there for us will ya, I have an idea."

Armed with all of the plans I needed, I jumped off the unit and walked towards the Shard. Opened back in 2013, The Shard is a 1016ft glass covered building, the tallest in Western Europe with offices, hotels, restaurants and apartments within its 95 floors. Its entrance is further along St Thomas's Street and from a number of familiarisation visits I'd carried out there, I knew they had extensive facilities in the security and fire command centres.

One of the security guards looked up in anticipation as I approached.

"Hello mate, I need some plans I've got on a memory stick printed off to assist us with the layout down at the market."

He nodded enthusiastically and spoke urgently into his radio. Within minutes, another guy in a smart suit came out and greeted me, I explained my predicament and he ushered me into the lobby.

Within minutes I was marching triumphantly back along the road towards the control point with A1 and A3 sized plans showing individual street and building detail rolled under my arms. The response had now been added to by a unit of special forces Soldiers who were waiting outside the pub, their commander had joined the command team inside as I walked among the group and announced.

"Plans."

There were lots of mumbles of approvals as I laid them out on the desk and took a couple more outside for Tony who was again briefing teams.

One thing I noticed in the street now crowded with even more responders was a Special Forces soldier with a Belgian Malinois dog on a short leash. Despite the crowds outside the pub, this Solider had a perfect 6ft circle of space around him as no one dared get within range of his dog. Belgian Malinois are like the elite athletes of the Service dog world. Frighteningly quick and strong, as courageous as a lion they can take an armed man down effortlessly.

Armed with their plans the Special Forces guys left with a team of Police Specialist Firearms Officers heading across the road and into the warren of tight streets around the market. Shortly afterwards a number of loud bangs, the first of which made me jump out of my skin came from within the market area as the more detailed search went ahead. Shortly after I witnessed the most bizarre sight I'd even seen on the streets of London.

Armed Police escorted dozens of revellers, dressed in shorts, T-shirts, party dresses with heels and other Saturday night 'going out' clothes across the road all with their hands held on their heads like a troop of captured soldiers. Obviously, a tactic employed to guarantee the safety of everyone, I had to double take and they snaked their way across the road and past us into an area of safety.

With the area now clear, but with further information coming into us that many of the restaurants had been left in a hurry, often with cooking ranges still burning, we now had a problem with the potential for unintentional fires to break out and in those tight streets, without the advantage of a full fire service response it could have been really embarrassing with the eyes of the World on us.

Plans for the initial threat of fire were hastily adapted and a team of specialist responders from the LFB buddied up with a team of armed Police made their way to a number of addresses within the market equipped with thermal imaging cameras to turn off the cookers in each of the premises and make some checks that fires hadn't started and spread unseen into the buildings.

Meanwhile we laid out enough equipment at the ready should it be required to make a quick attack on the fire to try to contain in. I'm happy to say the teams returned in around 20 minutes, their job done, and no fires found. One last severely injured casualty was brought out on a stretcher and then it appeared we now had a grip on everything.

In reality the whole thing only lasted a matter of minutes. There were only three terrorists and thanks to the quick response of Metropolitan Police and City of London Police firearms teams, were dead within 6 minutes of the start of the attack. 8 people were killed, not including the terrorists, two by the van being driven into them and 6 who were stabbed by the attackers. 48 people were injured.

However, none of this is clear in the frantic minutes and hours after the attack. If we were blessed with hindsight, once the Police had dealt with the attackers, the area could have been flooded with dozens of responders and treatment given immediately. But the reality is, the chaos and confusion they wreak within a few minutes takes hours to unpick before it can be declared under control.

June continued and was typically warm and dry but mid-month it had got even warmer. I like warm sunny weather, sot it always leaves me feeling happy. My Saturday 24 shift hadn't brought anything particularly interesting but on Sunday morning, I was keeping my eye on a developing fire in Golders Green in NW London that had started in a row of shops around breakfast time and had required first arriving crews to carry out some rescues. The number of appliances attending had crept up gradually, so all wasn't right.

Sometime around 11am, the job got made up again, this time to a 15-pump fire. That was when it was my turn to go, the additional appliances were ordered and more officers to support them. Two Officers of my rank were already attending, the jump to 15 pumps put that number up to three, with me being the next nearest, the only one left available north of the Thames by that time, I was on my way.

It's a relatively easy journey to Golders Green on blue lights on a Sunday, from where I lived up through Romford to the A12, down to Redbridge and then pick up the North Circular Road all the way around until a left turn into Golders Green Road and the fire was a couple of hundred yards down on the right. I figured somewhere to park that wasn't too far away, wouldn't block anyone in and most importantly not block me in.

Walking down to the control unit, Rick was the DAC in charge and Richard was the Assistant Commissioner monitoring him. They were deep in discussion but looked up as I walked in and greeted me simultaneously.

"Hello Gents, how are you?" I said by way of a greeting. They both smiled and said hello and finished their conversation. Seeing a point to jump in I spoke.

"There aren't many of us on today, in fact I was the last GM in the North, so if you don't need me, I'll make myself available again."

Rick looked and Richard replied.

"I don't know Steve, we might use you, can you do me a favour?"

"Of course I can, what is it?"

"Can you have a look around the job, see what's happening and let me know what you think and if we need to change anything," he said.

"No problem, leave it to me," I replied.

I was quite humbled by this, they were both senior to me in rank, albeit Rick was acting up into the DAC Rank. But that an Assistant Commissioner had seen me arrive, even though there were others on the ground in my rank, including Paul from the Operational review team, whose job it was to look at how the incident was progressing. But Richard, recognising me as one of the most senior and long serving in the role had wanted my eye cast over things.

Jumping off the control unit and walking towards the fire I was met by a typical row of high street shops, well burnt out, but with thick lazy grey smoke drifting out of them. Suggesting a fire deep inside and not at the front of the shop. Tons of debris had been pulled out and littered the pavement out front. I greeted Sami, who was the Sector Commander at the front and he gave me a run-down of exactly what was happening in his sector. I peered into the shop and as I suspected there was no immediate fire, but the hot smoke was drifting from deep inside.

Walking into Hazel Gardens the side street towards the back of the shops, a Turntable ladder was parked there, its ladder lowered down onto the ground with water dripping from the monitor fixed to the cage at the head of the ladder, indicating it had been used to deliver water from above. Oddly, at the rear of the shops was a strange narrow three storey building which looked residential, a mini block of flats. This was showing signs of being alight on the upper floors with angry smoke pushing from the eaves of the roof and upper windows.

I couldn't make out how a fire in a well-constructed 1930's row of shops, with dwelling above, all substantially brick built had spread back to this other building. Looking at the flats above the shops, a couple of these were also showing signs of fire and a couple of teams of Firefighters were working with jets up on the open balcony dealing with those fires.

Neil was the Sector Commander at this side, and he joined me.

"What on earth has happened here Neil?" I asked.

"Hello Steve. If you have a look behind the wall, what has happened they have opened up the rear of the shops and joined it to a series of metal ISO shipping Containers which run right across the back and behind this building, which is three single flats one on top of the other," He explained.

"Yes, I did think it was an odd-looking building," I observed.

"It's going like a train inside the shipping containers and we can't get into them. They have 'Cobra' on its way to try to punch through the walls, but it's a dog as they are all lined. We've used grinders to try to get it, but then there are layers of insulation. The containers are all joined ad-hoc and end up in the garden of the next house along." He pointed over his shoulder and I craned my neck to look beyond the odd block of flats to a large detached house.

We continued to discuss how he felt the operation was going and what he thought could be done. I then peeked into the front door of the flats to see that the hallway also went straight into the containers, explaining the unusual and unrestricted fire spread. The fire was raging deep inside and said a silent prayer that I had been ordered on a Command Officer and not the Fire Safety officer, who would have to start picking up the threads of what had gone wrong in terms of the occupiers legislative duties and build a case for what I though was certain prosecution. Into the house and out into the garden, I finally saw the mishmash of containers with pockets of Firefighters trying to access them to extinguish the fire.

"What's over that wall?" I asked Neil.

"Dunno Steve, I haven't been over there." He replied with a shrug.

Back out in the main road, I asked Sami if he'd been out the back on the left side. He said he had and if I entered the block of flats next door, I could get out to the back. Doing so, I came out into a courtyard and noticed a small access road with the wall of side of the shops and original storage areas facing me. I had an idea.

Back at the Command unit, I was frank with Rick and Richard.

"Speaking to the sector commanders, I don't think the Ops Commander has a particular grip on the job. Both sector commanders have different ideas and I don't think he is being effective. I think you should take charge Richard and make Rick the Ops Commander."

"I also think we need to see if we have a USAR Officer on one of the FRU's as I think if we breach the wall on the far side of the shops, as well as breaking into the containers, it's the only way we'll get to the middle of this lot."

Richard pondered, while Rick looked on the plan to visualise what I was talking about.

"I don't really want to take the job over to be honest Steve, I'd rather Rick remained as IC and me as MO. Would you take over as Ops Commander?"

"Yes of course, but what about the current Ops Commander?" I asked, feeling a little guilty about my honest assessment.

"You said we are short of GM's. He's been here since quite early on, he can get away, get some food and get back on the run to give cover. I'll deal with him… John, can you call the Ops Commander to the CU please," He said calling over his shoulder to the radio operator.

I did a handover with the outgoing Ops Commander and then did a tour of the fireground with Richard and Rick, discussing plans. It was a pig of a job, but we now had a plan. Ronnie, who I'd been on the Westminster terror attack with back in March arrived with the Cobra unit. This is a high-powered system, like a commercial jet washer, but much more advanced. It uses an extremely high-pressure water jet, ten times more pressure that delivered through normal fire pumps, and an abrasive cutting sand is introduced into the water stream giving it the power to cut through walls, doors and roofs. Ronnie was part of the team that responded with this equipment as it was still on a trail period with LFB. Unfortunately, at one of its first proper outings, it kept tripping out, so the plan went back to crews with grinders cutting holes into the sides of the containers.

At the other side, I had my USAR Officer. "Do you think we'd be able to breach that wall with the kit you have on the FRU's or will we need to get a USAR unit down here?" I asked of him. He sized up the wall and also examined some block work where a window had once been.

"That'll be a piece of piss, breaking through that blockwork Guvnor. We'll have to work a bit harder on the rest of the wall, but we've got enough with us to make a few holes to get jets inside," he said to me proudly.

"Good man, get your crew to make a start on that and I'll get a couple of crews here to help you." I walked back out of the block of flats into the main road and saw one of my Officers from Shoreditch with two Firefighters in tow.

"Shaun, just the man, have you got a job?" I said as I walked up to him.

"Hello Guvnor, no we haven't. we've just been tidying some hose." He replied, looking expectantly at me.

He stepped to one side, revealing a Firefighter who I hadn't seen before.

"Guv, this is April, she is our new trainee. Today is her first day and she'd keen to get in the thick of it. April, this is GM Dudeney, our Borough Commander for Hackney."

"Hello April, nice to meet you, what a great way to start," I said pulling off my glove to shake her hand. She replied shyly and smiled as I gave Shaun the instructions to get Shoreditch's machine around the back and to assist with breaking open the walls and getting some water onto the fires.

Within an hour I had everything in place and we were getting somewhere. Another FRU crew from Bethnal Green, had done a fantastic job cutting the sides out of the containers. I made some time to talk to Sam, one of the Firefighters from Bethnal Green whose Dad, Clive had been a Station officer at Bow for many years and who I'd known since I first joined. The odd block of flats in Hazel Gardens had become a little unstable, but the TL crew were working on opening that up and extinguishing the remaining fires in there. Back at the other side, I caught up with Shaun and was pleased to see April's head poking out of a hole that had been made in the wall, a big grin on her now blackened face as Paul and John, two of her more experienced colleagues guided her.

It had taken hours, but we had got there. Any smoke now drifting from the web of interlocked buildings was now white and light in volume, Richard and Rick were also pleased with how we'd gotten a grip on it having walked around with them both a couple of times each time progress getting better and better.

Golders Green is the heart of another of London's large Jewish Communities, not dissimilar to Stamford Hill over on my patch. The local community were friendly and very generous that day. Instead of the barbed comments or complaints about closed roads that we usually endure, local businesses had kept us well fed and watered all day, despite the usual attendance of the Salvation Army canteen van that was always sent out to fires of 8 pumps and above.

Me and Sami were sitting on a low wall opposite the fire having a breather as relief crews had arrived and were changing over. We'd just finished a big slice of Pizza each that a lovely rotund Jewish Man had insisted were the best in the area and we were pondering the fire and life in general. I was about a month or so short of thirty years with LFB, Sami had done 33 years at that point and was still enjoying himself.

"They have worked their nuts off today Sam," I said.

"Yeah, especially on such a warm day," he replied.

"I have to say, that has to be one of the most complex jobs I've ever been on. For hours, every gain we made, another problem would pop up. So many hidden voids and such odd construction. Still, we are pretty much there now mate, well done and well done to the crews, this is definitely one of the hardest fires most of them would have dealt with." With a slap on his leg, I stood up and said farewell to Sam, as his relief had arrived and he was off home.

It had been an incredibly complex fire that had taxed our combined experience and been a physical effort. Sunday June 11th was Red Watches first day duty. The crews who attended the fire at Golders Green had come from across London. Little did we know that on their first night duty, just sixty hours or so later, in the early hours of Wednesday 14th June, over 200 of them would come together again, at the scene of the worst peacetime fire in British history.

Grenfell Tower

Grenfell Tower, June 2017, the scene as I arrived defied belief.

My wife came into the bedroom and woke me up at about 6am. "There has been a really bad fire in West London, in a block of flats, apparently people are missing."

"Where?" I asked.

"Grenfell Tower, near Ladbroke Grove," she replied.

I thought I knew it, there had been a serious fire there a couple of years ago when I was on duty, I didn't attend but I was aware of it. I had a mental picture of it in my mind. I was wrong, that was Adair Tower on the other side of Ladbroke Grove, Grenfell Tower must be a name buried deep in my mind from my days doing the 'Knowledge'.

The weather had been hot, so I'd had quite an uncomfortable night trying to keep cool as I slept. As I lay there waking up and stretching, her next words caused me to gasp and throw back the quilt to run downstairs. "They are saying there are 40 fire engines and 200 firefighters on the scene." My heart was racing with adrenalin. That was unprecedented and unknown in terms of modern-day UK firefighting in a residential building.

"Fuck me," I exclaimed as I ran into my study and saw the images on Sky News. Jittery mobile phone images of an entire council tower block blazing from top to bottom against the night sky. The screen then changed to daylight images as the sun was rising. I did know the block, it was behind the old West Kensington Leisure Centre, I'd been past the block hundreds of times in the years I'd been driving the cab.

I was completely gobsmacked, I had a particular interest in high rise buildings and firefighting in them. I was seen as something of an 'expert' because of my technical interest and experiences, having attended more fires in high rise buildings than most, due to my fire service geography, time in and pure fate, that more often than not, I was on duty when a significant high rise fire came in.

I couldn't see how a whole building could be engulfed. The whole principal of fire safe high rise living in the UK was based on the fact that each flat was in effect a self-contained concrete box, so one flat could completely burn out without any effect on the rest of the building. Of course, there had been exceptions, we'd all seen and attended fires where flames, breaking out of the windows would crack the windows above and allow heat, smoke and sometimes fire in. Open windows in summer were also an issue. But the worse I'd ever seen was flames jump from a very serious fire in the first floor of a block in Mile End, East London. It had spread four floors higher as a result of 'auto-exposure', the term used to describe flames coming from an opening and spreading vertically as a result.

"It must've spread up the outside via the surface, whatever the building has been clad in must've burnt," I thought to myself, being aware of previous cladding fires, but not in the UK. It was unthinkable that such materials could be used in the UK, thinking how strict our fire safety and building regulations were. How naive I was, how naive all of us were, trusting as professionals, let alone members of the public, that reputable responsible organisations naturally adhere to codes and regulations.

I quickly showered and got changed into my uniform, I knew the number of Senior Officers on duty overnight were limited and just about everyone who was on duty would be there. Having no idea at that point of the horrendous night my colleagues in the LFB Control room had been through, I rang through to the Officer of the Watch and a shattered female voice answered me. I asked if any additional Officers were required, she tiredly replied that I should ring one of the Deputy Assistant Commissioners on duty.

I did that and found out they were going to put out an early pager message asking for people to come in early, many more of us were due on duty from 8am. It was getting on for 6:30am now, I was frustrated no one thought to put out a pager message earlier… although many of us were off duty. Quite a few people kept their pagers on and lived within London so could have responded. I added my name to the list and waited.

Shortly afterwards, my pager went off and I was ordered onto the incident. It was probably around 7am by now and I'd sat there, days short of 30 years' service, thinking I'd just about seen and done everything that any firefighter could reasonably expect to attend. As I left home it was a perfect summer day. The temperature was already rising and for a brief second as I walked from the house to the car, I felt the glorious soothing rays of sun wash over me. I knew exactly were the RVP was that I was told to head to on Ladbroke Grove, and I mentally planned my route, as I stuck the magnetic blue light on the roof of my car and jumped in, turning my handheld airwave radio and switching the car radio to LBC to try to listen to messages coming from the fire and the latest updates on the live news.

I raced through the warm sunlit, but already busy, streets of Hornchurch and then Dagenham as I made my way towards the A13 and the torturous route into Central, then West London. I struggled down the A13, eating slowly through the three solid lanes of traffic heading into London. Grabbing a lane to my left or right as the traffic tried to open up and make way for me. Blue light drives were always adrenalin fuelled and I always enjoyed them. This one though, was gloomy despite the beautiful day outside, and alongside the beating heart adrenalin, I felt an ominous grumble in the pit of my stomach, as I mentally prepared for what was ahead of me.

As I came to the top of Canning Town Flyover, I looked ahead to the west and briefly saw a dirty smudge of sky far in the distance heading north, to my right. I'd seen it before, many times, the line of smoke, now cooled as it gets ever further from the fire. I'd seen it before, smoke from massive warehouse or industrial fires, I had never, nor did I expect to see it from a fire in a residential block that was still eight miles away across our capital city.

From there I disappeared into the East India and Limehouse Link tunnels, emerging onto The Highway, tentatively edging the whole way on the opposite side of the road, defensively ducking in, sirens blaring, as one or two oncoming motorists were looking elsewhere and hadn't seen me. Thinking about the nightmare that Lower Thames Street had become since the introduction of the cycle lanes, I opted to head north into The City and work my way continually westwards with a slight northerly bias to get to Ladbroke Grove. I had similar thoughts about the A40, Euston Road, a direct hit to where I needed to be, but another dual carriageway, so ultimately undesirable as it left me with no options.

So, on I went through Holborn, Oxford Street and Bayswater Road, due to the height of the buildings and the warm southerly breeze blowing smoke from the fire to the north, I never got any further clues or indications as to the situation at Grenfell Tower.

I pulled into Ladbroke Grove from the Holland Park end and slowed through the lines of emergency vehicles. It was apparent I was never going to get to the RVP, obviously set hours earlier and now gridlocked. So, I opted for a side street, Blenheim Crescent, where I parked my car and rigged quietly in my fire kit preparing myself for what I was about to face. I was parked outside a beautiful multi-million-pound Townhouse in a street full of similar houses. Birds tweeted and the warm sun glinted through the trees. I thought of the "Who will buy this wonderful morning" song from the film Oliver, because of the tall houses, the shape of the road and the weather.

I walked away from the car, the map in my head telling me I was just southeast of Grenfell and had to make some rights and lefts. I turned into St Mark's Road and left again into Cornwall Crescent. There were more people now, stood outside of smaller more modest council houses and entrances to flats. They spoke in small groups, some dressed, some in nightclothes, talking quietly, occasionally looking up and giving me looks, oddly sympathetic in the main, which wasn't a good omen, and the occasional polite smile and nod. I noticed one or two other officers walking down the road, this was usually a signal for a bit of banter among colleagues and playful backslapping, but this was different, we kept our head down and remained silent.

I then turned right onto Clarendon Road, there was a fire engine parked in the middle of the road and a few yards in front of it a police van. I looked up and for the first time I saw it and my stomach flipped. A block of flats I'd seen many times before. The top of it matt black with thick soot. Most of the windows of the 12 or so floors I could see above the trees were emitting rolling dark grey smoke, occasionally punctuated by a flame here and there. The few windows that did not have smoke coming from them were even darker blackened holes. I could not believe what I was looking at and I swore quietly. I stopped to take a photograph on my phone. Not to be macabre, but I know where this was certain to head in terms of an inquiry and statements being taken, so I resolved, as did many others, to keep a visual/time stamped record of my day.

Turning left again into Walmer Road, walking around the perimeter of the new Kensington Leisure Centre, I reflected back to my teenage years when I'd attended a swimming gala at the old pool that stood in this site. A few of us had got talking to some girls from the estate, overlooked by Grenfell Tower, which at that point was less than ten years old, I remember seeing it, but didn't take any notice of it other than it being there. Not in my wildest imagination did I think that I'd be back here under such circumstances, 35 years later.

I turned right into Bomore Road and was directed towards the Command Unit further down on the right. I started to see pockets of exhausted firefighters, their faces blackened and almost glowing red, knowing full well all of them had been exposed to incredible heat whilst attempting firefighting and rescues inside the tower. There were hundreds of people, emergency services, civilians, officials in fluorescent waistcoats. All strangely silent, the only real noise was from the birds obliviously enjoying this beautiful summer morning. I nodded to a couple of people and stopped to talk to a few of those I knew well. Placing a protective arm around them and reassuring them. Small words of comfort, I didn't yet know the full story, but their faces and what I'd seen of the building told me all I needed to know.

Walking past the canteen van, which was parked under a tree where a street had been paved over, making it a dead end, among the crowds, I saw a senior officer colleague. He was stood alone, holding a cup of tea with a cigarette in his hand. His face was dirty but streaked with tears, I tried to make eye contact, to then go over and comfort him, but he looked right through me, lost in the horror of the past hours. I carried on.

I arrived at the Command Unit and met with a crowd of other officers, silent nods and greetings.

"Have we lost anyone?" Having seen the block, the look on the faces, the news on the way here, I was convinced we must have lost some firefighters. I was relieved and amazed that we hadn't.

Grenfell Tower, June 2017, burnt cladding that had fallen from the building during the fire.

I looked into the Command Unit and saw Andy, the Assistant Commissioner who was now in charge in a meeting with others, I reasoned, correctly, that a

'Silver' meeting was in progress. While waiting, with sweat already trickling down from under the brim of my helmet and feeling hot inside the coat, I removed them both and placed them on a hedgerow next to the CU. I thought to myself, "I'm going to have a shit and uncomfortable day, why not keep cool while I can."

I walked the few yards to the corner of Grenfell Road to get another look at the block, I looked up at it, I could see the whole of the south and east sides from here. Incredibly, even now, over seven hours since the fire had started, there were flats, mid-way up the building where the cladding fire had burned past them, that were now slowly catching fire inside. First, dark grey smoke began to push out around the edges of the window, then it got thicker and the windows cracked allowing thick black smoke to come out, then the room would flashover, a flame would roll out and up the building. It was fascinating from a fire development point of view, but horrific in terms of what we were facing. I concluded that the building must by now be alight completely on the inside and these previously untouched flats were now burning from the inside out. That in itself completely went against every assumption I had, based on experience and extensive knowledge of the way these blocks should have been constructed.

I walked back to the CU and made some small talk with a couple of the others, but again was drawn back, to watch the way the building was burning. Shortly after that, the group inside the CU left, I was near the door so got Andy's attention.

"Alright Steve?" he said, looking tired but quite collected.

"Yes, I'm OK Andy," I replied.

"I'll be with you all in a second," he said and closed the door. Presently, he came to the steps of the CU and addressed us. He outlined what had gone on and what was going to happen going forward and that most of us would be required, but that we'd have a presence here for days to come, so others would be released and called back later in the day or beyond.

He looked straight at me and held a stare for just a second too long before giving various officers their roles.

"Steve," he said to me at last.

"I have a particular job for you. I recognise, that you more than most will want to get into the thick of this job. But I have dozens of crews here who don't want to leave. They need to get away and they need to rest, a lot of them will be back here tonight. They really want to stay and help, we are having a hell of a job to get them to go. I need someone of your stature and reputation, who can talk to them and get them to realise they have done all that they could and need to let others step in now."

He outlined my task solemnly and continued.

"We also need to work out which appliances can't leave, those that are boxed in or are set in and pumping. We'll need to organise crews from their stations to be brought to the site and have them taken to Paddington. Everyone leaving here is being sent directly to Paddington for an immediate debrief. Sabrina is running that, make sure you tie in with her and let her know who is coming and when."

I was disappointed and relived in equal measure, I clearly remember the feeling. I saw the point of what he was saying and reasoned I'd know quite a few people here and would hopefully have the 'fatherly' ability to encourage people that they needed to go. But I also wanted to be in the tower and to take command of some aspect of the firefighting. It was what it was, I began my task armed with a list of who had already been released and who needed to go.

I walked closer to the block down Grenfell Road, looking up at the block, still, despite my experience, in awe at how this fire had developed, was still burning and still breaking out. I made a left turn and Grenfell Road went under a pedestrian deck with the block to my right. Drawn back across the road was Paddington's turntable ladder, it was wet and covered with debris that had fallen from the building, as it had been used to try to quell the flames in the cladding, which was ultimately unsuccessful due to its waterproof outer aluminium skin.

Walking around the TL, I glanced to my left and saw a body, covered by a sheet that had been dragged inside an empty garage. To my right was the newly refurbished entrance to the block. The large plate glass window had been removed to allow ease of access to the multitude of crews who had been in and out making rescues and firefighting in the previous hours. I saw a solitary figure in the lobby. It was Nick who had been one of my Station Commanders in Hackney, he had recently been promoted to Group Manager and by his location in the lobby and the surcoat on his back I identified he had the role of lobby Sector Commander. As I walked through the gap that had been left by the glass, I noticed another body, again covered with a sheet, that had been carefully left to one side with as much dignity as possible.

Nick looked exhausted. His usually warm smile tinged with sadness, nonetheless we greeted each other as best we could. "Alright Nick, are you OK?"

I stood close to him and held a comforting arm partly around him. "I'm OK thanks Steve, cheers." I found myself unusually lost for words; what words could I possibly say that would even begin to cover what we were dealing with here. I shook my head and looked down at my list.

"Are any of these crews still in the building, mate?"

Nick looked down and pulled on his reading glasses. "I'm not sure, most people are slowly being relieved, none of them are in my sector but may be up at the Bridgehead, have a look on the wall over there, I've been trying to keep everything up to date."

There was a door in the middle of the wall with a white sign that read 'Grenfell Tower Community Room'. On the wall between the door and the glass entrance wall was lots of spidery scrawl made in black chinagraph pencil. I had seen this used many times at fires, a large clear wall makes an excellent whiteboard for urgent note taking, but never this much. As I got closer it became clearer, at the top; in large block capitals 'Above 10 EDBA below 10 SDBA'. This meant that extended duration breathing apparatus, which can last up to one hour in optimum conditions, was being used on the floors above the 10th and standard duration BA, around 30 minutes, much less in difficult conditions, was being used on the lower floors.

There were crude diagrams of the layout of the floors and tables divided up with floor numbers and what crews were where. Other details recorded the plight of some people who were reported as trapped and the crews sent to rescue them, lots of these had some comforting words written next to them such as 'three people out' or 'two rescued' and so on. Sadly, many more had nothing written against them. Another table on the wall had details of what appeared to be reports coming from outside of the block '7th, 1 male' '9th, people waving' '11th, people hanging from floor' another just had 'baby' scrawled in bold capitals. I shook my head sadly as I compared my list to the crews still up at the Bridgehead.

It appeared this data was now somewhat out of date, so I decided to make the climb up into the tower towards the Bridgehead. I confirmed its current location with Nick and let out a deep sigh as I started to make the climb. The first flight was within the large open lobby, then I found myself walking along an open corridor and into the centre of the building and the main staircase. The heat and smell of smoke gave an immediate feeling of claustrophobia. My animal instinct was to turn around and walk out of the building. But like so many others that night, many of them putting themselves at great risk, not knowing if they'd ever come out, I kept going as I had a job to do.

Just after the initial emotional response to turn around is overcome, my well developed and now well used mechanism of defence kicked in. The shutters came down behind my eyes, what I might be seeing would be processed in a binary way to allow me to gather information and make decisions as a professional, with Steve being shut away, as best as I could manage, behind those shutters. The stairs were wet and littered with hose and other equipment. Enclosed within the tiny dark staircase I picked my way through, as distant and strangely comforting sounds of human activity, that of my colleagues, echoed down from above. I looked into a couple of the floors and respectfully acknowledged the bodies of those who were beyond help and had been moved to one side to make room for those who may still be alive, to be removed from the building with as little delay and further distress as was possible.

Arriving at the Bridgehead, I was confronted by a scene that was still amazingly busy with a group of officers deep in conversation in the middle of one of the floors, obviously doing a handover as a couple of them had arrived with me. Not wishing to push through, I pulled at the arm of a Watch Manager who seemed to have a coordinating role and asked after the crews that I was looking for. "Not up here Guvnor, here's everyone who we have at the Bridgehead currently or deployed above," he said, turning to check against the details written on a forward information board. I thanked him and walked back towards the staircase and headed back downstairs, checking an unusual feeling growing in me that I needed to get out, reminding me of being small and wanting to get to the next lamppost, door or other landmark before an approaching car caught up with me. Like something ominous and unseen was creeping up behind me.

On the way out, I exchanged a few more empty words with Nick, comforting him that he would surely be relieved sometime soon. Walking back into the bright warm sunlight, I felt relieved as the sunlight washed over my now sweat soaked body. I turned right following the service road, removed my fire helmet and wiped my head. On the north west corner of the block I saw large groups of firefighters in breathing apparatus, some stood, some sat against the wall getting relief from the strengthening sun. With them were groups of TSG police officers in full riot kit holding full length riot shields.

They were being used as escorts for firefighters making their way into the building, with an officer at the front and back, shield held over them, this formed a protective barrier against the large bits of burning cladding and debris that were still falling from the building. I felt my eyes sting a little as pride welled up inside me. Pride at these firefighters, young and old, black and white, male and female, doing whatever they could to save lives and our police colleagues, bravely doing their bit to protect the rescuers in this most unreal and tragic spectacle.

I was now walking along a pathway next to the railway line that led up to Bramley Road, I noted a team of HART paramedics and police in blue overalls who I assumed from previous experience were from the Police Disaster Victim Identification team. They were laying out sheets and putting up tables, assembling some sort of a temporary mortuary I guessed ominously.

Out in Bramley Road, I found another Command Unit and met up with Lee, the DAC who was in charge of the logistics operation of ensuring fresh crews, equipment and supplies were being brought to the scene. We had an exchange over what was going on and I started to tick off crews that were on my list as I discovered who had been relieved and who still remained. Pretty much everyone was taken care of, apart from a number of crews, Kentish Town, Richmond, Greenwich, Dockhead and Chiswick as I recall, who's appliances were set into hydrants pumping water to the fireground and could not be moved.

We decided that we'd need transport for them to be taken to Paddington for the initial debrief but also to get fresh crews brought immediately on blue lights to the incident ground from those stations. Getting them to Paddington was simple enough as there were plenty of vehicles we could use, but getting personnel urgently from stations was a problem. We had representatives from Transport for London on the scene who could provide us buses, but that would take far too long for buses to get from all of those locations.

Outside were a small group of police officers who had been allocated to us to assist. I approached a young PC and asked him. "Have you got a link to GT young man?" GT being the Police Gold Command room at Lambeth where the strategic level of this operation would be run from. "Erm, yes, yes, sir."

"Good man, can you get onto them and let them know that one of the LFB Commanders working on logistics needs, hold on, one two three, four, five… five of your TSG vans to blue light to these stations," I held the list for him to see, "and pick up fresh crews to come to the scene." He acknowledged taking the paper from my hand, making the call.

Shortly after, looking a little embarrassed, he came back to me and said, "GT have told me I don't have authority to request that."

"Christ," I replied and resisted the urge to tell him he was of no use unless he had the ability to get things done for us. "OK, who is in charge here on scene." He gave me the Police Commanders name and I asked where he was. Another inaudible conversation later, he told me that the police 'Silver' for the incident was in Kensington Leisure Centre. "OK, thanks for that." Confirming his name again, I retraced my steps to find him.

Passing back down Station Walk, the alleyway back towards the block, I noted that there were now several body bags lined up in a neat row in the makeshift mortuary area with the DVI Officers and HART paramedics busy around them taking notes. Back past Paddington's TL, I looked up at the block to confirm I wasn't going to be struck by anything falling and cut across the dry yellow grass area that acted as a break between the Tower and Leisure Centre. Dozens of exhausted firefighters were laid out on this grass, seeking shelter where they could under trees or in the shadows of the buildings. I saw lots of faces I knew, these were crews from many of the nearer stations so had obviously been here during the thick of it.

I took time to say hello to a few where I could, offering words of comfort or praise, reassuring them where their eyes seemed to beg a question of "have we done enough?" I saw Pav, who I'd been in training with 30 years previously. As our thirty years was going to be up in a few weeks, I knew he only had a short time to go before he retired. I gave him a big hug and repeatedly slapped his back hard. Few words were exchanged and once again I felt a sting in my eyes, thinking back over the years and how we never could have imagined the horror of today back then as fresh-faced recruits.

Recovering I made my way into the leisure centre and asked for the Police Commander. I was directed into a side room where some desks had been hastily assembled and identified the Commander by his rank markings. "Commander, I'm Borough Commander Steve Dudeney, I need to ask you a favour."

Getting up from his chair and offering me his hand he said, "Steve, I'm Stuart, what can I help you with?" I explained my predicament and he assured me they could help. He rang the Police Gold at GT, an Assistant Commissioner and I rang our own Gold, Richard the Assistant Commissioner I'd worked with at Golders Green just a few short days ago. Between us, we explained the situation to the respective Gold Commanders at Lambeth and they agreed to have an immediate conversation. I took the opportunity to remove my fire coat, the helmet already looped through my hand like a large round handbag and went to get a cup of water.

While I was greedily gulping down the water, Stuart walked over to me and confirmed, "We now have TSG vans, driver only, heading to those fire stations," he showed me an identical list of stations to what I had written down, "to bring your day shift crews to the scene." I thanked him with a shake of hands and grabbing my coat and helmet and walked back outside.

The first person I saw, looking as exhausted as everyone else was Shaun, my Watch Manager from Shoreditch. Immediately remembering the last time we had met at Sunday's fire I asked, "How is your crew, where are they?" then I remembered young April who had only just started on the Sunday, a pang of fear ran through my stomach. "What about April, is she OK?"

Shaun confirmed they were all OK. Terry and Jon had gone in first and had been involved in a number of rescues, while rescuing a mother and daughter they came across some other people and ended up having to drag and carry several people out. April was with Paul, who is her mentor, they were initially helping in the staircase but got sent up to the tenth floor where they were then involved in rescuing people.

I was really impressed, this fire was the worst incident I'd seen in thirty years, yet alone a couple of days. I hope and pray none of us will ever see a fire like Grenfell Tower again. The fact that April had thrown herself into the thick of this so early in her career was a great testament to her and her training.

I had eventually managed to locate all of the remaining Red Watch crews and got them home. Greenwich were at a loss as to how they were going to get back so I asked their Watch Manager if they had money in their petty cash back at the station. He confirmed they had about £100 so I told them to hail a black cab and take that back. I'd authorise the payment and getting out my small notebook I wrote a small note to that effect and signed it for him to attach to the expenses claim form. A while later, I heard that they had found a personnel carrier and actually drove that back to Greenwich, that would cause me a headache later in the day as it had been brought to the scene by a fresh blue watch crew from Wembley who themselves would need taking back at some point.

As the day progressed, I had been given a slightly different task. I was to meet another Command Unit at a new RVP in Ladbroke Grove and brief all of the crews who were now being sent in on three hourly rolling reliefs. I was again equally disappointed not to be getting more involved but also relieved to be away from the immediate scene, it was a strange feeling that left me conflicted. I decided that I'd collect my car and drive up to Ladbroke Grove, only a few hundred yards away, but thinking about unpicking myself from it all later on, I thought it would be useful to be parked out on the main road next to the CU.

Back in Clarendon Road, walking back to my car, I had a sudden and urgent desire for a cigarette. I hadn't smoked for quite a few years, apart from the odd 'social' cigarette on a night out. Scanning the street, I noticed a row of shops. I walked into a newsagent shop, fully dressed in my soaking stinking fire kit and the lady didn't so much as bat an eyelid as I bought myself a pack of Marlboro lights and a box of matches. Stepping outside I immediately pulled at the wrapping and took out a cigarette and lit it. It tasted awful as many previous smokers who fall back into smoking will testify, but was hugely satisfying, so much so I lit another straight after which tasted even better.

I spent the rest of the afternoon overseeing the arrival of fresh crews every few hours, briefing them on what would likely be required and telling them to gather their breathing apparatus and report to another officer outside of the leisure centre, pointing them along a route on a hastily drawn map that I had stuck to the outside of the Command Unit. At around 2pm a large rumbling noise was heard within the building and an emergency evacuation was called.

As I had all of the nominal roll boards from the appliances with me now at Ladbroke Grove, I had to urgently commandeer two Station Commanders, who had finally been relieved from the scene, to help me to work through the 20 or so crews and tick off each one to ensure all personnel had been accounted for.

Throughout the afternoon, well-wishers were stopping by and thanking us. People were dropping off food, drinks and one man went into a shop and brought a box of various ice creams for us. I was initially telling people we hadn't been involved in the rescues and were just carrying out a logistical role, but it became harder to refuse and explain than to simply thank them for their kindness and store the ever growing piles of goodies inside the cool interior of the Command unit. To be fair, I was distributing the drinks and food to crews who were arriving on the reliefs and being firefighters, nothing was wasted or not well received.

As evening began to draw in, the Incident Commander who had taken over mid-morning began to look at getting some officer reliefs. I'd been on scene for over ten hours now and although I hadn't physically worked hard, I had been juggling crews, appliances, resources and other things to try to keep the incident ground moving and ensuring supplies didn't run short. At around 8pm I made my way back towards the Tower for a meeting of all of the senior officers on site.

As I came within site of the tower again, it looked completely different. The sun was setting behind it casting an odd light around the building, the fires had been pretty much extinguished or had burnt out and the top two thirds of the building as I approached from the east were as black as hell, like nothing I'd ever seen. We worked on a plan going forward overnight. Every flat on every floor had now been checked and sadly no one was left alive inside. So, the number of crews would be reduced overnight and built up again in the morning. Our specialist Urban Search and Rescue teams would come in and begin to shore up any compromised parts of the building and along with the police DVI teams, begin the necessarily slow, deliberate and forensic task of collecting evidence and recovering the bodies of those who had been lost.

Having been relieved, I wearily sank into my car and cleared my thoughts for the drive back home. I left just before 9pm, having spent twelve hours on the scene and used my final bit of energy to heave myself out of the car an hour or so later. Joanne and the girls met me at the door, the same worried look across all four faces. They knew by now when I had my "I don't want to talk" face on and each gave me a reassuring touch or hug as I came through the door.

I went into my study, kicked my shoes off and poured myself a healthy glass of single malt and went and sat in the garden, reaching again for the pack of cigarettes that had taken quite a beating since I'd bought them earlier. Joanne was the first to come out after ten minutes or so, she asked if I was OK and if I wanted to eat. I was starving but opted for a couple of sandwiches, as I didn't have the energy to eat a large meal. I watched the News on catch up at around 11pm, watching the whole thing from the early hours right up to live night-time shots of the building, with small flames flickering behind a number of windows in the blackened hulk of the building. After that I fell into my bed where I surprisingly found sleep washing over me instantly.

I woke up early the next morning and had a few seconds of normality before the images of the past 24 hours came crashing back into my mind. I expected to be ordered back to the Tower but never was, not until a month or so later in fact when I visited with some officers from FDNY who had been sent over by New York City's Fire Commissioner to have a look at the building and understand what had happened, in case they were faced with a similar fire.

Meanwhile, I decided to work from home, and as expected, well before 9am, when I was drafting an email to the Chief Executive of Hackney Council, the Mayor, the head of Hackney Homes and the Police Borough Commander, the first of many telephone calls come in regarding the situation with high rise buildings in Hackney. The following weeks were a frenzy of activity and meetings, I'd never felt so in demand within Hackney and we gradually picked our way through the condition and likely risks associated with similar buildings within the borough. Thankfully there was nothing similar to Grenfell, although lots of urgent surveys were carried out around street doors, compartmentation and fire stopping within blocks.

As soon as the inquiry was announced into the fire, everyone within the fire industry was perplexed by the fact the inquiry would look at the night of the fire, before it got to the point of how the building came to be covered in flammable cladding with poor fire stopping in the first place. That was the most logical and natural place to start. The cynical among us saw a stitch up on the cards and as the first stage of the inquiry unfolded day by day, it became clear that a lot of the blame would unjustifiably fall at the feet of the London Fire Brigade. Sadly, when the first stage of the Grenfell Tower Inquiry reported a year and four months later in October 2019, I was proved right.

The details of the first stage of the enquiry are well known and as I predicted, used an element of smoke and mirrors to present the facts in such a way as to make the LFB look ill prepared and incompetent.

The learned experts, who scrutinised the events of the night second by second, with great hindsight and in the cold light of day, came to conclusions after hours of detailed analysis, whereas the firefighters on the ground that night only had seconds to make those same judgements. The incident was completely unprecedented, and was disastrously and uniquely coupled with a total failure of the compartmentation and fire stopping. This fact alone makes the Grenfell Tower fire an event not seen anywhere previously.

The report details that the 'stay put' advice should have been abandoned between 1:30am and 1:50am. It is a matter of fact and record, that no Senior Commanders from LFB were in attendance at the incident until after this time. A couple of middle ranking Station Managers had arrived and were immediately swamped with trying to make sense of the multiple fire survival calls they found themselves in the midst of.

So, the only command personnel, through an absolute mist of shock and horror, trying to make sense of information that was changing, for the worse, second by second, were the handful of appliance commanders on the scene. These brave individuals, who the organisation expects to command incidents where four fire engines and around 20 firefighters are in attendance, were expected to have the clarity in the 'fog of war', of a small military platoon facing a sudden unexpected onslaught from several regiments of the enemy, and to recognise that 'stay put' had failed and should be reversed.

In the midst of that constantly changing environment, where every second of change required a minute of thought it was so desperate, I implore anyone to explain to me how you come to that decision. Again, as discussed previously, even if by some miracle of divine intervention that decision was made at 01:30 to give them the best chance, how was that to be communication to the hundreds of residents still in the tower at that time?

There was, for very good reason that I will not go into here, no public fire alarm. In the noise and confusion would people, especially those who were still blissfully unaware at that time, have heard or taken notice of loud hailers used from the ground hundreds of feet below them? Evidence from some survivors and tragic testimony from some of those who were trapped clearly demonstrates some people did try to escape and facing choking blinding smoke and fumes either went back, went further up into the building to escape the poisoning atmosphere or got no further than opening their front doors.

It is true that a number of people took that brave decision and were able to escape, some barely conscious as they got to safety, others collapsed and were rescued by firefighters on the stairs. But if the order to evacuate had been communicated and heard, how were the LFB meant to encourage those people to make an orderly escape?

Witness testimony from many firefighters, for those who have been bothered to read it, is littered with reports of crews who did reach people in flats on upper floors where they often refused to open doors or found escape untenable and remained in their flats, or most tragically firefighters, physically exhausted from the climb to those higher floors in heat, smoke and debris quickly realised that to remove people was to condemn them to a certain death within minutes of leaving, at that time, a relatively safe environment, not being able to comprehend the spread of fire that was to follow.

I am afraid, for all of the great minds and detailed analysis and investigation into the night of the fire, this seems to have been overlooked. The facts I mention above have been overlooked in what appears to be conclusions built solely on technical analysis, without any consideration of human behaviour and emotions, lack of experience of this type of failure anywhere previously and no understanding of the utter horror those responding, trapped or witnessing had to endure.

In summary, I can only conclude with as much objectivity as I can muster, having been involved in the incident, that although mistakes were made by LFB, these were not reasonably predictable in terms of the rapid deterioration of events on the night, and as such the conclusions of the report have, in my opinion almost been pre-determined to scapegoat the London Fire Brigade and its personnel, to what end?

Systemic Failure. Those are the headlines that were written in relation to the LFB. I'd argue that systemic failure has appeared everywhere in the sorry tale of the Grenfell Tower fire. From deregulation of fire safety laws in the early 2000s, and the apparent cost cutting and poor oversight of the refurbishment of the Tower, to the way in which the inquiry was set up and the conclusions drawn at the end of phase one.

Grenfell Tower affected me deeply. Some of my colleagues took it very badly, especially those who were there early on in the incident, and many now have PTSD. For me it was different, as a so called 'elder statesman' of the LFB, reasonably high ranking and one of the longest serving operational fire officers, I felt a responsibility for those who had been there and tried so hard. Like most people, I am haunted by the images of the tower whenever I see it and by what I saw on the day. But the worse thing is the looks of exhausted desperation I saw on the faces of the many firefighters and officers who attended that day, and how none of us can ever answer the questions behind those masses of tormented eyes.

Life was clearly going to be different, with the inquiry due to go ahead in the coming months, the way it had been planned, LFB was going to be turned on its head in a way that would make all of the previous new regimes, political about turns and good ideas look like pebbles in the ocean.

I was tired, I certainly wasn't the oldest person in the organisation, but I was approaching 50 and had been doing this since just before my 19th birthday. I'd seen as many, if not more fires, accidents, deaths, loss and pain as pretty much anyone who did this job during the same time period. Getting up in the middle of the night to attend a fire or deal with pager message after pager message as duty ILO relating to sieges, armed incidents, bomb scares or prisoners on rooftops. Then having to sit in the London traffic in my car with everyone else the following morning, after little sleep, and put in a full day at the office was also beginning to lose its shine.

I had become tired of the petty politics a long time ago. As much as I loved those I worked alongside at all ranks and levels, there were enough of them who were a pain in the arse to make my life difficult, in managing their petty arguments and demands.

So, with all of this in mind, added to the fact that the pension changes back in 2015 held me hostage to a 'now or never' choice, I decided that I'd retire on my 50th birthday, which was the earliest date I could take the pension. In the early years, I never thought of retirement, there was so much to do, so much to see and that point in my life was so far ahead it was almost unimaginable. Later on, as I grew up a bit, I always planned to stay until I was 55, when Imogen, my youngest, will be 18. But here we were, everything changes and the best laid plans and all that. As late July 2017 passed and I turned 49, I was now into my final year as a London firefighter... but the fun wasn't over yet.

Back to Where It Started

With the Boss. Steve and LFB Commissioner Dany Cotton at a fire in South London in 2018.

The months after Grenfell had pretty much consumed me as a Borough Commander in terms of dealing with the local authority and the numerous social landlords in Hackney who had high rise residential buildings that everyone was now very suspicious of. Dany, the Commissioner was doing a fantastic job in making sure everyone who had been involved and was suffering was being taken care of.

If ever the stars align and the right person is in the right place at the right time, this was it. Dany had been made interim Commissioner in January 2017. Ironically as she was attending the Grenfell Tower fire with hundreds of her officers and Firefighters on June 14th, that, coincidentally was the day she was confirmed as having got the Commissioner role permanently.

LFB had been through some awful political turmoil in the previous years. The last Commissioner, himself a very capable and extremely intelligent man had been tarnished by the Machinations and political circus that had seeped into every crevice of the Brigade. Now with a new Mayor in City Hall from May 2016 and Grenfell having rocked us to our foundations, Dany was a long serving experienced officer with a big heart who was exactly what we needed to heal the organisation.

Tom her immediate deputy was also an experienced and people focussed officer who was also very well regarded. I knew them both well and felt that even though my days were now numbered with LFB, things were going to get better.

Al, my boss who was North East Area Commander rang me one afternoon. "Steve, Pat has been given Temporary DAC and they want you to go into Tower Hamlets as Borough Commander from November 1st," he said in a sombre voice down the phone.

"What? That's ridiculous, I've only got 8 months to do, It takes six months to get a Borough where you want it and get to know how it works and all of the personalities in the council," I replied flabbergasted.

"I know, I know, but Tower Hamlets Council has just come out of measures and it's one of those Boroughs you can't just give to a new officer."

"I get that Al, but Christ, we are all in the middle of the post Grenfell work and how can I just abandon Hackney and leave them to it?"

"Look, I was thinking, I might approach them and ask if Rod can act up as interim BC for Hackney with you overseeing it and you can take Tower Hamlets as well. You'd get an ARA for doing both Boroughs, they are doing exactly that over in the West with two Boroughs." He offered this as a means of compromise that made sense for Hackney and the organisation.

I agreed that sounded better. It wasn't all bad, I'd been brought up in Tower Hamlets and started my career there, so part of me liked the idea. I'd be reluctant to leave my lovely office at Shoreditch, but the BC's office at Millwall was a lot closer to home and would make my travelling easier. In the end I got a hybrid of

351

both… Rod was going to take over Hackney on a temporary basis, and I was to assist and mentor him, but from a distance. I was to be Tower Hamlets BC in name and publicly I'd have no more to do with Hackney.

I was stood outside of a burnt-out house in Green Lanes in Ilford one afternoon. I'd been called to the fire as a Senior Fire Safety officer because the house was being used as a House in Multiple Occupation and as such came under the rules of the Fire Safety order. My phone rang and I saw it was the AC in charge of Fire Stations for LFB. My Boss' Boss if you like. "Hello Dom, are you OK," I answered.

"Hello Steve, are you OK? Can you talk?" Came the reply.

"Yes of course, I'm on a job on Ilford's ground, but it's all quiet, what can I do for you."

"Steve, I need you to take over at Tower Hamlets, we need an experienced BC and someone who knows the Borough and the area." I was expecting the call, all of the negotiating had been done already so it was what it was. "Yes, of course I can Boss, Al has already mentioned it to me. November 1st isn't it?"

"Yes mate. Pat is starting as DAC on that date so that'll give both of you time to do a proper hand over and for you to get Rod up to speed."

And with that it was done, after 30 years and four months, I was heading back to where it all started for me as a young kid chasing the Fire Engines. I would have Bethnal Green, Bow had been closed in 2014, Millwall, Shadwell, Whitechapel and of course my beloved old Poplar.

My time at Tower Hamlets started on Wednesday November 1st 2017, not even having a chance to get to my office, the day started with a meeting with the Council and other partners discussing the final stages of a project that I had inherited and was about to be rolled out. That took me until lunchtime where I saw the on duty watch at Shadwell and then over to Millwall to see the on duty watch there as well as trying to unpack the boxes I had dropped of the previous weekend to try to get myself into a position where I could function. At the end of the day, when I should have been going off duty, I headed over to Poplar's ground to a community hall where I had a 'Health and wellbeing' board meeting that had been dropped into my diary in the weeks previously.

Over the next few days, I managed to get around to all of the watches in the Borough. Four Watches at five stations. It was an effort, but I absolutely believed that it was essential for every Firefighter and Officer, whether they know me, as most did, or not, to meet me personally and discuss their issues over a cup of coffee in the Mess.

I worked the Saturday, so I could finish the visits and was just pulling up at Whitechapel when they came racing out of the doors and disappeared towards the City of London. Parking in the bay, I walked into the Watchroom and noted from the printer they had been called to an automatic fire alarm actuating at the offices of a multi-national investment bank in Fleet Street. Deciding they wouldn't be too long, I opted to find my way up to the Station Commanders office right up on the top floor where I could long onto the computer and catch up with some emails.

Just as I opened the office door I felt the pager vibrate on my hip followed in a second by its high pitched bleeping. I pulled it off my belt and focussing on the small lettering noted I'd been informed of the same incident that Whitechapel had just turned out to. The first arriving crews had made the incident up to four pumps. Scrolling through, I saw I'd been informed as a Fire Safety officer and not a command officer. So as this was a commercial building that fell under the Fire Safety Order, I'd inevitably have to attend.

Walking round the desk I sat down and immediately logged on before ringing control. They confirmed I'd been informed as Fire Safety officer and Dowgate had made pumps four pretty much as they'd arrived. Knowing the size of the building and how quick it had been made up, I suspect it had more to offer. I told the control officer I'd be attending and quickly looked at the live incident log to see who was attending and if any further messages had been received. I recognised the name of the Station Manager as a new Officer who had just transferred into LFB. I didn't know her personally, but in any case as FSO I wasn't likely to get involved in incident command.

I ran down the stairs, opened the bay doors and placed the blue light on the roof before jumping in the car. I turned on my radio and pulled out of the station into the Saturday morning traffic. I'd hardly covered 50 yards when Dowgate came in again with another message making pumps six and confirming the fire was in the basement by the declaration of a "Basement procedure implemented" message.

The traffic was light and typically with my heavy accelerator foot and knowledge of London's streets I got there in a very short time. I got out of my car and was slowly getting rigged, taking a briefing from the Watch Manager from Soho who had now taken over, I explained I was here as FSO, but nonetheless as the most senior officer present, I still had legal responsibility for the incident.

Just as I was finishing another car tuned up and a Woman Officer who I didn't know got out. I assumed this was the new Station Manager who I hadn't met yet. I walked over to her and introduced myself to her and let her know although I was here as FSO, I would monitor her until her actual Monitoring officer arrived.

I stood with her and the Watch Manager as they carried out a handover of command, offering a few words of advice or asking the odd question to complete a picture in my own mind. I noted that the building security staff had provided an incident grab bag with all of the relevant information including detailed plans. It appeared the fire was within a bank of large batteries in a UPS room in the sub-basement. This was one of a number of uninterruptable power supplies in the building that guaranteed power to all of the important IT equipment no matter what was going on with the main power grid.

Shortly after this the Monitoring Officer arrived, and I was able to get back to my role. I was satisfied the construction within the sub-basement was to a very high standard and compartmentation was excellent. Although for good reason our crews still followed the strict protocols for firefighting within basements. In actual fact they were able to walk down two very well-lit flights of stairs and along a corridor also well-lit before arriving at the secure fire doors with the fire behind.

Reading the plans, I recognised the same of the signature of the person in overall control. Trevor had been my instructor at training centre as a recruit for the first training squad I was in. He had retired from the LFB and was now the European Head of Fire Safety for the organisation. Thinking briefly to my own upcoming retirement I allowed myself a smile at the potential opportunities out there.

Just after this, he actually rung the duty manager and asked to speak to the Fire Safety officer. He was most surprised to hear my name and voice on the other end of the phone and even more surprised that I, as one of the recruits he had trained decades before was now on the cusp of retirement myself.

With more personnel and some watches less settled than those in Hackney, I had my share of dramas to deal with. It seemed that Sara, the HR rep was in my office discussing one personnel issue or another more than my own Station Commanders. By and large though they were a great bunch at the five stations. I knew many of them from old and kind reports were made of me from those to the newer staff who I didn't know.

I was also short of Station Managers, but thankfully two of the Watch Managers at Bethnal Green, Chris and Emma were both looking to go for promotion in the coming months. Looking for more 'strategic experience' they volunteered to assist with some of the external liaison roles within the Borough. I was happy to give them both that opportunity and where I could, I found a bit of overtime money here and there to ensure it wasn't all 'voluntary' work.

They, working alongside my Station Managers made my life really easy. Obviously, I wasn't going to be around for very long, so it made sense for me to stay in the shadows as much as possible and let those who were going to be around a bit longer be the outward face of LFB Tower Hamlets. I'm glad to say, both of them got promoted after I retired, I hope I played a small part in that and I'm sure they'll go on to do great things.

Operationally, I wasn't about to be let off without several final and quiet exceptional outings. In fact, I don't think I could have imagined a better way to end my career. A couple of years previously a system of formal overtime had been agreed between LFB and the representative bodies, the Fire Brigades Union and the Fire Officers Association. This wasn't ideal, as organisations shouldn't run on overtime and the required number of staff should be employed to cover the vacancies.

On a personal level though, it wasn't too shabby for the individual officers. Our hourly rate of pay at that level was decent, so a twenty four hour shift at time and a half a couple of times per month could put a not insignificant amount of extra money in your pocket, even after the eye watering amount HMRC took out of it. 1986 and 1987 had been quite big intake years for LFB in terms of recruitment. So unsurprisingly, a lot of those took their retirement thirty years later. Quite a few of 'my generation' had also risen to the senior ranks, so by early 2018, with so many of my peers recently retired the shortage of officers and subsequent overtime availability was quite significant.

It was one of these overtime shifts on a cold February evening I was sprawled across the sofa at home, full after a nice dinner a couple of hours earlier, watching the TV. The tell-tale tickle in my hip came as the pager started to vibrate yet again followed by the bleeps. I had been ordered to 6 pump persons reported fire in Hackney, my old Borough were there had been multiple rescues from a sprawling block of low-rise flats. As this overtime shift was due to a shortage of officers with the Fire Safety tag, I had been expecting it to be fair as there were only two others on duty. One way down in South West London, the other up towards Wembley in the North West.

I drove along the main road in Hackney that had a long lazy curve in it. The first thing I saw were flashes of blue bouncing off the houses as the bend opened in front of me, then a Police car across the road with a line of tape set up in front of it and a solitary Police Officer stood there, his head seemingly shrunk down inside his jacket to spare him the worst of the cold. Beyond were the usual line of fire engines parked both sides of the road with the command unit, its blue beacons still flashing marking the focal point of the incident.

I jumped out of the car and quickly got rigged in my warm fire kit and then I took a few moments to examine the scene. Checking I was unseen, I lit up a cigarette. I'd still been trying to give up after starting smoking again at the Grenfell Tower fire, but reasoned with just a few months to go, retirement and my 50th birthday would be the time to finally draw a line under it.

Standing behind my car in the shadows of the trees I saw a number of Firefighters rolling hose in the middle of the road. Two more, with steam coming off their fire kit and their heads were at the side of an appliance, servicing their BA sets, they'd obviously been one of the BA crews, the heat they had absorbed in the fire now evaporating in the cold night air. Beyond them, more trees and between them bathed in gold light from the street lights the lower floors of the block involved. Lights came from windows on the lower floors and more starkly where the trees hid the light from further up the block, the light from the windows there appearing brighter.

A ladder, its bright shiny metal also reflecting the streetlights was pitched to the third floor of the building. A darkened window and a curtain hanging over the window ledge blowing in the cold breeze. A reminder of the desperate rescue that had taken place half an hour or so earlier. Next to that darker than anything else, the blackened soot stained windows of the rooms that had been on fire. A flash of brilliant white light from within the room as the torch of a Firefighter moved around the room and then again it was lost into the blackest of black.

Finishing my cigarette, I popped a chewing gum in my mouth, I was an awfully self-conscious smoker. Embarrassed at the constant and justified criticism of my family and conscious of the smell of cigarettes on my breath, once so familiar it was unnoticeable, now seemingly identifying me as a pariah of a bygone era. I ambled across the road and jumped up into the bright and warm interior of the Command Unit where I greeted the officers inside, handed over my role board and got a briefing as to what had happened.

Stoke Newington, followed by Homerton on multiple calls had responded to the fire in the third floor flat. Unusually, as although it was late evening, most people were still awake, the fire had remained undiscovered until the window in the burning bedroom had broken. A member of the family had ran out into the hallway and was immediately consumed by the smoke and heat and fell to the floor. The remainder of the family, now trapped, managed to shut the door and opened the window where they screamed for help.

Arriving within minutes of the call Stoke Newington sprang straight into action, throwing the 13.5m ladder expertly up to the third floor, a Firefighter running up it the instant it crashed against the wall. Four people were rescued and handed down the ladder by the crew who had pitched the ladder, while the others, having squeezed their Pump into the courtyard pulled off the hose reel. A line secured to it, it was pulled up to the third floor landing and passed to the two Firefighters who without waiting had entered the boiling black atmosphere in search of victims.

The man was found instantly, unconscious, partially burned but alive he was unceremoniously dragged out of the flat and passed to the crews on the open external balcony, now joined by Homerton where vital lifesaving first aid was given to him. He was conscious now but in quite a bad way. I saw the paramedics working to stabilise him inside the brightly lit interior of the ambulance.

Up on the landing it was now quiet. I said hello to a young Firefighter who was looping up a long line over his arms. I saw splinters of fresh wood from the door frame on the now wet landing along with a discarded mask and wrappers from the resuscitator and first aid kit. As I peered into the flat a large composite security door was laying in the passage. Large dents and cracks near the hinges, the door had survived but the frame had given way to the hefty blows of the sledgehammer launched at it by a strong adrenalin fuelled Firefighter. Covered in wet footprints from the dozens of feet that had been inside since I trod on it and added my own to the mix.

The walls from about three foot up were blackened and blistered, below this they retained their light painted colour, but tellingly flashes of black where Firefighters in BA and crawled in and felt their way along the wall in complete darkness, pinned low by the heat yet trying to scuttle as fast as they could in search of the victim and to attack the fire. The familiar scent of smoke and burned material, still hanging in the air mixed with steam, my torch beam highlighting it like car headlights cutting through mist in an atmospheric scene from a horror film.

The small hallway was T-shaped, turning left and right out of sight. Some movement and then a bright light, possibly the one I'd seen from outside I raised my hand to shade the light and saw a battered white helmet from one of the Fire Investigators I knew. We greeted each other and he explained the story in more detail. We entered the bedroom; the air was still hot and sauna like in here. I blinked my eyes and coughed slightly as I adjusted to the atmosphere.

The ceiling and walls were clean concrete and brickwork, the plaster having spalled and fallen to the floor which was now debris covered. A small wire hung from the ceiling indicating where the light had been in the centre of the room. The undulating carcass of a mattress was in one corner above some black debris that has once been a bed. Damaged most at one end with some other charred fragments the FI, using his bright torch as a pointer indicated that his preliminary examination and witness testimony from one of the householders who had been rescued had led him to believe that a charging laptop placed on a small bedside table may have been the cause. The witness stating that he laptop charger had bene getting quite hot recently.

Peering closer, I managed to pick out some molten plastic and small metal components which appeared to be similar to those found inside a laptop. I turned around and a collapsed wardrobe faced me. It's thicker supporting timbers still standing and tapered like four giant burnt matchsticks. The thinner panels charred, twisted and covering a soaking pile of partially burned clothes, several metal hooks that had been attached to plastic coat hangers and a handful of twisted wire coat hangers sat among the mess in defiance of the heat that had consumed most of the room.

Walking out of the bedroom I looked in the other rooms, these old GLC blocks were constructed of reinforced concrete with brick walls. They were sound and no fire was likely to compromise the structure. Still although this had been a residential fire, people had been injured, one severely and as a block of flats the 'common areas' the hallways and staircases were within the scope of the fire safety order so I had to make a report working with the FI to ensure between us we fully understood what had happened and how the building had performed.

Happy that the building had performed as expected and there had been no compromise or fault with the general fire precautions, I reassured the representative from the Housing provider all was well. However, I cautioned him that had they have had smoke detection in the flat, they'd have become aware of the fire much earlier and would have got out quickly through the front door unharmed.

March started as February ended, cold with a few days of light snow here and there. Things began to look up by mid-month and spring looked very promising. It was around mid-April the weather turned very warm and dry with the temperature reaching 29°c on one of the days. What I didn't know was that we were in for an absolutely stunning warm summer and with that things usually got really busy for LFB.

It was during one of these early hot days in April I attended what would be my last fatal fire. Called to a '10 pump persons reported' fire up in Chingford at about 3am one morning I made my way quickly through the streets of East London to the address just off Hatch Lane. I knew it was some sort of care home and having been ordered on as the second Group Manager when the job went to ten, guessed I'd not have much to do.

I arrived and parked up and after making my way to the command unit to book in, I spoke with the Chris the GM who was in charge and he told me my boss Al was on his was at the monitoring officer. Chris wanted me to have a look around and tidy up any loose ends. The two Station Managers also in attendance were good officers. Dick, who was one of my mine in Tower Hamlets and Terry another capable officer who was part of the Redbridge Borough team.

I got the story of the fire, it had been what appeared to be a regular fire in one of the rooms. It was more of a specialised care facility for people with mental health problems than a care home, and the flat involved was a supported living unit, part of the building but the person living there essentially had their own flat. Unfortunately, one person had already been found deceased in the flat where the fire had started but everyone else managed to escape from the remainder of the building when the alarms went off. Worryingly for a new build, especially a commercial residential building, was the fact the fire had spread irregularly and jumped from the ground floor into the first floor and up into the roof void, which was pumping out dark grey smoke above me as I ducked low and scuttled into one of the main doors to try to work out what had happened.

Looking up there was a heavy smoke layer, but it wasn't fast moving smoke or particularly hot. Listening to the building, nothing indicated to me that anything particularly ominous was about to happen above my head, so I pressed forward. I continued to crouch as I made my way up the corridor and made a left turn where I saw what appeared to be a front door. With the damage beyond the front door, I could tell this had been the fire flat. Looking into the door, the fire had been pretty much extinguished but a fog of steam and smoke still hung heavy inside. Walking in, I looked to my left and saw the badly burned body of the resident, getting lower, I crept forward and looked into the burned-out living area.

In one corner of the burnt-out room I saw a boxed plasterboard partition that had been burnt away. I went up to it and inside saw the remains of a melted plastic drainage pipe. Looking up following the beam of my torch, I looked into the cavity that disappeared into the murky darkness above. This I concluded was how the fire had spread out of the room. It appeared the partitioning built to protect the pipework in a fire resisting enclosure had failed allowing flames, heat and smoke to spread out of the room.

That was a fundamental failure of the building and with this being a residential care facility and a person having died, this would most likely lead to a prosecution. I offered small thanks I hadn't been ordered to this incident as the Fire Safety officer because this would no doubt entail a lot of investigation and report writing. I stuck my head out of the broken window to get a breath of fresh air and then retraced my steps, offering a silent prayer as I passed the body in the hallway.

Out the back of the building, the large dining room, the neat grounds of the building and the houses behind were lit up bright orange. The fire had now broken out of the roof properly and was moving quickly across the ridge with loud pops and crackles. A crew in the garden opened a jet up and aimed it at the flames. I ducked down the side of the building and saw Tottenham's ALP was unfolding and taking up a position to attack the fire from above while other Firefighters connected hose to the base.

I look around at a group of Firefighters stood at the back of a machine, two of them holding a large 70mm jet which was turned off. I was incredulous, the group of them were like spectators. "What are you doing?" I demanded.

"Well the ALP is about to get to work Guvnor."

"Yes, it is, but they haven't even got water to it yet so why the fuck have you turned the jet off?" Five faces looked at me, no one had an answer. "Get that fucking jet back into position and start putting water on the roof until the fucking ALP has water on," I roared at them. "For fuck sakes," I spat as I turned my back on them and walked across the face of the building. The next two people I came across were Al and Chris. Chris was showing Al around the fireground and they both got an expletive laden version of the events 30 seconds previously.

I was always known as being very calm on the fire ground, not one to shout and scream and always quite friendly as I truly believe it got the best out of people. But seeing what I did at that second, with one person dead inside and the roof now burning merrily across the roof absolutely incensed me. I wandered around the corner and found the Sally army van had set up. I had a quick chat with the Fire Safety Officer, delighting in telling him how he'd have his work cut out and then had a quick coffee and a sandwich before the hordes descended onto us.

Once the ALP was up and running, the fire darkened down pretty quickly. As I was the second Group Manager sent on Chris soon got me away. Peeling myself out of the wet kit I jumped back into my car for a very quiet ride home along the still deserted roads. Dawn was breaking and by the time I got home the sky was light, I dragged my wet kit out of the car and as I usually did I hung it in the garden over the furniture so it would dry in the warm morning. I was going to be off duty from 8am for a couple of days, so I sat there in silence in the garden watching the day come alive and the sun slowly rise from behind the trees.

With only three months left, I wondered if that was going to be the last dead body I saw whilst in service. It was as it happens, but I couldn't know that at the time. Death had been part of the job for my whole career and as I sat there, I found myself trying to remember how many I'd seen, I had no hope of recalling them all, but I couldn't even get a firm fix on the number. I knew the last year with The London Bridge attack and Grenfell had been the worst by far. But there are only some you remember… Driving down a road, a sound or a smell can bring a memory into sharp focus. Some stay with you and occasionally visit you in your dreams, I don't mind that so much, they don't haunt me, and I feel comforted that I remember a handful among the many.

Week after week of increasingly dry and warm weather drew the inevitable comparisons with 1976 and 1995. It was getting busy and I noticed I was getting paged and going out to calls more often. My friend Jim, a Firefighter from

Fitchburg in Massachusetts in the USA was coming over to spend a week with me before I retired. I picked him up from the airport and took him to the accommodation I had arranged for him. I promised him that it was going to be busy and as an exceptional photographer, who worked professionally outside of his Fire Service role, that he'd get some great photographs. In the two days before he arrived, I'd been to a 10 pump fire at a large plumbers merchants in Sidcup, in South East London, a large fire that had burned across the roof of several terraced houses in nearby Blackfen and back over my side of the water a hazardous materials fires in a large industrial complex beside the river in Dagenham between Barking Reach Power Station and the old Ford Engine plant.

I had his visit coincide with my weekend 24 shifts followed by the Thursday/Friday 24 shift four days later. So, he'd have four opportunities to ride with me to incidents. Expecting much, the weekend shifts disappointed. I couldn't remember the last time I'd had a weekend shift where it wasn't busy. It was Sods law, the same had happened a few years earlier when he came over, but I had him riding the pumps at Poplar and Euston that time so at least he saw a bit.

A few jobs occurred during the week when I was only working day shifts, so I was hopeful, and I gave Jim the usual tours around London and various activities including him witnessing and taking part in a large hazardous materials drill that NE area had planned at a bus garage. Thursday came along and again I went to bed disappointed.

I blinked my eyes open as the pager woke me. It was light in the room but unfamiliar. I had stayed at the Officers accommodation at Shoreditch, so I was initially confused, blinking the sleep out of my eyes I called to Jim who was asleep in an adjacent room. He acknowledged me in his Boston accent and we were soon on our way to a house fire in Bethnal Green so it was a very short ride. To be fair, I was only informed of the four pump fire as a Group Manager as the incident was commanded by a Watch Manager with a Station Manager monitoring, but control know I had a colleague from the USA with me so had no problems when I let them know I'd be attending. There was still quite a bit to be done when I arrived, I spoke to Mick from Homerton who was in charge and he was more than happy with us being there. The Station Manager who arrived after me was surprised to see me there but he soon understood as well.

Thankfully, Jim managed to get some great shots, one of which he got of me when I didn't notice him, as all brilliant photographers seem to manage. He arranged with my wife to have blown up and framed as a surprise retirement gift, on top of the wonderful personalised US style fire helmet shied he had commissioned for me. *That photo is the one used on the back cover of this book.*

It didn't pan out as we expected, but Jim, always cheerful got back onto his aeroplane satisfied with the week he'd spent with us again. Ironically just hours after dropping him off, there was a decent sized factory fire that broke out in East London that would have been fantastic for him to witness.

Final Fires

The last fire. Steve with members of the White Watch at F22 Poplar at his last fire, just hours before he retired in July 2018

At the end of May, we had the first rain in weeks, but with the atmosphere hot and unstable, this came as heavy thunderstorms. I was working from home as I had been quite a lot lately. With all of the overtime shifts and the 'day job' pretty much left to the remaining Tower Hamlets team because of my imminent departure, I was keeping all sorts of weird and wonderful hours. It couldn't be sustained under normal circumstances, but I had a big and very final way out now less than two months away.

I'd been to drop a signed fire safety witness statement at the Fire Safety Offices at East Ham and was heading back home along the A13 when the sky flashed, cracked and then the heavens opened. The radio was very busy with lots of crews already out and it went manic as flood call after flood call started to come in, these calls chasing their way across London as the storm progressed.

I heard an appliance get called up to a house fire in Rush Green on Dagenham's ground. It was Harold Hill's machine, quite a way from Dagenham so I guessed the local stations were already busy. Less than a minute later, more calls and appliances now being ordered on due to the multiple calls were from stations that were much further away. I then began to get quite interested, not only because I thought it would be quite a while before anyone got there, but also because I was now near the Bull Roundabout at Dagenham and less than a mile from the fire. Heading north through Dagenham East and through Rush Green also got me home, but it wasn't the most direct route from where I was.

So I found myself heading north off the roundabout instead of east and I also noticed I'd sped up a bit. I got to the lights at The Eastbrook at Dagenham and was now only about half a mile away. Still no messages, I cursed impatiently at the lights which are an annoying four way set at this junction. I was nothing to do with this call, so I had no justification to put my lights and sirens on, so had to sit there. The lights changed and I made the right turn and quickly passed the car in front that had slowed to pull into a side turning. Picking up the pace, I made the series of bends past the Eastbrook pub and as the road straightened, I could now see the smoke.

I reached for my radio, it was a bit of a cheat but I wasn't technically wrong. "FE from Foxtrot one, one, zero priority, running call over."

"Foxtrot one, one, zero from FE, go ahead with your running call over," The tinny female voice replied from my radio.

"FE, from Foxtrot one, one, zero, running call to smoke issuing from house, Rush Green Road, Rush Green, request full attendance and show me status three over."

"Foxtrot one, one, zero from FE, we already have an attendance on its way to this fire and have received multiple calls over."

As it happens, I had seen the first appliance approaching from the opposite direction, but by the sound of things they'd be on their own for quite a while so I pulled the car up on the opposite side of the road and got out into the heavy rain scampering to the back of the car to get rigged.

I spoke to the Watch Manager from Harold Hill as his crews got ready to go into the house to start to attack the fire. I told him that I'd been on my way home from East Ham when I came across the fire, technically correct, and here I was.

I began to think the fire wasn't as a result of a lightning strike after all because as the crews pushed in, there was heavy smoke on the ground floor.

The WM had made the job a four pumper and also ordered an aerial on. With Dagenham just down the road, their ALP was soon set up outside the house should it be required. The rest of the attendance was now on scene including Terry, the SM from Ilford, who knowing me as well as he did was not at all surprised that I was already here when he turned up.

What had actually happened was that the lighting strike had hit the house and blown all of the electrics. The main distribution board was on the ground floor under the wooden staircase and was already well alight as we'd arrived. All of the electrics were blown, quite literally on the first floor upstairs where some of them had blown out of the wall.

The crews soon had the fire under control and reported that because the damage under the staircase was so severe, the supply couldn't be isolated and all of the burned wiring was still live coming into the house and now exposed due to the damage. UK Power were called and once all of the crews were out Terry and I decided to go and have a look.

Now I am not small, I am just under 6ft and quite well-built so I hover around the 17-stone Mark. Terry, a very well-built Rugby player, was slightly taller than me and a lot heavier. He made his way in and gingerly tested the stairs for their integrity. Feeling confident, he stamped hard on them and with no reaction he put his weight on the first step, then his other foot on the second and so on. By the time he got to the fifth step, as if in slow motion the stair very slowly began to sink in front of him.

The remainder joined and unlike a 'crack' with a sudden collapse he slowly sunk into what had been the cupboard underneath, as the wet stair treads made contact with the exposed incoming electrical supply the area around us lit up banged and arced angrily. All of this was happening in slow motion and Terry had now disappeared up to his thighs he looked round at me, didn't say a word as if he was trying to process what was happening.

In a matter of microseconds I'd processed the entire horror of it. Here was I a GM, less than two months from retirement at a four Pump fire, where realistically I should have been remotely monitoring it. I was watching a very well-built Station Manager on a soaking wet and now collapsed staircase about to be electrocuted by a raw 240-volt direct supply from the street.

Without a hope of any success, but deciding I'd rather go with him than do the paperwork I reached around Terry's waist and pulled. He weighed nothing, nothing that I registered and I managed to pull him right out of the hole and backwards down three or four steps and laid him down in the passage with me still holding him and he lying between my legs.

"You alright Tel?" I said to him.

"Yer, I think so," Came his reply. I then heard voices behind me and as I once again became aware of my surroundings clearly heard, "Did you see that, The Guvnor just pulled the ADO out of a hole in the stairs."

Quickly getting up and husting out of the door we were surrounded by concerned if not somewhat amused faces as we retold the strange story to ourselves more than anyone else. Both Terry and I were somewhat shell shocked and also lightly amused by it. "I've no idea how the fuck I pulled you out of that hole Tel…" I said to him in disbelief. "I knew I had to grab you but didn't expect you to just come out, I didn't even feel your weight." We agreed it must have been a purely adrenalin driven situation and that adrenalin somehow gave me the strength to lift Terry as easy as if he were a small child.

Obviously, this had changed things. We had to request a call from the duty Senior Accident Investigator and that soon got people interested and phones ringing. Not least Adrian, the DAC who had been informed of my attendance. He rang to get a run down and congratulated me as "Terry is a big lad", before we parted, he said to me, "Steve, it's only a four pumper isn't it? What are you doing there anyway?" I let the question hang, he didn't say anymore and with a chuckle said goodbye and to try to keep myself out of trouble.

In the days following Grenfell Tower LFB had put out a communication that satisfied me entirely as someone who had always had an interest in high rise Firefighting and had fought long and hard, often at a cost, for an increase in the attendances.

The initial attendance to high rise fire was no be increased to five pumps and an aerial. If multiple calls were received, which was three or more, then that would be upgraded immediately to a full 8 pump attendance including all of the Officers that would attend an eight-pump fire. If the building was known to have an external cladding system on it, that went up to ten pumps.

A number of UK Fire Authorities were not happy with the precedent LFB had set. Many of them, most in fact apart from maybe the other large Metropolitan Brigades such as Greater Manchester or West Midlands would struggle to get the eight with an aerial. But this wasn't the time for worrying about the feelings of others.

As a Group Manager I'd be part of the attendance to an eight-pump fire as well as a Fire Safety Officer. Therefore, I had double the chance of being ordered onto a high-rise fire with multiple calls. And that had been just what had happened. I had never been to so many high-rise fires in my career, not all serious thankfully. In fact with only three calls required to get an incident to 'multiple calls' and trigger the large attendance, sometimes something like some rubbish burning on an open landing of a medium rise block of maybe seven or eight floors would get everyone, myself included on the road.

So, I wasn't surprised sitting in my office at Millwall on a hot day in late June when my pager went off and I was ordered to a high-rise fire with 'multiple calls'. It was to Grafton House just off Bow Road. It had previously been on Bow's ground, but since the closure of Bow in 2014 was now on Poplar's ground. I'd attended a few incidents there when I was at Bow, a handful of fires, persons shut in lifts, the usual story. Just a couple of years before I'd been called to a six-pump fire there from Shoreditch when I was BC of Hackney.

Making my way quickly past Canary Wharf and off the Isle of Dogs, the radio was very busy with chatter about this fire as well as one or two other things going on. Bethnal Green had arrived first and as I was heading along Burdett road I caught a glimpse of smoke in the sky as Bethnal Green came over the radio with a priority message making Pumps Ten, this clearly was now something unusual. Every now and then I got a glimpse of smoke to my right as I headed north and soon scattered the traffic at the busy Mile End junction and I made the right turn into Bow Road.

With the job being a ten pumper, I decided to park up on Bow Road and not even attempt to get down Wellington Way which was the side street off Bow Road where Grafton House was located.

As had become so typical of this summer, I was already sweating and uncomfortable as soon as put my heavy fire kit on and walked down the road. It was a hive of activity, dozens of people had left the block, no doubt terrified by the incorrect and unhelpful narrative being peddled about the 'Stay put' strategy by the media and other actors in the fiasco.

Crews were busy but calmly getting on with their work and seeing nothing on this, the east side of the block I walked down the side and looked up the west side. Thick clouds of grey smoke were rolling from a flat about halfway up around the tenth floor, the grey voluminous smoke told me that crews had already managed to get inside and were now flowing water onto the fire.

Mick from Homerton was taking care of this side of the building from the outside and he told me he was going to set up the TL to cover the outside. I could see the outside of the building was covered in a concrete render, so the chances of fire spread were minimal, but the fire above had completely burned out the flat and flames had extended a couple of floors above so it was a good call.

Walking back to the front, I met with the Watch Manager from Bethnal Green who was in charge, Chris was very capable and was just in the throes of handing over to a Station Manager, but I stepped in told them I'd take over straight away because it was now a ten pumper and it was mine to run by definition of rank anyway.

The fire was dealt with pretty quickly thanks to the speedy and efficient work by the crews. I had a quick chat with the initial BA crew who entered first and they confirmed it was "Fucking red hot in there Guvnor." I thanked them and told them to go and have a breather and drink plenty of water. Walking into the block, one or two stragglers still made their way out hurriedly, there was little point in anyone coming out but I wasn't about to have that argument with anyone.

Up on the fire floor, there was a slight haze on the landing and as I walked in the door I was immediately swamped in a sauna of steam as the concrete walls still held immense heat inside them. The flat had been absolutely consumed. The living room, the seat of the fire was typical of the damage from a severe burn out. The walls and ceiling were now clean steaming concrete, the remains of anything else was now a thick damp carpet of blackened steaming charcoal on the floor.

Going out on the balcony I looked over around and above me to see that the concrete render was scorched, but unlike the flammable cladding on Grenfell Tower, this much more severe fire had not even began to have any effect on the structure of the building itself. I bade my companion to join me upstairs in the flat directly above. Entering this flat it was completely untouched. A lot of smoke had got in through the open windows leaving the living room slightly darkened as if it was coated in a light black dust, but it was fine. I was happy everyone apart from the occupiers of the flat that had been burned out would be back in the building in no time.

From here, I spoke to the Command Unit Officer and along with Steve the ORT officer and Pete the DAC who had turned up we formulated a stop message that would be sent in my name. I was then asked by a Police officer to go to the rest centre where dozens of evacuees had been placed and speak to them. Lots of families were gathered and very concerned by the fire. Once I'd had a chat with a representative from the Housing Authority and a local councillor and reassured them, I spoke to the crowd and told them how the fire had been very bad inside the flat but had not affected any other property. The flames that had scorched the external walls had done no damage at all and the block had behaved exactly as it had been designed to.

I toyed with the idea of telling them that they'd not needed to evacuate and that in fact several people who had been unaware of the fire had stayed in their flats and were fine. But reading the room, I decided not to get into that debate, feeling reassured myself that I had no worries about the block and the biggest risk which we'd avoided would have been someone tripping as they rushed down the stairs and causing a crush as others fell onto them.

Two weeks and a few more fires later I was off a gain to another large high rise fire in Edmonton. I had a retirement party to go to. Graham had joined back in 1987 like me and had just reached his 50th Birthday so was another '68 baby that had become a teenage Fireman in '87 and was now leaving it all behind. Looking forward to his do that evening, I was working until 8pm so decided to stay down and drive over there as I came off duty. I'd actually been at Bethnal Green that afternoon doing my farewell tour with the watches. I'd got changed out of my uniform at about 7:30 into a pair of jeans and a nice clean polo shirt and jumped into my car with only half hour left on duty and headed over to his party.

I'd only got as far as Cambridge Heath Road when again my pager interrupted me. Pulling over and unclipping it from my hip, I swore to myself as I read the details that I'd been ordered again to a high rise fire where 'multiple calls' had been received. Considering only three calls to the same fire deemed it a multiple call incident, which for a high rise now attracted the full 8 pump attendance, I prayed as I rang through to control it wasn't going to be much.

The girl I spoke to at Control confirmed the address in a 25 floor building in Plevna Road in Edmonton Green. She told me that they'd had about fourteen calls to the fire, which indicated to me that it might be a bit more than I'd thought. But, nonetheless, it was a warm and sunny Friday evening with lots of people about, so even the smoke from a relatively small fire in a tall building would be seen from a distance. So, with a sigh of resignation, I flicked all of the switched to my blue lights on and U-turned the car in Cambridge Heath Road and Headed my way north, mentally figuring the route ahead.

Ever hopeful, I was waiting to heard Edmonton's callsign, Alpha Three Four One for their PL that would then be followed by a stop message. By the time I turned half left from Mare Street into Amhurst Road in Hackney I did hear their callsign… followed by a 'priority' that wasn't so good. Again they made pumps ten, and again I was resigned to spending the next couple of hours at least at a high rise fire.

The Fire was pretty much dealt with by the time I arrived, but this block was built above the Edmonton Green Shopping Centre. There had been a couple of issues with access and again the vast majority of those in the block had self-evacuated, which left us, the Police, Ambulance and Enfield Borough Council's emergency planning team with a logistical nightmare. Dealing with this was more time consuming than the fire itself.

It was approaching well past 9pm as I walked back to my car having excused myself as quickly as I reasonably could after an hour or so on scene. I was soaked with sweat, but with a sniff inside my open jacket hoped my deodorant was fulfilling its 48 hour promise, it was only a couple of hours since I'd put it on? That was fine, the pleasant smell mingling with the smell of some from my fire tunic. What wasn't so fine was the state of my dark red polo shirt. Already drying from my exertions inside the building it was horrendously creased and now covered in white stains as the salt in my sweat remained on it as it was drying. That was the end of my hopes of getting to Graham's retirement party. I rang Tony, another of the ILO's who was there and after he stopped laughing, he promised he'd pass my apologies on to Graham. In this time of lasts for me, that was the last high-rise fire I'd ever attend.

Tony who was in charge of the ILO group had pulled me to one side earlier in the summer. In his gruff but business like voice he asked me, "When are you off Dudes?"

"24th July is my last day, it's a 24 for us, but I'm only working a 9 as I retire at Midnight why?"

"POTUS and FLOTUS are coming over for a state visit in July, I thought you could be my 'Johnny on the spot' working with the Secret Service and The Met in sorting out all of the back-up and fallback locations for the visit."

"That'd be great. Thanks Tone," I replied gratefully.

"See how I look after you and yet you are leaving us," He said with a wink.

President Donald Trump was due in London on 12 July 2018 and would be staying until July 14th when he moved on to Scotland. As usual for a sitting president, they stay at Winfield House, the US Ambassador's residence in Regents Park in London. You won't be surprised to realise months of planning goes into these visits and an advance party of Secret Service agents arrive a couple of weeks beforehand.

Along with a few members of one of the Met Police's specialist teams we were told to meet at a Military barracks in London. There we were introduced to one of the advanced party of Secret Service agents who I will call 'Grant' The first day we formed into a convoy of police vehicles and did dry runs across London and Essex of a number of routes the President's motorcade would take.

The following weeks I met with Grant on a couple of occasions. He'd been a Firefighter/Paramedic in the US and was a 'Hazmat' expert. He'd applied to transfer to the Secret Service and after a difficult selection he had been successful and was now one of the close teams working with the President. We got on pretty well as we had clicked as two Firefighters in what was essentially a Police World. He gave me a tour of the president's 'side' of Winfield House, so I could get an understanding of the layout and any tactical considerations should a fire occur.

When the President was in London, I was required to be at Winfield House or nearby overnight. Accommodation was arranged for me at nearby Paddington Fire Station and my car given special clearance to be waved through the gates that had been erected several hundred yards either side of the large house in Regent's Park.

They travelled in two Sikorsky White Hawk Helicopters, the one the President fly's in being called 'Marine one'. The entourage followed in two Ospreys that were 'tiltrotor' aircraft that could take off and land like a helicopter but fly like a fixed wing aircraft.

Once all of the planning was done for the potential possibilities around the Presidential visit, my job basically became a glorified plane spotter. Every time a series of aircraft movements where scheduled, Paddington's crews and machines were sent to the house and driven into the gardens, incidentally the second largest private garden in the UK after Buckingham Palace. They'd standby next to lines of hose that had been discreetly hidden in the well-kept bushes so hose lines and a team of Rescuers could be deployed if one of the aircraft got into trouble. There was as you'd imagine a lot of down time, but as usual of American Hospitality, we were treated very well whilst on this little patch of the USA in London. Food and drink was always available, everyone was very friendly, including the US Ambassador himself who often walked round to say hello to us.

On previous Presidential visits, I'd been stuck in the Police Control room or some other dull remote place, so being 'Johnny on the spot' as Tony called me was a nice little acknowledgement of my service by the ILO group.

Tom was the Deputy Commissioner, a lovely man who I'd known for several years and yet another '87 recruit, he'd had a request from the Fire Brigade Society. A group of Fire Service enthusiasts who did a valuable job in photographing and collating lots of information as time passed by relating to the different types of fire engines that were in service, the stations and equipment. They'd written for a tour of a number of East London stations to photograph some of the newer appliances and Tom decided I'd be their perfect guide. I was to meet them at Romford Fire Station on the morning of Sunday 15th July 2018 and go ahead of their minibus to all of the stations they were due to visit to ensure the crews and appliances were ready to receive them as efficiently as possible without interrupting the stations day too much and without unnecessary delays to the group.

The day had gone swimmingly and by mid-afternoon, I was in the lobby of Millwall Fire Station having given them a short presentation about the changes to Firefighting in the East End over the past three decades. They'd presented me with some nice gifts and our goodbye and good lucks were interrupted by the bells. Millwall's crew came tumbling down the pole and onto the appliance as the Driver and Officer went to the Watchroom to see what they'd got. The delay for them to leave was a little too long for my liking and slightly embarrassed in front of my guests I excused myself as I went to see what was happening.

As I walked through the door towards the Watchroom I found them consulting the larger map in the corridor. "What's up?" I asked them impatiently.

"We are going onto a fifteen-pumper guvnor, a grass fire at Wanstead flats," Came their reply.

"What, when did that kick off, I've been out that way all day, it was busy but I had no inkling…" I was shocked.

They had traced their route to the RVP, the cause of the delay as they looked it up as this was over on Leytonstone's ground, four stations to the north east of

Millwall. I went back and told the group what was going on and made my excuses as I could feel a call to control coming on. Back in the office, I rang the Officer of the Watch at Control. "Hello, it's Steve Dudeney Foxtrot one, one, zero here. I'm on a 9 duty today, but I've been off the run hosting some visitors for the Dep, will you need me?" I asked hopefully.

"Oh yes Steve, we will. We've got a couple of bits going across the Brigade and we are short of Officers. Can you make your way to Wanstead flats, the RVP is Blake Hall Road at Aldersbrook Road. I'm still trying to sort out the Officer attendance for the fifteen but get going and I'll get it sent to your pager." And with that I was off. I jumped in the car and got on my way.

It didn't take long to see this was looking a bit special, As I came out of Canary Wharf and turned right onto Aspen Way behind Poplar, a large cloud of white and brown smoke was blotting the bright blue sky to the north east. Recognising the RVP for the fire was to the north of Wanstead Flats, I didn't retrace the route I took from Poplar to the grass fire I attended there back in 2003, instead I got onto the A12 just after Blackwall tunnel and chose to follow it as I headed up through Bow and past the Olympic site, past Hackney Marshes and through Leyton coming off at the Green Man Roundabout in Leytonstone.

Pulling up behind a line of cars with blue lights on the roof parked near the Control Unit, I thought back to the 2003 fire where I was the first officer there and alone for a long spell. I chuckled that at least this time it would be someone else with the headache and I'd hopefully be a bit more involved on the front line.

The first person I came across was Richard, I'd last worked with him operationally at the large fire in Wembley in 2017 and he'd recently been made DAC. He was in charge. He told me the fire had started between Centre Road and Lake House Road and had threatened the houses in Lake house Road but crews had got on top of that. However, it had spread across that smaller part of Wanstead flats, jumped Centre road and was now heading across the much larger side of the 'flats'. They had a couple of crews that side and were deploying those who made up the fifteen-pump attendance, but could I try to get an idea of the extent of the fire.

As luck would have it, back in March another officer had taken on my lease car and for these final few months I was using one of the Mini Countryman cars that the Brigade had used during the Olympics. Although it was a manual and a noisy little thing it had four-wheel drive and was very robust so ideal to take off road across the flats. The fire was also beginning to threaten the area the

Command Unit was parked in down at the mini roundabout where the four roads met at the top of Wanstead Flats.

Squeezing through the larger fire engines that were jostling for position to get themselves set up in water relays or water shuttles I manged to make my way down Aldersbrook road on the east side. Entering the small car park where the football pitch changing rooms were, I negotiated through another gate onto the flats themselves that had been opened by one of the park rangers. I bumped my way across the field kicking up dust and stones from the yellow dried grass and headed towards the nearest column of darkening smoke, which usually indicated quite a lot of heat and fire growth from a fire on heath land. Getting as far as I dared to go, thinking of the paperwork and notoriety if the Mini was to go up, I got out, pulled on my boots and leggings and strapped my two radios to the thick red braces as it was generally accepted that half rig with helmet and gloves was appropriate for this type of fire in the open.

Wanstead flats has a lot of peat soil and is very uneven. A nightmare as unlike other places we regularly get fires in the open such as Hornchurch Country Park, where the fire tends to burn on the surface, it gets underground here. The uneven surface also makes it difficult to walk over and is a recipe for a broken ankle if you don't mind how you go.

I hobbled across as far as I dared go and took in as much as I could looking over the long grass bushes, trees and shrubs from my limited 6ft vantage point of the direction of fire travel. One very angry looking arm of fire was heading towards me through a thick growth of gorse bushes nosily crackling as it went. What was beyond me was the relatively short dry grass of the football pitches over my left shoulder, but over my right was a continuous run of larger bushes and trees that grew in height until they surrounded a petrol station and small close of private houses. That was a concern.

I radioed this to Richard who told me that Richard the AC was now in charge and was going to make the job up again and what did I think I needed. I did a quick calculation that I saw two already over here, Homerton and Ilford, I'd need crews to lay in from the main road, but meanwhile I'd need a three to do a water shuttle whilst the relay was being laid. I told Richard I'd need six pumps in addition to what I already had and then another two when they arrived to give me some resilience.

Richard the AC then came on the radio confirming I wanted eight more pumps and then told me he was making Pumps up to Thirty. I was surprised, this was the largest fire I'd ever known over here at Wanstead Flats, but thirty pumps was a record in my time. I worked my way across towards Homerton and Ilford and established they both still had over three quarters of a tank of water so we had a little bit of time. Mick from Homerton said he'd take the southern flank of this arms of the fire that was spreading east and Ilford were going to try to tackle it head on.

I watched as Lisa, one of the Firefighters from Ilford who is very fit lifted the hose reel over her head and pulled it, a considerable feat to drag dozens of metres of this hose reel, charged with water across such uneven ground. I was glad she did as the fire suddenly turned and was headed straight for us. Lisa was lost in a swirl of hot smoke and sparks which seconds later overcame me in a warm blast the smoke immediately stinging my eyes and forcing them shut. I stood my ground, worried for Lisa but she had the hose reel at least. Trying to peer through one eye I estimated the progress of the fire towards me and sidestepped the path heading across to where I'd last seen Homerton and Ilford's machines before getting enveloped in this smoke.

Clearing the smoke, I saw a couple of the Ilford lads peering into the fire and calling for Lisa. Taking big steps over to where we'd last seen her the smoke parted and she emerged, her face blackened and her shoulder length hair stuck to her face, but a reassuring smile on her face. She'd cut a decent sized arc into the fire but beyond the length of the hose, it was still spreading. I made my way back to the car, jumped in and drove to where the longer wilder grass met with the shorter grass near the football pitches and where the larger trees were that surrounded the houses and petrol station. "This is where we'll hold it," I decided with more confidence than I should have in the circumstances. But hold it we did.

The first crew to me were from Shoreditch. I ordered them over to the tree line and gave them the "no matter what" line about holding it back. "Make sure you don't spread out to far, don't worry about the flanks and whatever you do, keep one line of your hose reel and the machine near the point where the big trees start as the fire cannot jump to them otherwise, we are bollocksed."

Edmonton were next, I briefed Jimmy the Guvnor and pointed the extent of his little bit. "Work within this area Jim, this is the crucial point, do your best either side but I'm less bothered if it spreads down to the south, I just need you to keep your eye on this side of Shoreditch's flank and this next lot of trees. Let it burn up to you, I know the lads will want to get into it, but I'd rather the longer stuff burn right up to the short stuff then we have no worries."

Then two crews came in. I sent Deptford in to give their water to Homerton and the crew to help out and kept Dockhead back to be ready to give their water to Shoreditch or Edmonton. Eventually over the next half an hour, which seemed more like a few minutes we got all the flanks of the fire covered. It had spread out in tree like tentacles in a number of directions, more than I expected to be fair. The fire had now risen to forty Pumps. For the third time in my career, the fire in Dagenham on the day of the Olympic closing ceremony, Grenfell Tower and now here. Wasn't I a lucky boy?

I saw another car coming towards me kicking up dust from the dry grass. It belonged to John the Borough Commander for the City of London who was on my Rota group so I was surprised to see him, it transpires he was on Overtime as one of the Operational review Team officers and had Dany in the passenger seat next to him.

I'd seen Dany twice on the fireground in the past Month. Once at a very difficult deep-seated 15 pump fire in a row of shops in Welling in South London, where we'd had a sudden an unexpected rapid development of the fire whilst BA crews inside causing even me and another very experienced Station Manager who were at the back of the building reach for our worry beads until the crews drew back to the door and dug in to knock the fire back again.

Two days after this, I'd been called in the early hours to a 20 Pump Fire in a large distribution warehouse in Orient Way Leyton, where again she'd got out of her bed in the middle of the night to come and see her crews doing battle. Walking over to John's car as I got out I greeted them both. "Guvnor, in three weeks I've seen you on the fireground three times. I've only ever seen one other Commissioner or Chief Officer on the Fireground once in the previous thirty-one years, good to see you again."

"I'm just here to keep my eye on you Steve, how is it going over this side," was her friendly reply.

Within no time at all, Monday 23rd July had come around. I slept quite well, despite it still being warm and I woke feeling quite normal despite this being one of the most significant days of my life. After breakfast, I got showered and for the last time changed into my London Fire Brigade Uniform.

I'd been told to 'report' to Poplar Fire Station that morning for my final roll call. It was another gloriously warm and sunny day in London as I made the journey down the A13 towards Poplar as I had done so many times over the previous decades.

I found myself lost in thought, thinking of the journey down in the fog on my bike, excited about my first day driving a fire engine back in 1991. I also thought about a similar warm sunny morning heading down this road on the day Billy and Adam had died 14 years previously.

As I arrived at Poplar and pulled into the yard, I was humbled. Most of my Senior Officer colleagues from NE area were there as was most of the ILO group. The yard was almost full, but nonetheless I performed a theatrical turn in the car and jumped out of it leaving it in right in the middle.

I got dressed in my undress uniform and we all walked out to the front of the Station where the off going and oncoming watches were also lined up for my final roll call. Al, being my immediate Boss took the roll call and at the end gave me a few small tokens of my service before handing over to me. I expected to be emotional but found a strength to address the assembled group. I passed on a few nuggets of wisdom attained over the years and was then interrupted by a noisy aeroplane taking off from nearby City Airport which thankfully lightened things at the right moment. I gave them a little more flannel and raised a couple of laughs before bidding them all to "Stay safe and be lucky." Before I called them up to attention for the final time and fell them out to a round of applause.

The White Watch, my old watch kindly provided everyone with fresh tea and coffee as well as some pastries and I sat there holding court for a while until the group naturally broke up. Alone with just the White Watch a while later I felt a bit weird. I had already done a handover with my replacement and although I was still Borough Commander of Tower Hamlets for one last day, I'd already moved out of my office at Millwall and now felt a little homeless and unneeded as I sat in the Station where it had all started for me as a 14 year old visiting 36 years earlier on that bonfire night in 1982. Feeling sad I went and found myself a spare computer in one of the offices and just sat there sending important, personal or nostalgic emails home and taking some sick delight in deleting all of my folders and the hundreds of emails relating to those things where I thought I'd better keep them just in case.

As was the tradition, my own rota group were going to meet up at Shoreditch that evening so I could buy them one last meal, we'd planned to go to a nice Thai restaurant in Hoxton. Feeling a little melancholy at Poplar, I decided to leave mid-afternoon and drove over to Shoreditch. My old office there was still empty as they hadn't formally replaced me and Rod was still looking after the Borough running from his own office downstairs.

As I'd stated, I loved my office at Shoreditch, it was a great space and I'd missed it. The day was passing slowly and I honestly wanted it all to be over now. I took a few telephone calls from Rod and Pat who had been arranging things and was just ambling about when I sat back at the computer to look at the live incident screen. I was still on call, would be until 8am the next morning, I wondered if I'd have another call before I retired.

Another grass fire had started, when hadn't they this summer, every day come the afternoon the usual suspects would start. Hounslow Heath in West London, Bromley Common to the south, The Chase in Dagenham to the east... This one though was Woolwich Common in SE London just south of the army barracks and east of the Queen Elizabeth Hospital. That was a first, for this year at least. I'd know that to go up a few times in the past.

The job was quickly made up and then made up again and again. It had gone to 15 pumps in about half an hour as I looked south east from the balcony of the office at Shoreditch, yet again I saw the ominous large smoke clouds that fill the sky from these large heathland fires.

Not long after I saw Wanstead flats had gone up again, a slightly different part of it. *No,* I thought to myself. *"No, this is not how it ends for an inner-City Firefighter. I'd had an amazingly busy run in the past couple of months. Possibly more fires than some people in quieter county Fire brigades see in their whole careers. But a nice 6 Pump 'shop and dwellings' flames out of the windows, no life risk somewhere in the End tonight is how I'd imagine it.*

Wanstead flats was made up to a four pumper as soon as they crews arrived, but seemed to be holding. Nothing else from Woolwich, but I didn't expect it to stay that way. I called Pat up on his phone. "We need to cancel it Pat," I said.

"What you frickin' talking about?" Came his reply, amazingly for a Firefighter Pat never swore.

"There's a fifteen going at Woolwich Common and a four at Wanstead Flats again, that is likely to go up. Johnny Swish and a few of the others are already at Woolwich, there's no point I..."

My pager went off. I'd had my radio on channel four listening to our side of the River keeping an ear out for Wanstead Flats again. But meanwhile south of the River on Channel two, The Command Unit at the Woolwich Common Fire had Made pumps twenty and I was now on my way. "What did I tell you?" I said to Pat.

"OK," he conceded, "I'll ring around anyone who is left, and we'll postpone it" and with that I clicked off the phone and headed down the stairs to my car.

So I got in the car and pulled out behind Shoreditch's Pump ladder that I originally thought was going elsewhere as they are a busy station, but by the time we'd driven down Commercial Street, onto Commercial Road and past Whitechapel fire station I guessed they were headed the same place as me. After a relatively relaxing drive through the East End, south through Blackwall Tunnel and up towards Woolwich, relaxing at Shoreditch's PL was doing all of the work in front of me. I left them to go to the RVP while I pulled into the large parade ground of Woolwich barracks where I'd seen the Command Unit had set up.

"Isn't this your last shift Steve?" Andy the AC who had taken charge of this incident said to me.

"Yes, it is, another fourteen hours or so and I'll be off duty forever," I replied.

"We'd better keep you safe then," he said with a glint in his eye this time, the last time he'd given me a job was a year and a month earlier at Grenfell Tower.

In the event, I never left the parade ground of the barracks. True to his word, I was given a logistics job and ended up working out the oncoming relief appliances with one of the other Command Unit crews. Dany turned up again. This time to make sure I went home and finally retired she told me as we had a photo together and she gave me a tender hug and wished me well.

It must've been sometime around 9pm when I got back in my car. Not the end I wanted, but if this was to be the end, then a 20 pump fire on your last night, albeit a grass fire and one where I only saw the fire burning a hundred yards or so in front of me, wasn't a bad way to sign off. I got home and after a hastily arranged dinner, as I should've been eating out, I had a shower and went to bed. Placing the pager in its usual position on my bedside cabinet and I looked at it before my eyes closed and wondered what else it would bring.

The pager stayed silent. I slept through the night and unfortunately, I actually slept passed 8am when I officially came off operational duty. I was annoyed as I wanted to be awake to mark that point. But it was done now. My very last day, 31 years and 13 days from when I reported to Southwark to become a London Firefighter was now upon me. My 24 shift had been removed and an EA code for Excused absence was put in against my name on the system. My final duty was to take all of my kit and the Mini I'd been using to Stratford and Al as my line manager would administer my last duty, signing the forms ensuring I'd returned all of my fire kit, radio equipment, laptop, pager etc.

I logged on to the LFB IT system for the last time, opening the daily News bulletin to look at the larger incident in the previous 24 hours. I'd missed nothing overnight, a trick hadn't been played on me, London had been free of large fires since I left Woolwich Common. I ignored the handful of other administrative emails that had come in and went straight to my 'drafts' folder and sent an email out to all of my stations and senior officer colleagues. I'd drafted it some days before and left it there. I didn't want to get drawn into the replies as they'd likely embarrass me or upset me.

After I got showered, I changed into my own clothes and drove to Stratford. Joanne had insisted she followed me and brought me home, but I was nervous I'd be a wreck and just wanted some time alone. Al and I did what we had to do with dignity, as he detailed all of the returns on the form, I thought back to the Counter at the GLC depot at Tottenham Hale all of those years earlier when I'd got my first issue. After a short while we were done. Al knew all that needed to be said had been said or was going to be said at my retirement party in a few days' time but I was done. I gave him a big hug and feeling the need to get out slipped out of the door of North East Area HQ, across the yard and out into the World Outside.

I put my headphones on and walked towards Maryland Station to get the train home. I felt sad and a little numb but any emotion I'd imagined wasn't there. Joanne met me at Gidea Park, her big eyes looked at me and asked me if I was OK. I was. We got home and the Girls were also a little edgy around me but I was fine. I pottered around for the rest of the day, a few people rang me to wish me good luck and that was it.

Everyone went to bed but I sat up alone, I had one final duty. At the stroke of midnight I'd turn 50, that would also be the moment I was no longer a London Firefighter. I sat there, alone in my study, the minutes ticking away, looking at the photos on the walls marking various highlights of my career. The clock past midnight, that was it. I was now no longer part of the London Fire Brigade, I had now become part of its history.

Epilogue

It's been two years and ten months since I retired as I sit here and write these final pages on an unseasonably cold Saturday night in May 2021. A lot has happened. Most notably Covid-19, which no one could have predicted and something that has seemingly altered the whole world.

My own family's little drama in all of it was my eldest daughter Charlotte's wedding that was due to go ahead in Texas in April of this year. The whole family were going to fly out and see her get married. As the Covid-19 emergency grew, our anxiety continued to rise until it became obvious around mid-March, we were not going to get there. They cancelled the wedding and elected instead to get married in a private ceremony in Austin where they were living. They are one of the many 'Covid couples' who had their dreams shattered this year.

Following that, Charlotte was diagnosed with breast cancer in November 2020 and had to immediately return to the UK for treatment. I am pleased to say she is fighting like a warrior and responding well to treatment. Autumn 2021 should see her fully recovered.

From my point of view, I'm doing OK outside of the Fire Brigade, well, sort of outside. I started my own company just before I retired and now spend a bit of time working in the fire protection industry. I'm sometimes carrying out fire risk assessments on buildings, checking their fire precautions are where they should be and that they are managing their fire safety well. I also act as a consultant for a number of landlords of high-rise residential buildings, assisting them with some of the post-Grenfell requirements.

I still do a bit with LFB. I am a visiting speaker on the national ILO course that is held at the Fire Service College for new fire, police and ambulance ILO's or NILO's, as the ILO role is now well embedded nationally across the UK. I also have a contract with LFB's training provider as their 'fire safety and high rise' subject matter expert. A title that sounds much grander than it actually is.

I spend a bit of my time visiting fire stations across London, some that I've never been inside before, training the crews in fire safety and high-rise buildings. Some people still recognise me, even with the customary retirement beard. "Didn't you used to be Steve Dudeney?" is the standard joke. "Yeah, that was me, I used to be Steve Dudeney."

The other thing I needed to do was finish this book. It has been eighteen years since I typed the first words. I made quite good progress at the start, and even had some interest from a publisher who had read the first 40 or so pages. But back then, the new politicised LFB was in its infancy. Around the time, I'd not endeared myself to many of my more senior colleagues anyway, and it became apparent that to publish a book would have meant the end of my time with LFB.

It sat doing nothing for many years after, having vowed to finish it when I retired. I added a few pages here and there over the years, but honestly, I didn't even look at it for a long time as it migrated from one computer to another as I upgraded them. After I retired, I started well, but life and holidays, lots of holidays, got in the way and in fact, just six months ago, I'd still only gotten up to telling the difficult story of when Billy and Adam died at Bethnal Green.

But since then, I've plugged away at it and here I am at the end of my story. I hope you have enjoyed it. It isn't the first, the last or the best firefighting memoir that has been written. In fact, it was a brilliant firefighting memoir that set me on this road about 40 years ago. As a fire service nut, I was always borrowing the same old fire service reference books from the local library. I liked them because of the photos in them of fires and fire engines from all over the UK and the world.

One day, when I was about 12, I visited the Tower Hamlets Central Library in Bancroft Road and as usual headed for the small collection of fire service books. I saw a bright cover, a coloured photo of a warehouse fire in the London Docks as I pulled it from the shelf. I was instantly disappointed as I opened it and saw it was a reading book. But, I read a few words and minutes later, I was sat in the aisle cross-legged reading this fireman's story.

The book was *Going to Blazes*, by LFB ACO Arthur Nichols. I borrowed it, took it home with me and read it from cover to cover. I couldn't believe what I had been missing. That book really told me the story of being a fireman beyond the pictures, and really inspired and fed my dream to become a fireman. Arthur Nichols had retired a decade before I joined LFB and sadly died in the early

1980s. But wherever you are now, I salute you, and the words in this book are only here because I picked up your book forty years ago.

A Warehouse Fire looking like a vision from hell, North London 2016.

I went on to read many good and one or two not so good firefighting memoirs, all of which encouraged me. After *Going to Blazes*, I read the book that launched a thousand firefighting careers, *Red Watch*, by the late newsreader and author, Gordon Honeycombe. That was a fantastic book about the Red Watch at Paddington and a fire they fought in 1974 where one of the Watch was sadly killed. A multitude of books by one of the firefighters in *Red Watch*, Neil Wallington, are also on my list; Neil is the most published firefighting author in the UK.

Report from Engine Company 82 is a best-selling book written by New York fireman, Dennis Smith, who worked in the South Bronx in New York in the early 70s when the 'Bronx was burning'. I was lucky enough to spend some time with Dennis in 2007 when he visited London, a lovely man who went on to write many more books.

Last and by no means least, I have to mention Dave Pike. Dave started his career in LFB as a junior fireman in the 1960s. By the time I joined, he was already a Divisional Officer and as far as I know, our paths never crossed before he retired in 1996. However, Dave published his first book, *Beyond the Flames*, in 2013, which really got my juices flowing again to finish this book. As well as publishing some more firefighting books since, Dave also runs the LFB retired members group on Facebook, so we've become 'friends' since and I regularly communicate with him.

I felt it only right that at the end of my book, I mention the books that most influenced my career, as well as my desire to write a book about my time as a firefighter. As I sit here typing this last paragraph, I just heard a familiar siren a quarter of a mile or so away up on the main road. Hornchurch are on their way to something; I wonder what they've got?

Steve Dudeney
Hornchurch
May 2021